Setting up in Business as a Mediator

Setting up in Business as a Mediator

Stephen Walker MA (Oxon), FCIArb
Solicitor and Accredited Mediator

Bloomsbury Professional

Bloomsbury Professional Limited,
Maxwelton House,
41–43 Boltro Road,
Haywards Heath,
West Sussex RH16 1BJ

© Stephen Walker 2015

Bloomsbury Professional is an imprint of Bloomsbury Publishing plc

All rights reserved. No part of this publication may be reproduced in any material form (including photocopying or storing it in any medium by electronic means and whether or not transiently or incidentally to some other use of this publication) without the written permission of the copyright owner except in accordance with the provisions of the Copyright, Designs and Patents Act 1988 or under the terms of a licence issued by the Copyright Licensing Agency Ltd, Saffron House, 6–10 Kirby Street, London EC1N 8TS. Applications for the copyright owner's written permission to reproduce any part of this publication should be addressed to the publisher.

Warning: The doing of an unauthorised act in relation to a copyright work may result in both a civil claim for damages and criminal prosecution.

Crown copyright material is reproduced with the permission of the Controller of HMSO and the Queen's Printer for Scotland. Any European material in this work which has been reproduced from EUR-lex, the official European Communities legislation website, is European Communities copyright.

A CIP Catalogue record for this book is available from the British Library.

Every effort has been taken to ensure the accuracy of the contents of this book. However, neither the authors nor the publishers can accept any responsibility for any loss occasioned to any person acting or refraining from acting in reliance on any statement contained in the book.

The views expressed in this book are those of the author and do not necessarily represent the views of the publishers.

ISBN: 978 1 78043 993 8

Typeset by Phoenix Photosetting, Chatham, Kent

Printed and bound in the United Kingdom by CPI Group (UK) Ltd, Croydon, CR0 4YY

Preface

So you want to be a mediator?

What is stopping you? Thousands of people all over the world are trying to answer this question.

More and more people want to become mediators, are trained as mediators and are failing to mediate. What is the problem and what is the solution?

Mediation in crisis?

Bernie Mayer, the well-known US trainer, mediator and author of *Beyond Neutrality* tells us in an interview with Aled Davies of the Mediation Academy that mediation is in crisis (see **Chapter 1**). Paul Randolph 'a well-known UK based trainer and barrister-mediator' tells us that mediation is like communism – a blip in history whose time has passed (see **Chapter 8**)

Is that really right? But even if it is, this book is not addressing the global problems of Mediation. Instead it deals with the particular issues of individual mediators who just want to mediate.

Who is this book for?

Anybody who wants to start or develop their practice as a mediator whether they are dreamers, apprentices, intermediates or snowballers.

Dreamers are people who are thinking that they would like to be a mediator. But they are not doing anything about it. They are not sure what to do or where to go.

Apprentices have done their mediation training and now want to start mediating and get their first 10 mediations under their belt. They need to get their observations out of the way and some appointments so that they can they gain experience.

Intermediates have completed between 10–30 mediations in total. They want to be doing 10+ paying mediations a year. How do they push on? What resources do they need?

Snowballers have completed more than 50 paying mediations as a lead mediator. They are appointed because they have been appointed before. Their business is essentially repeat business. But the market is changing and the old ways are under threat.

Preface

The book concentrates on:

- The market in England and Wales but draws on the experiences of mediators who have successfully developed practices in other countries.
- Civil and commercial mediation but draws on the experiences of those who have developed mediation practices in other areas such as family and workplace mediation.

It provides support, tips, guidance and know-how to:

- complete beginners who have completed their training but not done a mediation;
- those who have done some mediations but want to progress more quickly;
- those who have been accredited for some time and have a fair number of mediations under their belt but feel that they have plateaued;
- those who did their training some time ago but were not able to push ahead with developing their practices, and now want to kick start their dormant mediation businesses; and, finally
- those who have not yet decided whether to try and become a mediator and want to know what they might be letting themselves in for if they do go ahead.

Why write this book now?

When I told an experienced barrister mediator and arbitrator that I was writing this book he asked me: 'Why do you want to give all your trade secrets away?'

I am not sure I have any trade secrets. I do have experience and we live in a knowledge sharing world now thanks to the Internet. The motto now is 'Dare to Share'.

I have two main reasons for writing this book now, in 2015.

People want to know:

I have not written this book for the reason that Tammy Lenski gave for writing her well-known book: *Making Mediation your Day Job*. She explained in an interview on the Mediation Academy website that:

> 'I kind of wrote that book to ... *this is going to sound terrible, to get mediators off my back because I could just hand them the book.* What was happening is that I have been mediating full time for about a decade. At that point I was getting a lot of mediators contacting me and saying, 'How did you do it? What can I do? Where can I look....?' [my italics]

Courses and workshops on the subject are well attended. At any gathering of mediators the number one topic that they talk about is how to start and how grow their businesses. I want to help mediators get mediating.

Preface

The origins of this book lie in a pub in Fleet Street called the Old Bank of England. An experienced solicitor, a senior partner, Member of the Council of the Law Society and a Deputy District Judge had been mediating for three or four years. He had just completed a mediation for me which had gone very well.

He asked if we could have a drink. He wanted to know how to develop his practice. He enjoyed mediation. He liked it much more than being a Deputy District Judge because as a mediator he could try and achieve a just outcome. But he was frustrated. But he could not generate enough mediations. Ideally, he told me, he would like to do 20–25 year and earn about £50,000.

We chatted and batted a few ideas back and forth. He told me that there were lots of other people he knew who were experiencing the same frustrations. He suggested that we meet with them one evening in the pub over a pie and a pint and discuss problems and solutions.

We did. The ADR Group kindly paid for the food and drink. We ended up running several sessions. They went quite well. Over the years I have been asked from time to time to talk about developing a mediation practice.

PEAR

I summarised my essential message in an acronym: PEAR. These are the four factors that individual mediators can control in developing their practices. They are: Price, Experience, Availability and Reputation.

PEARL

At one workshop a non-lawyer mediator suggested adding a further letter to make the acronym read PEARL. The 'L' stood for lawyers. The suggestion was spot-on for those developing practices as civil and commercial mediators in England and Wales in 2014/15. You cannot ignore the lawyers. I discuss PEARL and its implications in greater detail in **Chapter 21**.

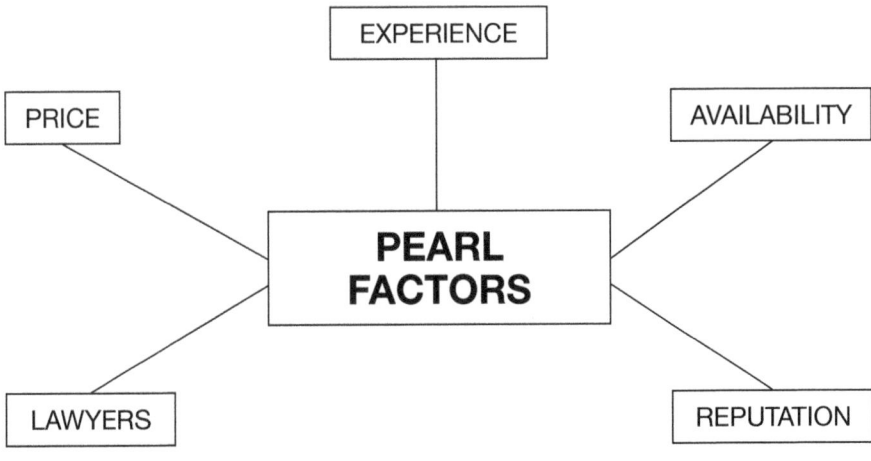

Figure 1

Preface

There is not much available:

Surprisingly little has been written for the UK as opposed to the USA market about developing a mediation practice. For example one of the country's leading civil and commercial mediators, David Richbell, recently published a book called *'How to Master Commercial Mediation'*.

Hailed as a masterpiece by some, it is a comprehensive treatise on all aspects of commercial mediation. It has 84 authors and runs to 549 pages. Chapter 9 is entitled :' Setting Up a Mediation Practice'. It runs from pages 89–91. So 3 pages out of 549 on what for many mediators is the key question.

It may well be asked if you can't practise mediation how can you develop mastery?

Blogs

USA

Plenty of blogs give hints and tips. Usually they are briefly annotated bullet point lists of headings. For example a blog from The American Bar Association by James E McGuire entitled *Twelve Tips For Launching A Mediation Practice* includes:

- '9 **Write something**. Articles written by you on topics important to you also will find a receptive audience. Avoid the disturbing current trend of paying some organization lots of money to write and place articles that are 'yours' in name only.
- 12 **Web awareness**. In the twenty-first century, marketing any services requires consideration of the Internet for marketing and communications.'

Both are sound suggestions, as were the other ten. But where do they get you?

UK

Aled Davies is a non-lawyer mediator and trainer and founder of the Mediation Academy, 'home of the passionate mediator'. He has posted an entertaining and useful 26-page pamphlet *'Becoming the GO-TO Mediator'* on his website MediatorAcademy.com. It says that it contains lessons from mediators with track records of success.

His key tip is that you should spend the first 100 minutes of every single day on a Marketing Activity. And he emphasises: 'Mediating isn't a marketing activity'. Really? (see para **16.3**).

The same marketing suggestions recur. They usual suspects are:

Preface

THE USUAL SUSPECTS

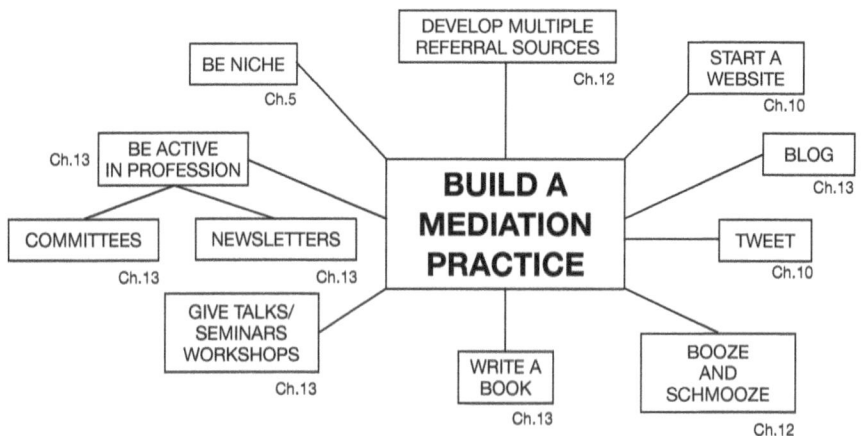

Figure 2

Digital exiles: digital natives

All good suggestions but no one tells you how to actually do anything.

Perhaps you are a digital exile, ie someone over 45 years old who was not brought up on computers, iPads and iPhones. You are not on LinkedIn. You have never tweeted and you do not have a website. Where do you start?

Perhaps you are a digital native but you don't read books, let alone write them. You don't talk to people on the telephone any more, you email or text. How do you write a book or give a talk or make a phone pitch?

IRL questions
- What is a niche anyway? One's man niche is another man's rut.
- How do I find observations?
- Are panels worth joining?
- What should I charge?
- How long will it take?

All these questions and many more are investigated in this book.

In real life

Some of the topics covered in this book were also covered in my previous book, *Mediation Advocacy: Representing Clients at Mediation (Bloomsbury 2015)* and some of the material is reproduced or adapted from there.

Finally: luck does play a part in mediation as in everything else. But remember what Louis Pasteur, pioneer of pasteurisation, said: 'Fortune favours the prepared mind.'

Preface

Work through this book and your mind will be well prepared.

As in my previous books I have respectfully followed the practice of Tom Bingham in *The Rule of Law* and have used 'he' rather than 'he or she' and in his words 'hope that this will be understood in an unchauvinistic, gender-neutral way'.

Stephen Walker

October 2015

Dedication

To Paul, Jane and Andy with thanks for all those mediation sessions in Old Trafford.

Contents

Preface	v
Useful websites	xix
List of acronyms and abbreviations	xxi
Chapter 1 Introduction	**1**
The question stays the same – does the answer?	1
7 Basic Premises	5
How do I get started?	7
How to use the book	7
Things to do	12
Stories	12
In a nutshell	12
Chapter 2 What are you getting into?	**13**
What is the mediation scene?	13
In summary	18
Who are mediators?	19
In a nutshell	28
Chapter 3 Accreditation – how to get it	**29**
Do I need to pay for mediation training?	29
Accreditation: where do I get it from?	29
Who regulates the trainers?	30
CPD	32
What to look for when seeking training	33
Looking ahead: observations	38
Looking ahead: CPD	40
In a nutshell	40
Chapter 4 Know yourself	**41**
Socrates	41
Question 1: Why do I want to be a mediator?	41
Question 2: Where do I want to be in three years' time?	52
Question 3: How will you get to where you want to be?	55
Question 4: How much money, time and effort can you invest?	55
Question 5: Why would you choose yourself as a mediator?	56
Question 6: How well do you cope with rejection?	57
In a nutshell	59
Chapter 5 Know your product	**61**
What am I selling?	61
The product line	61
Facilitative	63
Evaluative	66
Transformative	68
Narrative	68
Are transformative and narrative mediation methods relevant for commercial mediators?	69
Indicative	70

Contents

Evaluative winning the day?	70
Free marketeers	71
The paradox of choice	71
Be flexible	72
Interventions	72
Are you selling mediation at all any more?	75
ARB/MED	75
MED/ARB	76
MEDALOA	76
Mediator's recommendations	77
Arbitration	77
Ombudsman	77
Expanding your range of activities	77
Mediation – the client asks: what's in it for me?	79
In a nutshell	79
Chapter 6 Know your market	**81**
Who are your clients?	81
What do clients want?	83
What do clients look for when choosing a mediator?	84
How do clients choose a mediator?	85
Reasons to reject you	88
Prepare yourself	88
Do clients, lawyers and providers want the same thing?	90
Lawyer and non-lawyer mediators	92
Generalists or specialists?	94
What do clients need?	97
Segmenting your market	98
What is the focus of your market?	99
In a nutshell	99
Chapter 7 Business plan	**101**
Do you have a business plan?	101
Why do mediators not have business plans?	101
Why do you need a business plan?	102
The advantages of a business plan	102
Keep it short and simple	103
Why is it important to write things down?	104
Business plans made easy	105
A template for a business plan	108
Narrative business plan	114
Backup plan – plan B	126
All is not lost: a true story	127
In a nutshell	128
Chapter 8 Marketing – what is in it for mediators?	**129**
Cleaning toilets	129
What is marketing in a VUCA world?	129
Marketing made easy	136
Next step	136
In a nutshell	137
Chapter 9 Profile is all: is it?	**139**
The mantra: 'Profile is everything'	139
Profile as a CV	139
Profile as reputation	145

Marketing Groups	149
Directories	151
In a nutshell	153
Chapter 10 Social media	**155**
What? You don't have a website?	155
LinkedIn	156
Twitter	160
What to Tweet?	162
WEBSITE	164
Checklist of website design questions	166
Google Analytics	172
Facebook	174
In a nutshell	177
Chapter 11 Selling – the necessary mindset	**179**
Selling is a perfectly natural activity	179
How to influence people: the Big Six	181
Transferable skills for mediators	185
In a nutshell	190
Chapter 12 Selling – the necessary skill set	**191**
'Networking is not working'	191
What is networking?	191
Networking plan	193
11 tips for better networking	195
Follow up	200
Where to network?	202
Online networking	202
Selling for mediators.	203
Body Language	206
Pitching	208
In a nutshell	217
Chapter 13 Making a noise	**219**
Profile as brand	219
How to establish your brand?	220
How to write a blog	220
How to write a book	225
Self-published e-books	225
Traditional print media	229
Template for a book proposal	229
Contract	230
How to give a talk or lecture	231
Getting gigs	233
Seminars and workshops	233
Advertising/advertorials	234
Newsletters	235
Podcasts	235
In a nutshell	236
Chapter 14 Who can help you?	**237**
Mentors	237
Coaching	244
Support groups: other mediators	245
Clinics	247
Co-mediation	248

Contents

References and recommendations	249
Referrals	251
Returns	252
Reputation maintenance	252
Resilience	252
In a nutshell	253

Chapter 15 Online dispute resolution — **255**

What is Online Dispute Resolution ('ODR')?	255
Types of ODR	256
ODR is here	261
What's in it for mediators?	262
The Russian pencil?	263
Will ODR bring mediators work?	263
Will it make money for mediators?	264
In a nutshell	267

Chapter 16 Money — **269**

What should you charge?	269
Cash on the nail – do you extend credit?	282
Overtime	283
Conditional fee agreements ('CFAs') and funding arrangements	284
Insurers	284
Unpaid bills	284
In a nutshell	285

Chapter 17 Administration — **287**

Administration is boring	287
Diary	288
Mediation agreement	289
Terms and conditions	289
Billing	290
Credit control	290
Mediation report form	291
Feedback/satisfaction questionnaires	291
Complaints	292
Premises	294
Standard correspondence	294
Database	297
Bank account	298
VAT: pain, gain or marketing tool?	298
Tax	301
Expenses	306
The pros and cons of being self-employed	306
Being a limited company	307
Insurance	307
In a nutshell	309

Chapter 18 Mediation Agreement — **311**

General	311
Send the agreement in advance	311
Going through the agreement on the day	312
Standard form Mediation Agreement	312
In a nutshell	325

Chapter 19   Settlement agreement — **327**
   The danger zone — 327
   Heads of agreement: a solution or a problem? — 329
   Heads of terms: avoiding pitfalls — 331
   Contingent agreements — 332
   Conditional agreements — 333
   Pre-action mediations — 333
   Post-action mediations — 333
   Checklist for settlement agreement — 335
   In a nutshell — 339

Chapter 20   Help I've got a mediation — **341**
   Refreshing yourself – feeling a bit rusty — 341
   First mediation: help — 341
   The mediation lifejacket — 342
   First stage — 345
   Fast track through the mediation stages — 347
   FAQs for your first mediation — 347
   Remember — 365
   In a nutshell — 365

Chapter 21   Conclusion – bringing it all together — **367**
   Kissing frogs and strangling babies — 367
   Some amber lights — 371
   Takeaways — 372
   The buzz — 372

Appendices
   1 Mediation record form — 373
   2 Mediation crib sheet — 375
   3 Mediation Terms and Conditions — 377
   4 Mediation kit — 379

Index — **381**

Useful Websites

ADR GROUP	www.adr-group.com
AMATI	www.amati.org.uk
CEDR	www.cedr.com
CMC	www.civilmediation.org
FMC	www.familymediationcouncil.org.uk
IMI	www.imimediation.org
MEDIATION ACADEMY	www.mediationacademy.cm
SCMA	www.mediationadvocates.org.uk

List of acronyms and abbreviations

BATNA	Best Alternative to a Negotiated Agreement
CMC	Civil Mediation Council
CPR	Civil Procedure Rules
FMC	Family Mediation Council
HNP	Harvard Negotiation Project
ICC	International Chamber of Commerce
IMI	International Mediation Institute
ODR	Online Dispute Resolution
PI	Professional Indemnity
PEARL	Price, Experience, Availability, Reputation and Lawyers
WATNA	Worst Alternative to a Negotiated Agreement

Chapter 1

Introduction

> In this chapter you will learn:
> - How to cope with the 'mediation crisis'.
> - The importance of PEARL.
> - How to get the most out of this book.
> - The seven basic premises.

The question stays the same – does the answer?

1.01 No mediator even says that they are too busy. Lawyers, surveyors, doctors, accountants do. But not mediators. Why not?

Mediation has been established in the UK for over 25 years. In business terms, this is long enough for a product or service to become established. But still people in all jurisdictions say that mediation has not achieved market penetration. They even say it in the USA, the home of modern mediation and marketing.

Most people who train as mediators cannot make a living as mediators. Even if they do not want to make mediation their full-time day job they want to make it a satisfying part-time one. But they struggle to do even that. Why?

In 2004, Bernard Mayer diagnosed the problem and prescribed the cure. In his book, *Beyond Neutrality* he said that mediators were wrong to be mediators and that we must reinvent ourselves as Conflict Resolution Professionals. So his answer to the question is: stop being mediators and become CRPs.

Eleven years on and he is saying the same thing. Nothing much has changed. There are still too many mediators and not enough work. Mediation is in crisis.

Crisis? What crisis?

1.02 As you will see from what Professor Robert Cialdini advises in **Chapter 11**, always ask 'why is this expert giving me this opinion at this time?'

Bernie Mayer is a therapist as well as a mediator. Therapists thrive on crisis. If people are not in crisis what do they need therapy for?

1.03 *Introduction*

Other commentators disagree. They say there is plenty of work.

For example:

- Jesan Sorrells, Conflict Engagement Consultant, said in his blog (8 July 2014) 'In the current connection economy, building a mediation practice is easier now than it has ever been before.' (www.hscconsultingandtraining.com)
- Professor Ethan Katsh, the Online Dispute Resolution (ODR) guru, says that conflict is a growth industry (see **Chapter 15**).
- Stephen Ward, founder of Clerksroom which claims to be the UK's largest mediation provider, told the Civil Mediation Council (CMC) Conference in 2014 that there was plenty of work around.
- David Liddle, founder and CEO of TMC Group, one of Europe's leading private sector mediation companies (LinkedIn 24.10.2015) said in a interview with Mediation Academy that there's never been a better time to be a mediator.

Supply and demand

So is the problem just a mismatch of supply and demand? In fact there is enough work but it is not being distributed efficiently? Certainly the 2014 CEDR Survey shows that the commercial mediation market is asymmetrical, with only 130 mediators doing 85% of the cases (see **Chapter 6**).

Is the only measure of crisis that you have underemployed mediators who are expressing frustration? According to Bernie Mayer (see above) there is a more fundamental problem with mediation. He diagnosed it in 2004 and he repeated his diagnosis in 2015. Mediators, he says, define their role too narrowly.

Don't make peace: make war

1.03 According to Bernie Mayer in his interview for Mediation Academy (mediationacademy.com):

> 'We are not just about resolving conflict. We are about helping people engage in it as productively as possible and sometimes that means upping the ante, in fact. Sometimes that means escalating the conflict.'

Challenging thoughts for those mediators brought up on win-win, facilitative mediation where the only purpose of attending mediation is make peace not war.

People are said to find mediators boring (see para **8.12**). Does Conflict Resolution Professional sound more interesting? Possibly – it certainly sounds more complicated and possibly even pretentious. But the idea of developing the application of mediation and even strangling some of our favourite children, as John Harvey-Jones advised businesses often have to do, is a sound one. That is one of the themes of this book.

Expand the role

The Mayer solution is for mediators to widen their role and area of activity. As he says in his Mediation Academy interview:

'Rather than understanding maybe we have to understand the part of the role we can play lies as allies to people in conflict, not just as third party neutrals.

'We need to feel this part as helping people engage constructively sometimes, meaning in escalating conflict, using power effectively, not just settling things down, which is how people see us.'

Tammy Lenski says something similar, but in less inflammatory terms, when she advises mediators to seek out areas where they can become a meditative presence (*Making Mediation Your Day Job p 49*).

Narrow the focus

1.04 But the 'Sorrells solution' is different. He asks himself the question:

'what is holding back professional mediators from establishing a thriving professional practice?'

He replies:

'The answer is the same as in other industries. A lack of niche-ing a mediation practice.'

So there are two approaches: widen your focus and/or narrow your focus.

There is one aspect of the current environment which Sorrells mentions and Mayer does not. He refers to the 'connection' economy. In other words the Internet.

Guilds are dead: long live chat rooms

1.05 We live in a knowledge-sharing environment. The Internet is full of people offering and sharing advice. Often they do it for free. Chat-rooms, forums and discussion groups proliferate. They display a completely different mindset from the mediaeval guild approach of the traditional professions, crafts and trades. Access was restricted and knowledge fiercely protected and not made available to those outside the Guild.

We still see this even in a new craft like mediation. This explains why, for example, many experienced mediators are reluctant to take along new mediators as observers when they are mediating. They do not mind telling people how to do it but they do not want people seeing how they actually do it.

Is this proprietorial, protectionist approach the best way to develop business? It must be better to restrict competition and new entrants than to open up the floodgates and saturate the market. Monopolists make more money. Don't they?

1.06 *Introduction*

The more the merrier

1.06 There is a story of a young, newly qualified attorney who travelled from the East coast in the US to the West to set up in business. He got off the stage in a one-horse town and hung out his shingle. For two years he waited and waited. There was very little business. He was becoming desperate and poor. He was even thinking that he might have to give up.

Then one day the stage pulled into town and another newly qualified attorney climbed down. He hung out his shingle. Two years later they were both flourishing and looking for bigger premises.

In other words supply can create its own demand. Look at the success of the Apple iPad. When it was introduced the world asked why would anyone need one? We already had laptops and smartphones. Can mediators do the same thing and create their own demand? (See **Chapters 6** and **15**.)

The more mediators there are out there trying to find target markets, the more the buying public will be aware of mediation. So in fact is it really a case of the more the merrier? (See **Chapter 8**.)

Online dispute resolution

1.07 And what about ODR? Will it transform mediation, as some claim? And, if it does, will it be a saviour or a destroyer of what we have created over the last 25 years? Without doubt it will have an impact (see **Chapter 15**).

'Strangling children'

1.08 John Harvey-Jones, former Chairman of ICI, presented the *Troubleshooter* series on BBC. He went into ailing businesses and gave them a dose of reality therapy. Sound familiar? He famously said: 'Business is often about killing your favourite children to allow others to succeed.'

Mediators in 2015 have to decide whether to indulge in virtual infanticide. There are some dangerously out-of-date notions that are being promulgated by some of the thought leaders in the mediation community.

Here are two recent examples both reported in the mediate.com blog.

> On 28 August 2015 Ian Macduff a well-known mediation guru, in a piece called *'Laying the table'* about pre-mediation contact with the parties, referred to: "the signing of a mediation agreement (ie an agreement to mediate) that will also address the tacky but necessary question of fees…"

There is nothing tacky about fees. Without fees you have no income and without income you have no business (see **Chapter 16**).

> In July 2015 Bennett G Picker under the heading *'How to Become a Successful Mediator'*, in his keynote address to the newly-launched Florence Mediation Chamber, identified eight keys to building a successful mediation practice.
>
> Key 3 was 'Tell People What You Are Doing – Put Yourself Out There.' Under that heading he concluded: 'Finally, consider the use of social media including possibilities such as LinkedIn and even Twitter."

The reality is, don't bother *considering* it. Just *do* it, because if you don't you will not engage with the growth areas of your market (see **Chapter 10**).

7 Basic Premises

Seven basic premises underlie this book.

Basic Premise One

1.09 Setting up as a mediator is no different from setting up any other sort of practice or business.

You have to ask the same questions and make the same preparations. Mediators face the same challenges as many other businesses of too much competition for too few jobs, and the Internet.

Basic Premise Two

1.10 If you find it difficult to sell you will find it difficult to mediate at all, let alone develop a practice as a mediator.

Selling is not as difficult or alien as many think. Mediators have transferable skills (see **Chapter 11**).

Basic Premise Three

1.11 Marketing and selling are different but the same.

See the five main conventional differences in para **8.04** – but in the end, for mediators selling is the thing. It is where the theoretical rubber hits the commercial road.

Basic Premise Four

1.12 Negotiation is at the heart of both marketing and selling and mediation.

Negotiating is what we do when we are trying to get the work and it is what we do when we do the work.

1.13 *Introduction*

Basic Premise Five

1.13 You need a written business plan.

If you do not know where you want to get to, how will you know how to get there or know when you have arrived? It does not have to be complicated. The Geoff Sharp Model described in **Chapter 7** will do.

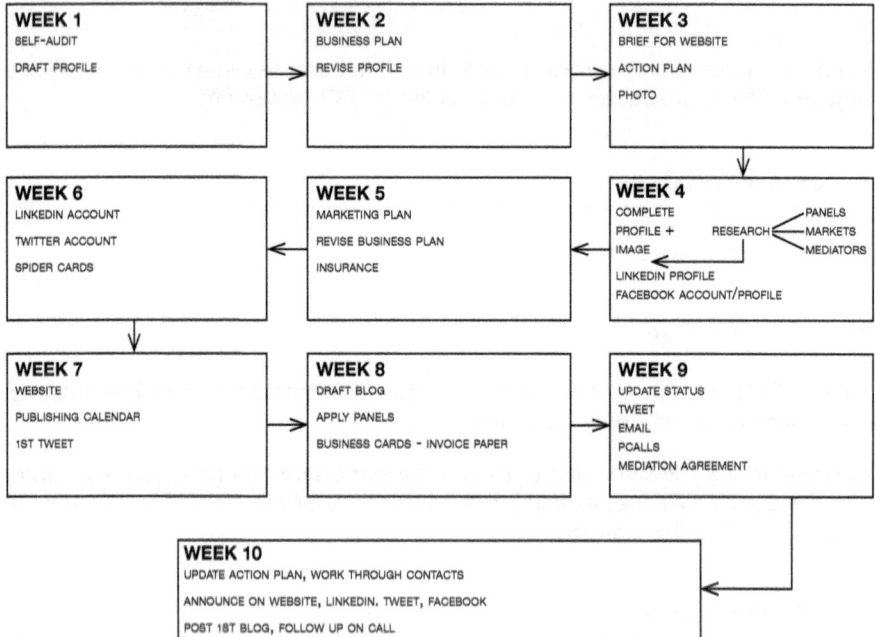

Figure 3

Basic Premise Six

1.14 There is a Mediation Timeline (see **Figure 4**).

Overnight success can take ten years. You need to know:

- where are you on the timeline; and
- how to move along the timeline.

To find out see **Chapter 4**.

Basic Premise Seven

1.15 Mediation is a business not a calling.

Mediation is a service provided by professionals to the paying public. It is not an ideology to save the mankind from itself. Ignore what the market wants at your peril.

Introduction **1.18**

How do I get started?

Route map

1.16 Look again at **Figure 3**. This is your route map. It takes you in ten weeks from a standing start to lift-off. You will not suddenly be doing lots of mediations. But you will be able to start attracting them.

In airline speak, you have taxied from the holding bay to the runway, turned on the power, passed through V1 and reached Rotate. You have not run out of runway. You are airborne.

MEDIATION TIME LINE

DAY DREAMING		HAVING A DREAM	LIVING THE DREAM
THINKING ABOUT IT TRAINING	A C C R E D I T E D		

	APPRENTICE	INTERMEDIATE	EXPERIENCED	SNOWBALLER
TOTAL NUMBER OF MEDIATIONS	0–10	10–20	20–30/40	50+
MONTHS	18–24	24–36/42	42/48–60	60–72/78
MEDIATIONS PER YEAR	5–7	6–10	10–15	12–20, 25/30+

Figure 4

PEARL

1.17 Now you are flying you need **PEARL** (see the **Preface**).

The mediation community cannot live without acronyms. PEARL is:

Price	see **Chapter 16** on Money
Experience	see **Chapter 9** on Profile
Availability	see **Chapter 4** on Knowing Yourself
Reputation	see **Chapters 13** and **14** on Making a Noise and References
Lawyers	see **Chapter 8** on Marketing

How to use the book

1.18 You can dip in and out depending on what topic most interests you. There are plenty of practical suggestions, checklists and precedents. But to get the best out of it:

1.19 *Introduction*

- Study the visuals which organise the topics.
- Complete the self-audits which show you where your gaps are.
- Follow the schema at **Figures 3** and **4**. Adapt them to suit your circumstances. They provide a structure for taking you from a standing start to take off.

Where to find what you want.

1.19   First check with yourself: is mediation, for you, a business or a calling? This book will be more helpful for mediators who want to develop a mediation practice as a business rather than a calling.

Anybody in business needs to know:

- What does the marketplace look like?
- Who are their competitors?
- Who are their customers?

1.20   In **Chapter 2** we discuss the current mediation scene.

- What are you getting into?
- How is the mediation industry structured?
- What are the points of entry?
- What are the barriers to entry?
- What are the emerging opportunities?

1.21   In **Chapter 3** we cover training, qualification and accreditation.

- Do you need it?
- Where do you find it?
- How do you get the best out of it?

1.22   In **Chapter 4** we discuss the key questions, which all mediators have to ask themselves. You need to 'Know Yourself'. Mediators certainly need to do this when they start. They also need to ask these questions throughout their business career just to make sure that they are on track for their destination. After all what is important to you in Year One will not always be the same as what is important in Year Ten.

Any business needs to know:

- What are they selling?
- Who are they selling it to?
- What is the route to market?

1.23   In **Chapter 5** we discuss the importance of knowing your product and review the different and developing types of mediation services now being provided.

1.24 In **Chapter 6** we discuss the importance of knowing your market. Who buys mediation services, what do they want now and what might they want in the future?

1.25 In **Chapter 7** we discuss the importance of formulating a plan to achieve your goals. Nearly every mediator, when asked if they have a business plan, says no. Why do mediators think that they can develop their businesses successfully without one of the basic tools that every other business uses?

1.26 **Chapters 8–12** analyse the route to market.

In **Chapter 8** we discuss what marketing is for mediators. At every business development get-together for mediators they talk about social media and the Internet. In this chapter we discuss what this means in practice.

1.27 In **Chapter 9** we discuss the mantra of business development advisers, namely that your profile is everything. Is this true? Is it more than just a CV? What about raising your profile on Panels and Directories? Do they make any difference?

1.28 In **Chapter 10** we grasp the nettle of social media. This chapter is particularly for 'digital exiles' ie those born before 1975. We cover LinkedIn, Twitter, Facebook and Websites.

- We do not just discuss the theory of social media we actually tell you how to set up a Twitter account or form a group on LinkedIn. You will learn where to click.
- Setting and running a website. What do actually you have to do in practice?
- What for example is Search Engine Optimisation (SEO) and how do you achieve it?

There is much, much more that could be said. But you can have too much of a good thing.

1.29 In **Chapter 11** we discuss selling. Advertisers and marketeers distinguish between marketing and selling. They overlap but they are not synonymous. In practice for mediators, marketing and selling are the same thing. Many people who become mediators are more comfortable with the concept of marketing than with the concept of selling. Not only does it sound more sophisticated and less grubby, it seems to carry less risk of personal rejection.

This may be true. But remember **Basic Premise Two**: that if you find it difficult to sell you will find it difficult to mediate at all let alone develop a practice as a mediator.

In the book we refer to promotion which is the combination of marketing and selling as it is relevant to mediators.

Chapter 11 deals with the mindset.

You will learn why mediators have less reason to be afraid of selling than most.

1.30 *Introduction*

1.30 **Chapter 12** deals with the skill set.

- Networking has a bad image. But if you want to attract commercial mediations or observations you have to put yourself in the opportunity flow. You can do it digitally but face to face is still better.
- How to pitch. Like it or not you will find yourself making pitches.
- People will raise all sorts of objections to mediation in general and to you in particular. Actual examples are given, with scripts which will help you overcome them.

1.31 In **Chapter 13** we develop the idea of making a noise. You learn how to:

- blog;
- publish an e-book;
- make a podcast; and
- give a talk.

1.32 In **Chapter 14** we discuss who can help you.

We discuss:

- *Mentors*. Many successful business people pay tribute to a mentor at some stage in their career. It is no different in mediation.
    - How do you find one and what do you do when you have?
    - What do you do if you cannot find one?
- *Coaches*. What is the difference between mentor and coach? People sell their services as coaches to mediators. Is it worth using a coach?
- *Support groups*. As discussed at para **4.14**, being a mediator can be quite lonely. Mediators, because they practise by themselves, can feel isolated. There are ways to combat this.
- *Direct action*. As discussed in **Chapter 9** you cannot rely on mediation panels to feed you. You will learn how to form your own marketing group.

1.33 We also discuss the 3Rs of mediation practice development: references, referrals and reciprocity.

- *References*, which are essentially endorsements about the quality of your service are gold dust. They are what reputations are made of.
- *Referrals* are the single most important source of most successful mediators' businesses. People give your name to mediation users and they contact you. It is the same in every other business.
- *Reciprocity* is an essential element of the whole mediation process. In this chapter we discuss how it applies in developing your practice. As noted at para **1.05** some mediators are defensive in protecting their patch. Even in the unstructured free market world of contemporary mediation something of the mediaeval guild mentality persists. As described in **Chapter 2** there is growing competitive pressure for work.

1.34 In **Chapter 15** we discuss Online Dispute Resolution (ODR).

Ethan Katsh says ODR is the future of ADR (in his 2014 interview on MediationAcademy.com). He might be right. But the question is what sort of future. As Nobel Prize Winner Niels Bohr said: 'Prediction is very difficult, especially if it's about the future'.

It will create opportunities and jobs for mediators. What sort of jobs – and do you want them?

1.35 In **Chapter 16** we discuss the paradoxical issue of money.

Some mediators say that the problems which they mediate, even in commercial disputes, are not really about money. They may be right. Although money is often the vocabulary of the dispute.

But if you regard mediation as a business, not as a calling, you will be interested in money.
- How do you charge?
- How much can you invest in your business?
- When will you get your money back?

These are key questions at all stages in a mediator's career. *Pace* Ian Macduff (para **1.07**) fees are not a tacky subject.

1.36 In **Chapter 17** we discuss the more prosaic aspects of the magical process of mediation, namely administration.
- Invoicing, paperwork, feedback forms, complaints handling etc.
- If you are carrying on business on your own account you have to deal with all the associated issues such as: tax, VAT and insurance. This again is true of every other business.

1.37 In **Chapter 18** there is a commentary on a key document for mediators: *The starting place: The Mediation Agreement.*

1.38 In **Chapter 19** there is a commentary on another key document for mediators: *The finishing place: The Settlement Agreement.*

1.39 In **Chapter 20** we discuss what happens when a mediation comes along. It may be your first for some time. You may feel that you are a little rusty. This revision chapter with checklists and flowcharts will help you tone up.

We also deal with the day that no mediator ever forgets: their first mediation. You have had the training. You have read the books. You will be nervous and unsure of yourself. Don't panic.

Read the answers to the FAQs. Follow the flowcharts and steps in this chapter. They will help you to give yourself the best chance of it being a success?

1.40 *Introduction*

1.40 Even if you are a busy mediator with regular work coming in there are still times when you are under pressure and a quick reference to a checklist is very helpful either before you go to the mediation or during it.

Things to do

1.41 At various points in the book there are:

- top tips
- action plans;
- self-audits; and
- questions to ask yourself.

Stories

1.42 We all love stories. All the ones in this book are based on real life mediators who are trying to develop their mediation businesses. Some are just starting. Others have been doing it for some time. One or two have been very successful. Their stories have been anonymised but they are authentic and based on real people.

In a nutshell

1.43

- The number of mediations is growing but the number of mediators is growing even faster.
- The market is opening up to mediators who are not lawyers, women and people under 45.
- Fees are falling.
- Mediation is still a cottage industry and is a second career for most people.
- ODR is both a threat and an opportunity.
- Adapt or go out of business. Who dares wins.

Chapter 2

What are you getting into?

> In this chapter you will learn
> - What the mediation scene looks like.
> - What are the barriers to entry.
> - Who are mediators.
> - What are they doing.
> - How are they organised.
> - What are the trends.

What is the mediation scene?

2.01 The mediation scene is made up of mediators, trainers, commentators, academics, regulators and users. Much of the most useful information about the mediation scene comes from the biannual audit carried out by CEDR. The latest available is the Sixth Audit published in May 2014. Although it only covers civil and commercial mediations it provides the best data that we have. The statistics referred to in this chapter are from the CEDR Audits unless otherwise indicated. They can be viewed on the CEDR website.

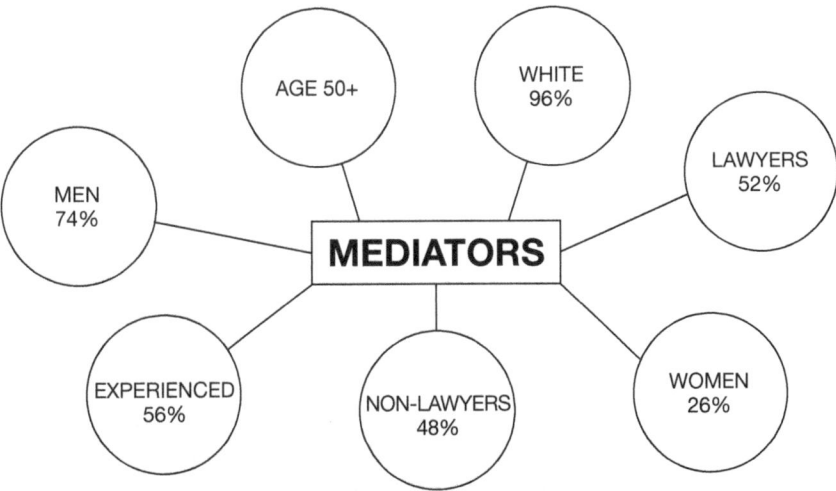

Figure 5

2.02 *What are you getting into?*

As a mediator you need to know the barriers to entry into this mediation community.

Barriers to entry

2.02

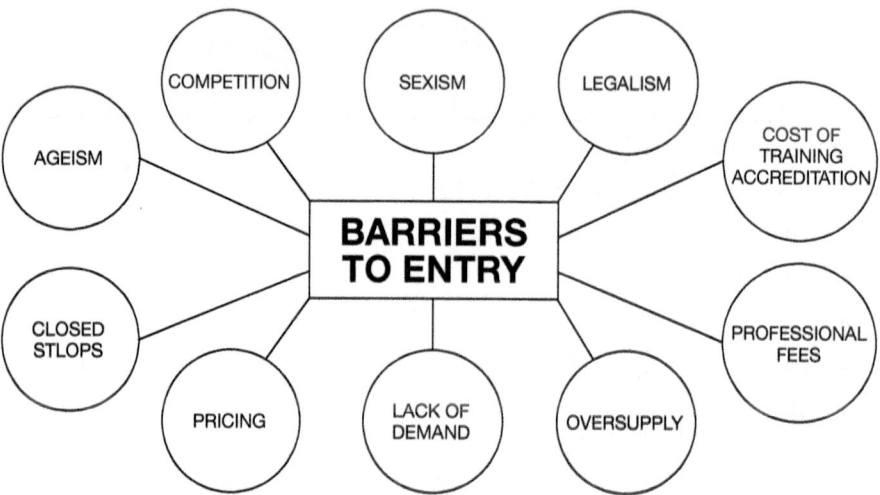

Figure 6

Ageism

2.03 Ageism, in the traditional sense of bias against older people, is not a barrier to entry in mediation. Most mediators are over 50. In fact there may be a reverse ageism with there being a bias against younger mediators.

Younger mediators can find it harder to convince customers that they have both the necessary life and professional experience. Building networks and connections takes time and they may not have had that time.

2.04 More and more people are seeing mediation as a primary career choice. For example, an increasing number of mediators are under 50. Many of them are women who see mediation as a career that they can combine with bringing up a family.

2.05 Many younger mediators want to be involved in inter-generational disputes. This is particularly true amongst ethnic minority communities where the younger generation are born and brought up in the UK and exposed to different cultural influences outside the home from those of their parents' generation.

An entry point for many mediators into civil and commercial mediation has often been via community or workplace mediation. Community mediation has offered been on a voluntary basis – mediators supply their services for free. Most community mediations are co-mediations which can make it easier for the novice mediator to get started. Lawyers are not usually involved. So some of the entry barriers for inexperienced non-lawyers do not exist.

Some mediators have found when offering their services that their emails or calls were not returned. This is often because the organisations offering mediation services are under-resourced. So stick at it. Do not give up because people do not reply the first or second time.

Workplace mediations has been seen as an easier point of entry for non-lawyers. But the market is more developed, sophisticated and competitive than it was ten years ago. For an excellent discussion on this, see Lewis *How to Master Workforce and Employment Mediation* (Bloomsbury Professional, 2015).

2.06 Looking ahead, the growth of ODR as described in **Chapter 15** offers opportunities for young mediators. For these jobs you need to be very familiar with computer systems and be prepared to work long hours for low wages, a situation which is not unique to young mediators. Young journalists, filmmakers, fashion designers and teachers often find themselves having to work for long hours on low pay.

Sexism

2.07 According to the 2014 CEDR Audit, female mediators do not seem to find it harder than male mediators. Women now make up over 25% of commercial mediators. That is a 36% increase over four years. Many of the most successful and high profile civil and commercial mediators are women.

As mentioned above an increasing number of women in the age bracket 35 to 45 are choosing to become mediators.

In some areas of mediation women predominate, for example in family. They make up more than 26% of community and workplace mediators. More and more successful women family mediators are converting to civil and commercial mediation. And the ones who seem to find the transition easiest tend to be lawyers who have carried out hybrid mediations in their family practice.

Legalism

2.08 Lawyers dominate civil and commercial mediation in the UK. As they do in many other jurisdictions. They dominate in two senses:

Most civil and commercial mediators are lawyers. But in England and Wales the percentage of non-lawyer civil and commercial mediators is growing. According to the CEDR Audits the percentage of non-lawyers is:

in 2007	43%
in 2010	40%
in 2012	38%
in 2014	48%

2.09 *What are you getting into?*

So this is becoming less of an entry barrier. But it cannot be ignored that generally the civil and commercial market prefers lawyer mediators (see para **6.35** for the reasons).

2.09 Lawyers, and particularly solicitors are frequently described as the 'gatekeepers' of mediation. In other words most appointments come from lawyers.

A non-lawyer market exists. So far it has been relatively untapped. Direct access from business clients to mediators is growing and can be encouraged. ODR will make it easier. Several online services have been set up offering this direct access approach to sorting out problems. The 2015 consumer ADR regulations which came into force on 9 July and 1 October 2015 may well reinforce this tendency (see **Chapter 15**).

2.10 For example a successful accountant mediator receives most of his appointments direct from companies and small businesses who are in dispute over sums typically under £100,000. He offers a fixed two-hour mediation for £250 plus VAT. 70% of his mediations have no lawyers present at all. If the dispute is, for example, between a company and its departing directors the company will tend to bring a lawyer with them but the director will not.

Most of his mediations last between three and four hours, by which time an agreement is reached and recorded in simple English in a short document.

2.11 You do not have to follow the advice of Alan Limbury who when asked how to become a successful commercial mediator replied: 'Become a retired judge'. But having a legal qualification helps. Several non-lawyer mediators have qualified as barristers (see para **7.39**).

And as much as you may want to follow Shakespeare's mission statement in Henry V1 Part 2: 'The first thing we do, let's kill all the lawyers', this will not remove a barrier to entry. Lawyers are your market.

You will have to work with them. Leave the lamentations about the over-legalisation of mediation to the academics who are not trying to make a living doing civil and commercial mediations

Cost of training

2.12 All accredited mediators need training. What is available is discussed in **Chapter 3**. To become an accredited civil and commercial mediator is likely to cost between £3,000 and £4,000 plus VAT. There are cheaper options. Some trainers are now supplying training online and say that it is just as good as face-to-face. Not everyone is convinced.

Realistically new mediators can expect to wait at least 18 months and possibly longer before they recover the cost of their initial training through their mediation fees.

In addition the Civil Mediation Council (CMC) and most other panels require some CPD each year. This does not have to be expensively acquired although there is a thriving training industry supplying courses for intermediate and advanced mediators.

What are you getting into? **2.16**

However, you do not have to have any sort of qualification or training to call yourself a mediator and to practise as one. There is no regulation (see para **2.33**).

Professional bodies and fees

2.13 These are increasing. The two professional fees that all new mediators will have to contemplate paying are:

- Membership of the CMC.

  Most of the most successful civil and commercial mediators are members of the CMC, but by no means all. The current fees can be found on their website at www.civilmediation.org.

- Panel membership

  Some are free. Most charge directly or indirectly. The charges vary.

These are discussed in more detail in **Chapter 9**. Membership of the CMC or indeed any panel is not compulsory.

Oversupply

2.14 Mediators are not known for agreeing with each other. But they do agree on one thing: there are too many mediators and not enough work.

More and more mediators are coming onto the market each year. This oversupply of mediators means greater competition for each appointment. You have to take that into account when framing your assumptions as you draw up your business plan. See **Chapter 7**.

Price

2.15 Mediation is price-sensitive except for the really big ticket mediations. Competition is driving down prices, as is commoditisation. And when something stops being a service and becomes a commodity the price drops. So usually does the quality but not always. Trainers are of course particularly exercised by this possibility.

Monopolies

2.16 A small group of civil and commercial mediators have for many years dominated the market in the UK. As the CEDR survey shows, that group is growing but the market is still skewed. A very few mediators at the top earn significant amounts of money. Most mediators do not. How different in reality is this from tennis players, footballers, actors and authors?

Family mediators complain about closed shops. The local family solicitors refer their clients to each other for mediations.

2.17 *What are you getting into?*

Panel members complain about favouritism in the allocation of mediations (see **Chapter 9**).

Lack of demand

2.17 The development of mediation in the UK has been a series of false dawns.

Mediation has not taken off in the UK in the way that was predicted. According to the CEDR survey of 2014 there were 9,500 civil and commercial mediations carried out. Although this may be an underestimate, it is still a very small number. Consider that the Law Society Annual Statistics Report for 2014 (April 2015) showed that there were 9,542 private practice firms registered in England and Wales, 160,394 solicitors, over 700 sets of barristers and 15,716 individual barristers.

The post-Jackson boom has not taken hold. Although already there does seem to be an increase in lower ticket mediations as a result of the increase in court fees in April 2015.

However, there are emerging new markets such as ODR and public engagement mediations (see **Chapter 15**).

Geography

2.18 London and the South East still dominate the commercial sector. Most of the large law firms and barristers' chambers are represented in London. But plenty of mediations take place outside London. One large mediation provider reported that they found London, and in particular City, firms were more reluctant to engage in mediation than the US offices of the same firms or large firms outside London.

You will have to consider how flexible you will be able to be. Can you travel to mediations? Will you charge for this travel? This is discussed in more detail in **Chapter 16**.

In summary

Low entry barriers?

2.19 At one level mediation has no real barriers to entry. You do not need to have any sort of qualification or belong to any sort of professional body or register. You can operate from your spare bedroom. All your marketing can be done on the Internet. The operating costs can be very low indeed.

All you have to do is attract work.

High entry barriers?

2.20 At another level there are significant barriers to entry identified above. At least they are barriers to entry to a full-time or financially sustainable mediation career.

It is a feature of the mediation scene that there are a lot of people who call themselves mediators who do not, in fact, do many mediations.

Who are mediators?

Civil and commercial mediators

2.21   The most up-to-date information is in the CEDR Sixth Biennial Mediation Audit available on the CEDR website (see **Figure 5**, at para **2.01**).

The survey reveals that:

- Most mediators are aged 50 or over. The average age of a female mediator is 50 and the average age of a male mediator is 57.
- Most are men (74% are men).
- Most are white (approx 96%).
- Most are lawyers (52%).
- 22% of the respondents are novices. Novice mediators are those who are accredited but have no experience as a lead mediator.
- 22% of respondents describe themselves as intermediate. Intermediate mediators are those with some, but limited, experience as a lead mediator.
- 56% of respondents describe themselves as advanced. Advanced mediators are those who are reasonably or very experienced as lead mediators.
- Nearly all those in the novice and intermediate categories carried out fewer than four mediations a year. Just over half the advanced mediators carried out more than ten mediations in a year.

This was the position in 2014. There are trends:

The number of women mediators is increasing:

2.22   The percentage of women mediators:

2014	26%
2012	22%
2010	19%

In addition, the percentage of women in the advanced category is increasing: in 2014 25%, in 2012 18%. Some of the most successful commercial mediators are women.

The number of advanced mediators is increasing.

2.23   For many years a small group of mediators have dominated the market and carried out most of the civil and commercial mediations.

2.24 *What are you getting into?*

2010	90 individuals	85% of the market.
2012	100 individuals	85% of the market.
2014	130 individuals	85% of the market.

Over a period of four years the group of 90 has increased to 130. Clearly the monopoly enjoyed by the traditional elite is under threat.

The number of mediators who are not legally trained is growing

2.24 This is both as a percentage and in absolute numbers. The first wave of non-lawyer mediators came from the traditional professions such as surveying and accountancy. Now there is a much more diverse intake including HR professionals, management consultants, ship brokers, IT professionals, diplomats and actors. They need to work out how they will be able to bring a distinctive contribution to their practice as mediators from their professional experience.

2.25 But still most of the commercial mediators are lawyers. Originally, when mediation was introduced into the UK 25 years ago, most were solicitors. Over the years barristers have qualified as mediators in increasing numbers. Now former judges, are following the example of their US brethren and have decided that mediation makes an attractive alternative retirement activity to golf. They have their own distinctive contribution to make. Some, but by no means all, have been very successful.

Mediators' earnings are falling

2.26 As is clear from the total number of mediations carried out each year, mediation will not be a viable full-time job for many people. Average earnings from mediation make it difficult to earn enough to pay the mortgage and bring up children without an additional source of income.

2.27 The increase in the number of mediators has led to downward pressure on fees.

	No fee	Less than £2,000 (for one-day mediation*)	Average fee (less experienced mediators	Average fee (experienced mediators)
2010	10%	57%	£1,390	£3,450
2012	7%	55%	£1,517	£4,279
2014	8%	51%	£1,422	£3,820

* Ie eight hours.

2.28 If the definition of an experienced mediator is one who carries out more than ten mediations a year this means that the threshold is only £38,000 a year.

Those carrying out between 20 and 30 mediations a year are earning about £70,000 a year.

For a one-day mediation the average time spent working with clients on the day is about eight hours (which is the standard mediation day) plus seven hours before the mediation in preparation and client contact and 1.7 hours after the mediation. In total about 16.5 hours are spent. In other words, for each day spent in mediation there is another day spent on related activities. Each one-day mediation is in reality a two-day job.

2.29 This means that, for the overwhelming majority of mediators, mediation is not a full-time job. Amongst the most experienced group 47% now describe themselves as full-time mediators. In 2012 the figure was 39% and in 2010, 37%.

In 2012 the former Lord Chancellor Lord Falconer told the Chartered Institute of Arbitrators that in five years' time (ie 2018) mediation would be a specialist skill performed by a cadre of specialist mediators. He thought that the cadre would be about 1,000 strong. After three years this does not appear to be happening.

The number of mediators is increasing

2.30 No one knows how many mediators there are but the Director of Training at the ADR Group estimated in 2014 that there were between 6,000 and 7,000 mediators in England and Wales with a further 900 being trained each year. This includes university students who complete a mediation module as part of their degree course, which leads to accreditation.

These trends give rise to the following questions:

What sort of people are mediators?

2.31 There has been surprisingly little research into what sort of people become commercial mediators in the UK and in particular what sort become successful mediators.

To date there has been much subjective observational research allied to demographic data that informs the reader but nothing in the qualitative field. However there is currently research being undertaken by Aaron Hudson-Tyreman at Queen Mary University London into the personality traits of commercial mediators in the UK. As far as one can tell the sort of people who are successful commercial mediators exhibit consistent traits across the spectrum. The final results are expected to be published in early 2016.

Can anyone be a mediator?

2.32 Another and more provocative answer to the question 'who are mediators?' is 'whoever wants to call themselves a mediator'. Anybody in England and Wales can call themselves a mediator. There is no restriction on the use of the term 'mediator' as there is for example with architects or solicitors.

There is no central unified regulatory body for mediators as there is for example for doctors (the British Medical Association), barristers (the Bar Council) or architects (RIBA). The Civil Mediation Council is gradually assuming a central role, but slowly

2.33 *What are you getting into?*

and with reluctance. It now maintains a register of mediators who have applied to join. There are minimum standards for entry onto the register. These can be found at the CMC website www.civilmediation.org.

Should mediators be regulated?

2.33 There are several mediation training organisations but not all are accredited by the CMC (see **Chapter 3**).

This does not apply to family mediators, who have their own regime. Details can be found on the Family Mediation Council website, www.familymediationcouncil.org.uk.

A debate has been going on for several years within the mediation community as to whether or not there should be central regulation. The arguments in favour focus on:

- quality assurance;
- public confidence; and
- inevitability.

Arguments in favour

2.34 The supporters of regulation argue that:

- In the end all new activities and markets end up being regulated.
- Sometimes the regulation is self-regulation and voluntary. But usually some degree of compulsory regulation is introduced.
- Over the last 40 years in the UK service industries have become regulated. Professionals in all sorts of sectors habitually complain about the amount of regulation that has been introduced. In the end they recognise that it is inevitable and a reflection of the rise of consumerism.

Arguments against

2.35 Those who are against regulation argue that:

- It is unnecessary as the market regulates itself.
- It will introduce an extra layer of costs.
- It will stifle commercial creativity.

2.36 Most successful mediators are in fact accredited in some way. This usually means that they have received training that is recognised by the CMC because it has been provided by a CMC-accredited trainer. Most also join the CMC as a member and agree to be bound by its Code of Conduct and Rules. These provide that:

- they have professional indemnity insurance in place;
- they will carry out and minimum of three mediations a year; and

- they will keep up-to-date with good practice by undergoing continuing professional development (CPD).

2.37 As part of the regulatory regime there is a limited system of accountability. Leaving aside more narrowly legal questions of negligence or breach of contract there can be complaints about poor service. The CMC and its affiliated mediation providers operate a complaints system. The redress is usually limited to a rebate of fees and/or the removal of the offending mediator from a panel.

2.38 Mediators who are also members of other professional bodies such as the Law Society, the Solicitors Regulation Authority, the Bar Council and RIBA are also liable under those organisations and systems for redress for poor service. Some mediators who practice, for example, as solicitors as well as mediators complain about this double jeopardy.

2.39 The International Mediation Institute (IMI) at an international level is also trying to bring in some degree of standardised accreditation. Details can be found on their website (immediation.org). One of the advantages of this scheme is that it will allow users of mediation to have access to a panel of mediators who they can be reasonably confident meet a minimum acceptable standard of experience and competence irrespective of where they originally trained or now practise.

Is mediation a profession?

2.40 At gatherings of mediators there is always reference to mediators being a profession. Those who think that it is mainly reason by analogy. They point to the main characteristics of a profession:

- training;
- codes of conduct;
- accountability;
- professional standards; and
- the nature of the activity.

2.41 In practice they seem to rely upon the fact that most mediators belong to another professional body such as solicitors, architects, doctors etc who have their own professional standards, which the mediators import into their practice as mediators. There is a lot of truth in this assertion. But it overlooks the following problems:

- Different professions have different norms.
- Some professions are closely regulated on an individual level, others are not.
- Most professions have mandatory requirements, mediators do not.
- There is little effective redress, unlike for most other recognised professions. Mediators cannot be banned from practising. The CMC complaints procedure consists of offering another mediation between the complainant and the mediator. There is no certainty that there will be final outcome if the parties cannot reach an agreement (see the CMC website (www.civilmediation.org/)).

2.42 *What are you getting into?*

Cottage industry

2.42 Mediation at the moment in the UK is not so much a profession as a cottage industry. There are thousands of mediators working from home. This is not necessarily a bad thing. Academic commentators such as Debbie Di Girolamo and Penny Brooker have recently criticised the institutionalisation of mediation. But they may be exaggerating its extent.

Most mediators are self-employed. Most are in paid employment for their main job, for example solicitors or accountants in private practice. They may provide their mediation services through their firm or they may do it, with the permission of the firm, as an outside activity.

2.43 Some organisations now use employed mediators. For example the Court Service employs mediators to operate their telephone mediation service.

Organisations such as Shelter and some local authorities have some employed mediators. Some NHS trusts require their therapists to provide workplace mediation as just another duty. Large retailers are likely to employ mediators to help them provide the ADR services under the 2015 Consumer ADR Regulations (see **Chapter 15**) or to outsource the service to service providers who will employ mediators.

Conflict advisers

2.44 Conflict advisers are already emerging as a separate category. In practice what they do is help people make complaints, for example James Walker and his company 'resolve'. In France there is a company that is essentially a call centre which helps people resolve local disputes. The employees are law students. It is not mediation as we know it but it is helping people solve their problems without going to expensive lawyers. That is after all the reasons why ADR/mediation was set up in the first place over 40 years ago.

Direct access

2.45 Nearly all mediators provide their services on a direct access basis. In other words they can be booked direct. Others provide their services through mediation providers for example the ADR Group, CEDR, the Academy of Experts. Clerksroom and JAMS. They do this by being on a panel. As discussed above that means that they have to comply with certain requirements about training, experience, PI insurance etc.

Others form marketing groups. For example In Place of Strife or the Panel of Independent Mediators. More and more of these groupings are being formed as mediators try to secure work (see **Chapter 9**).

5 emerging trends that will shape your mediation future

2.46 Here are five trends that will impact on mediation scene over the next five years:

1   Co-mediation: '2 for 1';
2   Morphing of facilitative mediation;
3   Growth of Ombudsman schemes;
4   Commoditisation; and
5   Growth of ODR.

Co-mediation: '2 for 1'

2.47   Co-mediation has been pushed by the mediation community but the market has not taken to it. Most co-mediation takes place in big ticket multi-party mediations. There are undoubted benefits in these types of cases (see **Chapter 14**).

There is limited market penetration for simpler and lower value mediations. Anecdotally more and more mediators appear to be now prepared to co-mediate. The rationale is that it is better to have a mediation and half the fee than no mediation at all. In community mediation after all co-mediation is the norm.

As mediators try to differentiate themselves from their competitors, offer something different from the online experience, and offer greater value for money, the use of 2 for 1 co-mediation is likely to grow.

Morphing of facilitative mediation

2.48   As described at para **5.04** facilitative mediation is the safe model taught and practised in the UK.

The trend in the commercial market has been towards a more adjudicative or evaluative style of mediation. As commercial mediators have been telling each other for years: mediation training might be facilitative but mediation practice is evaluative.

2.49   The growth of Ombudsman schemes and low-value high-volume consumer dispute schemes will lead to more people expecting their guaranteed outcome to be a decision of some sort (see **Chapter 15**).

Already commentators, trainers and practitioners agonise over this assault on doctrinal purity. You have to decide what you are doing mediation for. That is one of the questions you will be invited to consider in **Chapter 4.** Do you want to be an upholder of the faith or a practitioner of the craft?

Growth of Ombudsman schemes

2.50   As discussed in **Chapter 15** far more disputes are resolved each year through the Ombudsman system than are resolved through the courts, mediation, arbitration or adjudication. The Ombudsman Service reports that there were 66 million complaints about products and services in 2014.

2.51 *What are you getting into?*

There are already many schemes. More are being added. The Consumer Ombudsman, set up in operation from 12 August 2015, for example. Members of the public can obtain details from the Ombudsman Association or the Ombudsman Service.

Several commercial mediators who want to increase their income also act as Ombudsmen (see para **7.39**).

Commoditisation

2.51 An ugly word for an ugly phenomenon perhaps. Twenty years ago mediation was a novelty. Not many people knew about it and very few people knew how to do it. Today mediation is not a novelty. It has become part of the fabric of English legal system. Take-up may be disappointingly low for the many people who have trained as mediators but there is an increasing level of sophistication and awareness amongst users.

This has led to two clear trends:

LOWER PRICES

2.52 As people become more familiar with a product it ceases to be special and unusual. More and more people just want a service. They do not want the best – they just want one that is good enough. The requirement by the courts that parties to the dispute go to mediation before going to trial means that people just go through the motions. They just want it completed as quickly and cheaply as possible before they can get on with what they regard as the 'real thing', which is litigation and trial.

OFF-THE-PEG, NOT BESPOKE

2.53 More and more users are used to mediation. It has lost its novelty value for the lawyers who take clients to mediation. The consumers are less naive. Both lawyers and mediators complain about mediation becoming formulaic.

2.54 Many commercial parties do not want to be changed into better people for the future. They just want to get a problem off their desks. The clients may not have been to mediation before but the chances are their lawyers have. They tell their clients what the routine is and they indulge the mediators as they go through their carefully orchestrated steps in the way in which their trainers taught them.

But there is consumer resistance. As one leading commercial litigator and CMC Board member said at the 2015 CMC conference: 'My clients do not want to hear about their BATNA'. Heresy!!

The growth of ODR will reinforce this trend.

Online Dispute Resolution (ODR)

2.55 All industries are more dependent on online systems for delivery of their goods and services. Even doctors advise online. Why should mediation be any different? We discuss this in **Chapter 15**.

What are you getting into? **2.56**

Where are you?

2.56 Have a look at the mediation decision tree at **Figure 7**. This helps you to find out where you are in the mediation scene and the path to follow to get to where you want to go.

WHERE ARE YOU

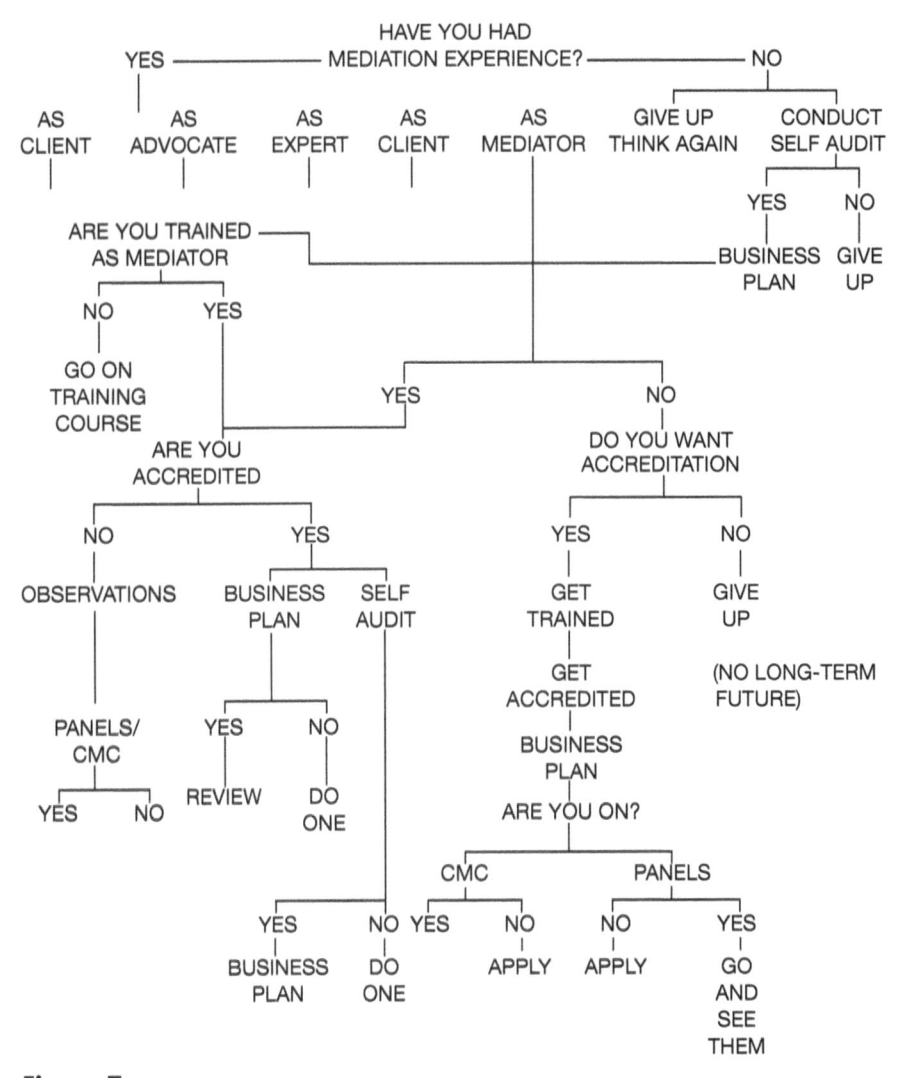

```
                            HAVE YOU HAD
        YES ──────────── MEDIATION EXPERIENCE? ──────────── NO
         │                                                    │
   ┌──┬──┴──┬──────┬──────┬──────────┐                  ┌─────┴─────┐
   AS   AS     AS     AS     AS      GIVE UP         CONDUCT
 CLIENT ADVOCATE EXPERT CLIENT MEDIATOR THINK AGAIN   SELF AUDIT
   │     │                      │                         │
                                                      ┌───┴───┐
                                                     YES      NO
                                                      │       │
   ARE YOU TRAINED ─────────┐                      BUSINESS  GIVE
   AS MEDIATOR              │                       PLAN     UP
    ┌──┴──┐                 │
    NO   YES                │
    │                       │
  GO ON                     │
 TRAINING              YES  │              NO
 COURSE                 │   │               │
         ARE YOU        │   │           DO YOU WANT
        ACCREDITED      │   │          ACCREDITATION
      ┌─────┴─────┐     │   │          ┌─────┴─────┐
      NO         YES    │   │         YES          NO
      │       ┌───┴───┐ │   │          │           │
  OBSERVATIONS BUSINESS SELF│           GET         GIVE
              PLAN    AUDIT│          TRAINED       UP
               │            │            │
               │            │          GET       (NO LONG-TERM
   PANELS/     │            │       ACCREDITED    FUTURE)
    CMC     ┌──┴──┐         │            │
   ┌─┴─┐   YES    NO        │        BUSINESS
  YES  NO   │     │         │          PLAN
        REVIEW    DO        │       ARE YOU ON?
                 ONE        │       ┌────┴────┐
                            │      CMC      PANELS
                            │     ┌─┴─┐     ┌─┴─┐
                           YES   NO YES    NO   YES
                            │     │  │      │    │
                         BUSINESS DO APPLY APPLY  GO
                          PLAN   ONE              AND
                                                  SEE
                                                  THEM
```

Figure 7

2.57 *What are you getting into?*

In a nutshell

2.57

- The market for civil and commercial mediation remains asymmetrical with a small group dominating.
- Most mediators do not earn enough from mediation for it to be a full time job.
- The market is changing; fees are lower, there are more non-lawyer mediators, and ODR is a potential game changer.
- It's an interesting time to be a mediator.

Chapter 3

Accreditation – how to get it

> In this chapter you will learn
> - Why you need training.
> - What training is available.
> - What you should ask your trainers.
> - How to get the best out of your training
> - Follow-up training.

Do I need to pay for mediation training?

3.01   The answer to this question is that you do not. You do not have to undertake any training. As explained in **Chapter 2** anybody can call themselves a mediator. There is no national accreditation scheme or restriction on the use of the title mediator as there is, for example, for solicitors, barristers or architects.

Plenty of people think that they do not need any training as a mediator. They say that in their day job they already practise mediation. People who say this come from a range of backgrounds including solicitors, barristers, judges HR professionals, psychotherapists, counsellors, doctors, nurses, managers, company directors and diplomats. In fact anybody that you can think of.

3.02   In a sense what they say is true. The same can also be said about negotiation. Everybody in essence negotiates all the time, every day. But there is a world of difference between day-to-day informal mediating/negotiating and the practice of mediation/negotiating as a business. The difference between formal and informal mediating/negotiating is discussed in more detail in **Chapter 11**.

The bottom line is that unless you are a celebrity negotiator/mediator such as the former Secretary General of the United Nations you will need to show that you have received some formal training in mediation if you want to be taken seriously as a mediator.

Accreditation: where do I get it from?

3.03   Qualification by experience itself is not sufficient. Increasingly you need to demonstrate reputable accreditation. Under the current system in England

3.04 *Accreditation – how to get it*

and Wales this is provided by accredited mediation providers/trainers who are themselves accredited by the Civil Mediation Council. You can find a list of these on the CMC website: www.civilmediation.org.

Just as anybody can call themselves a mediator so anybody can call themselves a mediation trainer or mediation provider. The Civil Mediation Council tries to provide some degree of quality control and regulation. But at the moment this is with a feather-light touch.

3.04 In addition there is the Association of Mediation Assessors Trainers and Instructors (AMATI) www.amati.org.uk/. This was formed by Andrew Goodman, who also founded the Standing Conference of Mediation Advocates (SCMA).

It is based in London but has an international Advisory Board consisting of well-known mediators and trainers from the UK, USA, Australia, the Netherlands, Italy, Germany, Romania and Switzerland. Its membership is global. Its stated aim is:

> 'Our aim is to promote best practice in mediation training and assessment and share knowledge through member forums and conferences. In particular we are keen to seek independent trainers and those from smaller enterprises to join our ranks, since they may benefit most from others, including those working mediation fields different from their own, through connected generically.'

It holds conferences and can be followed on LinkedIn and Twitter.

In addition the Law Society administers a list of approved mediation training providers (see www.lawsociety.org.uk.>supportservices>Accreditation).

Who regulates the trainers?

3.05 The CMC has requirements for accredited mediation providers who provide mediation services and mediation training.

Mediation Providers – Panels

In summary the requirements for mediation providers who operate panels of mediators are:

- *Adequate mediator training*: they must ensure that their panel members have completed appropriate training that meets the minimum training requirements of the CMC.
- *Code of conduct:* they must adopt a code of conduct which is at least as rigorous as the EU Model Code of Conduct for Mediators promulgated in 2004.
- *Complaints handling and feedback*: the provider must have a published procedure in place and keep written records of all complaints.
- *Supervision and mentoring*: they must provide appropriate supervision, mentoring, monitoring and observations for their mediators, as well as mediation-specific CPD policy.
- *Insurance*: they must have minimum professional indemnity insurance arrangements in place.

- *Efficient administration*: this includes being able to deal with enquiries, the recording of calls and accurate account of fees and the rendering of bills.
- *Allocation of mediators*: the provider must show that it operates an appropriate system to make sure that appropriate mediators are assigned to the cases.
- They must have a minimum of six members on their panel.

The mediation providers therefore must make sure that their mediators have been properly trained.

Panels are discussed in more details at paras **9.21–9.28**.

> **TOP TIP**
> - Most mediation providers can meet the above criteria. Be warned, many providers including some which are well-established, struggle from time to time to provide efficient administration.
> - Don't expect too much.

The minimum requirements for accredited training

3.06 The course must include training in ethics, mediation theory, mediation practice, negotiation and role-play exercises.

Mediators who are not professionally qualified in a discipline that includes law must demonstrate a grasp of basic contract law if they wish to undertake civil or commercial mediations.

3.07 Mediators who attended a training course before 31 March 2011 must have complied with the following requirements:

- Performance during, or on completion of, training must be assessed. The training course will include not less than 24 hours of tuition and role-play followed by a formal assessment.

Mediators who attended a training course from 1 April 2011 must have been on a course that met the following requirements:

- Assessors are to meet the criteria of the CMC accreditation scheme in terms of training, observations, CPD and practice requirements. Assessors are to be separate from those delivering the training.
- Performance during, or on completion of, training must contain at least one separate assessment phase of at least one hour where the assessment is continuous and at least two separate assessments of at least one hour each where the assessment is carried out on separate days.
- There is a minimum of 40 hours of face-to-face tuition and role-play followed by a formal assessment. In calculating the 40 hours, lunch and coffee breaks are excluded.

3.08 *Accreditation – how to get it*

- A minimum of 50% of the training course will be in role-plays. 50% of the role-plays must be supervised.
- A maximum of 40 trainees can attend in a classroom or lecture setting.

The minimum assessment criteria

3.08
- An appropriate and safe environment is set by the participant-mediator which is conducive to problem-solving.
- The role of the mediator is fully and properly articulated.
- The principles of confidentiality, neutrality and facilitation are evidenced.
- Trust and rapport is established.
- Necessary skills to explore issues, interests and options are applied.
- The ability to manage the parties and the process is demonstrated.
- The ability to advance resolution through the application of negotiation and communication skills is demonstrated.
- Proper consideration of ethical issues is given as they arise.

Supervision, mentoring and observations

3.09 The provider must
- provide adequate and appropriate supervision and mentoring.
- require its new mediators to have observed at least three civil or commercial mediations within the last 12 months before they are eligible for appointment as a lead mediator. One observation can be of a role-play.

3.10 Panel members must have current practice experience. This means they must have conducted at these two civil or commercial mediations within the previous 12 months.

As alternatives they can substitute for one actual observation:
- two simulated mediation practices of at least one hour each;
- one community mediation; or
- two telephone mediations.

The provider must offer the opportunity for mediators to consult experienced mediators before, during or after each mediation to discuss any issues on which they would benefit from advice.

CPD

3.11 Panel members must complete a minimum of six hours of mediation-specific CPD each year in addition to the other practice requirements.

Accreditation – how to get it **3.15**

These CPD hours may include:

- Courses offering practical role-plays;
- Attendance at seminars, conferences, tutorials and debates on mediation;
- Writing articles on mediation;
- Presenting mediation training, seminars or similar events.

Please note that reading articles, mentoring and supervising mediators and preparing for mediation do not count.

Insurance

3.12 The provider must have insurance in place with a minimum indemnity of £1 million to insure itself against claims it has negligently administered in mediation and must provide its mediators with similar cover or require that they provide it themselves.

Where mediators are doing work involving sums exceeding £1 million the provider must have appropriate insurance cover in place and be able to provide evidence of it.

CMC's secret weapon

3.13 The Civil Mediation Council reserves the right to limit the use of the phrases:

- Accredited Mediation Provider.
- Accredited by the Civil Mediation Council.

What to look for when seeking training

Is the trainer on the CMC list of accredited mediation trainers?

3.14 If they are not ask yourself: why bother using them? The usual answer will be they are cheaper. But you will get what you pay for. You will not be eligible to be a member of the CMC unless you are reassessed by an accredited mediation trainer/provider. You have to pay a fee for this.

How much will it cost?

3.15 The cost varies. For example:

3.16 Accreditation – how to get it

Provider	Cost £	Days	Notes
Academy of Experts	3,000	5	Modular. Discount for members
ADR GROUP	2,950	5	
CEDR	4,750	5	
CIArb	3,960	5	Includes assessment day fee of £1,560
CLEAR ADR	3,000	5	50% discount available
London School of Mediation	2,220	5	
Regents School of Psychotherapy	3,950	5	
RICS	2,950	5	2 separate modules – discount for members

When will it take place?

3.16 Some courses are continuous. Others take place over several weekends. You have to find the format that fits in with your diary.

Where will it be held?

3.17 Many courses take place in London but most providers also hold training sessions around the country and abroad.

If you have to travel away from home to attend the training session you will have to include travel and accommodation costs when working out the total spend on initial training. It can all add up.

What pre-training reading and work will there be?

3.18 Many providers insist that you undertake exercises and reading before you attend the course. These are usually assessed. You have to complete them and pass them.

You will want to be clear about what will be required so that you make sure you have enough time and energy to do it.

What materials will you be given?

3.19 You want to know what you will take away from the training course. Will you be supplied with a training manual in hard copy or will it be sent electronically? Is it something that you will be able to use after the training to help you during your apprenticeship period?

Who will the trainers be?

3.20 Ideally you should find out the names of the trainers so that you can look them up on LinkedIn. You can also ask to speak to them. If you do you will gain an impression of whether or not they are your type of person and whether their style is going to be a congenial one which will help you learn.

How much training have they done?

3.21 Everybody has to start somewhere but you do want to know that if you are going to have an inexperienced trainer that at least one experienced trainer will also be in attendance.

How much mediation have they done?

3.22 There is a suspicion shared by many mediators and would-be mediators that often mediation trainers are only doing training because they cannot get enough work doing mediations. Some mediation trainers have never done a civil or commercial mediation, even though they are giving training in it

Do you want practitioner-led training or would you prefer to receive training from people who are full-time trainers? The answer is not always obvious.

Non-practitioner trainers can probably adequately supply basic training. Advanced training is better supplied by people who are experienced and ideally currently active mediators as well. Otherwise it all becomes unreal.

As you will quickly learn, what happens on mediation training courses is not the same as what happens at mediations.

What to do during the training

3.23 *Accept that what you are taught is a safe model of mediation.* In the UK this will almost certainly be based on the facilitative model (see **Chapter 5**) and will be heavily influenced by the work of Fisher and Ury and the Harvard Negotiation Project.

3.24 *Watch out for the prescriptive trainers.* They do not just want you to meet the assessment criteria. They also want you to become 'followers' and do mediation in the way they think that it should be done.

3.25 *Be careful about the evangelists.* They, for example, tell you to put your pen down and not take notes. They use flip charts with lists of BATNAs and WATNAs. In real life mediators do take notes during private sessions with the parties and they rarely use the word 'BATNA'.

3.26 *Approach the mediation training with an open mind.* Do not assume that you know how to mediate because of what you do in your day job. Do not follow the example of one established commercial QC who turned up on the first morning of

3.27 *Accreditation – how to get it*

training and announced that he was there just to get the piece of paper. He knew how to mediate. He paid very little attention during the course Not surprisingly, he failed.

3.27 *Have faith in the process.* One recently retired High Court judge said after the first day that they doubted whether or not they could ever pass the course and were thinking of abandoning it. It was all so different from what they had done for the last 15 years, ie assign blame and tell people what to do. They stuck with it. They passed with flying colours.

3.28 *Be prepared to be tired.* A week's mediation course is intensive. You are learning a lot of new information and being asked to try out new techniques in the company of strangers. You are constantly being assessed. The days are long usually starting around 8–8.30am and finishing around 6.30–7pm. There will be exercises to do overnight to prepare for the role-plays the following day.

3.29 *Keeping in touch.* If you are still working, life will be going on in the office even when you are not there. People will want to speak to you. You will want to find out what is happening. Prioritise. Do not constantly be on your BlackBerry and iPad texting and emailing the office during the training sessions. Trainers recognise that you need to keep in touch and will make sure that there are 'BlackBerry breaks' so that you can stay in touch.

3.30 *Play your part.* Role-plays are a vital part of the training and of the assessment. You may not have formally role-played recently. They are performances. They have something of the quality of improv about them. To do well consider following the rules of improv performers:

- Take the suggestions – ie pickup cues and follow them. Do not go 'off piste' on frolics of your own.
- Make your partners look good!

3.31 On every training course there are those members who are frustrated thespians. They depart from the script. They over-interpret their role. They try and make the exercise difficult for the mediator. Don't follow their example.

If you do, three things happen:

- You make enemies, not friends.
- You are not learning.
- You are increasing your chances of failure in the assessment because you have not done what you are required to do.

You will be told that mediation is essentially a collaborative team effort. So is mediation training. It is not a competitive exercise.

Remember, as this book makes clear, a big part of developing a mediation practice is all about establishing relationships and networks. Start with the people on your course. You are all sharing an experience. You might as well establish productive relationships right from Day One.

Warnings for lawyers

3.32 On most civil and commercial courses lawyers are in the majority. Their biggest difficulty is stopping themselves working out what the answer is and telling the parties.

If you are a lawyer:

- Sit back.
- Let events unfold, even if the solution which emerges is not the one that you would have advised or chosen.
- Don't pre-judge.

Warnings for non-lawyers

3.33 The two biggest difficulties for non-lawyers are 'lawyer envy' and lack of self-confidence.

Do not be:

- Intimidated by the lawyers on the course.
- Frightened that you cannot help the parties because you don't know the legal answers.
- Scared to ask an obvious question.

Assessment

3.34 Different trainers have different forms of assessment, but they all try to teach core competencies. Here is a list of standard ones that any competent trainer will introduce you to. They are likely to form the assessment criteria.

1. Makes a clear opening statement.
2. Reminds parties of confidentiality.
3. Gathers information by asking appropriate questions.
4. Listens, paraphrases and summarises.
5. Demonstrates positive body language.
6. Empathises and develops rapport.
7. Shows understanding of each party's situation and feelings.
8. Reframes.
9. Mutualises.
10. Normalises.
11. Educates the parties (about each other's situation).
12. Engages in reality testing.
13. Enables parties to vent their feelings.

3.35 *Accreditation – how to get it*

14 Encourages parties to look at disputes from different angles.
15 Maintains confidentiality strictly in private sessions.
16 Clarifies and explores issues before developing options.
17 Gives parties relevant tasks.
18 Gives him/herself time to think between sessions.
19 Uses resources creatively.
20 Encourages problem-solving.
21 Suggests options without selling them.
22 Tests the workability of proposals.
23 Uses strategies to resolve an impasse.
24 Shows patience, perseverance and flexibility.
25 Is seen by all parties to be neutral and impartial.
26 Ensures that all parties have opportunities to express their views.
27 Deals effectively with power imbalances.
28 Moves parties from positions to interests.
29 Clarifies information to be disclosed.
30 Brings parties together to get affirmation of agreement, if reached.

3.35 Remember that you do not have to achieve a settlement. But you do have to demonstrate that you can:

- deliver an opening statement (see para **20.27**);
- at least move the parties to start to negotiate (see para **20.31**); and
- have conducted a minimum of three private sessions (see para **20.19**).

Do not worry about showing all 30 listed competences. But do make sure that you display the key ones. These are usually the ones numbered 1, 2, 7, 8, 9, 10, 15, 20, 21, 25, 27, 28, and 29 in the list above.

Looking ahead: observations

3.36 Many newly trained mediators complain about the delay in being able to attend observations. They become frustrated. This is understandable. They have paid for and completed the training. They have undertaken the assessment and passed. They are full of enthusiasm for their new skills and want to use them.

Some but by no means all training organisations will try and place mediators who they have trained on observations. Most say that they offer either a first come first served or a taxicab system.

- Under the first come first served system an email is circulated giving details of potential observation. The first one to reply is allocated to it. It is fair. But it does mean that you have to be alert to receive emails and be in able to respond promptly. If you are in court or in a meeting that is not always easy.

- Under the taxicab system the trained mediators wait their turn on a waiting list until they are called. You need patience.

If you want to obtain observations you have to go and look for them and ask for them. That means contacting mediators introducing yourself and asking them point-blank if they can take you on an observation. Some will ignore you. Others will prevaricate. Others will be happy to take you along.

Where to find mediators?

3.37

- On LinkedIn (see **Chapter 10**).
- In the Directories (see **Chapter 9**).
- At conferences workshops and support groups (see **Chapter 14**).

These are discussed in more detail in the section on mentors at paras **14.01–14.11**.

What to do at observations?

3.38

- Be on time.
- Pay your own fare.
- Take a notebook and pen.
- Keep your BlackBerry/iPhone in your bag.
- Ask the mediator what they would like you to do. Ask if it is alright for you to take notes.
- If the mediator asks you to do something, for example organise some photocopies, do it with a smile.
- Ask the mediator if you will have a chance of discussing things with them during the day for example in intervals between sessions with the parties.
- Always write and thank the mediator.
- Keep your views and opinions to yourself until the mediator asks you for them. Never volunteer them in front of the parties without the mediator's prior express consent.
- You will be surprised at how often people turn up to observations without a notebook and never say thank you.
- Do not sit like a pot plant in the sessions with the parties. Pay attention, show that you are engaged and take notes. Work out what you are learning even if you do not understand some of what is happening.
- Do not engage in proactive body language with the parties. You are observing not mediating.

3.39 *Accreditation – how to get it*

- If you have got on well with the mediator ask them if you can either attend another one with them or they could recommend someone for you to approach for another observation.
- Remember that you are bound by the same confidentiality provisions contained in the Mediation Agreement as everybody else.

Looking ahead: CPD

3.39 You pass your assessment. You undertake your observations. You have your first mediations under your belt. Keep taking the training.

There are three reasons for this:

- It is a CMC requirement.
- It helps prevent you becoming stuck in a rut and provides stimulation and encouragement.
- It fills in the gaps. The more mediations that you do the more you will realise how much more you need to learn. Once you stop realising that, you will switch to autopilot and end up crashing into the mountain of unconscious incompetence.

Be careful about attending expensive CPD training sessions and conferences in far-flung locations. There are plenty of low-cost and even free CPD training sessions available.

Keep looking on the CMC, SCMA and AMATI websites and use your LinkedIn and Twitter accounts.

In a nutshell

3.40

- In reality, if not in theory, you need to be accredited to be taken seriously as a civil and commercial mediator.
- Some trainers are better than others. Ask before you sign up.
- Include the cost of or initial training in your business plan. Don't forget the CPD.
- Work at getting your observations in early. Don't wait for someone to give them to you.

Chapter 4

Know yourself

> In this chapter you will learn:
> - The six key questions to ask yourself.
> - How to focus on your goals.
> - The opportunities and challenges at different career stages.
> - How to cope with rejection.

Socrates

4.01 Anyone wanting to be a mediator must ask themselves six key questions. In fact even those who are already mediators whether active or resting would do well to ask these questions as well. As Socrates said: 'The unexamined life is not worth living'.

Question 1: Why do I want to be a mediator?

4.02 Mediation has a lot of attractions as a career, whether full or part-time.

Here is a list of the main advantages and disadvantages. See which ones apply to you.

4.03 *Know yourself*

MEDIATION AS A CAREER	
BENEFITS	**DISADVANTAGES**
1. Worthwhile	1. Uncertain
2. Giving Something Back	2. Unpredictable
3. No Time-Sheets	3. No Repeat Business
4. More Fun	4. Insecurity
5. No Staff	5. Getting Work In
6. No Boss	6. Draining
7. Short Tail	7. Lonely
8. Flexi-Working	8. No Support Staff/Backup
9. Less Stress	9. Constant Marketing
10. Less Responsibility/Liability	10. Lower Pay
11. High Profit Margin	11. Less Travel
12. Work From Home	12. Rejection
13. No Commuting	13. Frustration

Figure 8

People decide that they want to be mediators for all sorts of reason.

Let us look at some of the most common ones.

An alternative to the 4 Gs: golf, gardening, galleries and grandchildren

4.03 Retirees see mediation as something lucrative and also more stimulating than the 4 Gs to do when they stop working full-time. They do not necessarily see it as a full-time replacement but as something additional to fill their time.

The obvious advantages

4.04 Mediation is:
- *Something that can be done part-time.* As described at para **2.42** the vast majority of mediators, even those who are actively mediating, are part-time. Very few mediators are full-time in the sense that they do not have any other paid employment or work.

- *A development of existing skills.* Some occupations clearly lend themselves to mediation. Obvious examples are lawyers who make up 52% of civil and commercial mediators and those professions which have a legal orientation such as accountants, tax planners, bankers, financial professionals, diplomats, contract negotiators, surveyors, architects and engineers. The overlap of skills and experiences is self-evident.

Others at the opposite end of the problem-solving spectrum such as the 'helping or healing' professions, ie psychologists, psychiatrists, HR professionals, counsellors and therapists of various persuasions also see obvious links with mediation.

4.05 But many people are drawn to mediation from professions with no obvious immediate overlap with mediation, for example airline pilots, musicians, actors, IT professionals and journalists.

All bring different attributes, experiences and expectations to being a mediator. There are some generic opportunities and challenges but also some individual ones depending upon your starting point. These are examined later at para **5.44**.

The opportunities for retiree mediators

THEY HAVE LIFE EXPERIENCE

4.06 Parties to a dispute are more likely to accept the intervention of someone who is obviously experienced as opposed to a recent university graduate of 22. Older mediators have dealt with a wider variety of people and situations. In short they have maturity.

THEY HAVE A RANGE OF CONTACTS

4.07 Many of these will be as a result of their work so they have occupational networks. Others will be personal or social contacts. Generally the older you are the more chance you have had of developing well- established networks. See **Chapters 12** and **14** for the importance of networks.

THEY ARE NOT UNDER FINANCIAL, PROFESSIONAL OR PSYCHOLOGICAL PRESSURES

4.08

- *Financial pressures*: Most retirees are not looking to mediation as the primary source of their income. They will have pension and investment income. Any money that they make from mediation will be a useful but not essential supplement. This gives them greater flexibility about pricing. In short they can charge less if they want to. This can be a potential price advantage. How much to charge is discussed in **Chapter 16.**
- *Professional pressures*: They do not have to justify the time they spend in training or carrying out mediations to anyone else. This is very different from mediators who are working for example in a firm of solicitors or surveyors. They still have to meet targets and make sure that their teams are busy.
- *Psychological pressures*: They have the freedom to fail. This is not a freedom enjoyed by those who are working full-time, either for themselves or others.

4.09 *Know yourself*

Having reached retirement, retirees will have achieved a certain level of accomplishment. They do not have to prove themselves to anybody but themselves. Of course they want to succeed in a new venture – otherwise why do it? But they can take a more relaxed approach. This can have an important influence on their mediation style. This is discussed in more detail in **Chapter 5.**

THEY HAVE MORE CHOICE

4.09   Retirees have fewer constraints on their time. They can pick and choose when to be available more easily than those who are engaged full-time in other occupations, whether self-employed or employed.

The challenges for retiree mediators

THEY LOSE TOUCH

4.10   Many retirees say that within the first 12 months of retirement old contacts still want to be in touch with them because they are of value and interest. This level of involvement falls off rapidly over the next 24 months. Annual reunions are not sufficient to refresh or renew old relationships which could be of value in developing a new business as a mediator. If you are off the radar why would people remember you when they are looking for a mediator?

THEY BECOME OUT OF DATE

4.11   Retirees are often surprised at how quickly they become out of date and de-skilled. For example many professionals are required to undertake continuing professional development training (CPD). Retirees are under no such obligation. Although the Internet provides plenty of opportunities to keep up-to-date there are two problems.
- Simply by not being in the daily swim retirees do not pick up on what is happening. The daily learning by osmosis stops.
- As time passes the motivation to keep up-to-date by reading professional journals, attending webinars and seminars or just scanning email updates can fade quite easily.

THE DON'T HAVE ENOUGH TIME

4.12   It is a clichéd paradox amongst retirees that they tell each other that they do not know how they found the time to go to work. Their days are taken up with other activities – some of them being the 4 Gs.

THEY LOSE OLD HABITS AND FIND IT HARD TO ACQUIRE NEW ONES

4.13
- Old habits may die hard but it is very easy to lose the habit of work, routine and deadlines. This can make it more difficult to stay committed to establishing a new venture.
- New habits can be harder to acquire. Although mediation skills may be a development of skills that have been practised and learned during a working lifetime they are not exactly identical. Indeed some are fundamentally different.

For example being a mediator and being a judge are the exact opposite of each other. Going through the evidence, working out what the right answer is and instructing people what they must do is not how mediators are trained to behave. Lawyers, of course spend their whole time doing this. That is why mediation trainers often say that lawyers find it more difficult than non-lawyers to acquire the mediator skill set and mindset.

THEY SUFFER FROM LONELINESS

4.14 Retirees often experience loneliness when they have been cut off from their world of work. But there is a different kind of mediator loneliness. By its nature mediation is a solitary pursuit. For reasons of confidentiality (see **Chapter 18**) mediators cannot discuss with each other in any detail what happens at mediations. They do not know what other mediators do. They have limited scope for discussing with others what they themselves do. If mediators are not regularly bumping into other mediators this can become dispiriting. And if there is one thing that mediators cannot allow to happen at any time, it is to become dispirited (see **Chapter 21** for the qualities of a mediator).

TOP TIP

- Don't leave it until you retire or are in the last six months before retirement before you decide to become a mediator.

- Research the market for training and accreditation. Talk to other mediators about how they are finding things see **Chapter 3** on training).

- Qualify before you retire. Your availability will suddenly improve once you have retired. If you are already trained and accredited you can start taking appointments straight away.

- Ideally you should be accepting appointments as a mediator before you retire. In practice this means that you need to have completed your training and accreditation at least 24 months before you retire. See the Mediation Timeline at **Figure 4** at para **1.16**. When people ask you, as they inevitably will: 'what are you going to do when you retire?' you will be able to say: 'I am going to concentrate on my mediation practice'. Immediately you have an introduction to them to ask if they will be able to supply you with any work.

Moonlighting

4.15 You are a moonlighter if you see becoming a mediator as an additional or ancillary activity. You are not starting out by thinking that mediation is going to be your main source of income or what you spend most of your time doing. It is something extra.

People want to do mediation as an add-on to their main activity or job for various reasons:

4.16 *Know yourself*

Stimulation

4.16 Doing the same thing for a few years can become monotonous. You enjoy it. You are well practised. But it is not making you learn new things. You are in danger of becoming stale. You need to be stimulated. For the same reason some people become Non-Executive Directors. This gives them opportunities for applying their existing skills in new contexts.

It can be the same with mediation. As discussed in **Chapter 11**, many of the skills that you need as a mediator are ones that you already have. And the skills that you need to be a salesman for your mediation business are the same ones that you acquire as a mediator.

Dipping a toe in the water

4.17 Many people feel occupationally jaded. They want to try something else.

They hear about mediation. It sounds ideal. You do not have to work five or six days a week. You work one or two days instead. You charge between £2,000 and £3,000 a day and work for yourself. No more bosses. No more staff. How much more attractive than the daily grind of the treadmill?

But they are not sure that they can make the financial and personal commitment to give up their full-time job and become a full-time mediator. They therefore want to test the opportunities by dipping their toe in the water.

4.18 Is this a good idea? There are at least two schools of thought.

- Andrew Goodman, a successful and well-known mediator, told a workshop organised by the Chartered Institute of Arbitrators in London on 3 February 2015 that you have to commit yourself. Once you have completed your mediation training you cannot go back to your day job. You have to make mediation your day job.

- On the other hand, Jane Gunn, another well known and successful mediator, writing in the Charted Institute of Arbitrators' magazine, 'Resolver', says:

    'I would advise that mediators don't give up their day job until they have built up their experience and knowledge and understood how they are going to carve a niche for themselves and market themselves.'

Both appear regularly on the platform at conferences and workshops and also have substantial training practices.

So are there any really full-time mediators?

4.19 As described in **Chapter 2** many mediators who describe themselves as full-time mediators could be said to make their money from mediation rather than from just doing mediations. In other words they have a portfolio of mediation-related activities. Actually acting as a mediator is only one of them.

Extra money

4.20 Most people are glad of the opportunity to earn some extra money. Freelancers can moonlight more easily than employees. If you are employed, then almost certainly your employer will require you to account for the money you earn from mediation. If you are a freelancer working for yourself, any money you earn from mediation on the side is yours.

See **Chapters 16** and **17** for a discussion of employment/self-employment and fees.

To give back

4.21 As noted at para **1.19** some regard mediation as a business and others regard it as a calling. Many people are attracted to mediation by the opportunity of doing good and giving something back. Or they want to make a difference or just try to make things better. There is nothing wrong with altruism. In fact behavioural research demonstrates that a key motivator of people, both in their personal and professional lives, is the sense that they are doing something worthwhile.

Unfortunately as the cliché says: 'Fine words butter no parsnips'.

But it is possible, as this book will demonstrate, to do something worthwhile and be paid for doing it.

The opportunities for moonlighters

THEY ARE ON THE RADAR

4.22 They are still working and interacting with colleagues, connections and competitors. People know who they are. They are making new contacts and refreshing old contacts all day long as part of their normal business.

THEY HAVE A SAFETY NET

4.23 If they are employed, they are working and being paid. They are not under financial pressure. This makes it easier for them to develop their practice in a relaxed and measured way. They do not have to panic if no appointments are coming in. They need not be tortured by a sense of failure if their mediation does not settle. They can go back and carry on with their day job. They are not investing their whole being and self-image in it. They can afford to fail.

RECIPROCITY

4.24 This is a key concept in all aspects of mediation and negotiation. If you are in business you may be able to offer opportunities for mediation or other things to people who can offer them back to you. The most obvious example are lawyers who may be able to refer cases for mediation either to mediation providers or to other mediators direct. If they can do that they can be reasonably confident that in time they will receive mediation appointments back.

4.25 *Know yourself*

Challenges for moonlighters

TIME

4.25 Your main activity, whether you are employed or a freelancer, has the main call on your time.

You will have to find the time to go on the training course. This can mean taking a full working week off as holiday. That is a clear investment of time and leisure, as well as money.

Having trained and become accredited you have to be available. This is the A is PEARL (see para **1.17** about PEARL). You have other demands on your time. Even when you are booked for a mediation something can crop up at work. It takes priority. If you cancel mediation appointments you can soon acquire a reputation for not being reliable or easy to book.

Solicitors can find this particularly difficult because of court dates, which crop up unexpectedly and can be very difficult to break. Paradoxically barristers can find it easier to juggle their diaries than solicitors.

CHARGES

4.26 This is the P in PEARL (Price). If you are employed or a partner in a firm there will be an established charging structure. As a new mediator you will not be able to charge the same rate. See **Chapter 16** for fees.

Even if your employer gives you some latitude because they are encouraging you to become a mediator you will still have to achieve your billing targets. Otherwise you will become extremely unpopular with your employers or partners. So you will still have to make up the chargeable hours somehow.

Freelancers have more flexibility, subject always to the demands of bank managers.

MOTIVATION

4.27 If mediation is an ancillary activity and you can afford to fail you might not be hungry enough to do what you have to do in order to succeed in building an active mediation practice.

> **TOP TIP**
> - It is a good idea to dip your toe in the water.
> - If you are moonlighting you simply have to accept that is going to take time to build up an active mediation practice let alone a financially viable one, which could offer you a full-time job.

Careerists

4.28 There are three categories of careerists:

- Those who want to make mediation their full time career from the start.
- Those who want to switch careers.
- Those who want to run parallel careers.

Early starters

4.29 This is a recent development. There are now 20 year olds who are contemplating becoming full-time mediators from the start of their careers. Typically they complete their tertiary education, which includes a mediation component. An increasing number of law courses, for example, include mediation practice and theory either as an optional or a compulsory module

Some university courses provide that, on completion of the mediation module, students are accredited as mediators. Students on graduating therefore come on to the market ready, willing and able to mediate.

Others complete their tertiary education and learn about mediation either from other students or mediators and decide that it is the sort of career that they would like to have.

OPPORTUNITIES FOR EARLY STARTERS

4.30 Early starters have energy and enthusiasm. In the immortal words of Arthur Daley: 'The world is their lobster'.

They are more open to new ideas. This includes new technologies such as ODR and new ways of thinking.

They are far more familiar with social media. They are digital natives not digital exiles (see **Preface**).

People tend to want to deal with people like them. Early starters will find themselves more accessible to the youth market. Entrepreneurship and start-ups are far more common amongst those in their 20s than they were 20 or 30 years ago. That could generate business.

CHALLENGES FOR EARLY STARTERS

4.31 They lack the E in PEARL (Experience). They do not have very much experience. The time simply has not been available to them to complete lots of mediations. They have limited life experience.

They lack the R in PEARL (Reputation). Experience and reputation go together. As can be seen from the discussion at para **6.08**, reputation is one of the main factors influencing customers when they chose a mediator.

NOT ENOUGH GREY HAIR

4.32 Reverse ageism as a barrier to entry was discussed in **Chapter 2.** Many people find it difficult to accept advice from people significantly younger than

4.33 *Know yourself*

themselves. This especially applies if they are having to take difficult decisions about what to do. Even more so, where it is a matter of choosing between unattractive alternatives or there is a high degree of uncertainty. People often draw comfort from hearing advice from those who have seen similar situations and previously advised about them in the past.

This is in addition to the well-known bias in favour of authority. This is discussed in more detail at para **11.10**. It is difficult to project authority, let alone acquire it, if you are only 25. It is much easier if you are 55 or 65.

Switchers

4.33 Many people, having earned their living doing the same things for 10 or 20 years, feel like a change. They can be all sorts of reasons for this:

- approaching a 'midlife crisis';
- plateaued with no obvious routes for advancement or promotion;
- shrinking business in the sector in which they work;
- boredom; or
- family commitments which mean they want to work part-time.

OPPORTUNITIES FOR SWITCHERS

4.34 They have a launch pad. They have fund of experience and contacts. They have life experience.

They may have transferable skills. This will be particularly true if they have worked in any sort of advisory capacity. Some are obvious, for example HR specialists will find it relatively easy to transfer to being workplace mediators.

CHALLENGES FOR SWITCHERS

Unrealistic expectations

4.35 Trainers tell stories of people turning up on their introductory training course having left their full-time job. They are full of enthusiasm. They expect to be earning a living from mediation by the end of the year. Almost all are doomed to disappointment.

Negative outlook: run in the right direction

4.36 If you want to change careers because you are basically dissatisfied with your lot, be careful not to transfer that dissatisfaction and sense of failure or grievance to your new career. Remember, mediators must at all times exude relentless optimism, energy and hunger for the future.

Mediation may, for most mediators, be a part-time job but when you are mediating you have to be engaged full-time with the clients and their problems and give 100% commitment.

In other words don't run away from something – run towards something.

Adjustment anxiety

4.37 Moving from an established career to being a freelance mediator can be very unsettling and stressful. You may have to re-engineer your whole way of working and, without exaggerating, your whole way of life. If you are used to working in a towering glass and steel monument to Justice or Finance you will find it difficult working from your spare bedroom at home.

All the support services that you took for granted such as someone to do your typing, filing, making appointments, ordering photocopy paper, sorting out your IT glitches disappear. If you don't do it, who will?

Some of these tasks can be outsourced (see **Chapter 17** on Administration). But you have to become more self-reliant. Working for yourself instead of working someone else is a fundamentally different way of life. Are you psychologically ready for it?

Financial pressure

4.38 You have to find a replacement income stream. That is not always as easy as you might imagine. This is why it is imperative that you have absolute clarity about what your objectives are, what is your route to them and what resources you have available to get you there. These are discussed in **Chapters 5** and **7**.

The sense of running out of money can be very debilitating, dispiriting and stress-inducing.

Lack of direction

4.39 Switching can be very disorientating. This arises from a combination of lack of clarity and the withdrawal of support services. Hence you must have a business plan and, if not a mentor, at least membership of support groups. See **Chapters 7** and **14**

Parallelists

4.40 One strategy for developing your mediation practice is to reinvent yourself (see para **1.03**). If you take this route you may find yourself also practising as a coach, teacher, counsellor, expert, arbitrator, therapist or change manager.

In other words mediation is only part of your offering. It may be the main part or just an ancillary activity.

OPPORTUNITIES FOR PARALLELISTS

Maximising complementary skills

4.41 Parallelists try to leverage their skills. Some skills are transferable and they transfer them. Bill Marsh, one of the UK's leading civil and commercial mediators, calls it 'vertical integration'.

4.42 *Know yourself*

Many mediators do not just mediate. They arbitrate and adjudicate as well. In other words they are in the business of helping clients solve disputes. Arbitration and adjudication are adjudicative. Mediation is not, at least the facilitative version is not. Lawyers who do this say that they find it easy to adopt this trinity of roles. Others are not so sure.

Other mediators offer, in addition to mediation services such as, coaching, counselling, mentoring and therapy. They tend to be offered by non-lawyers. There are overlapping skills required in all these roles such as: the ability to ask questions, to listen, to read between the lines, establish rapport, encourage perspective shifting and so on. Lawyers are parallelists as well. For example, John Sturrock, Scotland's most successful commercial mediator describes himself on LinkedIn as 'Mediator, Facilitator, Strategic Adviser, Innovator, Prompter of New Thinking'.

CHALLENGES FOR PARALLELISTS

Mixed messages

4.42 A harassed solicitor acting on behalf of a stressed client with a trial date approaching needs to go to mediation because the court is expecting it.

He looks for a mediator. Is he going to choose someone whose website says mediator or someone whose website says: 'Mediator, Peacemaker, Coach, Change Manager and Negotiator'?

Can you be all things to all men? Do you have, in fact, to limit your options and for example specialise in mediation? Remember the advice to be niche in **Chapter 1**.

Spreading yourself too thinly

4.43 You decide to appeal to different markets or different segments within the same market by offering different services. Will you have the time, money and energy to go to all the conferences, read all the websites and meet all the key people?

There are mediators who seem to attend every mediation conference, seminar or workshop and sit on all the committees and working groups. How do they have time to mediate? If you are also attending negotiation, coaching and change management courses and conferences you have even less time. It is all a matter of balance and priority.

Don't forget availability is one of the key factors when choosing mediators (see the A in PEARL at para **1.17**).

Question 2: Where do I want to be in three years' time?

4.44 This is a key – but difficult – question. Most of us find it hard to think about what we will be doing in the future and what sort of person we will be. Three years seems to be a time frame for thinking ahead that we can cope with.

For example, when trying to decide whether not buy a business or make an investment, three years is often the period in which people expect to see a return on their investment. Three years is the average length of a degree course in the UK. Staying in a job for less than three years can be seen as revealing nomadic tendencies.

To help you structure an image of where you want to be in three years' time consider the following questions:

How do I want my life to be different?

4.45 This is the big general question. It really depends on why you want to be a mediator in the first place. Which of the four categories do you fall into? Are you a retiree, moonlighter, careerist or parallelist?

How many mediations a year do you want to do?

4.46 Responses to this question at workshops on 'Developing your mediation practice' vary from '50', '12', 'twice as many as I'm doing at the moment' to the really helpful one: 'as many as possible'.

You do have to quantify and not just express your goal in aspirational terms. As the Business School maxim says: 'If you cannot measure it; you cannot manage it'.

When thinking about this you also have to ask yourself two subsidiary questions:

- How many mediations did I do last year?
- How many mediations have I done in total?

You can then compare what you have done to date with what you want to achieve in the next 36 months. That will help you do two things:

- assess how realistic your expectations are; and
- work out how you're going to get there.

How much money do I want to be earning?

4.47 **Chapter 16** is devoted to the subject of money. But also take a look at the section on average earnings at para **16.06**.

How much you want to earn is linked to how many mediations you are doing. Remember the conclusions from the 2014 CEDR survey in **Chapter 2**:

- the average fee per commercial mediation charged by less experienced mediator was £1,422;
- the vast majority of less experienced mediators ie those doing 10 a year or less, earn about £15,000 year; and
- those doing 20–30 mediations a year earn on average about £70,000.

4.48 *Know yourself*

If you want to earn £50,000 a year, in the current UK mediation market you will probably have to do 20–25 mediations. Just taking an average fee of £2,000 for a day's mediation means that you have to do 25 mediations. That is two every month of the year. Or one every other week. How long will it take you to reach that level?

How many days a week do you want to be working at mediation?

4.48 Again this question depends on why you want to be a mediator. Someone who is still working full-time will have less availability than a retiree.

Work out how many days a week you can devote to mediation. In **Chapters 13** and **14** we discuss how the time you are able to invest can be spent.

As a rule of thumb, for every day spent actually doing a mediation there is another day's worth of time spent in associated activity such as:

- setting up the mediation;
- making pre-mediation contact with the parties;
- preparation;
- general administration such as billing;
- writing confirmatory emails both before and after the mediation; and
- travel.

So if you are doing two mediations a month that means you will be spending a day a week on mediation work. But as the Managing Director of one of the world's largest providers of mediation services said, when talking about the UK market: 'It's much harder to get the mediations in than to do them'. So you may find yourself spending more time than this networking, marketing and blogging.

When you are not mediating how will you spend your time?

4.49 Again, how you answer this question depends on why you want to be a mediator in the first place. But take note that if you want to grow and maintain a practice of 25 mediations a year then you will have to spend time on marketing and selling (see paras **8.11** and **8.12**).

Retirees may want to indulge in at least some of the 4G's of gardening, galleries, golf and grandchildren. Parallelists will be coaching, training and juggling their complementary offerings.

This leads to the supplementary question of how many days a week do you want to be working?

For many people mediation is an attractive career as described at para **4.02** (see **Figure 6**). One of the reasons is the expectation that they can earn a reasonable income without working full-time. In practice many part-time mediators find they have to devote a significant amount of time to their business. How much do you have available?

Question 3: How will you get to where you want to be?

4.50   If you want to move from doing three mediations a year to doing 25 mediations a year you will need a route map (see para **4.65**).

- Where are the mediations going to come from?
- Where is the orchard in which the low-hanging golden mediation apples dangle?
- Having found it how you can you get into it?
- What is your input/output ratio? Would you rather do four mediations at £2,000 a time all eight mediations at £1,000 a time?
- Where are you on the Mediation Timeline? (See **Figure 4** at para **1.16**.) Are you an apprentice, an intermediate, an expert or a snowballer?

Question 4: How much money, time and effort can you invest?

4.51   Remember Basic Premise One in **Chapter 1**: starting a mediation practice is just like starting any other business. You have to work out what resources you have available to invest in it.

Many of those who have recently trained and been accredited as mediators think that they can establish a practice at almost nil cost. It can be done at a low cost but not for nothing. For example, if you are a retiree you will be able to work from home, which you have already paid for. The additional costs of being a mediator will be limited. If you are working for someone else and doing the occasional mediation there is probably almost no cost to you (see **Chapter 7**).

Headline costs

4.52   But there are costs. They are set out in detail and discussed in **Chapter 7** but the headline ones are:

- Professional indemnity insurance.
- Telephone and email.
- Professional fees – for example subscriptions to professional bodies, panel membership fees, conference and workshop fees. You can see from the analysis in **Chapter 7** how these can add up. Many a mediator ends up deciding not to renew a panel membership because they have received so little work from the panel and their earnings barely covered the cost of membership.
- Marketing – **Chapter 12** explores this in detail.
- If you are going to network – How many conferences and gatherings can you afford to attend? The fees, the hotel and meal charges all have to be paid for.

4.53 *Know yourself*

- How many lunches can you afford to buy?
- What promotional material are you going to give away? Pens, memory sticks, mugs, podcasts, video blogs all have to be paid for.
- Are you going to carry out surveys? Will you do it yourself or outsource?
- Administration – Will you do it all yourself? Will you have a virtual office? Will you have a telephone answering service? See **Chapter 16**.
- Additional training: you attend a basic civil and commercial mediation course. You successfully complete it and become accredited. Your learning and the need for training do not stop there. There are professional requirements for CPD (see **Chapter 3**). Even if you are not required to undertake further training you will need to keep yourself up-to-date and refreshed.

Where are all these questions leading?

4.53 The destination of all these questions is: a business plan.

Many mediators accept **Basic Premise 1** that setting up a mediation practice is like setting up any other business. Most also agree that when setting up a business you need a business plan. None of them, when asked, had a written business plan for their own mediation practice.

One recently qualified mediator who is successfully growing her practice said that she did have a business plan. When asked if it was written down, she said that it was not but it was all in her head. After a pause she started to scribble one on the back of the menu and said she would write one up when she returned home

The power of writing things down is well known to mediators. This is why they ask parties to write out their offers and proposals and confirm agreements in writing after mediation. Research shows the importance of writing down plans if you want to increase your chances of carrying it out successfully.

How to draw up a business plan is covered in **Chapter 7**.

Question 5: Why would you choose yourself as a mediator?

4.54 This is an easy question to ask and a hard one to answer. But you have to do it.

The process is as important as the outcome. In formulating the answer you have to examine exactly what you have to offer the mediation market. If you are struggling to do this find a sympathetic critic and ask them. Or look at the self-audit at **Figure 9**.

Being clear about what you are doing and who you are is essential. So is the ability to distil your message in a clear, crisp short way. The importance of this is discussed in detail at para **8.12** and in **Chapter 13**.

Know yourself **4.55**

YOU		CH	QUALIFICATIONS		CH
MALE/FEMALE			LAWYER/NON LAWYER		2
AGE		2	GRADUATE DEGREE – SPECIFY		
20			LANGUAGES – SPECIFY		9
30			PROFESSIONAL QUALIFICATIONS		
40			PUBLICATIONS	BLOG	9/13
50				BOOKS	
60				ARTICLES	
70					
STATUS	EMPLOYED	4	MEDIA	TV/RADIO	9/13
	SELF EMPLOYED			YOUTUBE	
	RETIRED			PODCASTS	
MONEY	SOURCE OF INCOME	16	MEDICAL		9
	CURRENT £		LEGAL		
	FUTURE		FINANCIAL		
	MINIMUM EARNINGS		PROPERTY		
12 MONTHS 24 36 60			COMPANY		
TIME AS	FULL TIME/	7	PSYCHOLOGICAL/		
MEDIATOR	PART TIME		BEHAVIOURAL		
ETHNIC BACKGROUND		2	I.T.		15
MARRIED/DIVORCED/		2	M.B.A		
SEPARATED					

RESOURCES	CH	EXPERIENCE	CH
TIME	7	INDUSTRY	2/9
MONEY	7	MAIN JOB	
		NON-EXECUTIVE	
PACE	7	VOLUNTARY	
I.T.	7/15	START-UP BUSINESS	
TRAINING	3	RUNNING BUSINESS	14/7/17
		SALES	
MENTORS/MEDIATORS	14	NEGOTIATION	
CONTACTS/NETWORKS/	12/14	H.R.	9
DATA BASES		POLITICS	9
		CONFLICT	9
		CRISIS MANAGEMENT	9
		MEDIATOR	

Figure 9

Question 6: How well do you cope with rejection?

4.55 Nobody likes to be rejected. As a mediator you will be rejected all the time even when you have become established and successful.

Rejection arises in the following circumstances:
- People are looking for a mediator. You do not even make the long list, let alone the shortlist.

4.56 *Know yourself*

- You are on the shortlist but somebody else is chosen.
- Having been chosen, you are mediating. You make various suggestions. Some will be innocuous and noncontroversial such as 'let us have a joint opening session'. Others are more interventionist. You see that the parties are stuck and you suggest a way forward. One or other of the parties rejects your suggestion. You cannot allow yourself to become dispirited.
- You are busy networking. Your suggestions for follow-up meetings or a coffee are either expressly declined or just ignored.
- You are trying to establish a presence. You make suggestions for seminars and talks. You submit ideas for articles and books. There are no takers.

And worst of all is the feeling of rejection when you have worked very hard all day to try and help the parties reach a solution and no settlement has been achieved. No matter how many mediations you do you always feel more cheerful and less tired when a mediation produces a settlement than when it does not. You feel disappointed at the rejection of your ability and effort.

As for coping with the rejection following a failed mediation take heart from the motto of Alan Limbury, a very experienced and successful international mediator. He advised at the 2015 IMI Mediation Roundtable that: 'All disputes that settle at mediation are because of you as the mediator. All disputes that do not settle are because of the parties'.

Our brains do not distinguish between physical pain and emotional pain. This means that we can use the same methods to deal with them. Taking painkillers works for easing emotional as well as physical pain. Jia Jang has investigated this phenomenon. See his book *Rejection Proof* (Random House, 2015). His conclusion is that the best ways of dealing with rejection are:

- Treat all challenges and rejections as a game.
- Don't underestimate the propensity of people to help when asked.
- When in pain turn to those who do accept you.
- Look for the humour in the situation – it will help you switch perspectives.

So you do have to ask yourself how you will cope with rejection. If you find rejection hard to accept you will have to develop some coping strategies. If you do not you will end up feeling disillusioned, bitter and out of work as a mediator.

Seven tips for coping with rejection

4.56

1 *Do not assume that the rejection is permanent and pervasive.* Everyone is rejected at some time, it is not just you. For example, freelance writers expect to have to pitch 12 ideas before one is accepted. Actors are rejected at auditions every day. The conversion rate for even well-established civil and commercial mediators is low. Figures are understandably hard to come by. But anecdotally it seems that, at best, 33% of all enquiries lead to a paid appointment. The working ratio is 25%. And many mediators report that this is dropping.

2   *Remember that it is only business.* Do not take it too personally. That is easier said than done when what you are selling is yourself but develop detachment.

3   *Be aware of how you respond to rejection.* Being rejected usually feels like your expectations have been violated in some way. So be realistic in your expectations.

4   *Do not over analyse the rejection.* If you can find out why someone did not appoint you as a mediator, well and good. But you will find it surprisingly difficult to do this. Research has shown that 50% of the damage done to us on rejection is by the rejection itself. The other 50% is what we do to ourselves in trying to cope with rejection.

5   *Move on and take action.* You can only control what can be controlled. So network, blog, make contact with potential customers. Do not dwell and whinge.

6   *Recognise that at the beginning you are likely to receive many more rejections than acceptances.* Take comfort that it happens to everyone. It's not just you.

7   *Take note that rejection is not as bad as you think that* is. The negative feelings do not last as long as you fear. Keep it in perspective. As far as possible follow the advice of Professor Martin Seligman (*Learned Optimism: How to Change Your Mind and Life 2006*) the expert in positive psychology, and regard rejection as:

    - temporary, not permanent;
    - specific, not universal;
    - external, not personal.

8   *Keep a photograph of your favourite person handy.* Look at it when you are feeling rejected and low.

In a nutshell

4.57

- All you can do is keep on keeping on. Eventually you will have some success. Latch onto the small wins and they will snowball.
- Accept that rejection is part of the mediator's way of life.

Chapter 5

Know your product

> This chapter discusses:
> - The different mediation styles and models.
> - The Big Four.
> - Are you selling mediation at all any more?

What am I selling?

5.01 The easy answer is 'mediation'. Unfortunately that does not take you very far. You run up against two other questions:

- What *sort* of mediation are you selling?
- Are you *only* selling mediation or do you have something else?

You need to have a clear understanding of these two questions and to be very clear in your own mind on what your response is.

The product line

Background

5.02 Twenty-five years ago in the UK there was only one 'flavour' of mediation: facilitative. That was the model that was taught and the one mediators were trained to use. There was another flavour proposed: evaluative mediation. These terms were coined in 1996 by Professor Leonard Riskin in *'Riskin's grid' (Understanding Mediators' Orientations, Strategies and Techniques: A Grid for the Perplexed* (1996) 1 Harv Negotiation L Rev 7).

Evaluative mediation was outlawed. Trainers told their students that evaluative mediation was an oxymoron. Mediators did not express opinions on the merits of the parties' cases. If you did that while being assessed on your mediation training course you would be failed.

5.03 *Know your product*

Too much choice?

5.03 Now things are very different. One result of the increasing sophistication and maturity of the mediation market is the proliferation of mediation styles. A recent literature review identified 25 different models of mediation (*Wall and Dunne* (2012)). Many seem to be examples of repackaging and putting old wine into new bottles but there are some new varieties. Mediators who complain that mediation is not as popular with the buying public as it should be perhaps ought to ask themselves whether they are putting customers off with too much choice.

Consider the plethora of styles in **Figure 10**, below.

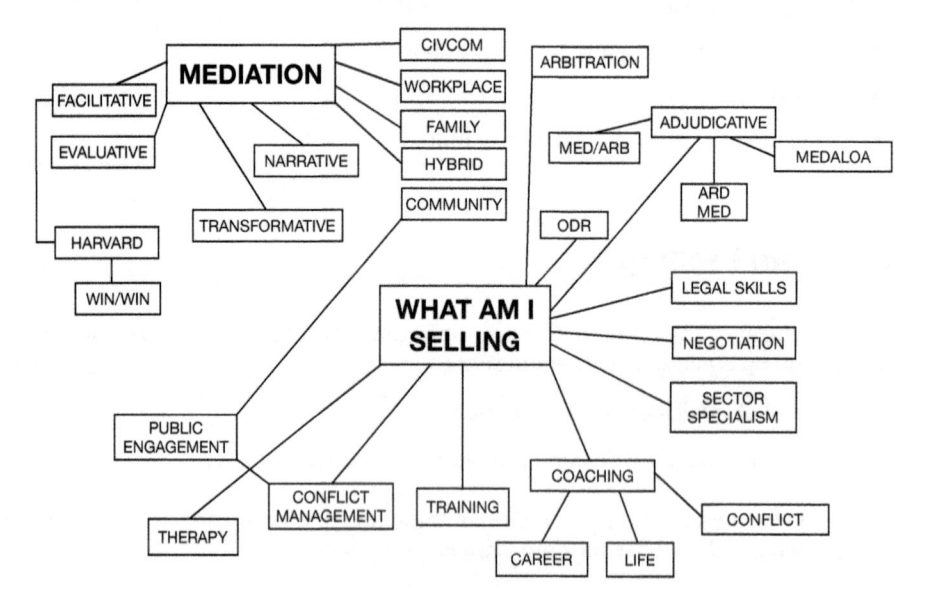

Figure 10

In practice there are five models of mediation that are currently used in civil and commercial mediations:

- Facilitative
- Evaluative
- Transformative
- Narrative
- Indicative

Know your product **5.04**

As a guide consider **Figure 11**, below.

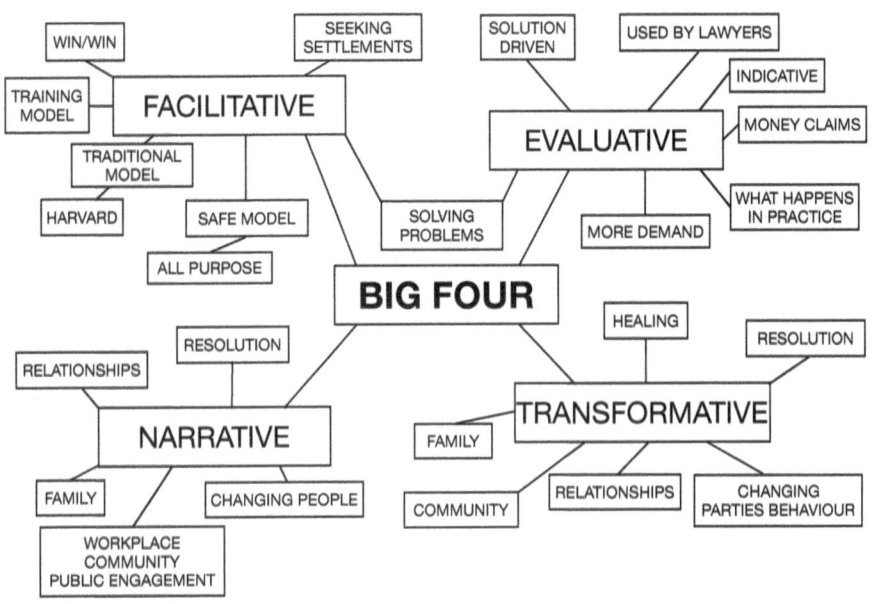

Figure 11

Facilitative

5.04 Facilitative mediation is the classic model. It is still widely taught by mediation trainers in the USA and Europe. It underpins the conventional definition of mediation namely: 'an informal, voluntary, confidential process in which parties to a dispute can with the help of an independent third party meet to work out their own solution'.

The key elements are:

- The mediator helps the parties to find their own solution by taking them through a process. He does not in any way evaluate their dispute, their case or even the proposed settlements.
- The facts are not as important to the mediator as they are to the parties. He does not require a lot of detailed background information. He may not want any documents at all.
- The mediator is in charge of the process but the dispute and the solution remain the property of the parties. Although there are some facilitative mediators who are so devoted to the idea of party autonomy that they tell the parties that the mediation day belongs to them and he will do what they wish.
- The mediator is not a judge and will not say who is right and who is wrong in general or on any particular point.
- The mediator will play Devil's Advocate and engage in reality therapy. This is not because he is taking sides. He is merely testing the parties' expressed positions.

5.05 *Know your product*

He will do the same in both rooms. Sometimes this is described as 'having challenging conversations'.

- By asking open questions the mediator will encourage the parties to tell him what is important in the dispute for them, why is it important and how they would like to see it achieved.

- The mediator will not devise solutions or settlement proposals but he will help generate them.

- The mediator will not give legal advice on anything.

- If asked the mediator will help draft the settlement agreement but the preference is to leave that to the parties' lawyers.

- In order to achieve this the mediator follows the three-stage process: Exploration, Exchange and Formulation (see paras **5.06–5.08**).

In practice

5.05 Facilitative mediators are seen by some commentators and also by some clients and their lawyers as wimps. The accusations are:

- They bring no value to the process beyond making sure that people do not swear at each other and acting as postmen taking messages from one room to another.

- They provide no direction or guidance on how to close a deal.

- They are disingenuous because in fact when acting as Devil's Advocate or applying reality therapy they are being evaluative without acknowledging it. Even if they are not giving opinions they disclose their views by the way in which they frame questions or by their body language when receiving answers.

This is why it is said that facilitative mediation is an oxymoron. It is simply impossible not to be evaluative to some extent. In any case, as the mediation day wears on, all mediators tend to become more evaluative. This happens for various reasons:

- The parties encourage this.

- The mediator feels more confident about his knowledge of the facts and the dynamics of the dispute.

- The mediator has got to know the parties better and feels that he can express an opinion without causing offence. He has built up some intellectual and social capital with them and he can now spend it.

Some types of dispute lend themselves to a more evaluative approach even if the mediator is expressly and consciously adopting the facilitative approach. It is often said that commercial disputes which are about money, with limited personal involvement for the people present at the mediation, fall into this category. They are contrasted with workplace mediations, for example between two warring employees both of whom want to remain in employment.

The three stages

Exploration

5.06 In this stage the mediator wants to find out what each party regards as important in the dispute and what it thinks the other party regards as important. He is looking for answers to three questions:

- what is important?
- why is it important ?
- how do you want to achieve it?

He does through a combination of open questions and active listening (see **Chapter 11**).

Exchange

5.07 The mediator is now finding out what each side needs to know about the other's position. He is trying to fill in gaps in each side's information and understanding. If people have different information they are more likely to have different opinions. The more shared information they have the less scope there is for differing opinions. In this way the mediator is already trying to expand the common ground.

By the time most parties come to mediation they are not communicating directly with each other. They are usually doing it through third parties and, in particular, through lawyers. In any dispute there is always a large element of misunderstanding arising out of poor communication. In this stage the mediator is able to correct misunderstandings.

At all times the mediator respects the confidentiality of the process and only discloses to each party what he has been authorised to disclose.

Formulation

5.08 In this stage the mediator is working with each party to formulate proposals for settlement. Settlements are achieved not by the parties arguing points of evidence or law, but by discussing proposals. The sooner the parties can put proposals on the table that can be discussed the more chance they are giving themselves of achieving a settlement on the day.

In both the Exchange and Formulation Stages the parties are negotiating. In the facilitative model of mediation the theory of negotiation which is most often used is the Harvard Negotiation Project model of Principled Negotiation.

Fisher and Ury in their book *Getting to Yes* set out five principles:

- separate the people from the problem;
- focus on interests not positions;
- invent options for mutual gain;

5.09 *Know your product*

- insist on using objective criteria; and
- know your BATNA (Best Alternative to a Negotiated Agreement).

This model emphasises:

- the primacy of people's interests, not their legal rights; and
- the need for parties to collaborate to achieve an outcome which is beneficial to both sides rather than trying to win something at the other party's expense.

In other words every dispute can be a win-win situation not a zero sum game.

This approach tries to achieve a solution, which is workable for the future. It is not trying to change people or their behaviour.

Evaluative

5.09   Evaluative mediators say that:

- Parties want an opinion on both the merits of their cases and the likely outcome in court and also on settlement proposals.
- As experienced lawyers or specialists (or sometimes both), mediators are well placed to know when clients and other lawyers are bluffing.
- It is useful for the parties to have an independent third party give their view on the merits of their case and their prospects at trial. It helps them concentrate on the realities of their situation.
- The mediators only give their views on the merits of the case if the parties ask for it.
- The mediators are addressing the major weakness of mediation: that there is no guaranteed outcome. The parties may work hard all day trying to reach a settlement, but if they do not succeed, the dispute or the case continues. This is the opposite of what happens in an adjudicative process such as arbitration. There will be an outcome and the dispute will end even if the parties do not like the results. At least there is finality and certainty, which they prize.
- The mediators admit that they are driving the process and the parties towards settlement but they say that is what the parties want them to do. That is why they hired them.

In practice

5.10   Evaluative mediators tend to give their opinions whether they are asked for them or not. QCs and former judges are particularly prone to doing this.

One successful barrister-mediator explains that he see his job as being to spread alarm.

Self-proclaimed and self-confident evaluative mediators can almost end up becoming Early Neutral Evaluators. But they do it:

- as they go along rather than in a considered fashion away from the parties; and
- on a partial understanding of the issues and the evidence.

Professor Di Girolamo quotes an anonymous CEDR mediator as saying:

> 'I meet them at the knees, ie will bring them down to size.... All mediators have to be somewhat evaluative. The parties expect it.'

Are evaluative mediators correct in what they say?

5.11 Do clients really wish to hear the advice of someone who has spent a few hours over the weekend 'reviewing', not 'studying' or 'working through', the documents. Do they prefer this to the advice of their own lawyers, including counsel, who will have spent considerable time on their case and know it much better?

Do clients and their advocates really welcome a mediator saying, after he has been invited to give an opinion on the case, that they are going to lose?

In practice what they want is for the mediator to go to the other side and tell them that they are going to lose.

Some clients want mediators to issue recommendations. Some mediators are happy to do this. Others are not. This is discussed in more detail at para **5.41**.

There is no doubt that, in some jurisdictions including the UK, the market for civil and commercial mediation services increasingly wants evaluative mediators.

Am I being evaluative?

5.12 There is, of course, disagreement in the mediation community about precisely what 'evaluative' means. For example:

- Is it evaluative to give an opinion on the likelihood of the other side accepting a settlement proposal?
- Is it evaluative to identify the legal obstacles which a party will have to overcome at trial?
- Is it evaluative to give an opinion on what is likely to happen at trial?
- Is it evaluative to give an opinion on whether a settlement proposal should be accepted?

Many mediators would say that:

- It is not evaluative to give an opinion about whether a settlement is likely to be accepted.
- It is probably evaluative to identify legal obstacles to be overcome at the trial, although some now would say that it was 'indicative' rather than evaluative.
- It is definitely evaluative to give an opinion on how the judge will decide the case, or whether a party should accept an offer.

5.13 *Know your product*

- It is definitely evaluative to give an opinion on whether a proposal should be accepted.

It is not evaluative to give an opinion on the form, structure and likely acceptability of a settlement proposal. The parties want guidance on how to close a deal. You as mediator are best placed to do this by virtue of your secret weapon, your knowledge of what is happening in both rooms.

Transformative

5.13 Transformative mediation is part of the reaction against problem-solving mediations. Robert Baruch Bush and Roger Folger developed it in 1994.

Like facilitative mediation it emphasises the parties' freedom to choose. The big differences are that the job of the transformative mediator is:

- to help the parties learn from their past experience; and
- to help the parties develop new skills for use in the future with an improved and better sense of control over their own lives.

It is more about changing how people see the world and each other than about finding a settlement or solution.

In other words the parties are being encouraged to examine their past, identify problems and work through them for the future. The primary objective is not a settlement.

It is not widely used in the UK outside community and workplace mediation.

Narrative

5.14 This also draws on the therapeutic tradition. It has its origins in the work of Michael White and David Epston in Australia in the 1990s. They pioneered Narrative Family Therapy. They have applied those techniques to mediation. Its main features are:

- It has a post-modernist flavour with its insistence that there is no such thing as objective truth. They assert that anyone's point of view is necessarily subjective, not objective and is derived from their socio-cultural context.
- It assumes that people see the world in terms of stories or narratives: their own and other people's. The role of the mediator is to encourage the parties to tell their own stories and then to try and understand the other side's. The mediator tries to unsettle and destabilise each party's belief in their own narrative and to try and adopt a new collaborative narrative for the future.
- It prioritises relational over substantive issues.
- It adheres to the post-modernist view that language creates reality and that language is a socio-economic construct, which betrays the power structure in the society in which it is used. This has led to it being employed by mediators working with marginalised groups.

The three stages

5.15 The three stages in narrative mediation are described differently from the stages described at paras **5.06–5.08**. Instead of exploration, exchange and formulation there are:

- engagement; and
- deconstructing the conflict-saturated story; and
- reconstructing a new narrative.

Engagement

5.16 In practice the Engagement phase is much like the Exploration stage. In it the mediator tries to establish a rapport with the parties and, once it is established, encourages them to tell their stories.

Deconstruction

5.17 In the Deconstruction phase the mediator tries to deconstruct the parties' stories and show them that there is another way of looking at things.

Reconstruction

5.18 In the Reconstruction phase the mediator, having helped a party to externalise the conflict, now works with them to co-author a new narrative. This is a narrative in which the parties work together against a common problem.

At this point there can be overlap between the narrative technique and the problem-solving approach. As Prof Toran Hansen summarises:

> 'Narrative mediation is thus interested in resolutions that go beyond simple settlement to consider the effects of the mediation on society at large and, like transformative mediation, considers mediation as a means for conflict parties to achieve a higher moral self.'

See his blog of September 2003 at www.mediate.com.

Are transformative and narrative mediation methods relevant for commercial mediators?

5.19 Both transformative and narrative methods are much more ambitious than the standard evaluative and facilitative models. They both draw heavily on the techniques of psychotherapy. As Professor G Neil Martin in his book *Psychology* (2008) says this is 'usually called the "talking cure" (although it rarely cures)'. Hence the considerable scepticism about these techniques amongst civil and commercial mediators.

5.20 *Know your product*

They doubt the value and relevance to what they do of unrestricted and undirected talk, which tends to be repetitive and self-serving. Its application to conflicts involving parties with on-going and deep relationships is more obvious. But whether it is more effective is a different matter.

Indicative

5.20 Indicative mediation is a newcomer to the mediation scene. It is a halfway house between the facilitative and evaluative models. In the UK judicial mediators practice it for example in the Employment Tribunals' mediation service. Mediators who are resisting their evaluative tendencies also often use it.

The Employment Judges emphasise that this is not the same as the evaluative model.

- They do not say what they think the merits of the case are or how one of their fellow judges will decide the case.
- They identify the hurdles that each side is going to have to overcome in order to win.

Apparently this causes both sides to focus on the realities of their legal positions.

In practice:

- An indicative mediator could easily become evaluative.
- Many facilitative mediators do identify issues that the court will consider at trial and invite the parties to say how confident they are that they will overcome them. They may do this in specific terms by addressing particular issues or more globally by simply asking about the overall confidence factor. They are usually at pains to say that they do not know how the court will decide the case.
- The indicative model is less of a stand-alone model and more of an advanced technique.

Evaluative winning the day?

5.21 The distinction between evaluative and facilitative mediation lingers on in some academic backwaters. But in practice it is redundant. Even Riskin has now said that the terms are obsolete. He has coined the words 'elicitative' and 'directive' as up-to-date replacements. The dichotomy between evaluative and facilitative has been replaced by a spectrum. It is all a matter of degree.

More than that, evaluative mediation is now, for many customers and mediators, the preferred model. Some describe it as 'facilitative mediation with muscle'. For many parties the big weakness in mediation has always been that there is no guaranteed outcome. With adjudicative processes such as arbitration or adjudication there is an outcome. The parties may not like the outcome much but they at least have a determination of the dispute. It is over. They have certainty and finality.

In fact many commentators, including celebrated practitioners, say that facilitative mediation is an impossibility. It is an oxymoron. All mediators whether they like it or not are to some degree or other evaluative. As a mediator you express a view by your gestures, the tone of voice in which you ask a question, your choice of vocabulary, even by the way you stand or sit. You cannot help doing it.

Commercial clients, especially those who are serial users of mediation services, say they welcome a mediator who gives a firm view on the merits of their case and even on what would be a fair outcome of the mediation. Whether they mean it in practice is another matter.

For other clients the last thing they want is an evaluative mediator. They do not mind a mediator who asks penetrating or tough questions but they do not want one who tells them that they may be wrong.

Free marketeers

5.22 Other mediators are free marketeers. By that they mean that they will provide the service that their clients ask them to provide. It varies from mediation to mediation.

The paradox of choice

5.23 One of the problems of this proliferation is that the terms used to describe the different approaches and styles are used almost interchangeably.

Mediation styles: a vocabulary list (this is in alphabetical not relevance order).

Bargaining	Directive	Elicitative	Evaluative	Facilitative
Indicative	Insight framework	Integrated	Interventionist	Narrative
Norm generating	Norm educating	Strategic	Social emotional	Task orientated
Therapeutic	Trashing, bashing and hashing			

Some of these appear to be distinctions without a difference.

Take your pick

5.24 As a mediator you must be clear what sort of mediation model you offer. This raises the interesting question of whether or not they are mutually exclusive. There seems to be an emerging trend where at least practitioners if not commentators say that you just use whatever technique seems appropriate to you in the moment on the day.

Proactivity

5.25 In the end, all this anxious debate may boil down to how proactive the mediator chooses to be. This will be influenced by the mediator's background,

5.26 *Know your product*

personality, comfort zone and, crucially, by the personalities of the parties and their representatives and the way they choose to behave.

It is very rare in any civil and commercial mediation for a mediator not to be asked at some stage during the day what they think. Sometimes the question is about the merits of the case or a particular argument. More often it is about what the party should do. For example:

- Is the settlement a fair one?
- What proposal should they put forward in response to one received from the other side, which they have rejected?
- In the end, should they accept the settlement?
- What would you do if you were them?

As a mediator you have to decide to what extent you are prepared to answer these questions.

This all becomes much easier when you have experience. Some mediators expressly state that they are evaluative. Others expressly state that they are facilitative and refuse to be evaluative in any way at all. Both mediate the same types of civil and commercial mediations and achieve success.

Be flexible

5.26 The only useful practical advice that can be given to a new mediator is: be flexible. Do what you feel comfortable doing. After all you are just starting out and feeling your way.

As explained in **Chapter 3** most mediation training courses in the UK teach the safe model. This is essentially the facilitative model based around the Harvard Negotiation Project philosophy of principled negotiation. See para **5.08**.

To start with stick with what you know. Do a few mediations. Develop your own style that people want to buy. Do not get hung up on doctrinal differences and debates about the One True Path.

As you can see from the following section individual commercial mediators are being inventive to what they perceive that their market wants.

Interventions

5.27 The current orthodoxy is that mediators actually do not evaluate or facilitate. They just make interventions. For these purposes an intervention can be defined as: 'an identifiable piece of verbal and non-verbal behaviour that is part of the practitioner service to the client.' This definition comes from John Heron who was a pioneer of cooperative enquiry in the social sciences. See *Helping the Client* (5th edn, 2001) in which he developed his six-category Intervention Analysis.

Know your product **5.29**

The Heron model

5.28 There are two basic categories of style: authoritative and facilitative.

A mediator making an authoritative intervention is giving information, challenging the other person and suggesting what they should do. A facilitative intervention is one designed to help draw out ideas and solutions from the other person and generally give encouragement.

The two basic categories subdivide into six styles. See **Figure 12** below.

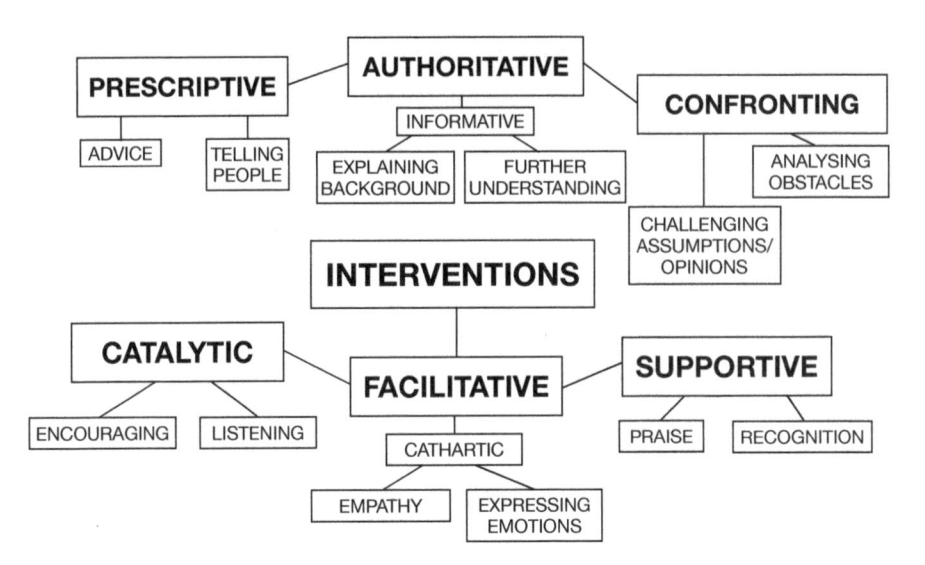

Figure 12

Authoritative

5.29

1 Prescriptive;

- Give advice and guidance.
- Tell the person what they should do.
- Tell them how to behave.

Examples

- 'I think that you need to reconsider ....'
- 'Being adversarial is not going to help ....'

2 Informative:

- Give your view and experience.
- Explain the background and principles.
- Help the person acquire a better understanding.

5.30 *Know your product*

Examples
- 'If you look at it from their point of view then you can ....'
- 'When I was a solicitor I used to take this sort of case to trial and ....'

3 Confronting:
- Challenge the person's thinking.
- Repeat exactly what the person has said or done.
- Tell them what you think the obstacle is.

Examples
- 'What message do you think you are sending when you say that? What message you think is being received?'
- How have you calculated your risk/reward?'

Facilitative

5.30

4 Cathartic:
- Help the other person express their feelings and emotions.
- Empathise with them.

Examples
- 'How do you feel about this?'
- 'Most people feel annoyed if that happens to them.'

5 Catalytic:
- Ask questions to encourage new thinking or generate new proposals.
- Listen and summarise.

Examples
- 'What would happen if you....?'
- 'From what you say it sounds as though you really want revenge.'

6 Supportive:
- Give praise and recognition.

Examples
- 'That's a very helpful suggestion.'
- 'Thank you for that. We are making progress.'

You need to recognise the different sorts of interventions that you, as the mediator, make. The impact of an intervention will be influenced by when and how you make it. You can smile and nod and be friendly while asking the most challenging and confrontational question.

The more authoritative your interventions the more you are likely to be regarded as evaluative or directive. Is this what you want to sell? If you do go ahead and sell it.

Are you selling mediation at all any more?

5.31 If you follow the advice of Bernie Mayer and Tammy Lenski you will be turning yourself into a Conflict Resolution Professional or a meditative influence. Mediation, in whatever model you were trained, will be only one tool in the Conflict Resolution Toolbox. Of course in order to do this you will need much more training. Lenski even suggests taking a Master's degree in conflict resolution.

This suggestion is likely to be unwelcome to newly trained mediators in the UK who are trying to get some civil and commercial mediations under their belt. But think about offering different models of mediation.

One of the themes that was identified in para **2.48** is that there is a growing demand for more evaluative and even adjudicative styles.

Mediators are now offering for example MED/ARB and ARB/MED. Both these hybrid techniques designed to deal with the biggest flaw in mediation, namely that there is no guaranteed outcome.

ARB/MED

5.32 The parties choose the same person to act as both mediator and arbitrator. The arbitration is held first in the normal way. The arbitrator makes his award but does not publish it. He keeps it in a sealed envelope. The parties do not know the outcome.

A mediation is then held in the normal way. There is no procedural change just because it is taking place after an arbitration of the same dispute. Time can be saved in going through the issues and facts because they have already been investigated and explained in the arbitration hearing. In theory at least more time and energy is spent on formulating and structuring settlements.

If the parties reach a settlement it is a legally binding deal. The award is not published. The arbitrator never reveals his decision. If they do not reach a settlement the arbitrator publishes the award in the usual way.

The parties will have a view after the arbitration on what the likely outcome will be. They will see how the witnesses performed and how the evidence came out. They will have closely observed the arbitrator's questions and reactions.

With the mediation taking place before publication of the arbitral award they have an opportunity to achieve an outcome more favourable the one they expect.

There are all sorts of theoretical philosophical concerns about the procedure. But there are mediators, for example Andrew Parsons, a successful barrister and commercial mediator who offers the service when clients request it. In his experience it works well.

At the Eighth Chartered Institute of Arbitrators Mediation Symposium on 8 October 2015 Jonathan Seitler QC explained how he offered what he called Med/Arb.

5.33 *Know your product*

The parties submit their position papers to him in advance. On the day of the mediation he holds a joint session in which each party has 20 minutes to make submissions to him. He can ask questions. At the end of the joint session he takes time for himself to write his decision. He places it in a sealed envelope.

He then conducts a mediation. He says that it is immensely empowering and enables him to sideline obstructive lawyers.

He has developed this model in response to a demand from clients, particularly insurers who are tired of meandering, drawn-out mediations that do not lead to a conclusion. He has done four mediations on this basis and the parties seemed happy with the process.

He conceded that although he called it Med/Arb it was in fact Arb/Med.

MED/ARB

5.33 Med/Arb is the opposite of Arb/Med. The mediation takes place first. If there is a settlement that is the end of the matter. No arbitration takes place. If there is no settlement the same person who acted as mediator conducts an arbitration in the normal way. At the conclusion of the arbitration he publishes his award.

This is seen to pose a bigger problem. Inevitably during the course of the mediation the mediator will learn confidential information. How can he not be influenced by that during the arbitration?

This matter has already been before the English courts which set aside an arbitral award that had been made by an arbitrator who had previously conducted a mediation: *Glencot Development and Design Co Ltd v Ben Barrett & Son (Contractors) Ltd* [2001] EWHC Technology 15.

MEDALOA

5.34 This stands for Mediation After Last Offer Arbitration. It derives from US baseball arbitration.

The key features are:
- If at mediation the parties cannot achieve a settlement, the mediator acts as an arbitrator.
- His sole job as arbitrator is to decide which of the proposals submitted to him by the parties is the most reasonable.
- He picks one and that becomes the arbitral award.
- The idea is that each party will have the incentive to put forward their most reasonable proposal in the hope that the arbitrator will choose it.
- The parties will have the benefit of having had discussions with the arbitrator during the mediation when he was acting as a mediator before formulating their proposal.
- It guarantees an outcome.

Mediator's recommendations

5.35 Many civil and commercial mediators are prepared to offer recommendations about settlement if the parties request this. Usually they require all the parties to request it. But some go further and give themselves the right in their mediation agreements to offer an opinion not just on settlement but on the various legal and evidential issues in the dispute.

Mediators should contemplate doing this. Experienced, rather than novice, mediators will find it easier to offer these three services. The following two suggestions will be possibly more useful for novice mediators as they try to find their mediation feet.

An elegant variation on this theme is where an experienced international mediator was asked in a cross-border mediation taking place in the Middle East to stipulate in his mediation agreement that he would certify any settlement that was reached as, being fair and reasonable. After some deliberation he agreed to do it. He found the process empowering and it made his job much easier as he was able to tell a party that he was not sure that he would be able to certify their proposal.

Arbitration

5.36 Civil and commercial arbitration, particularly of international disputes, is a well-developed and thriving industry. Starting and developing an arbitration practice is no easier than starting than developing a mediation practice. But as identified in **Chapter 15** there is a developing demand for the adjudicative resolution of low value disputes particularly consumer disputes. The new regulations require retailers for example to offer ADR as an alternative to litigation. ADR is not confined to mediation.

The online systems being developed to supply this service usually have the option of the mediator deciding the dispute.

Ombudsman

5.37 There are many schemes. They are often funded by a particular industry or sector. They deal with complaints from users. They try and resolve the dispute by conciliation and negotiation. If they cannot they issue a decision. That decision is usually binding on the industry member but not on the complainant (see **Chapter 15**).

Several mediators, while trying to grow their mediation practice, act as ombudsmen.

Expanding your range of activities

5.38 Traditionally civil and commercial mediators have mediated disputes referred to them by lawyers. In the UK solicitors are often described as the

5.38 *Know your product*

gatekeepers for mediation. You can see why. The dispute has already 'gone legal'. Proceedings may not have actually been issued, but the parties have sought legal advice. Usually proceedings will have been issued. Certainly this is true of court-annexed mediations. In any event the dispute will have been framed in terms of legal rights and remedies not commercial interests and opportunities.

The number of cases in which proceedings have been issued is a relatively stable and, in the UK, gently declining number. In other words court cases are a fixed and shrinking pie. Or in the words of company analysts a low-growth environment.

If you want to prosper as a mediator then you have to look for a high-growth environment. In other words seek out areas of life or a particular business where there is a need for a more efficient dispute resolution system outside that of litigation/arbitration. The ED-MED, ie Education and Health, sector is an obvious example. Both are expanding. But there is increasing competition and costs pressures. There are more and more disputes between providers and customers.

Examples include:

Workplace mediations

The number of workplace mediations has risen significantly. In recent years more rights have been given to employees. Employers are under increasing financial pressure to deliver on targets and cut costs. The potential for disputes between employers and employees or between employee and employees grows every day. HR departments have seen the value of having external mediators. They realise that it can be cheaper to employ an outside consultant to come in and defuse the situation rather than working through protracted disciplinary and grievance procedures. Having warring or disgruntled employees is bad for business.

Others have introduced systems of internal mediation using either full-time or part-time mediators. Local authorities and NHS trusts in particular have adopted this model.

Deal mediations

Deal mediation is now well established where, during projects, parties in the chain of suppliers have disputes. In large complex projects Dispute Resolution Boards have been used for many years. Other projects employ a monitoring system where outside mediators look at communications between the contracting parties and alert management to developing problems. Many such as Resolex use a traffic light system. When Amber is flashing there is a mediated meeting to prevent it turning Red.

This is part of a developing trend to use mediation as a preventative technique. The idea is to intervene early as relations deteriorate before disputes or conflict develop. By way of example one of the country's leading civil and commercial mediators, David Richbell, is now supplying this service through his new business DRP (The Dispute Resolution Partnership).

Change management

The impact of the Internet has led to fundamental changes in all sorts of workplaces. This can cause conflict. Consultants are brought in to help manage the process and minimise friction induced by dislocation.

Coaching

Life and business coaching has been a growth industry. Many of the skills required to be a successful coach are the skills that mediators routinely use. More and more mediators are also training as coaches. Some report that their coaching training helps them in their work as mediators.

Mediation – the client asks: what's in it for me?

5.39 Tammy Lenski makes the excellent point in her book *Making Mediation Your Day Job* that clients are not interested in mediation. Why should they be? What they are interested in is having their problems solved and their needs met. And sometimes a non-mediative or non-adjudicative process is what is required. But just as often what is required is a decision from someone who tells them what to do.

In a nutshell

5.40

- Choose your mediation approach.
- Have a flexible offering.
- Be prepared to use ODR more
- Be prepared to be more evaluative and even adjudicative
- Listen to what the market says it wants to buy. Sell it to them.

Chapter 6

Know your market

In this chapter you will learn:

- Who are your clients.
- What clients want.
- How to find out what clients really want.
- How clients pick mediators.

Who are your clients?

6.01

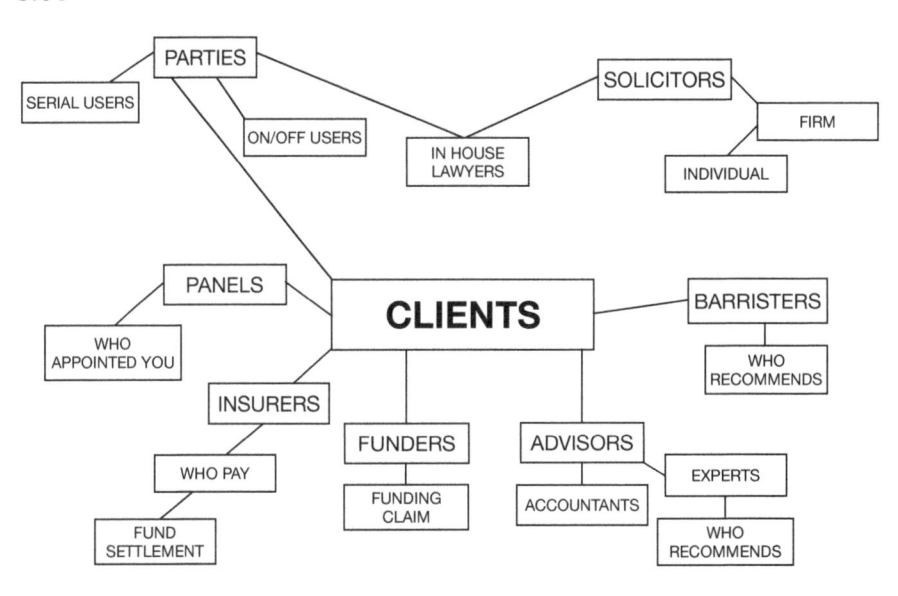

Figure 13

There are several possibilities.

6.02 *Know your market*

The parties

6.02 The apparently obvious answer is the parties to the dispute. In one sense that is absolutely correct. They sign the mediation agreement. They are the people to whom you owe the duties under the mediation agreement. Their representatives may also co-sign the agreement but they are only agents and the parties are the principals.

This is true but trite. And is it really helpful?

6.03 If you want to build a business as a mediator, how will you do it by appealing to the parties at the dispute? If they have representatives, professional etiquette usually prevents you from dealing with them directly, either before the mediation or after it. How do you secure referrals or repeat business from the parties?

Most parties to a mediation have never been to one before and are unlikely to go again. This is less true of commercial disputes especially if the parties' businesses are in a dispute-prone sector, eg insurance, lending, construction or property. Some parties are serial users of litigation and mediation. They are a potential source of repeat business.

In practice the business that they may have for mediators is usually channelled through lawyers. In the UK this usually means solicitors. But not always: in-house counsel, costs lawyers and barristers who are instructed on a direct access basis also contact mediators directly about appointing them.

Not all disputes that can lead to a mediation involve lawyers. Other professions advise clients. Accountants, surveyors, property managers, HR departments can all be advising clients on matters which might turn contentious.

The appointers

6.04 Another answer is therefore whoever appointed you as the mediator. But in reality who did appoint you?

There are several possibilities:

- The parties to the mediation.
- The lawyers who approached you direct to appoint you.
- The panel who secured your appointment.
- The insurers.

The parties to the mediation

6.05 In practice most parties to mediation play little part in the appointment of mediators. Usually they rely upon the recommendation of their legal advisers. This is less true of sophisticated commercial users of litigation and mediation. They often have their own opinions about mediators. Some, for example those who have in-house lawyers or the claims departments of insurance companies, may appoint the mediator directly.

Some solicitors consult their clients about the choice of mediators. More often than not they make a recommendation, which is usually but not always accepted.

The parties' lawyers

6.06 If the parties' lawyers approach you directly they are the ones who effectively appoint you. As discussed below, the process of selecting the mediator is not as straightforward as it might be (see paras **6.11–6.22**). The lawyers tussle over who should be appointed. More often than not this is a power-play between the lawyers or an illustration of the well-known cognitive bias of reactive devaluation, ie if you suggest the idea the other side must think there must be something wrong with it.

If the lawyers approached an appointing body they are still in the end the decision makers – although their choice will have been filtered by the mediation administrator at the panel.

The panel

6.07 Panels operate differently as discussed in **Chapter 9**. Some panel administrators see themselves as impresarios whose job is to develop your career. Others see themselves simply as administrators whose job is to allocate mediations efficiently and fairly. Either way they are the people that you have to impress.

The insurers

6.08 Insurers are serial users of both litigation and mediation. They may handle a claim in-house without using external lawyers. If they do they will have their own views on mediators and offer their suggestions as to who should be appointed. If they use external lawyers they may still make their views known and will almost certainly be consulted by the lawyers about who should be appointed.

There does seem to be a trend amongst insurers to prefer subject specialist lawyers as mediators. For example a professional indemnity insurer dealing with a professional negligence claim against a solicitor arising out of the administration of an estate will often prefer a solicitor mediator who has practised in that area. There seems to be a feeling that in some way such a mediator will have a more instinctive understanding of the problems faced by the policyholder solicitor. The unspoken assumption seems to be that in some way they will be more favourably inclined towards the defendant (see para **6.40**).

There are some mediators who do seem to be favoured by insurers.

What do clients want?

6.09 Different approaches will be needed for each of these potential clients or markets (see **Chapters 8**, **11** and **12** on marketing and selling). In reality, as a new mediator, you will have to rely upon lawyers and panels for your appointments.

6.10 *Know your market*

You have to find out
- What do they want?
- Who are they?
- How do I meet them?

In the end the only way to find out is to assess them directly. This takes time and a lot of effort. Even if you manage to speak directly to a client, whether this is the claims director of a large insurance company or the litigation partner, they may not actually tell you what they are looking for. They will speak in general terms about commercial awareness and the ability to handle difficult people. Whether or not they will be able to provide you with any specific information that will help you refine your marketing materials and your pitches is another matter.

In any case what one person wants may not be the same as what someone else wants. Discussions with the heads of litigation of large firms indicates that the appointment of mediators is to a large extent case-specific. As the Head of Litigation at one large City firm said: 'If you have a strong case you want a mediator who is prepared to stress test the parties' cases. If you have a less than strong case you will want a mediator who takes a more commercial view.'

Luckily there is some general guidance available.

What do clients look for when choosing a mediator?

6.10 Useful information can be derived from four surveys:
- the 2014 CEDR Sixth Mediation Audit;
- the Commercial Mediation Group (CMG) Survey of 2012;
- the 2013 International Mediation Institute (IMI) Survey of In-House Counsel;
- the City of London 2014 Survey undertaken at an international convention held by the Corporation of the City of London (which shows what users, as opposed to their lawyers, want from mediations, see para **6.31**).

In the CEDR survey the lawyers ranked the factors influencing selection as follows:

1   Availability
2   Professional reputation – mediation style
3   Professional reputation – experience/status
4   Fees
5   Sector experience

The CMG survey ranked the following factors

1   Personal recommendation of the mediator
2   Personal experience of the mediator
3   Sector expertise

4   Bedside manner
5   Legal expertise

The IMI survey ranked the following factors

1   Experience as a mediator
2   Past experience with a particular mediator
3   Mediator's personality and attitude
4   Independently verified feedback from other users
5   Experience in the core issue of the case
6   Evidence that the mediator's competency has been independently assessed.

The Big Three Factors

6.11   What the surveys show is that the three main factors influencing choice are:

- Reputation.
- Previous experience of the mediator.
- Sector experience/expertise.

How do clients choose a mediator?

6.12   From the surveys it appears that most people use all the following methods or a combination of them to find a mediator:

Previous experience

6.13   People tend to choose a mediator who has mediated a dispute for them before and has done a good job. Why not use them again?

The advantages are:

- You know what to expect from them and in particular you will know their style of mediation and their personality. That will make it easier to find a match with your client. A key factor is how well the mediator will get on with the client and in particular the decision-makers.
- You know that they can do a good job.
- You know what they will charge.

The disadvantages are:

- Familiarity can start to develop and breed discontent. Both sides start to take each other for granted. The mediator may think that he does not have to try so hard. The instructing solicitor may think that he can cut corners in the preparation because the mediator will not complain and will be able to fill in the gaps himself.

6.14 *Know your market*

- Some solicitors and clients become very sensitive if they think that there is a prior relationship between the mediator and the other side. They think there might be bias. In practice there is no more risk of bias than if counsel are habitually instructed.
- Personal preferences vary. There are some solicitors, including for example the Head of Dispute Resolution at a large international firm, who never use the same mediator twice. Other members of his department, which is over 200 strong in London alone, do.

Recommendations

6.14 This is the second most usual common way of finding a mediator. In many firms e-mails are circulated asking for suggestions or comments on names that have been proposed. Counsel, other mediators and clients as well as colleagues may have suggestions.

Talent spotting

6.15 Mediators seem to be everywhere. There are more and more of us. Just listening to mediators chatting at book launches, seminars, conferences can provide useful information on what they might be like as a mediator.

Some lawyers who regularly instruct mediators attend mediation gatherings such as the Breakfast Club, which meets in the Punch Tavern in Fleet Street, London (see **Chapter 14**). They meet lots of mediators and take note of those that impress.

So put yourself in the opportunity flow and attend these events. Talk to the lawyers present, whether they are mediators or not.

Directories

6.16 In a survey carried out in 2012 by the Commercial Mediation Group, 40% of respondents said they use directories. The two most widely used are *Chambers and Partners* and the *Legal 500*.

See **Chapter 9** for a discussion on Directories.

The Web

6.17 Going onto the web and searching for mediators will produce pages and pages of individuals and organisations.

You need to make sure that those looking find your website (see **Chapter 10**).

Registers

6.18 The CMC maintains a list of its members who have asked to be put on the Register. They do not recommend any particular mediator. They simply provide details.

The FMC does the same.

Panels/Mediation Providers

6.19 These are similar to but different from the registers operated by the CMC and the FMC (see **Chapter 9**).

They are operated by mediation service providers for example the ADR Group, CEDR and JAMS. Most, but not all, of them are also training organisations. Members of their panel have usually trained with them. Others are operated by professional bodies such as the Law Society, the Academy of Experts and the RICS. Most charge their members a fee to be included on the panel. They also charge users a fee for organising and administering the mediation.

In the 2012 CMG survey 56% of respondents said that they used specialist providers and 40% said that they used directories. As the 2014 CEDR Survey reported:

> 'There seems also to have been a halt in long-term trend towards commercial clients and advisers making referrals directly to their chosen mediators rather than working through providers.'

Many mediators join multiple panels. Others limit themselves to one or two (see **Chapter 9**).

Marketing groups

6.20 Increasingly mediators band together for marketing purposes. They form groups which are not attached to a training company or a professional body. They come together for administration and marketing. Examples are In Place of Strife or The Panel of Independent Mediators. They are independent mediators who share some common facilities. More and more marketing groups are being formed.

Many are by invitation only. But you can always ask if they have a slot for you. There will be a cost.

See para **9.19** for how to set one up.

Barristers' chambers and firms of solicitors

6.21 Barristers who are in chambers have a clerk. When acting as a mediator they are usually clerked in the same way. Some chambers identify specialist ADR groups within their set and offer mediation suites. Some mediators have become door tenants to chambers to give them this increased exposure. Others have re-qualified as barristers to acquire greater professional credibility.

Some firms of solicitors offer similar facilities and have set up specific mediation arms distinct from their litigation and/or dispute resolution services.

6.22 *Know your market*

Individuals/independents

6.22 Most mediators fall into this category. Some may also be panel members or work in professional firms. Many are not associated or affiliated with anyone. They rely upon their website and networking (see **Chapters 10** and **12**).

The 'little black book'

6.23 Many firms, especially as part of quality control programmes have databases listing approved suppliers. These will include barristers, forensic experts and now mediators. Many practitioners, after a few years, develop their individual little black book of favoured and trusted professionals who they can call upon.

You can contact the firms and ask how you can get on their list. Or you just get to know some of the partners and nudge them to include you. This takes time.

Reasons to reject you

6.24 Most lawyers adopt one of two policies when choosing mediators:

- They go with the other side's choice of mediator. The reasoning is that, provided you know nothing bad about the mediator and the other side like using him, you agree with their choice. This is because the other side have confidence in him and are more likely to take note of what he says.
- They look for a reason to reject the other side's choice. Any pretext will do. They look for reasons to reject you.

Prepare yourself

6.25 Here is a selection of questions that you may face. Work out your answers.

How are you accredited?

6.26 For civil and commercial mediations it can be dangerous to appoint someone who is not accredited either directly or indirectly by the CMC.

How are you regulated?

6.27 This is a similar point to the one above. The limited scope of regulation was discussed at paras **22.32–22.43**. Why choose someone who is not regulated at all?

Do you have professional indemnity insurance?

6.28 So far there have been few claims against mediators in the UK. There will be more. PI insurance for mediators is cheap. Make sure that you have it (see **Chapter 17**).

How many mediations you have actually done?

6.29 There is no agreed definition of an experienced or advanced mediator. Within the mediation community a rule of thumb is that mediators who have carried out fewer than ten mediations cannot call themselves experienced. Some providers rank their mediators by the number of mediations that they have done. Clerksroom for example have a category of elite mediators who have carried out over 50 mediations.

What you will be asked is how many mediations you have carried out as the lead mediator. This does not include observations, acting as an assistant or co-mediator or even being a representative at a mediation.

Do not lie but maximise your relevant experience. Ways of doing this are discussed in **Chapter 9** on preparing a good profile.

Can I talk to you?

6.30 As mediators we are only too happy to receive enquiries for our services. Make yourself available to talk to people if they ask.

Some of the sophisticated or habitual purchasers of mediation services hold 'beauty parades'. But this tends to be at the big ticket end of the market.

Whether you are in a line up or just being quizzed over the telephone have your pitch ready (see **Chapter 12**).

Some firms of solicitors offer similar facilities and have set up specific mediation arms distinct from their litigation and/or dispute resolution services.

What do you charge?

(See **Chapter 16**.)

6.31 The surveys show that mediators think that the level of charges is less important than their clients do.

- In the 2012 CEDR Fifth Mediation Audit, fees were listed as 2nd out of 17 factors that influence the lawyers' selection of mediators.
- In the 2014 CEDR Sixth Mediation Audit they were listed as 5th by the lawyers
- In both audits the mediators ranked fees at 5 or 6.

It may be that the level of charges is less significant as a criterion because the general level of charges is falling. Mediations are becoming cheaper.

When are you available?

6.32 In the Sixth CEDR Audit availability was numbered 2 in the list of factors, which mediators thought was important and number 3 by the lawyers.

6.33 *Know your market*

In practice availability is often the deciding factor. You may be the best mediator in the world but if the mediation has to take place on 4 July and you are not available you will not be appointed.

Keep your diary as flexible as you can. One very successful international commercial mediator who regularly does 100 commercial mediations a year makes it clear that mediation appointments prevail. When arranging lunch he tells people this is subject to his still being free that day. If a mediation comes in, lunch is cancelled.

Do clients, lawyers and providers want the same thing?

Client and representatives

6.33 Many responses to this question depend on individual experience and anecdotal evidence of others' experience. Fortunately, so far as the UK is concerned, help is provided by a recent survey.

As part of the increasing maturity and sophistication of the UK mediation scene more research is being undertaken as to what clients actually want. The results of the most recent survey undertaken on 29 October 2014 at a conference organised by the Corporation of London on 'Shaping the future of international dispute resolution' are illuminating.

The full results can be accessed on the IMI website, imimediation.org

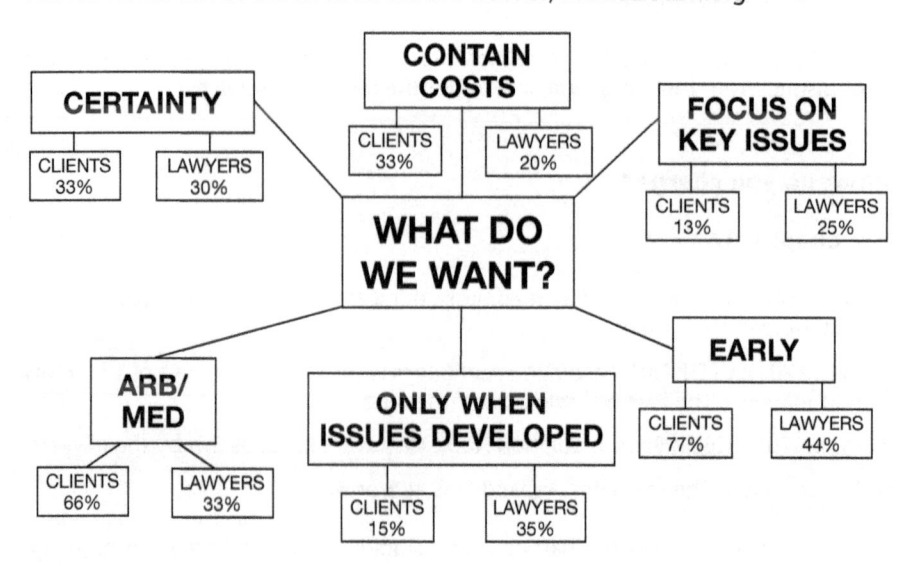

WHAT DO WE WANT?

- **CERTAINTY** — CLIENTS 33% / LAWYERS 30%
- **CONTAIN COSTS** — CLIENTS 33% / LAWYERS 20%
- **FOCUS ON KEY ISSUES** — CLIENTS 13% / LAWYERS 25%
- **EARLY** — CLIENTS 77% / LAWYERS 44%
- **ONLY WHEN ISSUES DEVELOPED** — CLIENTS 15% / LAWYERS 35%
- **ARB/MED** — CLIENTS 66% / LAWYERS 33%

Figure 14

The headline results are:
- 66% of end-users ranked achieving certainty and containing costs as the two key factors for choosing ADR. They rank them equally.

- Only 13% of end-users ranked focusing on the key issues, ie the legal issues in the dispute, as an important factor.
- By contrast, representatives ranked focusing on key issues as more important than achieving certainty.
- 77% of end-users thought that mediation should be conducted as early as possible and if possible before proceedings are commenced. By contrast only 44% of advisers thought this.
- 38% of advisers thought that ADR should only be attempted 'when issues are sufficiently developed, whenever that may be'. Only 15% of end-users thought this.
- 75% of end-users would use mediators as dealmakers even if there were no dispute between the parties. Only 38% of advisers would.
- 66% of end-users favoured the use of a cooling-off period during arbitration before the award is made to allow the parties to mediate. Only 33% of advisers were of this view.

What this survey does is confirm what many mediators say they have found in practice when talking to clients at mediations: What they want above all is certainty.

Businesses need to manage risk. If they cannot measure risk they cannot manage it. They want to cap their downside. This is also true of civil mediations where individual, as opposed to corporate, clients say how much they dislike uncertainty.

Build these learnings into your pitch (see **Chapter 12**).

End-users want to control costs and contain them

6.34 This applies in both commercial and civil mediations, but especially in civil mediation where individuals are paying legal fees out of their own pockets. The prospect of adverse costs orders terrifies them. At mediations they often say that if they had realised what they now face, namely the prospect of:

- not collecting the money that they think is due to them;
- having to pay their own legal costs; and
- having to pay a contribution to the other side's costs;

they would not have started proceedings.

They want to settle as soon as possible

6.35 End-users do not think that it is necessary for legal proceedings to be started, the pleadings to be exchanged and issues in cases developed in order for there be a negotiation leading to settlement.

What do clients really want deep down?

6.36 No solicitor has ever said that his client came into his office and said what they wanted was two years of litigation with an uncertain outcome and a large bill

6.37 *Know your market*

plus a unquantifiable level of risk, anxiety and wasted time. What they say they want is revenge, justice, or money. That is at the beginning of the dispute. But after the initial expression of outrage, as the City of London Survey results show, they just want an early solution that brings certainty.

And when inviting parties to consider the benefits of settlement ask them to remember that no one's last words are: 'I wish I'd spent more time in court'.

Lawyer and non-lawyer mediators

6.37 Two of current themes in the UK mediation market identified in **Chapter 2** were:

- the predominance of lawyer mediators; and
- the growth of specialist mediators.

Who make the best mediators – lawyers or non-lawyers? Mediators endlessly debate this question. Non-lawyers appear to be more interested in the answer than lawyers. They know that the market for civil and commercial mediations prefers to appoint lawyers rather than non- lawyers but they rail against this trend.

Being a lawyer is not always an advantage. One active commercial mediator who is also an IT specialist decided to remove his legal qualification from his website. He had been selected as the mediator in an IT dispute. He was deselected when one of the parties found out that he was a retired solicitor.

You will have to be able to deal with the issues arising. How you will do it of course depends on whether what you are a lawyer or not. As Winston Churchill said: 'Where you stand depends on where you sit'.

To help prepare your pitch here is a checklist of the pros and cons.

Lawyer mediators – pros

6.38 If you are a lawyer mediator you will say that the advantages are:

- If, as has often been said, mediation takes place in the shadow of the law, lawyers are better able to work in that shadow. You know the law better than non-lawyers.
- You are familiar with litigation procedure. You will not be confused by the language of litigation and references to Part 36, Tomlin Orders, counterclaims and Part 18 requests etc.
- You are better able to interpret what the lawyers at the mediation are actually saying about their prospects at trial and the merits of their case.
- You are used to assimilating large amounts of facts at short notice and to identifying the key points from a legal point of view
- You are better able to reality test and challenge the lawyers about the weak points in their case both legal and evidential.

Know your market **6.40**

- One of the obstacles to settlement at mediation is often the question of costs. You are much more familiar than non-lawyers with costs. You will have a better idea of the likely level of costs and the way in which the court applies the costs rules
- You can speak to the lawyers on both sides at the mediation on a lawyer-to-lawyer basis with mutual understanding. There is an instinctive understanding, which is not present with a non-lawyer mediator.
- Most civil and commercial mediations are initiated by lawyers. It is lawyers who instruct the mediator. They frankly admit that they are nervous about instructing non-lawyer mediators especially in disputes which have already become legal ones because they do not want to be criticised by their clients.

Lawyer mediators – cons

6.39 If you are not a lawyer you will emphasise the disadvantages of lawyers:

- They are lawyers. They are brought up to analyse facts in terms of legal categories and to argue their client's case. This is especially true of litigation lawyers. It is less true of transaction lawyers who are more inclined to be dealmakers.
- Lawyers are trained to analyse and advise. They find it impossible, when given a set of papers to read, not to form an opinion. It is second nature to them. Mediators who are senior barristers or former judges find it particularly difficult to avoid doing this. Indeed they often use a closing technique based upon their previous eminence. More than one former judge now a mediator has been heard to say at mediations: 'You know who I am and what I used to do. If this matter had come before me I would have decided as follows.
- Even if they are not adopting an overtly evaluative approach to mediation, they let it be known that they have views on the merits and unless forcibly stopped will express those views throughout the day.
- Lawyers have a tendency to believe that mediation will be resolved by a balancing of the legal arguments. Whoever ends up ahead on points will in some way be able to dictate the terms of settlement. The problem is that there is no one at the mediation to mark the score card.
- They overlook the fact that most disputes, even civil and commercial disputes, are not settled as a result of legal arguments. Personal and commercial considerations prevail. Non- lawyers understand this much better.

Non-lawyer mediators – pros

6.40 You will stress the advantages of non-lawyers:

- Not being lawyers you can sidestep the legal debate. You can simply speak directly to the non-lawyer decision-makers and say: 'I am like you. I am not a lawyer. I have sat in your position. I have negotiated commercial settlements which is what we are here to do today'.
- The lawyers may not feel able to speak to you as a non-lawyer mediator in the same way that they can speak to a lawyer mediator. But their clients may feel more comfortable in speaking to you as a non-lawyer.

6.41 *Know your market*

- When both sets of barristers or solicitors are saying that their client has a very good chance of settling a case, even as high as 80% on both sides, you can say: 'I do not know which of you is right but I do know something that is 100% right. One of you is wrong'.
- Having been in the client's shoes you will have a better insight into what is going on in the client's head.
- You may also have a wider range of commercial experience. If you have not been in business but have worked in the medical profession or as a psychotherapist or social worker or in HR you will have a wide range of experience in dealing with people under stress in a non-legal context.

Non-lawyer mediators – cons

6.41 You will point out the disadvantages of non-lawyers:

- There is distinctive school of non-lawyers who become mediators because really at some time in their life they wanted to be a lawyer. This is their chance. They make full use of it by engaging in what they call reality therapy and other people would call amateurish cross-examination.
- They under-estimate the influence which the litigation default position has on decision-makers. While it is true that personal and commercial considerations usually prevail at mediation, legal considerations are not entirely ignored. At the very least the decision maker may have to justify his decision to settle when he returns home – either to his wife or to his Board of Directors. He needs to be able to answer the question: 'Why did you settle at that figure when the lawyers told us that we could expect to get twice that at trial?'
- Even experienced non-lawyer mediators cannot have an instinctive and up-to-date feel for how cases turn out at trial. This makes it more difficult for them to challenge the predictions given by legal representatives.
- Very few non-lawyer mediators have a good working knowledge of costs. Some consciously try to keep up-to-date. Most do not.
- They are not as skilled as lawyers in making sure that the legal requirements for an enforceable settlement are incorporated in the settlement documents.
- They are not as useful as a lawyer mediator in resolving drafting difficulties in the settlement agreement, which is usually some sort of Tomlin Order in civil and commercial litigation and mediation.

If the mediation is about a dispute in a sector in which the non-lawyer mediator is an expert, for example dilapidations or property valuation, many of the disadvantages listed above do not apply. They are much more like a lawyer mediator in these circumstances.

Generalists or specialists?

6.42 Is it better to have an expert in mediation rather than a sector expert? This question overlaps with the lawyer or non-lawyer debate.

A specialist for these purposes is someone who has sector experience. In other words he has either advised as a lawyer or practised as a non-lawyer in the area of the dispute: for example hotels, IT procurement contracts, pension advice etc.

You need to be up-to-date with the issues because:

- As the surveys described in para **6.09** show, sector expertise is an important factor when choosing a mediator.
- One of the pieces of advice routinely given to those wanting to start or develop their mediation practice is 'be niche'. The usual definition of being niche is specialising in a particular area of dispute.

Here is a Checklist of the pros and cons.

Specialists – pros

6.43

- Parties think that a specialist will understand more quickly what the dispute is about. There will be less learning time. He will be familiar with the concepts and vocabulary of the sector. This will save time and therefore be cheaper.
- His prior knowledge means that he will understand the dispute better. In practice what parties who say this mean is that the more that the mediator understands the dispute the more likely he is to agree with us and disagree with them. This view is more prevalent amongst potential paying parties. In professional negligence actions for example the defendants often want somebody who has practised in the same area so they will understand why the defendant did what he did and why it is not negligent.
- He will be able to engage with any expert evidence much better and more quickly than the generalist. He will be better able to reality test what the expert says.
- He will be better at generating ideas for settlement based on his own technical experience.

Specialists – cons

6.44

- Like the lawyer mediator the specialist mediator finds it difficult to keep his opinions to himself.
- Like the lawyer mediator the specialist may think the settlement revolves around technical points rather than broader personal or commercial considerations.
- The saving in time and costs of briefing a specialist rather than a generalist mediator are exaggerated. Lawyers in particular are used to having to get up a subject quickly. Many mediators include their reading-in time in their fee with no additional charge.
- Sector specialists, because of their specialism, think that they are worth more and can be more expensive.

6.45 *Know your market*

- In practice at mediation decisions on whether or not to settle will not usually be taken for technical or legal reasons but for personal or commercial ones

Generalists – pros

6.45

- Generalists who are trained in mediation and have mediation rather than sector experience will concentrate more on the process than the substance of the dispute.
- At court the judge concentrates on the substance of the dispute, ie the legal and evidential issues. At mediation, the mediator does not act as a judge. He is there to find out what the obstacles to settlement are, how much common ground there is in fact between the parties and what are the real goals of the parties. As is repeatedly said, it is practical, personal and commercial considerations, not legal and evidential ones which drive settlements.
- He is more likely to be more interested in background or connected issues which are not aired in the correspondence, the pleadings or the expert reports.
- He is less likely than the specialist to allow himself to become a participant in the debate about the merits and the technical issues.
- Having no specialist knowledge gives the generalist licence to ask simple questions which a specialist may think beneath them. These simple questions can cause the parties to widen their focus and field of vision.
- He is less prone to the cognitive biases such as:
  - The curse of information. This is where so much is known about a subject it prevents people from thinking about it.
  - Authority bias, ie the tendency to allow the status and credentials of a person to influence the perception of information or advice he gives.
  - The hammer (aka déformation professionnelle) as Mark Twain said: 'and If your only tool is a hammer, all your problems will be nails'.
  - False consensus effect, ie the tendency for people to over-estimate how much other people agree with them.

Generalists – cons

6.46

- It takes them longer to bring themselves up to speed on the technical issues in the dispute.
- The technical experts on each side may try to blind the generalist with science.
- Where a party has simply misunderstood the technical issues and his lawyers have misunderstood the legal ones it can be easier for a specialist and a specialist lawyer to correct these misunderstandings. This is where former judges can have an advantage. In practice this total misunderstanding is very rare.

Know your market **6.47**

What do clients need?

6.47 As a mediator you will find out that what a client needs is not necessarily the same as what a client wants. Maslow's hierarchy of needs still applies. Everybody, he says, needs the following:

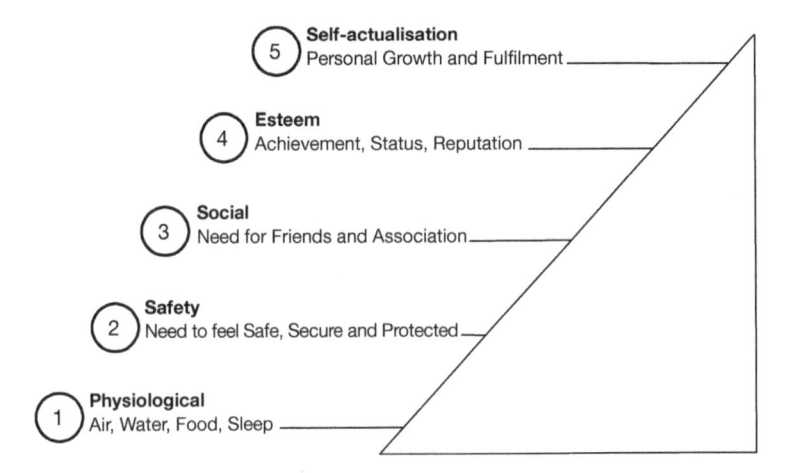

```
5  Self-actualisation
   Personal Growth and Fulfilment

4  Esteem
   Achievement, Status, Reputation

3  Social
   Need for Friends and Association

2  Safety
   Need to feel Safe, Secure and Protected

1  Physiological
   Air, Water, Food, Sleep
```

Figure 15

These are intended to help analyse human behaviour on a universal level. But they also apply very directly to what mediators do at mediations.

Even **Stage 1**, which is most fundamental physiological need for air, water food and sleep, is relevant. As explained at para **7.30** if you as the mediator can supply a venue you have a commercial edge. At the mediation if you as the mediator make sure that everybody has enough fresh air, water and food you will achieve better results and the thanks of the parties and their lawyers.

Stage Two which is the need to feel safe also applies to mediation. In commercial mediation this is rarely physical safety. In community and family mediations physical safety can sometimes be an issue. Usually it is more a need for psychological safety. As the mediator you have to:

- Make sure that everybody understands that the process is confidential and that they are bound to observe the confidentiality. See the provisions in the mediation agreement in **Chapter 20**.
- Provide the environment where the parties can experiment with new ideas and suggestions without fear of being rejected or ridiculed.

This is also where your skills in active listening and open questioning come into play (see **Chapter 11**).

You will be able to demonstrate these abilities once you are carrying out some mediations. The trick is to demonstrate them before you have received any mediations. In other words you have to do this in your marketing material and when you are promoting yourself. These are discussed in **Chapter 12**.

6.48 *Know your market*

The more that you can do this the greater chance that visitors to your website or people you pitch to will like what they see and hear.

Segmenting your market

6.48 Even if you confine your market to lawyers in England and Wales you have over 10,000 firms. They are not all your market. As discussed in **Chapter 8** on marketing, you need to focus on who you want to attract as customers. This means that you have to segment your market.

Conventionally markets are segmented by:

- Geography, eg. within the M25,
- Range, eg international companies engaged in cross-border disputes
- Sector, eg financial services or the leisure industry
- Age, eg people over 60 or young start-up entrepreneurs
- Size, eg businesses with fewer than 20 employees
- Age
- Nationality
- Religion
- Education
- Status
- Income
- Residence

Segmenting for Mediators

6.49 The above classification is not particularly relevant to mediators. Here is a checklist of relevant segments. See also para **7.2**.

Types of lawyer

Size

    Number of partners
    Number of legal staff
    Turnover

Type of work

    Litigation, insurance, construction etc
    Private client
    Non-contentious
    Employment

Location

In-house
>Legal departments
>Risk managers
>Claims departments

Barristers' Chambers
>Clerks
>Individual Barristers
>Direct Access

What is the focus of your market?

Lawyers

6.50 For civil and commercial mediators the main market is litigation lawyers, both barristers and solicitors. They are currently the main suppliers of mediation cases. Commentators, academics and non-lawyers might not like this but it is a fact in the current market. Ignore it at your peril.

As discussed at para **8.14** this is a limited pie. You need to find ways of increasing your slice of it. The trick is to find another pie to grow or try and grow this one. Where are there other suppliers of mediation work?

Non-lawyers

6.51 Other professionals such as accountants, quantity surveyors, HR directors, risk managers, commercial directors, finance directors, managing agents, IFAS insolvency practitioners and other mediator are all potential sources.

In fact anybody who has any sort of involvement in business will inevitably come into conflict with other people. The vast majority of conflicts are sorted out by negotiations between the disputants. They do not usually need any outside help. But when they do, you want them to think of mediation in general, and of you as the mediator in particular.

In a nutshell

6.52
- Lawyers dominate the market for civil and commercial mediations both as suppliers and customers.

6.52 *Know your market*

- Commercial clients and their lawyers increasingly prefer specialist mediators.
- Clients do not always want what their lawyers want.
- Commercial clients want speedy cheap outcomes.

Chapter 7

Business plan

> In this chapter you will learn:
> - Why you need a business plan.
> - How to make a business plan.

Do you have a business plan?

7.01 If you ask mediators if they have a business plan they nearly all say that they do not have one. Many looked puzzled as to why they should even be asked the question. Most mediators see mediation, at least to start with, as a secondary activity. They do not spend most of their time mediating. It is not their full-time job or occupation. Most of their income derives from other sources.

Why do mediators not have business plans?

7.02 Describing mediation for such mediators as a hobby is too harsh. But they do approach mediation in a casual way, not in the serious way that they would if they were setting up in business as their principal activity. They wonder why they would need a business plan at all. Common fallacies are:

- Business plans are for businesses, whether established or start-ups, who are looking for outside finance.
- You draft business plans in order to persuade a bank or a venture capitalist to invest money in your business.

This is all true but you still need a business plan even if the only person who is investing in your new business is yourself.

Apart from not really seeing the relevance, mediators are put off the idea by lack of experience and expertise. Most lawyers will not have had to draw up business plans. They may have compiled budgets, but that is only half of the job. Even those mediators who come from non-legal backgrounds or commercial backgrounds may have had limited personal experience in drawing up business plans.

7.03 *Business plan*

Why do you need a business plan?

7.03 The different answers to this question can be found in three quotations:

Benjamin Franklin: 'If you fail to plan you are planning to fail.'

Von Moltke: 'No battle plan ever survives contact with the enemy'

Spike Milligan: 'We didn't have a plan so nothing could go wrong.'

Franklin's quotation has become a cliché but it contains an inherent truth. As researchers from Cranfield Business School report:

> 'Time after time, research studies reveal that the absence of a written business plan leads to a high incidence of failure for new and small businesses, as well as inhibiting growth and development.'

(Barrow & Others *The Business Plan Workbook* (2008).)

The advantages of a business plan

Sharpens up your thinking

7.04 Preparing a business plan makes you concentrate on key factors which are otherwise easy to overlook or relegate to the back of your mind. For example precisely what are you selling, who are you selling it to and how much are you going to charge?

Test drives your ideas

7.05 By working through the steps and the resources needed you can make your mistakes on paper not when you are actually out in the marketplace trying to sell your services.

Gives you a route map

7.06 Having a route map gives confidence that there is a direction you can follow. Otherwise you can blunder about in a rudderless way.

Shows the costs

7.07 Drawing up the business plan shows you how much money you will need. Even mediating on a part-time basis as a bolt-on to your main job costs money. You cannot do it at nil cost. Being under-capitalised and cash flow difficulties are two of the most common reasons for businesses to fail, whether they are new or old, big or small.

Shows the time needed

7.08 The plan will show how much time you will need to invest. This is the biggest single investment that you make when setting up a business as a mediator. You have to be very clear how much of this limited resource you have available. Time is not a free good in limitless supply.

Manages your expectations

7.09 Self-esteem is the second biggest investment that you will make. You will face rejection and disappointment. All mediators do. But you can minimise it.

Mediators are trained to manage the parties' expectations. Unrealistic expectations are often seen as a barrier to settlement. You, as a new mediator, do not want your expectations to be so unrealistic that they become a barrier to success.

Provides a record

7.10 The plan will remind you of what you wanted to do and how far you have achieved progress.

Keep it short and simple

7.11 A business plan does not have to be a complicated multipage document of the sort that you submit to venture capitalists. As you will not be using it to persuade investors or borrowers you can ignore many of the usual ingredients of a business plan.

Geoff Sharp, one of the leading international mediators who regularly conducts over 100 mediations a year, carries with him his original business plan. It is a simple three-column document that he devised in 2000 when he decided to give up his job as a lawyer and become a full-time mediator. Of course he updates it every year but he still carries the original one with him so he can just reflect on where he started, where he wanted to get to and how far he has come.

I want	I will do that by	How I will achieve that

Figure 16

You can view it on his website geoffsharp.co.nz or mediatorblahblah.blogspot.com.

One of the biggest benefits of having a business plan is that you write it down. An unwritten business plan is, as Sam Goldwyn said about oral contracts, not worth the paper they're written on.

7.12 *Business plan*

Why is it important to write things down?

Memory is not enough

7.12 As Confucius said: 'The weakest ink is stronger than the most powerful memory'.

Research has established that memory is an act of re-creation. The repatriation is influenced by our beliefs, our emotional state at the time and our self-image. This explains why what one person remembers about event can differ radically from what another person remembers.

To guard against this write it down.

The other advantages are:

Ideas evaporate

7.13 Writing ideas down captures them.

Written goals are easier to achieve

7.14 Researchers have established that writing down a plan or a goal makes it more likely to be achieved. And the more concrete that you can make it the more likely you are to achieve it.

Not only does writing something down bring clarity. It also gives you focus and acts as a reminder of what you should be doing. It helps you keep your eyes on the prize.

Reduces stress

7.15 By being able to refer to a written goal you do not have to try and remember it or worry about what you thought you were trying to do. You can check any time that you want to. That leaves more mental and emotional energy for actually achieving the goals.

Prevents distraction

7.16 If you write something down you concentrate. It's impossible to write something down and think about something else at the same time.

Creates priorities

7.17 We are all more productive if we do the important things first. It is easy to confuse activity with progress. Having an orderly list of priorities counteracts the tendency that we all have to do the easy things first and neglect the more important and the more difficult ones.

Increases commitment

7.18 As mediators we are often encouraged to ask the parties to write down their proposals at mediation. In a sense you are putting your name to something. By doing this you are also making yourself more accountable. You have something to measure your progress by.

So why not do the same for yourself?

Business plans made easy

7.19 A business plan does not have to be a complicated document. Look at Geoff Sharp's after all. But it must contain certain fundamentals.

To start yourself get started the three fundamental questions that your trainers taught you to ask the parties:

- What is important to you?
- Why is it important to you?
- How would you like to achieve?

Acronyms

7.20 You cannot avoid acronyms in mediation. Hackneyed they may be, but they crystallise useful concepts.

SWOT	This is an analysis of your: • **S**trengths • **W**eaknesses • **O**pportunities • **T**hreats
SMART	This is the measure of your plan – it should be • **S**pecific • **M**easurable • **A**ttainable • **R**ealistic • **T**imely

7.21 *Business plan*

KISS	This is the measure of your message
	• **K**eep **I**t **S**imple **S**tupid
USP	This is the measure of what you take to your customer
	• **U**nique **S**elling **P**oint/**P**roposition
UVP	This is the measure of what your customer receives
	• **U**nique **V**alue **P**roposition

Goals

7.21 Goals are not the same as 'wants'. They are a combination of position, interests and needs, shot through with psychological imperatives and economic demands.

The more specific the goal the more likely it is to be achieved. For example there is a difference between saying: 'My goal is to travel to London' and: 'My goal is to stay in the Plaza Hotel on Duke Street, London'.

Once you establish your goal you give all your activities shape and focus. Does any particular activity help achieve the goal? Anything that does not help you achieve the goal should be abandoned.

Anybody can dream about having a successful mediation practice and hope to achieve it. But to do it you have to make living the dream your goal.

A key difference between having a goal and having a dream is you write down your goals. You do not just do it on a scratch pad on your bedside table when you wake up in the middle of the night. You do it in a focused, planned way. Here are seven tips to help you get there.

Checklist of goal plans

7.22

1 Do you really want the goal or is it just something that sounds good?

2 Goals need to be consistent with your values. If you set inconsistent goals you will find that you lack commitment to them.

3 Make sure that your goals do not contradict each other. For example:

In the mediation sphere saying that you want to do community mediation and earn £100,000 a year doing it is inconsistent. Psychologists call this non-integrated thinking. If you engage in it you will make your life so much harder.

4 Balance your goals.

Remember that there are goals in other areas of your life apart from developing a mediation business. When considering why you are doing mediation, and how much time, money and effort you can afford to invest in it remember these other areas such as family and home, physical health, social and cultural life.

5   Write your goals down as positives not negatives.

- Part of the importance of writing down your goals is to create instructions to your subconscious.
- But remember the subconscious does not distinguish right from wrong. It does not judge. The job of the subconscious is to carry out instructions.
- The more positive the instructions the more chance you have of achieving results.

6   Write your goal out in detail.

Make the description as complete as possible.

For example instead of writing: 'I want a new house' write : 'I want a three-storey detached house with five bedrooms, four bathrooms and a 200 foot garden in Kensington.'

Or

Instead of writing I want to do '25 mediations a year' write: 'I want to do a total of 25 commercial mediations in the UK by 31 December 2016. This is an average of 2/3 a month for 9/10 months of the year with an average fee of £2500 plus VAT'.

7   Make sure your goal is high enough.

- Expectation affects performance – this is the Rosenthal or Pygmalion effect.
- Aim high. If you miss you will still be up there. In other words even if you cannot become the World Number One ranked mediator earning £500,000 a year the attempt to achieve that ranking will be of value to you.
- So long as your goals are consistent with your values you will enjoy the challenge of trying to achieve them and benefit from it. Of course do not undo the benefit by completely abandoning all critical disbelief. Mindless optimism is no basis for entry into the mediation process at any stage or in any role.

8   Write down and review your goals.

- Remember what Sam Goldwyn and Confucius said as quoted above. But also remember to review your goals.
- Some life and business coaches say that you must review your goals every day. In practical mediation life this is unrealistic. If you cannot do this daily try and do it every week. Ask yourself once a week whether:
    - has what you have done that week helped you towards achieving your goal?
    - is what you intend to do next week a step towards your goal?

7.23 *Business plan*

If the answer to both those questions is no, then you should ask yourself why you are doing what you are doing.

A template for a business plan

Getting started: three steps

7.23

1 **Look at Figure 17.** Answer the questions. They help you to think about how realistic your expectations are and what you will need in order to achieve them.

2 Doing this will give you a skeleton of a business plan. Now flesh it out by writing a short narrative business plan. See **Figure 18** for an example.

3 Move to the financials. Photocopy **Figure 19**. Fill in the details. You have to guess some of the figures. Others you can work out or find out later.

Business plan **7.23**

BUSINESS PLAN

①	**WHY DO I WANT TO BE A MEDIATOR**	1. Money
		2. Stimulation / Challenge
		3. Give Back
		4. Do Good
		5. Change Career
②	**WHERE AM I NOW**	1. Employed as a _____
		2. Self-employed as a _____
		3. Not working _____
		4. Studying _____
③	**WHERE DO I WANT TO BE** 12 MONTHS 36 MONTHS	

Figure 17a

7.23 *Business plan*

④ HOW MUCH MONEY DO I WANT TO EARN A YEAR FROM MEDIATION

£0 – £10k

£10k – £20k

£20k – £25k

£25k – £40k

£40k – £50k

£50k – £65k

£65k – £85k

£85k – £100k

£100k+

⑤ WHAT IS MY DAILY CHARGE AND RATE NOW?

⑥ HOW MANY MEDIATIONS HAVE I DONE IN TOTAL?

Figure 17b

Business plan **7.23**

IN THE LAST 36 MONTHS

IN THE LAST 12 MONTHS

(7) **HOW MANY MEDIATIONS DO I WANT TO DO A YEAR?**

(8) **WHAT TYPE OF MEDIATIONS?**
   1. BY SUBJECT
   2. BY VALUE

(9) **WHAT WILL I CHARGE FOR A FULL DAY?**

(10) **WHERE WILL THE MEDIATIONS COME FROM?**
   1. PANEL
   2. WEBSITE
   3. OWN CONTACTS

Figure 17C

7.23 *Business plan*

(11) HOW MUCH MONEY CAN I INVEST?

1. NOW

2. IN TOTAL

(12) HOW MUCH CAN I AFFORD TO LOSE?

(13) HOW MUCH TIME CAN I INVEST?

1. UNTIL BREAKEVEN

2. UNTIL SNOWBALL

3. NOW – WITHIN NEXT 10 WEEKS (see fig 3)

4. EACH WEEK

5. EACH MONTH

Figure 17d

Here are the fundamental elements that you have to include in any worthwhile business plan. The business plan is where several of these elements which have already been discussed, eg in **Chapter 3 Know Yourself** and in **Chapter 4 Know Your Product** are brought together.

What is my business?

7.24 Your starting point – asking yourself why you are in the business of mediation at all? This was discussed in **Chapter 3.**

What are the activities that you particularly want to be engaged in?

- Is it, for example, helping people to avoid the problems in life that you have experienced yourself?
    - A well-known and successful barrister-mediator specialises in family mediation because he wants to help people avoid the pain that he suffered during his own divorce.
    - A well-known community mediator wants to help people who feel ignored and neglected in society have a voice. She has been very successful.

What are the values that are important to you?

- Do you want to feel in control of your own destiny, ie be your own boss.
- Do you want to feel that you have discretion over how you spend your time so that you can pick and choose when you want to work?

Is there a minimum amount of money that you need to make out of mediation?

- Do you need to make any money out of it at all?
- Is the practice of the activity sufficient satisfaction in itself?

Having thought about all of this, *write down* the answers. Writing them down is essential for the reasons given above.

What am I selling?

7.25 In **Chapter 4** we looked at different types of mediation services. If you are not crystal clear in your own mind about what you are selling, how can you expect your customers to know what you are offering them?

- Be specific. You cannot be all things to all men. You may have a different service for a different market.
- Are you going to be specialist? Are you going to be niche?
- Is mediation just one of the services that you offer?

What is my market?

7.26 As discussed in **Chapter 6** this is one of the most important questions for mediators and also one of the hardest.

7.27 *Business plan*

Many mediators just assume that they are offering mediation as a broad concept to anybody who wants to buy it. You can do this. Eventually given enough time and luck you will attract some work. But you might wait a very long time.

Not everybody is your market. For example:

- If you are a non-lawyer mediator based in Carlisle why do you think that a City firm of solicitors is going to hire you as a mediator for a big-ticket mediation for an international client?
- If you are the former senior partner of a leading City law firm specialising in financial restructuring for international bondholders why do you think that the HR director of the local NHS trust is going to commission you to intervene in a dispute between two surgical firms in their flagship hospital?

Your market will partly be defined by what service you want to provide e.g. the market for workplace mediators is different from that for commercial mediators. Are you looking for customers in the public sector or the private sector?

Narrative business plan

7.27

This is a device to help you unfreeze your thoughts.

Imagine that you are borrowing the money to start your new mediation business from a third party rather than from yourself.

My name is xxxxx yyy. I am a qualified solicitor but I have not practised as a solicitor for 10 years. Instead I have been a commercial director In a management consultancy and headhunting company.

The market for my services

The company that I work for has recently been bought out by a large American company. I do not wish to work for the new owners in the long term. I have to stay for three years with them under the Purchase agreement. They have agreed that in six months time I can reduce my hours and only work four days a week.

I have dealt with many businesses both large and small at director level and am aware of many of the reasons why they have disputes.

In particular through the head hunting side of the company I dealt with boardroom bust ups and internal management conflicts.

As a management consultant and head-hunter I was often brought in to sort out internal problems, which were often brought about by organisational change or to advise on how to deal with external challenges. I developed a specialism in crisis management.

I often provided coaching and training to senior executives in managing conflict, change and crisis management.

Many of my clients are concerned that the new owners will have a different way of doing business and will be too expensive. The smaller clients fear that they will be not as important to the new company as they have been to me.

I have had experience of mediation both as a client and as a client's representative.

I have seen that it has become increasingly popular amongst my clients as a way of resolving disputes and conflicts both internally and externally.

About myself

In addition to my above experience I set up a trust to work with disadvantaged teenagers who had been excluded from their family homes in the East End of London. I was also one of the original founders of a start-up business making computer games and smartphone applications for autistic boys and girls under the age of 12.

I do not have operational fluency in any languages other than English but my husband's native tongue is Urdu and I have visited Pakistan and Northern India many times.

I am 50 years of age and in good health.

How I will set up my business

I will be able to make very limited use of the office and administrative resources at my employers. I do not wish to use their facilities in such a way

7.27 *Business plan*

> as to give them the opportunity of accusing me of being in breach of my contract. I will be able to operate from my study at home.
>
> I will not rely upon income from mediations as my main source, or even an important source, of supplemental income for the next three years.
>
> **The future**
>
> After I leave my present employment my pension and investment income will provide me with a reasonable standard of living but not sufficient to maintain it at the level that I currently enjoy or wish to enjoy in my retirement.
>
> **How I will use the money**
>
> | | |
> |---|---|
> | Obtaining accreditation | £5,000 |
> | Buying a new laptop | £2,000 |
> | Designing a new website | £600 |
> | Insurance | £150 |
> | Professional and panel fees | £1250 |
> | Marketing | £2000 |
> | Total | £11,000 |
>
> **Paying back the money**
>
> I expect to recoup my investment within 36 months and after that to be making an operational profit each year of not less than £X.

Figure 18

Then you need to do a more detailed quantitative analysis of what is going to happen in your new business. For help with this look at **Figure 19**.

Business Plan Financials 4 Years

	Year 1	Year 2	Year 3	Year 4
Receipts				
Fees (A)	£2,000.00	£4,000.00	£8,000.00	£16,000.00
Capital Introduced (B)	£5,000.00	£1,500.00	NIL	NIL
Net Receipts (C)	-£3,000.00	£2,500.00	£8,000.00	£16,000.00
Less				
Expenses				

Business plan **7.27**

Training				
Initial	£3,000.00	NIL	NIL	NIL
CPD	£500.00	£500.00	£750.00	£750.00
Fees	£500.00	£500.00	£600.00	£600.00
Insurance	£150.00	£150.00	£150.00	£180.00
Subs	£150.00	£150.00	£200.00	£200.00
Mobile	£360.00	£360.00	£360.00	£360.00
Broadband	£300.00	£320.00	£380.00	£380.00
Travel	£150.00	£250.00	£1,000.00	£2,000.00
Car				
Hotels	NIL	£150.00	£750.00	£1,500.00
Conference	£500.00	£500.00	£500.00	£750.00
Food/ Drink	£450.00	£650.00	£950.00	£1,500.00
Stationery	£500.00	£100.00	£100.00	£350.00
Total (D)	-£6,590.00	-£3,130.00	-£5,740.00	-£6,770.00
Gross Receipts	£7,000.00	£5,500.00	£8,000.00	£16,000.00
Gross Expenses	-£6,590.00	-£3,130.00	-£5,740.00	-£6,770.00
Net Receipts	-£3,000.00	£2,500.00	£8,000.00	£16,000.00
Operating Loss/Profit (D)	-£9,590.00	-£630.00	£2,260.00	£9,230.00
Accumulated Loss/Profit (F)	-£9,590.00	-£10,220.00	-£7,960.00	£1,270.00

Figure 19a

7.27 *Business plan*

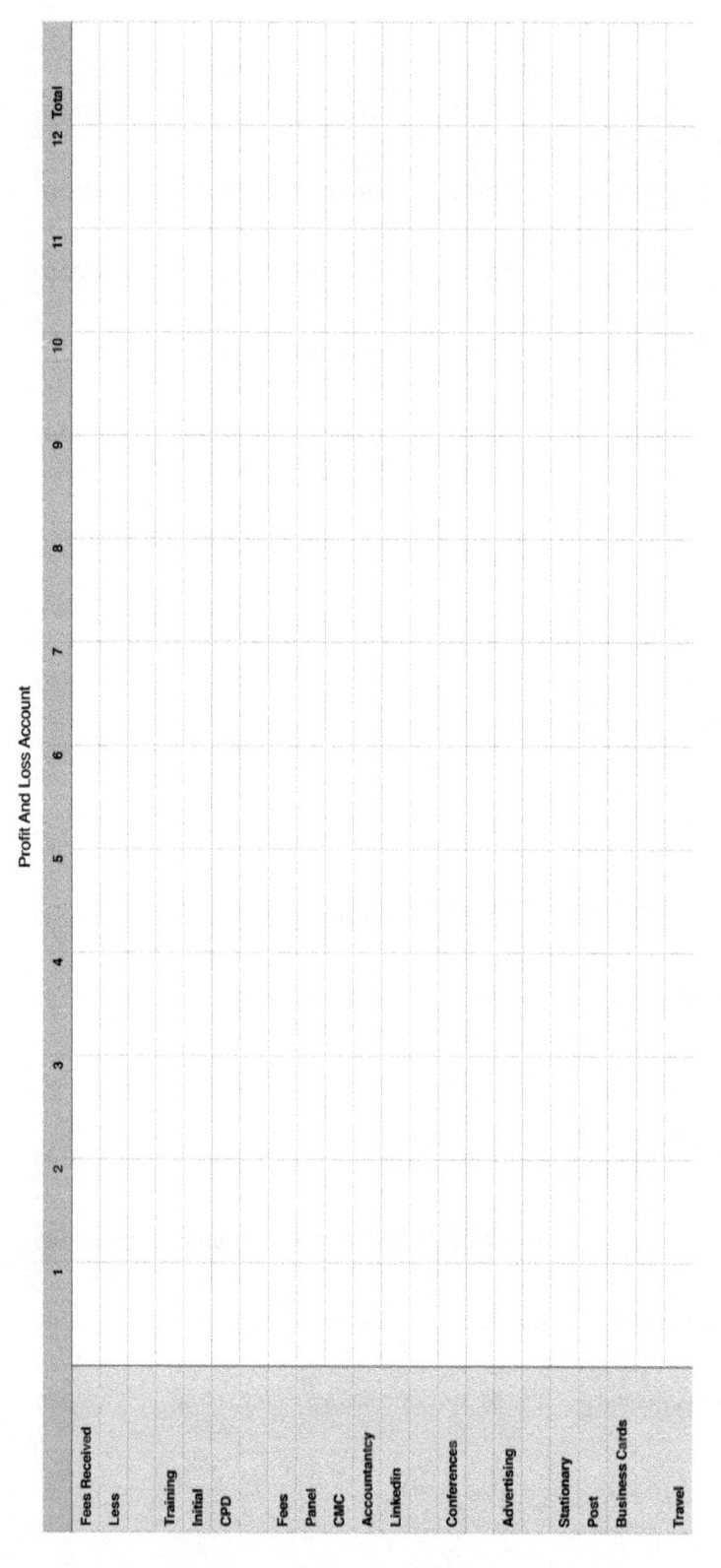

Profit And Loss Account	1	2	3	4	5	6	7	8	9	10	11	12	Total
Fees Received													
Less													
Training													
Initial													
CPD													
Fees													
Panel													
CMC													
Accountancy													
LinkedIn													
Conferences													
Advertising													
Stationary													
Post													
Business Cards													
Travel													

Business plan **7.27**

	1	2	3	4	5	6	7	8	9	10	11	12 Total
Car												
Mobile												
Broadband												
Insurance												
Room Hire												
Hotels												
Food / Drink												
Books												
Total												

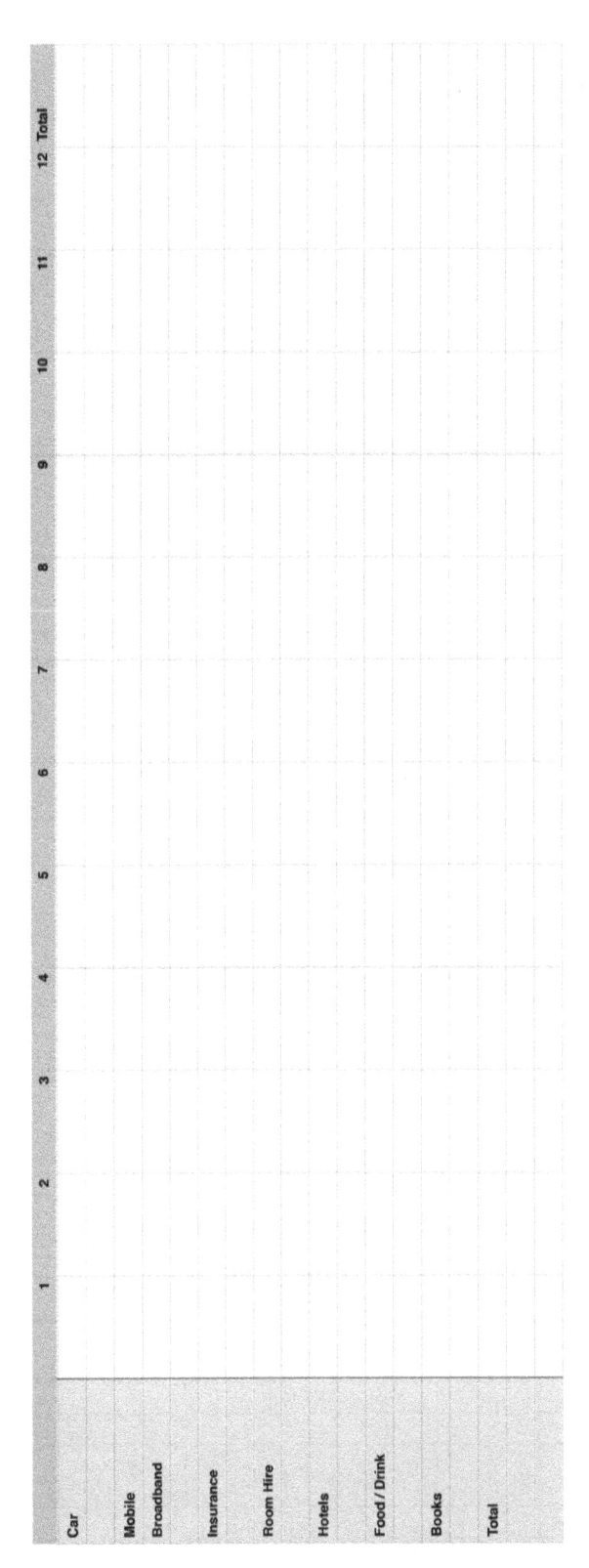

Figure 19b

7.27 Business plan

Cashflow forecast for 12 Months

	Jan B	Jan A	Feb B	Feb A	Mar B	Mar A	Apr B	Apr A	May B	May A	June B	June A
Income												
Capital Introduced												
Total Income												
Payments												
Training												
Initial												
CPD												
Fees												
Panel												
CMC												
Accountancy												
Subs												
LinkedIn												
Conferences												
Advertising												
Stationery												
Business Cards												
Postage												
Travel												
Car												
Mobile												
Broadband												
Insurance												
Room Hire												
Hotels												
Food/Drink												
Books												
Total Payments												
Net Cash												
Opening Bank Balance												
Closing Bank Balance												

Business plan **7.27**

	July		Aug		Sept		Oct		Nov		Dec	
	B	A	B	A	B	A	B	A	B	A	B	A
Income												
Capital Introduced												
Total Income												
Payments												
Training												
Initial												
CPD												
Fees												
Panel												
CMC												
Accountancy												
Subs												
LinkedIn												
Conferences												
Advertising												
Stationery												
Business Cards												
Postage												
Travel												
Car												
Mobile												
Broadband												
Insurance												
Room Hire												
Hotels												
Food/Drink												
Books												
Total Payments												
Net Cash												
Opening Bank Balance												
Closing Bank Balance												

Figure 19c

7.28 *Business plan*

Segment your market

7.28 The importance of segmenting your market was discussed in **Chapter 6** at para **6.46**. To get started try using a visual.

Say that you have decided that your market for commercial and civil mediation is lawyers.

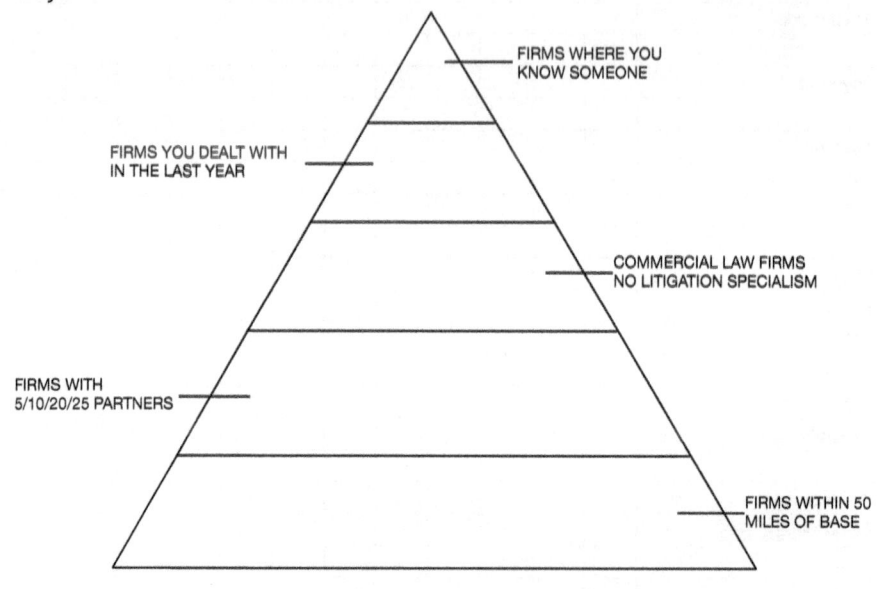

```
                    /\
                   /  \
                  /    \——— FIRMS WHERE YOU
                 /      \    KNOW SOMEONE
                /────────\
               /          \
  FIRMS YOU DEALT WITH ———/
  IN THE LAST YEAR       /
             /────────────\
            /              \
           /                \——— COMMERCIAL LAW FIRMS
          /                  \   NO LITIGATION SPECIALISM
         /────────────────────\
        /                      \
  FIRMS WITH ———/                \
  5/10/20/25 PARTNERS            \
       /────────────────────────\
      /                          \
     /                            \——— FIRMS WITHIN 50
    /                              \   MILES OF BASE
   /────────────────────────────────\
```

SEGMENT TRIANGLE

Figure 20

Examples

7.29 One successful Bristol solicitor mediator qualified before he retired. He told everybody whom he was dealing with that he would be carrying on mediating after he had retired. Once he had retired he went round and saw everybody that he could think of. He developed a very nice practice.

But on the other hand:

Another successful litigation solicitor in the Midlands who is a partner in a well-known small-to-medium-sized firm decided that he would become a mediator. He had learned about mediation through representing clients at mediations. He qualified and carried out his first mediations. He also approached everybody that he had dealt with. He was disappointed in the response. He wondered why this was.

He concluded that it was for two reasons:
- Many of the people that he approached were at firms that were still competitors of his own firm.
- He had been on the other side of disputes and engaged in hard fought battles with many of these people over a period of years. They were rivals with scores to settle.

What will it cost me to set up in business?

7.30 It can cost you very little. You may be an entrepreneur but you do not need a bank loan or a venture capitalist to invest in you. If you are operating from your home, as most mediators do when they start, you have very little extra expense.

If mediation is a secondary activity you may not need very much money at all to start with. But if you want it to be a self-sustaining business you need to be very clear what your costs will be.

In any case starting a mediation business, even on a quasi-hobby basis, still costs money.

It is easy to overlook costs that you will incur.

Checklist of start-up costs

7.31 *Training*: this covers your initial training and advanced training as you progress.

Membership fees: for example to be registered with the Civil Mediation Council or to be a member of a panel of ADR providers.

Subscriptions: Some of the services that you may want to use are not entirely free, for example the premium service for LinkedIn.

Conference fees: as described in **Chapter 12** attending conferences and workshops is a useful way of learning about the mediation market, what your competitors are doing and simply keeping yourself on people's radar. Not many of them are totally free. Even if they are there will be your fares and drinks to buy for people to build better relationships.

Networking expenses: this is linked with attending conferences but you can network to in all sorts of circumstances. One of the keys to networking as we discussed in **Chapter 12** is to follow up. This usually means inviting someone you have met for coffee/lunch/drink on another occasion. This will cost you money.

Stationery: business cards are essential. They may not be very expensive but it is still money. If you decide to have any sort of image of yourself on the card it is best to have a good quality, professionally-taken photograph. You may decide to print marketing material such as leaflets or booklets for distribution and the photograph could be useful for those.

Travel: you will need to travel to events and with any luck you will also need to travel to mediations. Certainly your observations while you are still in the apprenticeship stage and before you are fully accredited will be unpaid. You may also undertake pro bono work as a volunteer. Sometimes you will be paid your travel expenses; usually you will have to pay yourself.

Mobile phone and broadband: your usage will go up. You may have to buy a more expensive plan.

Insurance: most reputable panels and, certainly the CMC or IMI require their members to have professional indemnity insurance (see para **3.12**).

7.32 *Business plan*

Room hire: if you decide to stage events yourself to promote your business you may have to pay for room hire as well as refreshments. You need to budget for this.

Quite often the parties to a mediation will expect the mediator to provide premises for the mediation. This is usually where the parties are not represented. They often want a neutral venue. You will have a commercial decision to take: do you include the cost of room hire in your fee or charge separately? Certainly being able to provide room hire at no or very low cost is a definite commercial advantage in attracting mediation business.

Working out your costs is an essential step to calculating how much you will charge. We discuss this in more detail in **Chapter 16**

How much do you want to earn?

7.32 Set yourself realistic targets for 6 months, 12 months, 24 months and 36 months. Bear in mind:

- the comparative figures discussed in **Chapter 16** and
- the number of mediations that you think that you can complete at these milestones.

How many mediations do you want to do?

7.33 Set yourself realistic targets for 6 months, 12 months, 24 months and 36 months. When doing this, bear in mind:

- The number of mediations that you have done to date.
- The number of mediations that you have done in the last 12 months.
- The average number of mediations that people are doing in your sector – see **Chapter 2**.
- What other people say they are doing – take care to remember that they will tend to exaggerate.

What resources do I need?

7.34 The most important resource is time. This has two dimensions:

(1) How much time can I invest overall on this project?

In other words the question is how long are you prepared to devote to establishing a mediation practice before you decide whether or not you have failed or succeeded? As previously discussed, you have to give the project a commitment of at least three years.

Many mediators start to become

- impatient after 9/12 months,
- very impatient after 18 months,
- frustrated after 24 months,
- demoralised and disillusioned by 36 months.

Stick with it. Remember what Thomas Edison said: 'Many of life's failures are people who did not realise how close they were to success when they gave up'.

When developing a mediation practice, giving up too soon is more dangerous than hanging on for too long. Established mediators are often told by new mediators that it is all right for them because they are established. Many reply that it took them ten years to become an overnight success.

Very few mediators manage to achieve sustainable success, which translates into a regular flow of the sort of cases they want to do, without having spent a lot of years building a business. As Geoff Sharp says on his website: 'You have to do the hard yards'.

Go back to the Mediation Timeline at para **1.19**. It shows a 'snowball' figure. That is where you as a mediator receive work from people because you have done work for them before. The secret of success is to reach the snowball figure. How quickly you get there depends on the PEARL factors discussed in **Chapter 1.**

(2) How much time a day, a week, a month can you spend on developing your mediation practice?

This goes back to the questions that you asked yourself in **Chapter 4**. What would you be doing if you were not mediating?

If you are working full-time or are engaged in another activity, this will be limited. You might have to confine yourself to weekends and the occasional day's leave. Be realistic. You will have other demands on your time. You will receive setbacks and risk becoming discouraged.

Aled Davies of the Mediation Academy (mediatoracademy.com) advises that you spend the first 100 minutes of every day on marketing activities for your mediation practice.

There may be some mediators who do that. But bear in mind that if you have a successful busy practice you will not have the time to do it. Even when you are building a practice and therefore have lots of days when you are not actually doing a mediation or preparing for one, For most people it is a unrealistic target .

IT costs

7.35 Do not even contemplate having a mediation business without using IT and in particular the internet. The questions you have to ask yourself at this stage are:

- do you have the necessary equipment, software and expertise yourself; or
- will you have to buy it in or outsource it?

For example when you design your website will you do it yourself or hire a website designer? We discuss this and related questions in **Chapter 10**.

By going through the resources that you need in this systematic way you will highlight costs that you may have to incur. Web designers are not by themselves necessarily very expensive but do not forget 'many a mickle make a muckle'. They all add up.

7.36 Business plan

Legal and accounting costs

7.36 See **Chapter 16** for some of the legal and accounting issues that arise in running any sort of business even as a sole trader. Consider, especially if you are not a lawyer, whether or not you need any help in drawing up your Terms and Conditions and your Mediation Agreement. To help on this there are precedents in **Chapters 17** and **18**.

Administration costs

7.37 Someone will have to prepare and send out your mediation agreements and invoices. You can do it yourself. But don't forget that takes time and time is a resource. You also need to consider the following:

- Who will answer the telephone when you are not there?
- Are you going to hire a telephone answering service?
- Will your market expect you to have a respectable or even impressive business address?
- Will you hire a virtual office service to give yourself greater commercial credibility?

One of the few mediators in London who managed to successfully exchange his partnership in a large City Law firm to become a full-time mediator in mid-career did that. He thinks that it was money well spent.

Of course if you are attached to a firm of solicitors or barristers' chambers you will probably be able to come to an arrangement with them to use their administration services. They may expect a contribution to the cost. If you are relying upon appointing panels for your jobs they will undertake the administration. See **Chapter 9**.

Backup plan – plan B

7.38 Your business plan is your **Plan A**. This is what you are going to concentrate on and work to achieve. In formulating it you have to make all sorts of assumptions. Some of those may turn out to be wrong. Just as you are warned as a mediator to expect the unexpected at mediations so you have to expect the unexpected when building a mediation practice.

If things don't go according to plan in Plan A you need **Plan B**. Remember the Von Moltke quotation that no plan survives actually being used.

For example, your business plan may be is based upon operating costs of £3,000 a year and doing two mediations a month after two years. If it turns out that your operating costs are £5,000 a year and you are only doing one mediation a month what will you do? Will you be able to carry on?

You also need a **Plan Z**. This is for what happens when you fail. Nothing has gone according to plan. Your project has not worked.

What will you do? You could take comfort in the Spike Milligan quotation at para **7.03** or you could ask yourself some questions. Will you abandon it completely?

Will you cut your losses and put it all down to experience? Or will you think again and re-engineer your project?

A large part of the answer to this question will be found in the answer you gave to the questions highlighted in **Chapter 4.** These were:

- Why am I doing this at all?
- Where do I want to get to?
- How will I know when I get there?
- How much money time and effort am I prepared to invest in this project?

You can, and you should, always live in hope. But you cannot live on hope. There may be time when you just have to cut your losses.

All is not lost: a true story

7.39 Alan was 40 years old. He was running a building supply business online. This was the third online business that he had set up. The other two had been successes and been sold. This business was also a success but he had a dispute with his IT supplier. Alan was also a registered IT practitioner with the British Computer Society.

Proceedings were issued and a mediation was arranged in April 2010. Alan was not a lawyer but he was well educated and had sat for ten years as a lay magistrate. By the time of the mediation Alan had become disillusioned with the litigation process, given the risk-reward ratio that was emerging out of the cost-benefit analysis. He had not been to mediation before and did not know much about it. The mediation ran on past midnight but a settlement was achieved.

Alan was so impressed by mediation as a way of sorting out disputes that he decided to become a mediator. He took the training with one of the well-known providers in July. He passed the assessment and within nine months had completed three observations.

He concluded that not having a legal qualification was a disadvantage if you wanted to do civil and commercial mediations. He therefore decided to take the Bar exams. He had researched the various legal qualifications and concluded that the easiest and quickest way of gaining a legal qualification was to become a barrister. He successfully did this within three years.

He did not want to practise as a barrister and therefore did not undertake pupillage. He realised that he was not able to give legal advice but he could call himself a barrister.

He had sold his business when he decided to read for the Bar. He looked round for work. He quickly realised that it would take time to obtain mediations and to replace the income he had earned from his on-line business. He applied to various disciplinary and regulatory bodies to sit on disciplinary and investigatory panels. Within two years he had assembled a portfolio of appointments. With the

7.40 *Business plan*

experience he gained promotion to sit as a legally qualified chairman of some of the panels.

But he still wanted to do mediations. He realised that he needed a USP.

He also wanted to run a mediation provider business. His analysis of the mediation scene had led him to the conclusion that it is easier to make money by being a mediation trainer or mediation provider than by being a mediator. He also wanted to know more about mediation. He therefore enrolled on a Master's degree. His dissertation was on the business opportunities for ODR.

During this time he gained some practical mediation experience by undertaking mediations for one of the low-value dispute resolution providers. He was only paid £30 a mediation but at least he had some mediations under his belt. He also regularly attended conferences and workshops and became a member of several panels of ADR providers. He also set up his own small mediation provider. A few mediations came in but not enough.

Alan formed a company to provide ODR in a particular way, which nobody else in the UK is currently providing. His portfolio of disciplinary-regulatory appointments continues to expand. He is now finding it difficult to devote the time necessary to develop his mediation business either as a mediator or as a mediation provider.

Five years after he first encountered mediation and trained as a mediator he has decided that he is not going to make it as a practising mediator doing civil and commercial mediation which was his original objective. Instead he is optimistic about exploiting the opportunities in ODR and continues to develop a successful practice as a member of disciplinary-regulatory boards and as an Ombudsman. He attributes part of his success to his mediation training. He says that he often uses some of the techniques he was taught on his mediation course when sitting as the chairman of a Disciplinary Board.

Alan does not regret at all undertaking mediation training and trying to become a civil and commercial mediator. In fact he is grateful for it. By taking that path he found himself in an area of activity, which is giving him a good living that he had never thought of previously. It also introduced him to the world of ODR and mediation providers.

In a nutshell

7.40

- Draw up a business plan. Follow it. Update it. Follow it.
- Not being a lawyer can be a disadvantage if you want to do civil and commercial mediation.
- Qualifying as a lawyer is not as expensive, difficult or time-consuming as you might think, especially if you take the barrister route.
- You can earn an income from your mediation training rather than by being a mediator.
- Persevere and take the opportunities that come your way.

Chapter 8

Marketing – what is in it for mediators?

In this chapter you will learn:
- The difference between marketing, promotion and selling.
- Why mediators find marketing hard.
- How to find marketing easy.

Cleaning toilets

8.01 For many mediators, and others, marketing and, even worse, selling is regarded as a distasteful activity. As Daniel Pink describes it in his book *To Sell Is Human*, they are seen: 'as a white-collar equivalent of cleaning toilets – necessary perhaps, but unpleasant and even a bit unclean'.

But everything seems to have changed. New marketing and new selling have arrived. They seem to be less lavatorial.

What is marketing in a VUCA world?

8.02 What is a VUCA world? It is a Volatile, Uncertain, Complex and Ambiguous world. In fact according to the CEO of Saatchi & Saatchi, Kevin Roberts, we live a super-VUCA world.

Different people have different ideas about marketing in much the same way as they have about mediation. The new marketing has developed almost entirely as a result of the internet in order to cope with the VUCA world.

In this world things have changed:
- Strategy is dead. Nobody knows what is going to happen in a super-VUCA world therefore don't bother trying to work it out. Strategy has been replaced by ideas as the currency of business.
- Management is dead. The Chief Executive Officer is being replaced by the Chief Excitement Officer. Leaders have become emotional not rational thinkers.

8.03 *Marketing – what is in it for mediators?*

- Marketing is dead. Speed and velocity is everything. And the marketing job is to create a *movement to persuade* and inspire people to join in.

As Kevin Roberts told the IoD's Annual Convention in 2012:

> 'Everyone wants a conversation. They want inspiration. Inspire people with your website. Don't just interrupt, but interact. Asking about Return on Investment is the wrong question today. You should be asking about Return on Involvement.'

What does this mean for mediators?

8.03 Where does this leave a mediator trying to develop a mediation practice? Mediators are in a good place. They can use their transferable skills. As explained in **Chapters 11** and **12** many of the approaches and techniques espoused by the new marketing and the new selling are the ones that mediators and trained in and routinely use. After all what are mediations if not conversations? Don't be afraid.

Five differences between marketing and selling

8.04 Mark Twain defined a cauliflower as a cabbage with a college education. Traditionally that was the same difference between marketing and selling. Selling was carried out by people without degrees wearing polyester suits. Marketing is performed by people with degrees and mohair suits.

Prof Theodore Levitt who died in 2005 was a renowned Harvard-based economist famous for coining the word 'globalisation' and the concept of 'marketing myopia'. He said:

> 'The difference between selling and marketing is more than semantic.
>
> 'Selling merely concerns itself with the tricks and techniques of getting the customers to exchange their cash for the company's products, it does not bother about the value satisfaction that the exchange is all about.
>
> 'On the contrary marketing views the entire business as consisting of a tightly integrated effort to discover, create, arouse and satisfy customer needs.'

Levitt T *'Marketing Myopia'* (1960) Harvard Business Review

Apparently the Internet has changed all this, but distinctions are still said to remain.

In a nutshell they boil down to: marketing is about *pull* and sales is about *push*.

1.	Marketing speaks to many people at a time.	Sales speaks to one person at a time.
2.	Marketing tells the story of the business/brand.	Sales is where the story turns into an order.
3.	Marketing looks at the bigger picture – it is broad and shallow.	Sales look at the detail-it is narrow and deep.
4.	Marketing looks at the big data and averages and trends.	Sales does not deal in averages it deals with the particular.
5.	Marketing deals with relationships.	Sales deals with orders and products.

How does this apply to mediators?

8.05 These high-level views and definitions coming from the world of academia or advertising may have relevance for those promoting global brands or acting for multinationals. How do they apply to sole practitioner mediators working out of their back bedrooms?

Are there any brands?

8.06 In practice the distinction for individual mediators between marketing and sales is not important. They are practically synonymous. Most individual mediators do not have a brand. They have themselves. If they tell a story about the business they are telling a story about themselves.

Some mediation organisations such as CEDR, JAMS or ADR GROUP have a brand. They have been in business for 25 years. There are very few mediators in the UK who have been in business that long. There are a handful with a distinctive reputation and style that could be called a brand.

In **Chapter 9** we look at marketing groups, panels and other attempts to give a corporate image or presence in the market. There can be advantages in doing this. But how can individual mediators go about promoting themselves whether through marketing or selling?

Marketing barriers

8.07 Some of the problems remain the same whether or not you are promoting, marketing or selling. The three main ones are:

1 A psychological one

Most mediators face this. They do not like doing it, whatever you call it. They feel reluctant. You may think that this is partly because of a cultural reticence peculiar to the UK – the home of understatement, self-restraint and the stiff upper lip. Not so. In the US according to Tammy Lenski mediators feel just the same. Mediators just find it difficult to go and tell people why they should use them.

2 Habit

Although many mediators come from professional backgrounds where advertising is allowed and practised it is often on a non-individual basis. An organisation, practice or firm rather than a single individual is being promoted. There is not the same individual spotlight. There may be individual CVs of the firm's partners on the company's website. But this is part of a much wider offering and there is a feeling of safety in numbers.

Many people find it easier to sell a third party than to sell themselves. So they have relied upon someone else to do it for them in a way non-specific to the individual.

3 The perceived difficulty

This is understandable. Promotion, marketing or selling is hard. In fact mediation seems to be a particularly hard sell. But it is not impossible and it is necessary.

8.08 *Marketing – what is in it for mediators?*

Why is mediation a hard sell?

8.08 Many mediators find this a strange question. Why, they ask, is litigation an easier sell than mediation? The positive benefits of mediation are so obvious. Out comes the mantra.

Mediation is a voluntary process under which the parties can choose a neutral independent third party to help them create their own settlement and find solutions, which they could never find in court. It is cheaper and quicker than litigation or arbitration.

It must be a no-brainer.

Don't sell the benefits

8.09 This emphasis on the self-evident benefits of the mediation process highlights the first problem. Potential customers are not really interested in the process. Mediators swear by it and use it to great effect every day.

Potential customers see that they have a need or a problem. They want it satisfied or solved. They are not too concerned with who does it and how it is done. They just want it done in a satisfactory way at a reasonable price.

Mediators concentrate on emphasising the benefits to the customer. This is especially true of new mediators. They have been trained in the new techniques and ways of looking at and handling disputes and conflict. They have drunk the Kool-Aid. They cannot wait to start helping people.

Ask the customer

8.10 Practitioners of the new marketing and the new selling agree on one thing: emphasising the benefits of your product or service to your customers is the wrong way round. What you should be doing is asking the customers what they need.

The focus is on *needs* rather than on *problems*. Most people know when they have a problem although they may not realise its full extent or nature. The theory is that not everybody understands what they need. There may be unrealised needs.

Have a conversation

8.11 Everybody is talking about having a dialogue with customers and engaging in learning conversations with them. By digging through this conversational archaeology, layers of need in the organisational architecture will be uncovered. With luck you may even unearth the foundations.

The way that this is achieved is not by asking a potential customer: 'How can I help you?' or 'What are the problems that you need solving?'

Instead you ask them to describe their business. You encourage them to explain how they have arrived at where they are and to share with you their objectives and vision for the future. By sensitive questioning the prospecting mediator should be able to find out what is really important to the business and what potential challenges there could be. Things will emerge for example:

- In increasingly cosmopolitan workforces there will be different cultural expectations and behavioural norms.
- When IT systems are replaced or upgraded there will be problems with IT suppliers. That is a given.
- Expanding businesses often make changes to working patterns and practices. That always causes uncertainty amongst the workforce.
- If the business owns or leases property there will be problems. No one can own property without having problems with somebody at some time.
- Acquisitions are a fruitful source of disputes. Post-transaction warranty claims are routinely made.
- As businesses develop, and owners and shareholders become older, strains and tensions develop between different generations. The founders want to sell. The newcomers want to hang on to the business to enjoy the fruits of their labour. Shareholder and partnership disputes ensue

In practice here are some of the barriers that you will meet.

Barriers

8.12

(1) Poor image

Mediators constantly talk about why mediation is not more popular amongst the public, both professional and general. The usual comments are about

- resistance from lawyers; and
- lack of public awareness.

Both these factors apply but there are other difficulties, which mediators are not quite so ready to acknowledge.

(2) Mediation is boring

Mediators find this astonishing. For them mediation is endlessly fascinating. But consider what is actually happening. Very few articles about mediation appear in the general media, either in print or online. Mediation only became an episode in a soap opera last year. On 20 July 2014, in Coronation Street, Leanne and Nick Tisley went to mediation with Charlie Kemp the mediator. It was a family mediation. It did not produce a resolution. But at least it was a start. Sadly at the moment there is no sign of follow-through with greater interest being generated.

According to one well-known workplace and community mediator people are reluctant to admit that they have been to mediation. They see it as a sign of weakness. She contrasts this with coaching where people are keen to tell each other about their experience. Coaching is seen as a positive experience. Mediation can appear to be a negative experience.

8.12 *Marketing – what is in it for mediators?*

Again, anecdotally, there is the dinner party test. Guests ask each other what they do. Lawyers are accustomed to seeing their fellow guests eyes glaze over when they say what they do. People are more interested in barristers than solicitors. But, according to one experienced barrister-mediator, specialising in disputes in the wine trade, they are not interested in mediators.

(3) Confusion

When you say that you are a mediator the reaction is usually: 'Oh arbitration I know about that.' But at least they have heard of arbitration.

Or it is the standard: 'Mediation? Do you mean meditation?'

The more well-informed say: "Ah yes do you deal with divorces?' with an expectant air of hearing salacious gossip. When you tell them that you do not do matrimonial work their interest declines. If you do manage to explain what mediators do the response is often that it all sounds like counselling or therapy. As indeed it does.

(4) Faceless

In the UK there is no face of mediation. People know about courts and they see pictures of judges. For arbitration there is the Chartered Institute of Arbitrators, which has been around for 100 years. For mediation there is the Civil Mediation Council, which has been around ten years. Even the CMC does not include all types of mediators. Family mediators have their own organisation – the Family Mediation Council. Community mediators are not yet included.

The Chairman of the Civil Mediation Council, Sir Alan Ward, a former Court of Appeal judge, routinely says when making public speeches that the CMC speaks on behalf of mediation not on behalf of mediators. It is more like the GMC (General Medical Council) than the BMA. (British Medical Association). Establishing a face or voice of mediation will take time.

This is true. Perhaps over the next ten years greater progress will be made especially if mediation becomes mandatory for some disputes. But given that after ten years the CMC has still not appointed a marketing expert, do not rely upon it to raise the profile of mediation for you. For the present, individual mediators will have to bang their own drums because no one else is going to do it for them.

(5) Fear

People are afraid of something either because they do not know about it or because they do. Mediation for most people is still novel. Even for people in business it is largely unknown. They know about negotiation, litigation and possibly arbitration. They have not heard of mediation. Why should they have heard of it? The media does not give it much coverage. Any coverage that is given to mediation tends to be about family mediation, which is being actively promoted by the government as a cost reduction exercise. The CMC is not telling them about it. Are their own advisers telling them?

Lawyers are now under a duty to discuss mediation with their clients (see the Bar Code of Conduct and the SRA Principles and Code of Conduct). But many still see mediation as a challenge to the established ways of doing things. In times of insecurity challenges can be seen as threats. And we live in a VUCA world now.

Marketing – what is in it for mediators? **8.12**

(6) Too much choice

Herein lies another problem. Mediators present to the outside world a confusing picture of what they do. As described in **Chapters 2** and **4** there is a kaleidoscope of mediation styles and models. If mediators as a community are not agreed about what mediation is how can we expect the public to be clear?

All the marketing advice emphasises that if you want to get your message across you have to:

- be clear what that message is; and
- make sure that the message is clear.

Mediators have failed to do this and are continuing to fail. If you have any doubt about this go online and read the blogs and chat rooms. You will find perennial and eternal debates and arguments (or conversations as they are called) about facilitative, evaluative, therapeutic, narrative mediation and the rest. On an academic or theoretical level some of it is interesting. But if insiders who know about mediation find it confusing, imagine what it is like for outsiders trying to find out what mediation is about.

(7) It's unnatural

Some commentators go further. They say that mediation is not providing what customers want. This is not just a case of evaluative as opposed to facilitative styles of mediation. Paul Randolph, one of the UK's leading mediation trainers, told the London mediation day conference on 10 October 2015 that what people in conflict want is not what mediators provide. According to him mediation is not 'natural'. What people in conflict want is:

- Revenge – they want an eye for an eye.
- Vindication – they want to be proved right. This gives a great boost to self-esteem.
- Humiliation – they want to avoid being proved wrong and to show that the others were wrong.
- Retribution – they want something back.

Mediation either as a process or as an ideology does not provide these. Instead it emphasises looking forward to the future not towards the past, needs not interests or positions and seeing the other person's point of view. Compromise and collaboration, not conflict and competition, is the language of mediation.

This view is not universally shared. Paul Randolph, although a barrister, comes from the psychotherapy perspective on mediation. Other mediators and commentators who come more from the problem-solving perspective are not so defeatist. In practice, when mediators ask parties at a mediation what they want, revenge is rarely mentioned. Fairness is. Mediation can, and often does, provide a means of boosting self-esteem, allowing people to feel they have got something back, they have been vindicated by being acknowledged and have avoided humiliation.

8.13 *Marketing – what is in it for mediators?*

> **TOP TIP**
>
> Put all this debate to one side. Do not get drawn into. Work out what mediation model you want to sell and who you think will buy it.

Pies

8.13 Commentators constantly say that that the market for commercial mediations of litigated cases is finite and possibly getting smaller because the number of legal claims that are filed at court is falling. They refer to it as a fixed pie. This is a real problem for civil and commercial mediators. As described at para **6.19** lawyers, in particular solicitors, are usually described as the gatekeepers of mediation. In other words most civil and commercial mediations are brought to market through solicitors. They are the ones who advise their clients whether or not to go to mediation and are instrumental in choosing the mediator. This pool of litigated cases may be a fixed pie but at least it is food.

As mediators we are trained to grow the pie. Are the Internet and social media the growth hormones that mediation needs? See **Chapter 10**.

Marketing made easy

8.14 Having thought about what modern marketing is for mediators you need to know how you implement marketing. What do you actually do?

You work through the checklist.

Checklist of marketing tools

- You raise your profile; see **Chapter 9**.
- You establish an Internet presence: see **Chapter 10**.
- You use social media: see **Chapter 10**.
- You defrost your transferrable skills.
- You pitch: see **Chapter 12**.
- You network: see **Chapter 12**.
- You make a noise: see **Chapter 13**.

Next step

8.15 Before reading on, go back to para **4.66** and re-read the self-audit and to **Chapter 7** and re-read paras **7.33–7.37** about the resources that you have available to invest in your new mediation business.

Marketing – what is in it for mediators? **8.16**

In a nutshell

8.16

- If you want to mediate learn to sell.
- Mediators are salesmen.
- Ignore the macro picture and concentrate on the micro: sell what you are comfortable selling to the people who want to buy what you are selling.
- Leave the existential angst to others. Draft your profile (**Chapter 9**) and set up your website (**Chapter 10).**

Chapter 9

Profile is all: is it?

> In this chapter you will learn about:
> - Establishing your profile.
> - Raising your profile.
> - Drafting your profile.
> - Panels.
> - Marketing Groups.
> - Directories.

The mantra: 'Profile is everything'

9.01 Profile is everything.

These words are constantly repeated by every business development consultant who advises mediators. Profile means has different meanings:
- Profile as a CV
- Profile as a brand
- Profile as a reputation

Profile as a CV

9.02 Stephen Ward of Clerksroom told the CMC conference in 2014 that profile is everything. This was part of his talk on how to develop a mediation practice. He said that it was simple.

The first element is to have a good profile. By that he meant a good CV. He referred to mediators who have registered with Clerksroom and who attract work. One of the main reasons that they attract work is that they have a good profile. He gave examples of good profiles. If you want to see what he means, go to his website www.clerksroom.com/mediators.php and look at the profiles of mediators who are successful.

Not everybody agrees with this advice. For example Mark Belford, an experienced barristers' clerk who is now the administrator at the ADR Group, says that in his experience people who are looking for mediators paid very little attention to the profiles. What they want is to discuss with him is which mediators might be available and suitable for their mediation.

9.03 *Profile is all: is it?*

Having said that, if you are going to have CV/profile you might as well have a good one.

Inevitably there are many different views about what makes a good profile. Not everybody agrees with Clerksroom's style. Some find it too brash and self-congratulatory. Others prefer the more traditional profiles, which you can see on many barristers' chambers' websites. These often read more like a cross between an entry in Who's Who and an obituary than advertising material.

Is there a middle ground?

You will be asked for a CV/Profile from time to time. Your CV is a sales pitch for yourself. There are ground rules for drafting any profile/CV/biog.

CV ground rules

Have a structure

9.03 Inevitably different profile writers advocate different structures. Here are some examples:

Example 1	• Description: eg solicitor, business and legal consultant, mediator • Work undertaken • Experience • Personal • Education • Other experience • Feedback
Example 2	• Current position and background • Personal • Main mediation practice areas • Mediation experience • Mediation style code of conduct • Complaints process • Professional affiliations • The rates • Feedback digests • References • Mediation education and training • Professional indemnity insurance • Teaching • Publications

Example 3	• Introduce yourself
	• Educational credentials
	• Notable achievements
	• Closing statement
Example 4	• Introductory statement that defines who you are
	• Professional history
	• New professional affiliations
	• Awards
	• Volunteer activities
	• Credentials
	• Education

9.04 The two key questions to ask when drafting your profile/CV are

- How many words have I got?
- Who is the audience?

How to write an excellent profile

9.05 Make sure that you have clear answers to these four questions.

(1) How long should it be?

The length of your profile/CV will often be dictated by where it is going to appear.

If you are putting it on your own website you can, in theory, choose how long it will be. But visitors to websites do not have long attention spans. You have to grab their attention. Your key information must be 'above the fold', ie that part of the screen that the visitor can read without scrolling down (see para **10.24**).

You can refer the visitor for more details to another page within your website. That one can be of a more conventional printed media length. But it should never be more than two pages long.

Remember what it is for. To tell people about you and to give them good reasons for not rejecting you as a mediator. Do not bore them with:

- pages of coagulated prose;
- decades of achievements;
- reams of publications; or
- details of how you like to spend your time when you are not mediating.

Remember that this is a generic document. You are trying to give information, which will meet the information needs of a wide range of readers. When someone asks for your CV/profile you can always tailor it by highlighting or including specific information that is particularly relevant to the reader or the dispute to be mediated.

9.06 *Profile is all: is it?*

(2) What do I put in it?

Your CV/profile must be up-to-date. Readers are interested in what you are currently doing and what you have recently done. Awards for excellence as an innovative mediator 25 years ago will not impress anybody looking for a mediator today. A citation of an article written ten years ago will have limited eye appeal.

When writing your profile/CV for somebody else's website you will have to follow their stipulations on the maximum number of words, layout, headings and key information. For example some websites require you to specify which Code of Conduct you adhere to and whether or not you have professional indemnity insurance.

(3) How often do I update it?

As a rule of thumb, head-hunters/recruiters advise that your CV should be updated every three months as a minimum. If there is a major change in your circumstances update your CV promptly to reflect it .

(4) What are the essential points?

A photograph/image

CVs and profiles on the Internet usually include a head and shoulders passport style photograph. We live in a visual age. We all recognise faces more easily than names. We believe that we can tell something about the person from how they look. Some mediators persist in presenting CVs/profiles without an image of themselves. Choosing to be anonymous in this way is a bold decision.

An experienced litigation solicitor who regularly appoints mediators said that he would never hire a mediator without knowing what they looked like. It also turned that he did not like photographs that showed mediators with beards: 'You can't trust them' he used to mutter.

We all make judgements about people based on their appearance. Some people make very quick snap judgements, which become indelible. This might be thought a good reason for having a silhouette rather than a photograph. But overall we do live in a visual world. Websites and profiles without an image are the exception.

The passport style photo is being challenged. Instead of head-on shots there are now angled images. Other mediators are moving a further step forward and including caricatures or line drawings. They have a novelty impact. It is a matter of personal style and choice about what image of yourself you want to project.

A brief description

Think Twitter. In 140 characters say who you are and what you do. That is the hook. You can expand it in your sections about past experiences and current activities.

What to include

First or third person?

9.06   Here is the first decision. Do you write in the first or third person? If you write in the third person do you use

- Your first name, eg 'Rachel is an incisive and energetic mediator.'
- Or more formally, eg 'Rachel Smith is an incisive and energetic mediator.'
- Or even more formally, eg 'Ms Rachel Smith is an incisive and energetic mediator.'

Writing in the third person may suggest a more authoritative and objective description. Some panels require their mediators' profiles to be written in the third person.

Writing in the first person sounds less formal and possibly more personally engaging. Of course, it can also sound more self-obsessed and self-promoting.

Current mediation activities

9.07 Readers want to know what you are doing now as a mediator. What sort of mediations you are doing. How many have you done? How long have you been doing it for? What sectors have you mediated?

This section can be a challenge for new mediators who have not done any mediations. The golden rule is: do not lie.

Haven't done a mediation: what do you say?

9.08 Resourceful new mediators use various devices to get over this problem. For example:

- 'Catherine brings a wealth of recent financial experience to complex mediation cases involving derivative swaps'. This is useful for someone who has relevant professional experience but little or no actual mediation experience.
- 'Richard has wide/extensive mediation experience in a number of sectors including construction, professional negligence, boundary disputes etc.' This is a formula that could be used if you have attended mediations either as a client, expert witness or more importantly as a representative.

What you are genuinely trying to do is to emphasise the transferable skills that you have acquired in your previous professional experience.

- Former judges, for example, emphasise the fact that they are used to assimilating information, seeing the main point, isolating the key issues and weighing competing interpretations of the same facts and law.
- Contract negotiators can say: 'I have 25 years' experience in commercial negotiation and dispute resolution as commercial director of X CO.'
- HR professionals can say: 'I have ten years' experience of handling employment claims, workplace disputes and contract negotiation.'

Relevant non-mediation experience

9.09 This is the section where new mediators with limited mediation experience can sell themselves as described above.

9.10 *Profile is all: is it?*

When trying to work out what to include ask yourself: 'If I was looking for a mediator what would I want to know?'

Accentuating the positives and minimising the negatives is legitimate. Auctioneers when preparing their sales catalogues call this 'perfuming the provenance'. But do not actively mislead.

Rankings

9.10 If your profile appears in any Directories, tell your readers. The 2014 IMI survey of in-house corporate counsel revealed that rankings or peer review was one of the main factors they took into account when selecting a mediator. See para **6.09**. https://imimediation.org/imi-international-corporate-users-adr-survey/.

Achievements

Courses

9.11 The most relevant achievement is your mediation qualification. Readers want to know that you are accredited with a reputable body. If you have received additional specialised training mention that as well. You do not have to list every two-week course that you attended over the last 20 years.

Publications

9.12 If you have published something recently, especially a book about mediation, give the details. Be careful about overloading your publications list because the reader could think that you are an academic rather than a practitioner.

Training

9.13 The same warning applies to those mediators who also do lots of training. Readers are not looking for mediation training. They are looking for a mediator to mediate. For some clients, involvement in training, especially if it is linked to well-established organisations or associated with a prestigious academic institution, does confer status. You must be an expert because people are paying you to teach about mediation.

But bear in mind the warning given in **Chapter 3** about training. There is widespread scepticism, especially among lawyers, that mediation trainers are people who cannot attract enough work as mediators.

Speaking

9.14 Recent invitations to speak at conferences are worth mentioning especially if they are prestigious ones. But again, remember readers are not looking for a public speaker.

Education

9.15 Not all mediators include details of their education. Some mediators think that saying they went to a certain school is relevant. Most do not. But most include details of where they obtained their professional qualifications including their university degree. It has to be acknowledged that some institutions are more of a selling point than others. But for every reader who is impressed by the fact that you went to Oxford another will be put off and be thinking that you are an elitist snob.

Languages

9.16 If you have operational fluency, tell people. If you do not, but you have experience of working with interpreters say that instead.

If you have worked overseas and are therefore used to different cultural and professional environments mention it.

Feedback/testimonials

9.17 Include these if you have them. Some mediation providers stipulate that feedback information is included in profiles on their website. The use of references and testimonials is discussed in much more detail in **Chapter 14**. Do not provide six pages of them. Just pick the best and the latest.

Personal

9.18 Most people like to end on a slightly lighter note by mentioning the number of children they have or which football team they support. Possibly this personalises and humanises the document. But again for every person who is impressed another is probably put off.

You can't win 'em all

9.19 Although you are writing a generic document remember that you cannot appeal to everyone all the time. This does not matter because the maximum number of mediations that anyone can do in a year is 365. Even the busiest and most successful mediators do not do that.

Profile as reputation

9.20 See **Chapter 14** for how you build your business (through referrals, recommendations and returns).

See **Chapter 10** for how you establish your expertise and go-to status on the Internet, LinkedIn and Twitter.

In this section we discuss whether it is worth joining Panels or being included in Directories.

See **Chapter 13** for establishing your profile as a brand.

9.21 *Profile is all: is it?*

Panels

What are panels?

9.21 Most mediation providers operate panels of mediators. These are the people they put forward when they receive an enquiry about organising a mediation. Some of the bigger panels are associated with training organisations such as CEDR, the ADR Group, the Academy of Experts. Others are not, for example, In Place of Strife, Panel of Independent Mediators.

Most but not all charge a fee to be a member. Some, for example Clerksroom, do not.

Access

9.22 Some of the panels are open access like Clerksroom with limited requirements. Others require you to be assessed by them before you can join them either by having received your initial training from them or by being re-assessed at an assessment day. Others are by invitation only.

- Some panels are designed for full-time mediators, others for part-timers. In fact most panels consist of people who do not practice mediation either as their main job or on a full-time basis.
- Some panels differentiate between classes of mediators, depending upon their experience. For example Clerksroom divides them up into elite, experienced and intermediate mediators The By Invitation Only panels promote themselves as only having experienced and acknowledged expert mediators as members.

They can be mutually exclusive. One experienced commercial mediator with a particular and unusual specialism was invited to join one of the best-known By Invitation only panels. They told him that if he did join them he would have to give it up his membership of Clerksroom.

What do panels do?

9.23 All the panels say that they will help their members. Some also warn that they cannot guarantee appointments but only offer the opportunity to be selected.

Some panels stipulate in their terms and conditions that they cannot nominate a mediator unless the parties have not already chosen one or the parties cannot agree on who to appoint.

Reread para **3.05** to adjust your expectations.

Don't expect too much

9.24 Most newly accredited mediators expect that they will receive appointments as mediators as a result of being on a panel. After a year or two they realise that their fees from the appointments they have received from the panel do not cover their costs of training or even the annual joining fee. There is a high degree of churn on some of these panels.

Panel administrators

9.25 Some panel administrators see it as their job to act as an impresario for their panel members and help them develop their career as mediators. They act in much the same way as a traditional barrister's clerk. Others see their job as sorting out the logistics and to fairly allocate cases amongst the panel members.

Panels vary greatly in size. Clerksroom has over 500 panel members. CEDR has 150. PIM (Panel of Independent Mediators) has 22. Mediation 1st has 8. ADR Group has 127 Civil and Commercial mediators.

Some panels, such as ADR Group, can tell you how many mediations you have been put forward for. Others, such as Clerksroom, cannot.

Some panels offer help with drawing up your profile, or arranging for professional images to be taken.

Some try and help by finding out why you were not selected if they put you forward. Most do not.

The relationship with the panel of your choice has to be administered. Boxes of chocolates and bottles of whisky might help! Expressions of gratitude definitely do. So does the opposite. One active property mediator thought that she was not receiving enough appointments. So in her words she rang up the panel administrator and had a row. She claims that she then received some appointments.

There are different ways of getting on someone's radar.

Misgivings

9.26 Many mediators are suspicious about how mediation problems are allocated by the panels. One panel, which is that of the Standing Conference of Mediation Advocates SCMA, expressly says that it operates on the taxi rank principle, ie by rotation. Most panels explain that they put forward mediators who are most suitable for the proposed appointment and try to be fair.

There are dark rumours about favouritism. Some panels are more open than others and explain that they do operate on the principle of reciprocity. Panel members who can refer mediations to them will receive more appointments. Panels which are attached to another organisations such as barristers' chambers or law firms, even though they are open to mediators who are not members of the firm or chambers, are sometimes suspected of favouring them.

The golden rule is that you cannot rely upon panels to feed you enough mediations to live on.

9.27 Profile is all: is it?

Business model

9.27 Panels proliferate as they are seen by the organisers as a way of making money and by the mediators as a way of gaining access to market.

You also have to consider the business models of the various panels. They are not all the same. For example Clerksroom says that it does not charge its panel members for being a member of the panel or take a cut of their fee. Their mediators receive the full mediation fee. Clerksroom make their money by charging the customer an administration fee or for room hire.

Others quote a fee to the customers and pay the mediator carrying out the mediation a percentage of it. They keep the rest to cover their costs. Some mediation providers are coy about how much they retain. 30% seems to be the going rate. Some charge more and some charge less.

As the chart below shows the mediation provider is more likely to be making money out of the arrangement than the mediators. You have to decide whether or not what you pay to the panel directly and indirectly is worth it compared with what else you could do with that money in promoting your business.

This illustration assumes that there is an annual membership fee of £800 and that the provider retains 30% of the mediation fee of £3000.

	MEDIATOR	MEDIATION FEE	PROVIDER
Year one			
1	Fee (£800)	£800	
	£2,100	3,000	900
	1,300	1,700	
2	£,2,100	3,000	900
	3,400	2,600	
3	£2,100	3,000	900
	5,500	3,500	
Year two			
	(800)	800	
4	£2,100	3,000	900
	6,800	5,200	

Summary:

1   At end of Year One having done three mediations the mediator has earned a total of £5,500 and the Provider £3,500. His earnings per mediation is £1,833 and the Provider's £1,166.

2   In Year Two having done four mediations the mediator's total earnings are £6,800 and the Provider's are £5,200. His earnings per mediation are £1,700 and the Provider's £1,300.

If the mediator charged £2,000 a mediation and secured appointments direct by being 33% cheaper he would have earned £8,000.

3 The figures for the mediators improve the more mediations they do. But very few panel members receive more than a handful of appointments a year.

The big question is would you have got the jobs even at a much lower price? Only if people know who you are and where to find you.

Bear in mind that the use of panels for mediation appointments has been declining. But the decline seems to have levelled off (see the CEDR survey in **Chapter 6**).

Advantages of panels

9.28 As discussed in **Chapter 6** customers selecting mediators are more likely to approach mediators direct than through panels/mediation providers.

Not all do this because they like the definite advantages which can be offered by panel. These are:

- The mediators are vetted and can be assumed to be of a minimum level of competence and experience.
- The mediators will be covered by professional indemnity insurance.
- There will be a complaints procedure and redress will be available even if it is only the rebate of fees.
- The hassle of organising dates and rooms is taken away.
- Most panels undertake the administration of mediations. Some now offer administration services to independent mediators who are not panel members or who receive appointments independently and not through them. They charge a fee.

There is no doubt that some newly qualified mediators think that they establish commercial credibility by being on a panel. This is probably true. In practice what often happens is that their expectations are not met. They join a panel expecting to receive appointments as mediators. They often become disappointed. They realise that self-help might be needed. They consider marketing groups and directories.

Marketing Groups

9.29 As mentioned at para **2.45** many mediators consider forming their own marketing groups to try and secure work. Here is checklist of things to think about.

Structure:

- Many marketing groups are formed on the barristers' chambers model. An unincorporated group of people agree to share facilities and expenses. There is often no formal agreement. There is certainly no partnership agreement.
- Sometimes there is a limited company structure with each of the members being shareholders.
- More often a limited company owned by two or three founding members provides services to the others in exchange for a contribution towards expenses.

9.29 *Profile is all: is it?*

Decision-making:

Who takes the decisions? For example do you employ an administrator? How much do you spend on the website?

Funding:

In any activities this is always a tricky subject. The need for a business plan when you have a group of people trying to work together is even more obvious than when you are setting up business as a sole trader.

Premises:

- Where are you going to operate from?
- Several marketing groups operate from serviced offices. They buy in the telephone answering service, the address and the use of meeting rooms. They share the expenses amongst themselves.
- Others attach themselves to barristers' chambers or professional firms and user facilities.
- Others operate from a series of members' spare bedrooms.

Members:

- Who are you going to choose to work with? Do you want people who are like you in terms of experience, personality, age and values? Do you want a diverse group of people?
- Many marketing groups have a turnover of membership. People will be motivated by self-interest – enlightened self-interest perhaps – but still self- interest.
- Do you want an anchor or magnet member? Someone who already has a reputation as a mediator and might attract work?
- How many members you want? Three, six, twelve? What do you feel comfortable with?

Administration:

Who does it? This includes the routine and boring tasks like sending out agreements, bills, fixing up venues and dates but also two vital functions:

- Selling the group.
- Allocating the work that comes in. This will be where a specific mediator has not been requested. What system of allocation will you use: a rota, first-come first-served open outcry, the administrator's discretion? These are all points that, for example, barristers' clerks have coped with for generations.

This is why barristers' clerks are often recruited as administrators for marketing groups. Sometimes they are grafted on to barristers' chambers. If one of the members is working in a professional firm they may volunteer to provide admin through their office. There will always be the risk of a residual suspicion that allocation of cases is not carried out in an impartial even-handed manner.

Exclusivity:
- Are you going to insist that the members channel all their cases through the group even ones that they receive direct?
- If they do introduce through the group a case that they have received direct, will they receive a credit doing this for example paying a lower administration fee?

Charges:

How will you charge? This has two sides.

- How you allocate expenses amongst the numbers?

Is this strict equality of contribution? Always be linked to income derived from appointments administered by the group? Those who receive less work will always grumble more than those who receive more.

If some of the members undertake some of the administration work for the group will they be credited in some way?

- How much would you charge to clients who want you to provide the mediation service?

Will you charge the same level as your individual members do for their own appointments? If you do then their net receipts might be lower after deduction of their share of the group expenses. They will want to be assured that there is a benefit, ie they may be receiving less per appointment but they are receiving more appointments.

Time:
- It always takes longer than you think to set up a group in the first place and to manage it.
- You can consider and debate the above topics for months. In the end you have got to decide whether to form your own group or practise on your own and be a panel member. There are some mediators who seem to do both but none seem to ecstatically happy about the amount of work that they are receiving

Directories

9.30 There have been directories of lawyers, both solicitors and barristers, for many years. In the UK the two best-known are *Chambers and Partners* and the *Legal 500*. They have extended their range to include mediators.

Each year they issue their rankings. The *Legal 500* is published in September and *Chambers* in October. Applications for inclusion have to be made by February. There is a detailed application procedure, which can be found on their websites. As discussed in **Chapter 14** if you want to apply for inclusion, you will have to provide details of examples of mediations and references and names of referees.

Chambers has a wider reach of users beyond the legal market. *Legal 500* tends to be more limited to the legal market.

9.31 *Profile is all: is it?*

Applying for entry into directories is a painstaking business. Frankly it is probably quicker and cheaper and more efficient to employ someone to do it for you. There are various consultants who do this. You do have to pay them for their troubles. You can expect to be quoted a day rate of £250-500 plus VAT. It is not cheap but it is well worth it and you can put it down to your marketing spend.

If you are only going to apply for one *Chambers* is probably the better bet, especially if you are a not a lawyer-mediator or want to appeal to the non-lawyer market.

Are they worth it?

9.31 The process of applying is tedious and time-consuming. The outcome is uncertain. As explained in **Chapter 6** the use of directories in selecting mediators is not high but they are used.

If you are ranked you are entitled by for example *Chambers* to use a thumbnail image of the publication in your publicity material and to cite quotations from your entry. For an additional fee you can also have a more detailed profile.

Mediators who are not ranked in these directories say they are worthless and susceptible to manipulation and nobody pays any attention to them. Those who are included think that they are a valuable indication of their ranking, status and expertise and publicise the fact.

Marketing groups: a true story

9.32 Michael's thought process about Directories was typical. He is a 55-year-old solicitor in a major provincial centre who had built up a successful litigation practice. He has now reached the stage where he can hand over much of the work to others. He encountered mediation as part of his litigation practice. He liked the process. He decided to try it himself. He was accredited three years ago.

He did many of the right things. He attended conferences and spoke to experienced mediators and sought their advice. He went on several observations He joined two or three panels. Some mediation appointments came in but it was too slow.

He took one of the first Online Dispute Resolution ('ODR') training courses. He did ODR mediation for £500 in six months. He also advertised in his local newspaper for 12 months.

He would like to be doing 4/5 mediations a month. He realises from his discussions with experienced mediators that it will take time but, as he admits, he did not think that it would take quite so much time. By nature he is an energetic and proactive person who likes to get things done. Frankly, he says he has become a little jaded after 30 years and is looking for some stimulation.

He has recently decided to apply to the directories. He came to this conclusion because, as he put it, nearly everybody else seems to be in them. He likens being appointed as a mediator to an actor attending auditions. If you have a ranking in a directory it is another skill that you can demonstrate like being able to tap dance upside down. He has contacted one of the directory advisers who can help with the process. At the same time he is cancelling his membership of one of the well-known panels because he does not think that the annual fee is justified.

These are the sorts of decisions mediators constantly have to take as they develop their practice.

Being included in the directory is not conclusive of anything but it does not do any harm and it may do some good. Do you have the time and money to invest?

In a nutshell

9.33

- Prepare the best profile that you can.
- Keep your profile up to date.
- Maximise the positives, minimise the negatives.
- Never lie in your profile.
- Join the CMC and at least one other panel.
- Do not expect the panels to feed you with work.
- Form your own marketing group.

Chapter 10

Social media

> In this chapter you will learn:
> - How to have an Internet presence.
> - Why you need to have an Internet presence.
> - The basics of creating a website.
> - The basics of setting up a LinkedIn account.
> - The basics of setting up a Facebook account.
> - The basics of setting up a Twitter account.

What? You don't have a website?

10.01 'What do you mean, you haven't got a website?! How can you be a mediator?'

This was the enquiry addressed to a mediator at a workshop on how to develop your mediation practice.

'I know.' she said. 'I must get round to it.'

In the bar afterwards mediators huddled together confessing that they also knew that they had to 'get round to it'.

The basics

10.02 Be clear, if you want to develop a mediation practice you need three things:
- LinkedIn account;
- Twitter account; and
- a website

You set them up in that order.

10.03 Setting up a LinkedIn account is easy and free. Learn how at para **10.05**. You are immediately able to start building connections and asking for advice about building a website.

10.04 *Social media*

Twitter is second because, although setting up an account is also easy and free (learn how at para **10.06**), you only have 140 characters in which to announce yourself and ask for advice.

No one will find it very odd if you have a website Home Page saying: 'Site under construction'. Do not leave the sign up for too long. See paras **10.13–10.14** for how to get your website up and running quickly.

Mediators can also benefit from having:

- A Facebook account – a business rather than a personal Page.
- A YouTube account – if you want to use promotional podcasts and video.

But, compared with LinkedIn, Twitter and a website, they are second tier activities for mediators.

Getting round to it

10.04 Most mediators, according to the 2014 CEDR survey, are over 50 (see **Chapter 2**). That means that they are digital exiles. Even those of us in the age range 35–50 may also be digital exiles.

For the exiles this chapter is designed to fast-track you to a working knowledge of social media for mediators. You do not just receive the theory. You learn what buttons, tabs and icons to click.

For the digital natives it is designed to highlight the mediation-specific requirements of using social media to help you to develop a mediation practice.

LinkedIn

10.05 Mediators know that very few things in life are a given but for anybody wanting to develop a mediation practice joining LinkedIn is one of them. Why?

- It's free.
- It's just networking on the Internet. And as described in **Chapter 12** mediators who do not network, do not mediate.
- It drives traffic to your website. As described in **Chapter 9** mediators who do not have a website don't mediate very often.
- It's for professionals. It's primarily a B2B network that can easily be searched for potential connections.

You need to do the following:

1. Set up a LinkedIn account;
2. Take part in LinkedIn groups;
3. Create a LinkedIn group;
4. Provide answers/advise on LinkedIn;

5. Collect recommendations; and
6. Measure your LinkedIn success

Here's how you do it.

Stage 1 Set up a LinkedIn account.

1   Go to www.LinkedIn.com.
    - Be careful not to go to Linked.com by mistake
    - Register by entering your details in the boxes shown.
    - Complete the profile.
      There are prompts and straightforward step-by-step instructions.

      You will need a URL (Unique Resource Locator). Try and choose your own name. If that is already taken choose your name with a cluster of descriptive words such as stephenwalkermediator.
    - Go to the Profile box. Scroll down to Public Profile. Click Edit. On the right hand side of the page click 'Customise your public profile URL'.
      - Upload your image.
      - Fill in the sections:
      - Profile headline – maximise its impact by saying something like 'commercial and civil mediator' not just 'mediator.'
      - Experience section – say what you are doing now. Show from your previous positions what your expertise is and refer to any transferable skills if you have changed jobs.
      - Summary section – expand on your expertise. Give examples of what you have done for clients and, if the client permits, name the clients. Note confidentiality can restrict what you, as a mediator, can put on your LinkedIn page.

2   Include your Twitter ID on your LinkedIn profile
    - Be careful about sharing if you use your Twitter account for personal as well as professional purposes.
    - Click the down arrow next to your name in the top right hand corner. Click 'Settings'. Click 'Manage your Twitter Settings'.

3   Share status updates to your Twitter account.
    - Tick the box underneath your status update.

4   Add existing email contacts to your LinkedIn connections. You will then easily connect with anyone you know is already on LinkedIn.
    - Click Contacts. Click Connections.

5   Get Introduced
    - People are more likely to connect with you if you introduced by someone they know. Check if someone you would like to be introduced to is connected to one of your connections.

10.05 Social media

- Click on their name to bring up their profile.
- Click 'Get introduced through a connection'.

6   Add a link to your LinkedIn Profile on your email signature.

Stage 2 Using Groups

7   Join Groups relevant to mediation and your target markets, sectors and interests.
- Click on the Groups tab in the main header. Click 'Groups You May Like'.
- Review the LinkedIn Group Directory. Join from the list or a link to a similar group.
- Click 'Groups' on the homepage toolbar and then click on 'Directory'.

8   Choose groups that have lots of members and discussion activity.
- Click on the relevant group. Click 'Members'.

9   Join in Group Discussions – activity promotes awareness. When you comment on a discussion your profile picture is shown.

Stage 3 Start your own Group

10 Starting your own Group will generate new connections. If someone you do not know asks to join your Group ask if they would like to connect. But note if you start a Group you need to post to it and monitor activity frequently and regularly to gain maximum exposure from it.
- Click on 'Groups' and 'Create a Group'.

11 Share your Group with Twitter or Facebook by your status update or invite others to join.
- In the top right hand corner of your Group Page click the 'Share Group' button.

12 LinkedIn sends suggestions of Groups to join. You can find out this by clicking the Groups tab on your toolbar. Select Groups you May Like.

Stage 4 Use LinkedIn Answers

13 The LinkedIn Answers facility gives you a great chance to demonstrate your expertise. Look for questions and try to answer two or three every week.
- Click the 'More' button. Click 'Answers'.

14 Ask a Question
- In the Answers Section ask a question. This is a useful way to gather information.

Stage 5 Recommendations

15 Ask for a Recommendation
- Check on Premium Services when you complete a mediation for someone to see if they are one of your contacts. If they are ask them to give you a recommendation.
- Click 'Profile' on your toolbar.

Social media **10.05**

- Click 'Recommendations'.
- Click 'Request Recommendations'.

14 Give A Recommendation.

- People appreciate receiving a Recommendation even if they have not requested one.
- Click 'Profile' on your toolbar.
- Click 'Recommendations'.
- Scroll down the page to 'Make a Recommendation'.
- NB: If you receive an unsolicited recommendation always thank the sender.

15 Upgrade – LinkedIn offers premium services. It is worth subscribing to take advantage of Inmails, Premium Search Filters and enhanced Profile information.

- Click 'More' on your toolbar.
- Click 'Upgrade Your Account'.

16 Carry out a LinkedIn Poll.

- Click 'More'.
- Click 'Get More Applications'.
- Click 'Polls'.
- Search polls in your field of expertise. Check who is commenting on them and make a connection.

17 Blog link: sync your blog to your LinkedIn profile. Your connections then see your blog updates on their homepage.

- Click 'More'.
- Click 'Get More Applications'.
- Click 'Blog Link'.

Stage 6 LinkedIn analytics

18 Look at your LinkedIn analytics.

The upgraded services provide more information about who has been looking at your LinkedIn Profile, who has invited you to become a connection and tracks your activity levels so that you can see whether it is growing or not.

- Go to your Home Page.
- Click on 'Who's viewed you'.
- If you have Linkedin Premium go to Home Page.
- In the toolbar Click on 'Profile'. A drop down list appears.
- Click on 'Who's Viewed Your Profile'.

10.06 *Social media*

Twitter

10.06

1. Go to www.twitter.com:
   - Choose your Twitter ID. It is best to use your business name or something relevant to your business.
   - Upload your Profile Photo:
2. Keywords:
   - Make a list of keywords that will help people find your service. Include them in your tweets.
   - Do not use trade jargon. Imagine you are one of your customers.
3. Twitter Bio:
   - Make a list of keywords. Include some of them in your bio. Search engines will then recognise them.
   - Make the most of your 160 characters.
4. You want to tweet:
   - On the Home Page go to 'What's Happening'.
   - Click.
   - You have 140 characters. Type them in.
   - Limit your message to 120 characters. That gives room for anyone who wants to re-tweet your tweet to include a comment.
5. Hashtag #:
   - Type a #in front of a keyword if you want that specific word to show up if someone searches for that topic.
6. Who is following you?

   You can easily find out:
   - On your Twitter homepage under your name on the left-hand side there is 'Followers' and 'Following'. The number of how many is shown next to them.
   - Click 'Followers'.
   - A list of your followers with their twitter ID, photo, bio and follow button next to each one is shown.
7. Look for tweets that refer to you.
   - Make sure you reply. Twitter feeds on engagement.
   - Click '@Connect' in the top left angle of the homepage. Click 'Mentions'.
8. Re-tweets.
   - Re-tweet others. Be generous to competitors. It suggests authenticity and authority.
   - Place your cursor over the tweet. Four options appear. Click 'Retweet'.

Social media **10.06**

9   Being re-tweeted.
    - This is good news as your word is being spread.
    - To see who is re-tweeting you Click '@Connect'.
    - Click 'Mentions'.

    Or

    Set your Notifications so that you receive an email every time someone has re-tweeted you.
    - Click 'Settings'.
    - Click 'Notifications'. Tick the box.

10 Email Signature.
    - Include a link to your Twitter profile in all your emails.

11 Reply.

    Reply to tweets whenever you think that you can add value.
    - Place your cursor over the tweet.
    - Four options appear.
    - Click 'Reply'. A box pops up. Enter your reply in it.

12 Drop into a Conversation.

    When you see a tweet that looks like a reply you can see the whole conversation. Often says "In reply to...."
    - Place cursor over the tweet.
    - Four options appear. Click 'Open'.

13 Search Tweets.
    - Type a keyword into the Search box at the top of your Homepage.
    - A list of tweets that include the keyword appears.
    - Review for questions that you can answer people you want to connect with.

14 Save the Search.
    - In the top right hand corner on your homepage click the down arrow next to the "" icon.
    - Click 'Save Search'.
    - When you next want to search that keyword or phrase Click in the Search box at the top of the homepage.

15 Direct Messages.

    If you just want the recipient to be able to read your message:
    - Click the head and shoulders icon in the top right-hand corner of any page.
    - Click 'Direct Messages'.
    - Click 'New Message'.

10.07 Social media

16 Who to Follow

Twitter suggests people to follow based upon people you already follow.

- Click '@Connect'.
- Go to the 'Who to Follow' box on the left hand side of the page.
- Click 'View All'.
- Suggestions will pop up.
- Click those that you like.

17 Follow by Interests.

You can follow people based on the topics you have in common. Twitter provides a list of categories. It tells you how many people they have suggested in each category.

- Go to the bottom of the 'Who to Follow' box under '@Connect'.
- Click 'Browse Categories'.
- Click those that you like.

18 Favourites:

If you want to read a tweet later save it by adding it to Favourites.

- Place cursor over the tweet.
- Four options appear.
- Click 'Favourite'.
- When you want to read it Click the Head and shoulders icon in the top right hand corner.
- Click 'Lists' then Click 'Favourites'.

What to Tweet?

10.07

- Link to your own blog post. Include a few words on what it is about.
- Link to articles, videos that your target market may like. Include a few words why you think it is useful or interesting.
- Give your followers tips.
- Encourage engagement by asking a question – give them an either/or choice.
- Use the Twitter search facility to find out what questions people are asking in your field of expertise. Give helpful replies. Follow them and build relationships.
- Re-tweet interesting tweets from your followers.

How best to use Twitter

10.08 Be consistent.

Tweet each day or every other day even if time is short. It is much more effective to tweet a small amount each day than a lot on one day and then nothing for several days.

Invest the time.

Tweeting, even if a tweet is only 140 characters, takes time. So does reading other people's tweets. Plan to spend a minimum of two hours a week on Twitter-related activities.

Some people spend much more – at least 30 to 45 minutes a day.

Try and tweet at the same time each day.

Pick the best time to tweet.

The best times are between 7 and 8:30, 12.30 and 13.30, 18.00 and 20.00. This is when people are either going to or from work and looking at their Twitter pages on their mobiles or when they are relaxing after a hard morning's work and checking their inboxes.

Tuesdays, Wednesdays and Fridays are the busiest days for Twitter traffic according to Twitter's own analysis.

Between 11.00 and 15.00 is the busiest time.

Stay away from these days and times to maximise your impact.

Tweets fall into three main categories:

- Social chat.
- Sharing of resources, ie links, tools, information, ideas and opinions and comments.
- Answering and asking questions, which demonstrate your knowledge and expertise.

Balance them. Put the emphasis on the sharing of resources and asking and answering questions. Keep the social chitchat to a minimum but include some occasionally to show your followers that you are human.

Be interested.

- Joining conversations. Engage with others by answering questions.
- Re-tweet.
- Remember Twitter is not about selling your services directly. It is about building brand awareness and your personal credibility.

10.09 *Social media*

> **Top Tip**: research has shown that readers of tweets find that only:
>
> 36% were worth reading;
>
> 25% were not worth reading at all; and
>
> 39% were neutral.
>
> So only just over a third of tweets are likely to be read. That is a high wastage rate.

How to improve your hit rate

Avoid

10.09

- *Gripes and complaints.* If you have encountered a problem or difficulty pose it as a question. Suggest an answer and invite comments.
- *Look at my wonderful life.* If you have won the Nobel Peace Prize as a result of being the planet's best mediator then no one will mind you telling the world about it. Otherwise self-restraint is appreciated and preferred.
- *Non-stop self-promotion.* If every other tweet is about yourself and something you have done your followers will become bored. Empty vessels make the most noise' will spring to mind.

Everybody accepts that Twitter is about self-promotion but keep it proportionate and understated. As a rule of thumb limit your self-promotion to 10%. The other 90% should be follower/market orientated not self-orientated.

WEBSITE

A tale of three mediators

Mediator One

10.10 An established solicitor in her late 40s with a reputation as an expert in personal injury work decided to become a mediator. She undertook the civil and commercial training and was quickly able to undertake her observations. She had excellent personal skills and a proactive personality, having sat on various national committees and as a deputy district judge. Through her work she had established a wide and sound network of professional contacts.

She thoroughly enjoyed the training and was very enthusiastic about mediation as a technique and as a philosophy. A year later she was expressing her frustration at not having been able to do any mediations. She was acting as a consultant to a firm of solicitors and was able to devote time to mediation.

She attended a workshop on developing a mediation practice. She admitted that she needed to spend more time marketing. When asked if she had a website she said no. She knew that she must get round to it.

Mediator Two

10.11 A mediator in his early 50s who has been accredited for three years and specialises in financial services disputes was explaining how much he liked mediation. He still worked in the City as a consultant and was a non-practising barrister. He had mediated several interesting well-paid disputes but was frustrated that he did not have more of a throughput.

When explaining how he went about attracting work he said that he had closed down his website. It was more trouble than it was worth. He had no evidence that it had ever brought in any work. He complained that people who did contact him having seen his website tended to be, in his words, 'time wasters'.

Mediator Three

10.12 Another solicitor-mediator who has just turned 40 and is a consultant specialising in commercial litigation set up his own mediation business. He qualified and did several pro-bono mediations. He joined several panels. Some charged; others were free. After 18 months he was delighted to announce that he had received his first fee-paying civil and commercial mediation. It came to him direct through his website from a well-known firm of solicitors with whom he had had no previous dealings. They found him simply by searching the Net. He loves his website.

All these conversations took place with the author within the last six months.

You can run a business in 2015 without having a website. There are mediators without websites. There are even firms of solicitors and accountants without websites. But one thing is clear: if you do not have a website you are making it harder for people to know about you and find you.

Remember the Texas Paradox:

> 'There are two reasons why you don't get work as a mediator. People have never heard of you. Or they have.'

How to build a website

10.13 You want to have a website. What do you need to do?

Step one: are you going to build your own or hire someone to do it for you? If you are a digital exile there is only one answer. Hire someone. If you are a digital native and you have the time, you can do it yourself. Log onto WordPress and take it from there.

Step two: find a website designer. There are thousands of them. You find a good one in the same way that you find a good plumber, doctor or mediator. You ask people that you know for recommendations.

10.14 *Social media*

Look at some mediators' websites. If you like one take a note of who designed it. It will probably give the name at the foot of the pages by the © sign. If it does not send an email to the mediator or telephone and ask. If he will not tell you, make a note that he is a not someone to waste time on.

But warning: do not just copy the opposition. You are trying to establish a USP.

You will need to work out a website brief. Your designer can help with this but you need to have thought about what you want in advance. Find examples of other websites that you like and ones that you do not like and show them to the designer.

Here is a checklist of important questions to consider. You need to ask them even if you are building your own website.

Checklist of website design questions

10.14

1 What shall I call myself?

Choosing a domain name, (which is sometimes called a URL – uniform resource locator) is an important marketing decision. Your first problem is availability. Find out whether your name is available by searching one of the registration sites such as Network Solutions.

The characteristics of a good domain name are that it is easy to:

- Dictate –Try and avoid having to say digit or hyphen.
- Hear – Some words our easily confused. Letters such as D/T, M/N, B/P, V/B. The letter 'S' can be confused with 'ess.'
- Spell – Avoid eccentric spelling such as 'lite' for 'light 'and 'nu' for 'new'
- Type – The more characters there are in your URL the more typos there will be. Tests have shown that the average unskilled typist makes a typo every seven strokes.
- Read on-screen – Some colour combinations are easier to read than others. Black and white and red and white are good choices. Blue and grey and green and red are difficult.
- Read – In the address toolbar- some combinations of characters are are easy to confuse. For example m, n, r or l, I, 1 and I.

Remember: if you are using your name, as many mediators do, this is not always easy. Some people who use their own name have one that is easily misspelled. Therefore also register misspellings such as Maciver, McIvor, Macivor.

2 What do you want your website to do?

Websites can be used for different purposes:

- As a digital business card. At its simplest a website is a business card that potential customers can look at on a computer screen. They are sometimes referred to as brochureware. They give the minimum of information about the business in the same way that a business card or a small leaflet brochure does.

- To build your brand. Just by being there when people search for mediator they may find you. The main aim is not to generate leads or sales directly but to do it indirectly.
- To build relationships. This is usually achieved by blogs or podcasts being available to viewers.
- To generate leads.
- To give information about your services and how to book them. Sometimes this can be done online. More usually the site invites the visitor to contact the business through email or telephone.
- To generate revenue through sales. Some sites can offer other products and services, which can be purchased online, for example books or courses, podcasts and webinars.
- To generate revenue through advertising: although this is common in non-mediation sectors it is rare in mediation.
- To book appointments. More and more mediators offer an online facility for asking about availability and making a mediation booking. For the novice mediator this is probably an optional extra.

Who will host the site?

10.15 If you use a web designer they will often arrange hosting and support for your site. This will not usually be expensive. You can expect to pay from £XXXX to £XXXX.

A hosting service has been described as the online world's landlord. You rent space for your business in a building that your landlord owns. You rent space for your business online from a hosting service which operates web servers that are constantly connected to the internet.

Some are free. But most experts advise using a paid-for hosting service. These often offer additional facilities such as helplines and backup if the server goes down. You can find a hosting service by going online.

Who will maintain the site?

10.16 What does website maintenance mean? It includes the following:

Updating content

10.17 This is vital. See para **10.26**.

It is not difficult to do yourself but it does take time and self-discipline.

Backing up your website

10.18 Your hosting service should do this but it is well to have your own backup as well.

10.19 Social media

Link Checking

10.19 Links can be broken if you make changes to your site or references.

Testing website speed

10.20 Good download speed is crucial. You do not want visitors becoming bored waiting for content to download.

Software updates

10.21 If you use third-party software such as WordPress you will see that they are constantly updating. You need to install the updates promptly.

Search engine results

10.22 Use Google Analytics (see para **13.22**.).

Reputation management

10.23 Use Google Alerts to monitor your website name, your name and your content on the Web.

You can do this yourself or have someone do it for you. Your website designer again may offer this service. Many of them do for small businesses or individuals.

Or go online and see who is offering the service. There is a lot of choice.

What do I put on my website?

Content

10.24
Content is gold dust. You need it for websites and blogs. Search engines gorge on it. Content includes text, images, sound and video.

Marketing practitioners have developed ground rules for good marketing content. Pay attention to them because:

- Online, people scan, they don't read.
- People take 25% longer, on average, to read something on a screen than on a page.
- Four seconds is the average time that someone stays on a Home Page.

The 10 Commandments of websites:

1 **Use bullet points.** You are not writing feature articles or essays.
2 **Keep it short.** Use short words, short sentences and short paragraphs. You only need three punctuation marks – the hyphen, the full stop and the question mark.

3   **Put key information at the top.** Use the inverted pyramid. All the important information goes at the start of each page.

4   **Keep the key information 'above the fold'.** Screen readers spend 80% of their time reading what they can immediately see on the web page without scrolling down. That is 'the fold'. Avoid long scrolling pages. Readers' attention spans are measured in micro-seconds.

5   **Grab the readers' eyeballs with a headline.**

6   **Write strong leads.** The first sentence answers the six questions: who, what, why, when, where, and how? Mediators live on these questions at mediations. They use them with the parties to explore issues and generate solutions.

7   **Use the second person, not the first or third.** Using 'you' or 'your' focuses your writing on the reader. Talking a lot about yourself or your service is not what the reader wants to hear. Readers want to know what is in it for them.

8   **Use the active not the passive.** For example 'Mediation saves time and money.' is active. 'Money and time are saved by using mediation.' is passive. Cut down on using the verb 'to be'. Beware of the constructions 'there is,' 'there are,' or 'it is'.

9   **Limit PDF files.** The format is not user-friendly. Web designers like them because they preserve designs. Only use them for documents, which are intended to be read in print not online or which need to be seen in their original format.

10 **Include text links.** Use lots of links to other parts of your site within the text. These help readers find in-depth in information more quickly. Search engines like them.

Good writing rules

10.25   The golden rules of good writing still apply online. Remember:

1   Keep it lively – use specific nouns and verbs not general nouns and adjectives and adverbs.

2   Avoid jargon – use plain English.

3   Express your personality – this is difficult but do not try to be someone that you are not. Authenticity counts. Just write in a style that feels natural and easy.

4   Check spelling and grammar – use a spell check on your computer.

5   Proofread – it is difficult to proofread what you have written yourself. You see what you wanted to write, not what you have actually written. Read it out loud to yourself or have someone else do it.

Refresh your content

10.26   Online content is like fish. Once it becomes stale it has no appeal. It makes people turn away.

10.27 *Social media*

Many mediators think that once they have put up their website they can leave it. Visitors will be magnetically drawn to it. Business will just roll in. Not so. You have to keep updating your website. There are good reasons for this:

- Search engines thrive on novelty. The more often you update the higher your website will be ranked.
- Visitors are put off by out of date information. Seeing that the site was last updated two years ago will not impress. They will just go to another site.
- Up-to-date content impresses them. It reassures them that there is something substantial behind the website. There is still widespread suspicion about websites. Are they just a front? Anybody can have an impressive website without having an impressive business or service to offer.
- Refreshing content is good for you as well. You have to stay engaged in your project as you think of new material and review what you have done and what is going to be done.

How do you refresh content?

10.27 There are several options:

- If you used a developer for your website they can do it. They will charge but it is not expensive.
- Do it yourself. If you have a template or blog-based site this is straightforward.
- Buy a commercial CMS (Content Management System) or use an open source CMS. Open source simply means source code that is available to users without charge.

How often to update?

10.28 Timetable whatever you want to update. Work out what needs to be updated. How frequently you do it depends on the nature of the content.

A rule of thumb is: update some aspect of your website at least once a month. This is not as difficult as it sounds.

- If you have a blog, writing 750 words on a mediation related topic is not too onerous. It should not take more than three/four hours in total (see paras **13.04–13.07**).
- If you provide tips and advice to mediation users, refining them or adding new ones will not take more than 30/45 minutes.
- If you provide snippets of information and news, this takes only 15–20 minutes to update.

It really is all a matter of planning and sticking to your plan.

Website updating is another example.

From time to time you will need to revamp your website. Fashion and styles change. As mediators we do not have to be as cutting edge as graphic designers but we do not want to appear dated old-fashioned and out of touch.

> **TOP TIP**
>
> Look at your market's websites. Make sure that you are in tune with their look and overall style. And of course carry out a reconnaissance of your competitors' websites. Knowing what the opposition/competition is doing is always useful. Take care not to just copy them.

Example of Website Updating Schedule

Every two years	Redesign the site. Add new features and content. Incorporate feedback.
Every year	Review and update all content including photographs. In fact especially photographs. Often the person walking into the mediation room bears scant resemblance to the beaming face on their website.
Each quarter	Review your Profile/CV.
Each month	Update at least one page with for example a blog or testimonial.
Weekly	If you have received a new testimonial add it straightaway. If a significant development happens, eg a new Court of Appeal case about mediation tell visitors about it.
As needed	Big breaking news, eg you have just been awarded the Mediator of the Year prize.
	Changes in your charges, if you show them on your website (see **Chapter 16**).
	Changes in your contact details.

What do I update?

Updating checklist

10.29 Do not be overwhelmed. You do not have to do everything at once. Any small change updates your site. If you are stuck, use this checklist:

Home page

10.30
Profile: Review this every three months. If your profile stays the same year after year visitors will think that you are not active.

10.31 *Social media*

Testimonials: Seek them out and use them.

Blog: This is the obvious one to update regularly (see para **13.06**).

Terms and conditions: Keep an eye on what the competition is doing and make sure that you are not out of step with market trends. If you are not following a trend formulate a good reason in case a potential customer asks.

Rates: You have to stay competitive. In the end you can only charge what the market will bear. The market is dynamic.

Tips: Make a list of tips, say 20, and work through them by posting one on your website each week/month.

Publications: Tell visitors about publications that you have written or are working on.

How do I know if it is working?

10.31 If the number of people offering you mediations shoots through the roof you might reasonably infer that your website is working for you. But even that is not a safe assumption. Your increasing work may simply be result of two or three influential satisfied customers mentioning your name.

A quick, cheap and fairly reliable way of finding out if your website is effective is to use Google Analytics. The world refers to statistics but on the Web they are called analytics. They are the same thing: figures and numbers.

Google Analytics

10.32 The advantages are:

- It is free;
- It gives you more in-depth analysis on competing services; and
- You do not need their paid AdWords campaign to use it.

The disadvantages are:

- There is a danger of data overload. You cannot see the wood for the trees. In fact you cannot see the trees for the leaves.
- You have to tag every page of your site with the small piece of code that Google supplies. This is not as difficult as you might think. If you use a template or a SSI file (server-side include) you only need to place the Analytics code once and then it appears on all pages.

Lies, damn lies and statistics

10.33 Statistics/analytics are only of any use to you if in fact you can draw lessons from them to improve your profitability or your visitors' experience of your site.

Be careful about what you are being told.

Sometimes analytics are referred to as KPI's (Key Performance Indicators). KPIs can depend on what the website is for. If you are looking at your website as a lead generator the conversion rate is vital.

'Hits' is a word much used in the online world. These can be misleading. The definition of a 'hit' is any file that is downloaded as part of the webpage. Hit rates are not the same as the number of visitors. Conventionally they overstate the number of visitors by 10 to 1. (NB: 'Downloaded' in this context means displayed on-screen.)

These are the statistics to consider:

- **Visits**: the number of times that your website is visited/viewed.
- **Unique visitors**: this measures the number of user sessions from different computers. It is smaller than the total number of visits. The difference is the number of repeat visits. To see how successful you are in attracting people back to your site you can track repeats visits as a percentage of all visits.
- **Page views**: the total number of distinct web pages downloaded.
- **Page views per visit**. This is a key figure. It measures the 'stickiness' of your website, in other words how long visitors stay on it. This can be measured by the number of pages downloaded divided by the total number of visits.
- **URLs viewed**: this is the number of times each individual page is downloaded. You can see which pages are downloaded and, just as importantly, which ones are not.
- **Referrers**: these are the websites or pages that generated links to your site.
- **Search engines**: this tells you which search engines generated links to your site based on appearance in natural search results as opposed to paid ones.
- **Conversion rate**: this will depend upon what your business is. As a mediator it could be the total number of visits divided by the number of paid mediations carried out.

As with all statistics, there are different interpretations and you have to treat them with caution. The important aspect to concentrate on is relative change. Is the number of visits going up or down? Is your conversion rate increasing or not?

Try some qualitative analysis by:
- Going on to your own website and navigating around it; and
- Asking friends to do the same.

Then do the same thing with other mediators' websites and systematically compare the experience.

The silver bullet: Search Engine Optimisation

10.34 For digital exiles certainly, and possibly also for digital natives, Search Engine Optimisation ('SEO') is a mysterious and arcane practice. Consultancies

10.35 *Social media*

specialising in SEO will tell you that they can increase your page rankings. In other words when someone goes online and looks for mediators, your name and website will come up higher in the list.

They say that you won't achieve top ranking without paying for it. Actually this is not true eg Bill Black 's website is ranked second in Google searches (google Bill Black photographer, he's the Brighton one) and he has never paid anything for the privilege. He does it all himself. Wikipedia entries will always win out but otherwise a high rank is achievable. But you can achieve a higher ranking by using SEO.

If you ask SEO consultants what they do, they are vague. They assure you they can achieve great outcomes but are not specific about the methods that they use. This is not to suggest that they use underhand methods. Understandably they are reluctant to reveal their trade secrets. Other gurus are sceptical about the services offered by SEO consultants and have described them as 'snake oil salesmen'.

A good place to start is by downloading Google's SEO starter guide. It comes in Adobe PDF format. Google have done their best for digital natives to make it reasonably reader friendly, but it is likely that you will have to work through it more than once. There are useful and easy to follow diagrams to help you. At the time of going to press you can download it from www.google.com/webmasters/docs/search-engine-optimisation-starter-guide.pdf.

Google dominates the market. In practice you do not need to bother with any other search engines.

But Google don't tell you everything. They want to minimise others manipulating the rankings. If you want to try and gain an insight into the Google approach try going online and searching for blogs. Tom Demers writes a useful one. Go to @tomdemers. And you can follow him on Twitter.

If all else fails you will have to find yourself an SEO consultant. You find one in the same way that people find mediators. You ask colleagues for references, research the Internet and look in directories.

Good luck!

Facebook

10.35 Facebook is primarily a social rather than a business medium. It is used for business purposes. But note Facebook does not permit you to set up a personal profile in the name of your business.

Social media experts advise small businesses to set up a personal account rather than a business account. You can then set up a business page.

- Login to your Facebook personal account.
- Go to www.facebook.com/pages.
- Click 'Create a Page'.
- Choose the Page Category from the options.

Social media **10.35**

- Use Facebook as your Page.

You can comment on other posts as your business page rather than as you personally. The advantage is that every time you comment or like something your Page Photo is shown alongside your comment. This increases your business's visibility.

- Login to your Personal Account.
- On the toolbar at the top Click the down arrow next to Home.
- Click the Page you want.

Business Link on your Personal Account. Include the name of your business in the box on your personal account asking you where you work. Visitors can click this to go directly to your Page.

- Click Update Info.
- Click Edit in the Work and Education section.
- Enter the name of your Page. A list of pages pops up. Click yours.

Record a video. This is increasingly popular. You can record video directly to your Facebook Page. You need a WebCam.

- On your Timeline or Wall in the Status Update box click photo/Video. Click Use WebCam.

Upload a video to Facebook from your computer.

- On your Timeline/Wall in the Status Update box Click Photo/Video.
- Click Upload Photo/Video.

Ask questions. Asking questions is very popular. It is an easy way for people to interact. It is also a useful tool for market research.

- On your Timeline/Wall in your Status Update box Click 'Event, Milestone+'.
- Click 'Question'.
- Type in your question.
- Click 'Poll Options'.

Add a Link direct to your friends to your blog post in other media.

- Paste the URL into the Status Update Box.
- Comment why they should look at it.

Email Signature.

Include a link to your Facebook Page at the end of all your emails.

TOP TIP

Researchers show that Facebook Status Updates with fewer than 80 characters work best in engaging followers.

10.35 *Social media*

A maximum of 5,000 characters can be used in your Status Update. If you exceed this it will automatically be turned into a Note.

Notes: the Notes App is useful for articles and longer pieces. Google indexes notes. Include keywords for search engine optimisation.

- Click 'Edit Page'.
- Click 'Update Info'.
- Click 'Apps'.
- Click 'Notes'.

Like Button. Include the Facebook 'Like' button on your website. Users can then share pages from your website back to their Facebook Profile in one click.

- Click 'Edit Page'.
- Click 'Update Info'.
- Click 'Resources'.
- Click 'Use Social Plugins'.
- Click 'Like'.

Send Button. Include the Facebook Send Button on your website. Users can then your URL from your website back to their friends on Facebook or to an email address in one click.

- Click 'Edit Page'.
- Click 'Update Info'.
- Click 'Resources'.
- Click 'Use Social Plugins'.
- Click 'Send'.

Facebook Insights. This provides analytics on your Facebook Page.

- At the top of your Timeline/Wall see your Admin Panel.
- Click 'See All' from the Insights box.

View Shares. Knowing who is sharing your posts is useful.

When someone shares your post an icon appears in the bottom right-hand corner of your post. The number next to it shows how many times it has been shared. Click on the icon. You can see who has shared it.

What next?

Just Give It A Go!

In a nutshell

- Build a website. Do it yourself or get someone else to do it. But get round to it.
- A half built website is not a website.
- Open a LinkedIn Account.
- Join LinkedIn Groups and post comments. Be careful. It can be addictive.
- Open a Twitter account. Tweet regularly, at least once a week.

Chapter 11

Selling – the necessary mindset

> In this chapter you will learn:
> - How not to be afraid of selling.
> - How to make best use of your transferable skills.

Selling is a perfectly natural activity

11.01 According to Daniel Pink selling is something all humans do every day whether we realise it or not. We are constantly trying to persuade people to do something that we want them to do. He refers to it as 'moving' people (see '*To Sell is Human*').

People like Gavin Kennedy make the point about negotiation (see *Everything is Negotiable 2008)*. Far from being a difficult and arcane skill as many think we all do it all the time.

Everything that we do in our daily lives is in fact a negotiation. From buying a cup of coffee on the way to work to arranging lunch with a colleague. But do we really behave in the same way when trying to agree where to have lunch, negotiating the sale of a company or, more relevantly for mediators, settling a court case?

Apparently so, at least in the sense that when we are selling or negotiating we are 'moving' people. So we are all people movers now.

The good news is that mediators know that mediating is all about moving people. They know that mediating is certainly about negotiating. They are trained to do it. They have transferable skills (see para **11.14**).

11.01 *Selling – the necessary mindset*

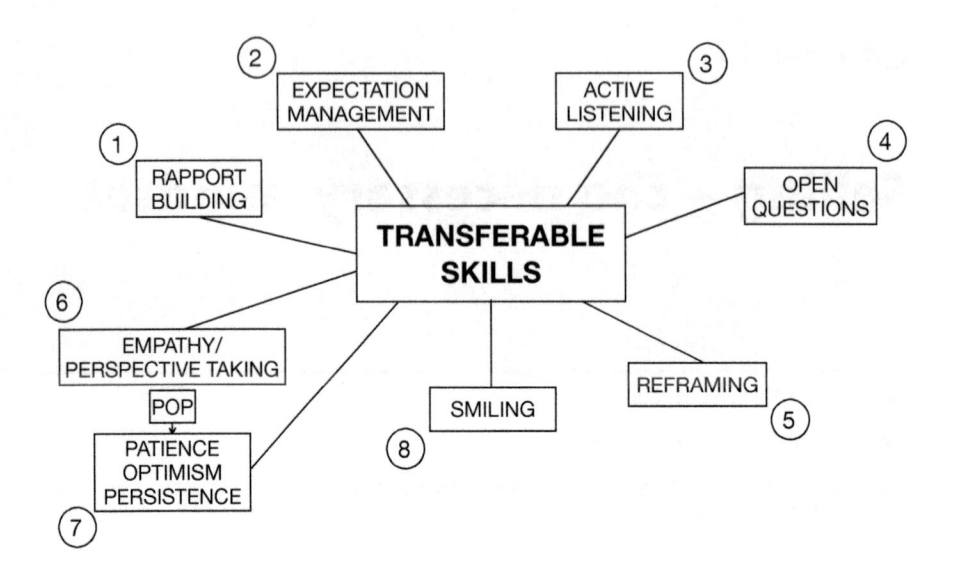

```
         ②                              ③
    EXPECTATION                     ACTIVE
    MANAGEMENT                     LISTENING
①                                                    ④
  RAPPORT                                          OPEN
  BUILDING          TRANSFERABLE                QUESTIONS
                       SKILLS
⑥
  EMPATHY/
PERSPECTIVE TAKING
    POP                                  REFRAMING
  PATIENCE            SMILING                       ⑤
  OPTIMISM              ⑧
 PERSISTENCE
    ⑦
```

Figure 21

- Rapport Building,
- Expectation Management,
- Active Listening,
- Open Questioning,
- Reframing,
- Empathy/Perspective taking.

All these techniques are now referred to as 'non-selling selling'. The fast talking always-be-closing manipulator has now been replaced by the consultative problem solver.

Basic Premise Three in **Chapter 1** was that negotiation is at the heart of marketing, selling and mediation. So before you can apply your transferable skills to marketing and selling you need to check whether there any transferable basic rules for negotiation

Can you brush up on your negotiation skills? The answer is yes and you can learn the six rules that you need to know (see para **11.02**).

Professor Robert Cialdini has identified and popularised six key principles for persuading people. (See *Influence Science & Practice* 5th Ed, 2009).

Selling – the necessary mindset **11.03**

How to influence people: the Big Six

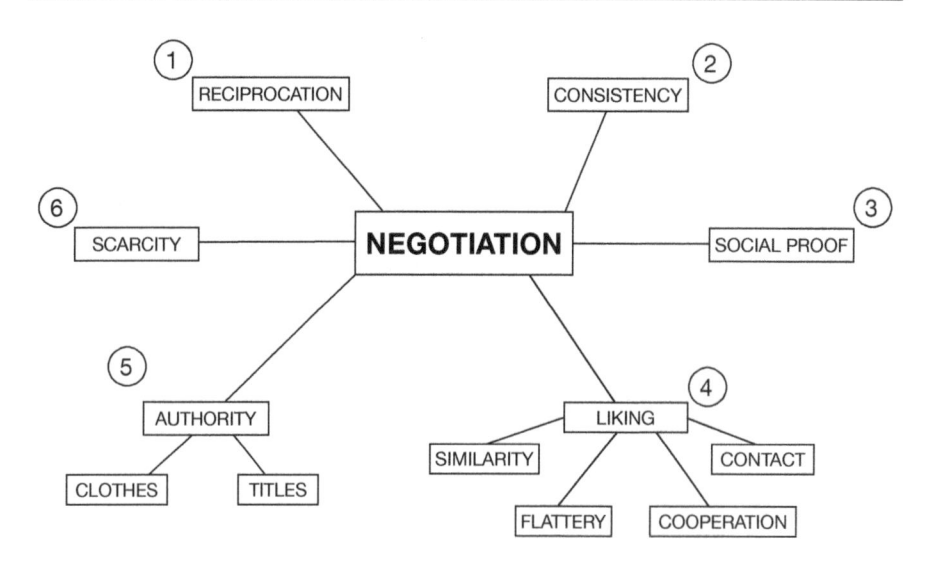

```
          1                           2
    RECIPROCATION              CONSISTENCY

  6                                                3
   SCARCITY         NEGOTIATION         SOCIAL PROOF

      5                              4
    AUTHORITY                      LIKING
                      SIMILARITY          CONTACT
  CLOTHES   TITLES
                         FLATTERY    COOPERATION
```

Figure 22

Reciprocation

11.02 Every human society follows the rule of reciprocation and the sense of obligation that it engenders.

It is now well established that

- If you do someone a favour they are more likely to do what you ask them to do when you ask them later. Fund raisers, for example, include small gifts such as a pen or an enamel badge with their letters seeking donations.
- Trading is after all the heart of any negotiation. Effective negotiators do not make concessions, they trade them.

So when selling or negotiating give the other person something first. A cup of tea, a pen or even just a compliment. One very successful non-lawyer mediator used to leave a copy of his book on mediation when he visited law firms to give in-house training. This was both a gift and an advertisement.

Warning: beware of the fallacy of thinking: 'If I am nice to them they will be nice to me.'

In negotiation you don't make concessions. You trade them. You give something in exchange for something.

Commitment and consistency

11.03 Some psychologists regard our desire for consistency as a key motivator for our behaviour. It can even lead us to act against our own best interests.

11.04 *Selling – the necessary mindset*

Consistency offers a fast track through the complexities of life and enables us to make decisions more quickly. We tend to assume that what we want now is consistent with our earlier decisions. That makes taking a subsequent decision much easier.

Our desire for consistency can lead us to make decisions simply to be consistent rather than to reflect on what we are doing and even change our minds and adopt a better alternative. We therefore need to be alert to the dangers of following consistency foolishly which is likely to cause us to make a poor decision. We rely on two signals:

- What your stomach tells you. In other words gut instinct.
- What your heart tells you. In other words what do your feelings tell you?

Rational and logical decision-making are replaced by instinct and feeling. Research into this phenomenon suggests that people experience feelings towards something in a nanosecond before they intellectualise them.

Social proof

11.04 Also known as the herd instinct. When trying to decide what to do we tend to see what others have done or are doing and do the same thing.

Negative consequences can flow from this behaviour. There are many well-documented examples of a group of people watching somebody being attacked or collapsing in the street and not doing anything about it. Instead people look around to see what they should do. Nobody moves. Individual responsibility is reduced or taken over by the group. They are waiting for a lead.

In para **12.27** we discuss using the 'feel, felt, found' formula. Researchers have found that referring to what others have done is a very powerful persuader.

Liking

11.05 People find it easier to say yes to people that they like. This bias towards being liked can have negative effects. Research has shown the power of the halo effect, particularly, in this context, in respect of personal appearance. People automatically think that good-looking individuals are more talented, intelligent, kind and honest.

Experiments have shown that good-looking people:

- are more likely to receive favourable treatment in the legal system;
- are twice as likely to avoid jail sentences;
- receive more compensation when they are victims; and
- receive more help when they are in distress, even from their own gender.

Mediators will want to consider to what extent in practice they can incorporate these findings in their own practices and promotion!

Our desire to be liked has four off-shoots: similarity, flattery, contact/co-operation and contact/association.

Similarity

11.06 People like people who like them. Mediators understand the importance of this at mediations.

- When establishing rapport, mediators spend time trying to find links such as knowing people in common, living in the same area, sharing the same educational background, supporting the same football team, having the same number of children etc. Small talk is rarely only small.

- Skilled persuaders mirror and match the other person's behaviour, body language, tone of voice and vocabulary.

This is exactly what skilled negotiators and salesmen do.

Flattery

11.07 People like to be liked. We are all susceptible to flattery, compliments and praise. We like people who give them to us.

11.08 We like what we know and we know what we like. Familiarity with something makes it more acceptable to us. Often this happens without our realising it.

Repeated experiments have shown that people get on better together when they have cooperated in a joint-venture of some sort. Conversely the more people like each other the easier they find it to cooperate.

So keep going to the events and saying hello to people. See **Chapters 12** and **14** on networking and support groups. Become part of the furniture.

Conditioning and association

11.09 It was established in the 1930s by Gregory Razran, in Psychological Bulletin Vols 35 and 37) that people liked each other more if they ate together and were more responsive and supportive of things that they experienced while they were eating together. Hence the importance of dinners and luncheons in negotiation and diplomacy.

Keep buying people coffee and taking them to lunch. You may have to sacrifice your waistline in the interests of business development.

Authority

11.10 The susceptibility of human beings to authority has been well demonstrated. The shocking conclusions of the Milgram experiment where people showed that they were prepared to inflict excessive pain on victims when ordered to do so are well known (see p 175–180 in Caldini, see para **11.01**).

11.11 *Selling – the necessary mindset*

So if you become an authority on something you can expect people to defer to you. This is the rationale behind the advice of the social media gurus to become a trusted expert and go-to person.

Start writing and blogging.

Titles

11.11 These can influence people's perceptions. They can cause people to look up to someone, sometimes literally.

> - In one experiment a visitor was introduced as someone from Cambridge University.
> - To one group of students he was introduced as a professor.
> - To the other group of students he was introduced as a postgraduate researcher.
> - The two groups of students were then asked to estimate the height of the visitor.
> - The professor was estimated to be to three and half inches taller than the postgraduate researcher.

This explains why several well- known mediators are careful to display their visiting Professorships. If you have a title use it.

Clothes

11.12 Experiments show that someone wearing a uniform can control more people than a person wearing ordinary clothes. A person in a security guard's uniform telling people to pick up litter will be obeyed more than someone in ordinary clothes.

Less obvious uniforms have the same effect. A suit and tie will do. Researchers found that more people will follow someone wearing a suit and tie in crossing traffic lights at red than will follow someone wearing jeans and a sweater.

Other accessories such as expensive watches, pens and cars can reinforce this effect. Many studies have shown that motorists are more deferential to drivers of big expensive cars. Hence the proliferation of oversized Mont Blanc pens and luxury leather iPad covers at commercial mediations.

One of the UK's most successful and unstuffy mediators recalled how he was conducting a big-ticket mediation for a construction dispute in the Middle East. Everything went very well. A settlement was achieved and relations restored. One group of clients thanked their solicitor for his choice of an excellent mediator but said that they had noticed that the mediator obviously did not like expensive watches.

Think about what you wear and what messages your clothes send out. When mediating, dress up not down. When networking, dress like everyone else (see **Chapter 19**).

Scarcity

11.13 We see examples of the scarcity principle every day. People talking to someone face to face will interrupt the conversation to take a call from an unknown caller. Why? The availability of the person they are speaking to is guaranteed. The availability of the unknown caller is not.

People in general:
- regard an opportunity as more valuable when its availability is limited.
- are more motivated by the thought of losing something than by the thought of gaining something of equal value.

> The Worchel experiment is the classic example
>
> Identical biscuits were placed in two jars.
> - He put ten biscuits in one jar and two in the other.
> - People were asked to say which tasted better.
> - They rated the biscuits in the jar with only two in it as better.
> - They were exactly the same as the biscuits in the other jar, which contained ten.

In summary, when the freedom to have something is limited, the item becomes less available, and people experience an increased desire for it.

Hence the limited offers, deadlines, exclusive access and other scarcity triggers that populate websites. Think about this if you plan to offer free seminars webinars, podcasts, e-books or training. Some people are already offering a free online mediation for a limited time.

Now that you have brushed up your negotiating basics have a look at your transferable mediation skills.

Transferable skills for mediators

11.14 Go back to **Figure 21**.

Rapport Building, Active Listening, Open Questioning, Expectation Management, Reframing and Empathy. The first three are the most important and help you do the last three.

Rapport building

This starts with
- Talking
- Listening
- Smiling

11.15 *Selling – the necessary mindset*

So does selling.

Many salesmen think that their job is to sell by talking. In fact listening and smiling are more important. Most people prefer to talk than to listen. They talk even more when under stress. Talking can relieve tension. Let the prospects do the talking. If you do you will learn what they want and are prepared to offer. Listen to them. Listening and hearing are not the same thing.

Active listening

11.15 Mediators are trained in active listening. You do not just nod and smile to encourage people to keep talking. You pay close attention to what is being said and let the talker know that you are absorbing what is being said.

Are you good at active listening? Check yourself with this self-audit.

Active listening – self-audit

11.16 Circle the numbers that apply to you.

Do you:
1. Think about what you're going to ask next before the talker has finished
2. Nod
3. Talk over the talker
4. Smile
5. Finish their sentence
6. Paraphrase (aka reframing)
7. Interrupt
8. Say nothing
9. Fill the silence
10. Maintain eye contact
11. Make notes
12. Clarify to check that you understood what has been said
13. Have a pen or pencil in your hand
14. Use phrases such as: I understand
15. Glance at your mobile
16. Encourage speaker to say more

The more even numbers that you circled the better you are at active listening. Don't worry if there were too many odd numbers. You will become better at it by practising it every day.

What are your ears for?

11.17 As the American philosopher Mortimer Adler in his book *How to Speak/ How to Listen* said: 'Is anybody anywhere taught how to listen? How utterly amazing is the general assumption that the ability to listen well is a natural gift for which no training is required. How extraordinary is the fact that no effort is made anywhere in the educational process to help individuals to learn how to listen well'.

That book was written in 1997. Nearly 20 years later things have changed. Thanks to mediation thousands of people are now trained how to listen well.

You practised active listening during your initial training. Now you use it. See below for a checklist reminder.

Checklist for active listening

11.18

- Maintain eye contact
- Encourage the speaker to say more
- Clarify that you have understood what has been said
- Use phrases such as:
- 'I understand'
- 'Tell me more'
- 'What happened next?'
- 'What did you do then?'
- 'How you feel about it?'
- 'Anything more?'

Talking

11.19 Most salesmen spend most of their time making statements rather than asking questions. Don't they?

Listening helps us learn about the other person. Asking questions does the same thing. Questioning is essential and fundamental to any sort of successful communication. We are all asked and ask questions when engaging in conversation.

Open questions

11.20 Why do we ask questions?
- To obtain information.
- To engage with or show the other person that we are interested in them. This is important for rapport building and empathy.
- To clarify a point.

11.21 *Selling – the necessary mindset*

- To find out what they feel about an issue. This is very important in mediations where each side is trying to find out what the real problems are for the other side.
- To test knowledge: our own and theirs.
- To encourage further thought.
- To show acknowledgment by asking for an opinion or reaction. In groups, this helps people feel engaged in a group activity and to keep attention.

Remember your training and the practice that you were given in asking different types of questions.

11.21 Open questions are questions which cannot be answered with a yes or a no. Mediators and skilled advocates use them a lot.

- Who?
- What?
- How?
- Why?
- When?
- Where?

They are used to open up discussion, thought or lines of enquiry.

Closed questions

11.22 Closed questions are those which can be answered with a short, often one word, answer, usually yes or no. For example:

To get simple information:

- 'Do you drink coffee?'

To make a choice from a list of options:

- 'Would you like tea or coffee?'

To confirm a certain piece of information:

- 'Where did you will study law?'

Closed questions can close down discussion, thought or lines of enquiry. They are a staple of cross-examination. Good mediators do not cross-examine parties. Good salesmen do not cross-examine prospects.

Smiling

11.23 In negotiation progress is made if trust develops (which is another name for rapport building) and people start to like each other more. The simplest way of

Selling – the necessary mindset **11.24**

starting this process, and maintaining it, is to smile. Smiling is really a shorthand form of engaging in empathetic behaviour.

But remember there are two types of smile: the genuine and the fake. There has been a lot of research into this.

A genuine smile is both voluntary and involves the contraction of two sets of muscles: the zygomatic major (raising the corners of the mouth) and the orbicularis oculi (raising the cheeks and producing crows' feet around the eyes).

This genuine smile is known as the Duchenne smile after the French physician Guillaume Duchenne who studied the physiology of facial expressions in the 19th century.

The fake smile is known as the 'Say Cheese' or polite smile

It has been discovered that the Say Cheese smile is controlled by the motor cortex in the brain's left hemisphere, while the emotion related to the Duchenne smile is controlled by the limbic system (the emotional centre of the brain). The conventional wisdom is that you cannot voluntarily engage the orbicularis oculi but you can voluntarily engage the zygomatic major.

Recent research has cast doubt on this. It suggests that people can fake a genuine smile in certain conditions. But it is far from clear whether in a real life in the heat of an interaction as opposed to a laboratory, people can actually fake a Duchenne smile.

So do not follow the advice to fake it until you make it.

Remember emotions and feelings do not always just follow facial expressions. Facial expressions can create emotions and feelings. Research has established that smiling makes you feel more energised and optimistic.

Opening up

11.24 Your job is to establish rapport and to encourage the other person to open up. You **do not** do this by

- explaining the mediation process to them;
- describing your background and experience; or
- asking them what disputes or conflicts they have experienced.

You **do** it by asking:

- What is important to them;
- Why is it is important; and
- How they think they can achieve it.

You are in receive mode not transmit mode. The single most important thing that you can do is to listen. When you are selling, it is not about your product or services. It is not about you or your business. It is about the customer and their interests

11.25 *Selling – the necessary mindset*

In a nutshell

11.25
- Mediators use the same skills as salesmen and negotiators.
- Remember Cialdini's Big Six of Negotiation and use them.
- Listen and Smile at all times
- Selling is not about the service or you. It is about the customer.

Chapter 12

Selling – the necessary skill set

> In this chapter you will learn:
> - How to network effectively.
> - How to follow up.
> - How to actually sell.
> - How to pitch.
> - How to overcome objections.
> - Direct action.

'Networking is not working'

12.01 You need to reread this sentence before you can be sure that you know what it means.

It could mean:

- If you are networking you are not really doing any worthwhile work. You are pretending to work. Networking is a displacement activity. You will not make any money doing it.

Or:

- The networking that you do doesn't produce any results for you. You are not making any money doing it.
- If you do not network you do not work. We live in an interconnected world, economically, personally and psychologically.

What is networking?

12.02 Inevitably there is an industry of consultants advising on how to network. According to Ivan Mizner, named as the 'Father of Modern Networking' by CNN in their Newswire of 19 February 2008, it is:

> 'The process of developing and activating your relationships to increase your business, enhance your knowledge, expand your sphere of influence or serve the community.'

12.03 *Selling – the necessary skill set*

Networking can take place online or face-to-face. Either way it is something that anybody building a business, and especially mediators who are in the relationship business, must do. For mediators face-to-face is better than online. But many mediators, especially the digital natives or digital immigrants, are making more use of online networking. They are finding it successful.

Networking is a displacement activity

12.03 This view might well be true if for example you are a farmer or a writer or a coal miner. Your main activity is not to mingle with people it is to actually do something. Farmers tend animals and grow crops. Writers put words on the screen or page. Coalminers dig out coal and load it onto wagons.

What do mediators do? They attend mediations. They meet a group of strangers who are not getting on very well and build relationships with each person present. This is creating rapport. Out of those relationships they generate trust. And out of trust comes deals.

In order to win the job in the first place they will have made themselves known to someone. They may simply rely upon being on a Panel or on their profile on their website. If they do just that and nothing more they will receive some jobs eventually if they are lucky. But they will not build a mediation practice, let alone a business.

For mediators, going out and meeting people is not a displacement activity. A displacement activity is reading about going out and meeting people and then not doing it. If you read about networking and then go and do it that is preparation.

And you have to actually do it. As the famous economist, EF Schumacher, said: 'An ounce of practice is worth a ton of theory'.

Networking doesn't work

12.04 Undoubtedly this is true for everybody at some time. You need to avoid it being true for you most of the time.

Mediators who complain that networking is a waste of time are usually making the following mistakes:

- They are going to the wrong events/They are going to the right events.
- They are not going to events often enough/They are going to events too often.
- They leave too early/They stay too late.
- They do not hand out business cards/They do not ask for business cards.

But the biggest mistake is:

They go with a 'What can you do for me?' approach.

No networking: no work

12.05 Mediation is all about connections. Building a mediation practice is all about making more connections.

Remember the Texas paradox:

> 'There are two reasons why as a mediator you don't get work. People have never heard of you or they have.'

Networking plan

12.06 It is no use saying that networking does not work for you. So many people throughout the world have proved that networking works. The trick is to find the right plan.

Rushing from networking event to networking event collecting business cards and email addresses and never following up and making relationships is a waste of time and energy. Inputting lots of new information into your database is a good start. But networking does not finish there.

Spider cards

12.07 Databases are fine but Spider Cards are better.

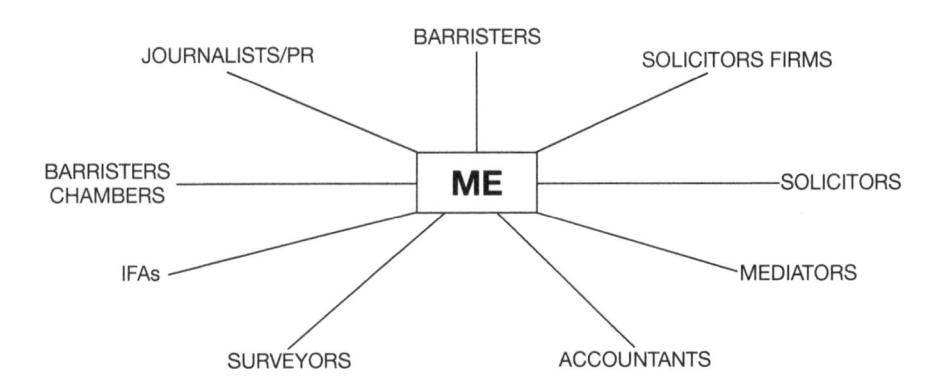

Figure 23a

12.07 *Selling – the necessary skill set*

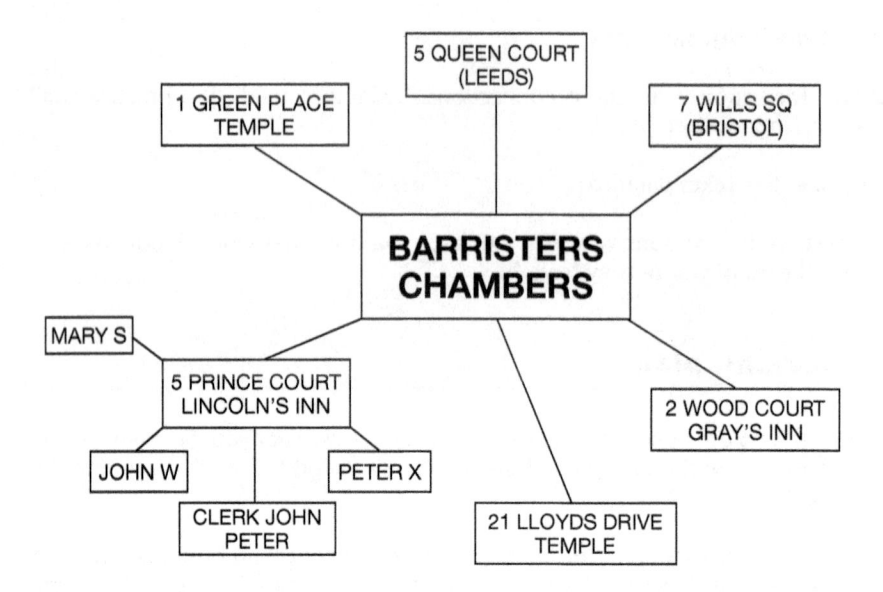

Figure 23b

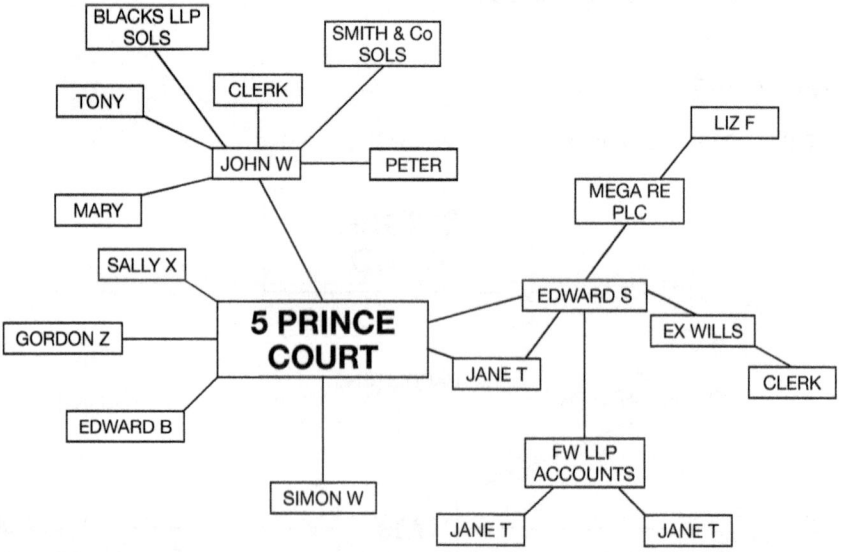

Figure 23c

As you can see they are a variation on the mind map theme.
- You put one name in the centre of the card and just draw lines to the other people that they know. You build a web or network.
- The simple act of just drawing the links prompts memories of fresh connections.
- Use 5 x 3 cards for convenience. You can conveniently carry them in your handbag or inside pocket.
- Make a list of the type of people that you want to meet. You may know some of them by name. Check your spider cards. Otherwise describe them by groups. Then work out where they go?

If you want to be a property mediator go where surveyors, architects, managing agents and builders, as well as construction lawyers go. Attend their events, which will not be ones specifically aimed at lawyers, arbitrators, adjudicators or mediators.

A good way of doing this is to get yourself on the mailing lists for firms of professionals who hold free seminars. They aim them at their clients or potential clients. It is rare but not unknown for them to refuse to put you on their list. They only usually do that if they think that you are a competitor in some way. Generally the Marketing Department which is in charge of promoting the firm through seminars is only too happy to add another name.

Once you have established a few relationships you can ask yourself who and what you want to know and who you know who could help you. Remember the well-established theory of six degrees of separation. In other words any one of us is linked in six steps from anyone else in the world. If you do not believe this try it. It is fun and it is illuminating.

Opportunity flow

12.08 Brokers and venture capitalists talk about 'deal flow'. They need to see a constant stream of deals for them to consider. The more that they see the more likely they are to spot something worth investing in. It is much the same with mediators. The more that you are in the stream of activity, ie people talking about what they have done, what they are doing and what is going to happen, the more opportunities will be around you.

Remember the definition of luck: it is where opportunity meets the prepared mind. You can have the best mind in the world but you still have to place yourself in the stream of opportunities.

11 tips for better networking

12.09

1 Turn up

If you are invited to an event, say yes. Write it in the diary. And go. Do not find a reason not to go.

Try and find out in advance who else is going. Ask around the people that you know whether anybody is also going.

2 Name badges

Wear your name badge on the right hand side. Most people, or at least men wearing suits or jackets wear it on the left-hand side as they have a pocket there to clip it over. Try it. It is more difficult someone approaching you to read it if the name tag is on your left than if it is on your right.

Women need to try and not obscure their nametags with their hair, scarves and necklaces. Easily done.

12.10 *Selling – the necessary skill set*

3 Join in

Remember what Woody Allen said about: 'Half of life is turning up.' That is true. The other half of life is: 'When you turn up join in.'

Nobody finds it easy to walk into a room of complete strangers. So don't do it. Arrive early. Find out who else is going to the event.

Different networking events have different arrangements. That is a truism. Let us take some examples.

You attend a conference on mediation

12.10 The last session of the day is drinks and networking. You know who will be there. Conference organisers publish lists of attendees. If there are lists, good. If there are not, go to different conferences.

During the day you chat to people. Some will stay on for the event. Others will not.

You have the perfect opening line when you have received your drink and are standing next to somebody: 'What did you think of the day? What was the best session for you?'

There is a book launch

12.11 You have been invited. There is no list of invitees but there are name badges. Again you have the perfect opening question: 'What did you think of the book?' Nine times out of ten the answer will be that they have not read it yet. Or 'how do you know the author?'

There is a seminar

12.12 The same rules apply. There may be list of attendees, which is distributed. Or there may be simply a master list of attendees at the front desk as you arrive. You sign your name on it so that can collect your CPD points. Have a quick read of the names while you are doing this.

You may be given a name badge or not depending on how formal the event is.

Again simple opening questions are there to be used:

'What did you think of the talk?' 'Who do you use in these chambers/this firm?'

It's a happening

12.13 People get together. It is all informal and unplanned. Pick up a drink. Look for someone who is not actually talking animatedly or who is by themselves, walk over and say 'Hello my name is xxxxx'.

Some people describe themselves as shy. They say that they are not natural networkers. Extrovert personalities will find this sort of activity easier than introverted ones. But it is not unnatural and most importantly it can be learned and practised.

You will receive the occasional snub, embarrassing silence and awkwardness. Don't dwell on it. Be like a jockey who has just been thrown. Dust yourself down and get back on the horse. Read the section at para **4.67** again.

What you have to remember is as Mark Belford, arch networker and keen observer of the legal and mediation scene, once said to me:

> 'I was always taught to remember that as much you may hate attending those meetings (or approaching people), so do the people hosting the event. Ie in reality, no one really wants to be there and often people are pleased that you have approached them so that they don't have to worry about approaching someone themselves.'

4　Your 10-second intro

Practise this over and over again before you go to your first networking event.

'My name is XX. I am a mediator. I do commercial and civil mediation etc etc. if you are attached to an organisation you will probably also say: 'I do commercial as mediations. I'm with ADR group/ Sue, Grabbit and Run etc. What about yourself?'

They tell you their name. This is where the trouble can start. Five seconds later you realise that you cannot remember their name. How can you avoid this? What do you do when it happens?

5　Forgetting names

People forget names as soon as they are introduced because:

- You did not hear the name. There was too much noise. They mumbled or spoke into your bad ear.
- You are distracted at the time. Something else caught your attention at the event or you are thinking of something else.
- You were not paying enough attention or showing enough interest. This is the biggest problem.

3 tips for remembering names

(1) Make sure that you hear the name.

   If you don't, just say immediately: 'I'm sorry. I did not catch your name.' When they tell you to you again repeat it and say sorry again. They will not take offence.

(2) Fix the right name to the right face

   This happens when you are introduced to a group quickly. The introducer says: 'Stephen, this is Susan, Jeremy, Peter, Pauline, and Mark.'

   Trying quickly think of something about them. Susan – glasses, Jeremy – beard, Peter – bald, poorly – red hair, Mark – stripey tie. Not always easy to do but practise and it becomes easier.

12.13 *Selling – the necessary skill set*

(3) Always repeat the name

Even when you know that you heard it correctly, repeat it. Try to do this out loud. If you cannot do that repeat it to yourself. Do it several times.

After the introductions, when you are sitting down, you can quickly write down the name and the prompt, eg Jeremy – beard.

Use business cards and check them. If they hand you business cards, at the same time take them and as you are reading, ask them something about themselves saying their name.

6   Remember your mediation training: ask about them

'But enough about me. What about you? What do you think of me?'

Bette Midler raised a laugh with this line in 'Beaches'. Funny perhaps but it also touches a nerve.

Most people prefer to talk than to listen. People feeling uncomfortable or stressed are more likely to keep on talking.

Extroverts are more prone to this than introverts. As the conversation develops they become more energised. They speak more and more quickly. They start to talk over you or interrupt. They are not meaning to be rude. They are just being enthusiastic. But how does the other person know that?

Professor Hugh Trevor-Roper's (of the Hitler Diaries fame) maxim: 'The beauty of conversation consists in the mute, attentive faces of one's fellow talkers' may apply to Oxford dons at High Table. It cuts no ice at networking events.

So restrain your stress and inner extrovert and listen more than you talk.

7   Give, don't take

Go back to Ivan Mizner's definition of networking. The core value of networking is to establish and activate relationships. The best way doing that is by establishing rapport (or trust). The best way of doing this is by being open and sharing and in giving to the other person not by demanding or taking. Mizner calls it 'Givers' Gain'.

Reciprocity is one of Robert Cialdini's Big Six. Through your listening and questioning you are trying to find out what you could do for them. You are not trying to find out what they could do for you.

If they offer something to you, whether it is an introduction or a meeting for lunch, you have of course to acknowledge it with thanks. What you need to avoid is then immediately offering something back. It looks obvious and insincere.

Don't force the reciprocity. Let it grow out of the mutually developing level of intimacy through your conversation.

8   Ask for a card

Asking 'Do you have a card?' is politer than saying 'Can I give you my card.' But this is perfectly permissible. What can seem crass to some people is taking out half a dozen cards and saying 'Let's swap cards.'

When receiving a card, take it with both hands if you can. Not always possible if you are holding a glass or a plate.

Always use your right hand not your left hand to take a card. Hold it in both hands and look at it. Do not just put it into your inside pocket or handbag. Make some comment on it such as: 'How long you have you been at XYZ?'

When you get home write on the back of the card where you met them and any other point that will help you fix them in your mind.

Without delay enter them in your Contacts. Make a note in the Notes section of where you met them and any other key points.

File away your business cards. Do not throw them away. Flick through them from time to time.

9 Smile

Nothing works better than a smile. Go back and read para **11.23**.

And remember the power of the smile. It energises and emboldens you. So smile, step forward, give your name and shake their hand.

10 Firm handshake

Give a firm handshake and look them in the eye.

Most people prefer firm handshakes to limp ones. They just feel nicer.

Researchers at Harvard have established that firm handshakes send a message about confidence, trustworthiness and openness. Or as the researchers put it firm handshakes were 'positively related to extraversion and emotional expressiveness and negatively related to shyness and neuroticism.'

Further research has also established two important conclusions for networkers:

- People who shake hands were more likely to be open during negotiations.
- People who gave a firm handshake were more likely to receive a job offer after an interview those who did not.

This does not seem to be gender specific.

Avoid:

- Bone crushers: they cause physical discomfort and can easily be seen as dominance behaviour.
- Hanging on to the hand too long: this causes psychological discomfort and suggests social gaucherie.
- The double handshake: it smacks of dominance behaviour and synthetic sincerity. American Presidents do it all the time but they can get away with it.

11 Don't look over their shoulder

Networking consultants always advise you to work the room. You have to circulate. Networking meetings are not group therapy meetings. Nor are they speed-dating sessions. Pace yourself but keep moving.

12.14 *Selling – the necessary skill set*

Be careful not to hog people. They may feel trapped. But when you are talking to someone they have to feel that you are really interested in what they are saying. So give them your undivided attention.

This is not always easy. The networking environment is distracting. People are coming and going. You overhear other people's conversations. People bump into you or tap you on the shoulder.

If someone shouts your name to you across the room of course you acknowledge them. Ask the person you are talking to whether they know the person who has just hailed you. If they do, exchange words about how you both know the other person and suggest that you go across to meet them together. If they do not, you can briefly describe the other person and ask whether or not they would like to meet them.

What you must not do is look over people's shoulders while they are talking to you.

Maintaining eye contact with your companion while scanning the room with your peripheral vision is an art and skill that you will develop over many hours of networking events.

Follow up

Making appointments

Be specific

12.14 If you are leaving a networking event with a promise to have coffee/lunch within the next two weeks, try and arrange it on the smart phones there and then.

If that is not possible say you will send an email the next day with some dates and times.

The 11am rule

12.15 If you meet someone at a networking event and you want to follow up, send them an email before 11am the next day. Tell them that you enjoyed meeting them and that you are interested in what they said. Say that you would like the opportunity of talking further. Ask them if they will have a window for a cup of coffee/lunch within the next two weeks.

Similarly do your thank you emails or telephone calls made before 11am the next day. Otherwise their impact is lost in the welter of the next day's activities.

The 36-hour rule

12.16 If you receive an email try to respond on the same day. Remember the 36-hour rule. Emails that are not answered within 36 hours get lost. Rarely do they resurface.

Reconfirm

12.17 Once the meeting is confirmed always reconfirm. Do this the night before or first thing on the morning of the date of the meeting. Being cancelled at short notice is demoralising and time wasting.

We all know the diaries are subject to change. But you want to minimise the ping-pong over times and dates and the irritation.

Be punctual

12.18 If you promise to telephone somebody always give the time by which you will do it, eg at 10am or before lunch etc on the specified day. Stick to that time. Do not miss it. Your prospects have commitments and busy diaries as well. Think of them.

Be grateful

12.19 Always send an email to the organisers of events that you attend to tell them how much you enjoyed it.

Being polite costs nothing. Being rude can cost you everything.

Be persistent

12.20 If you send an email and it is not answered, follow up within three or four working days, all that you need to do is send an email with your original email attached and the message:

'Dear Pat,

Good morning.

I hope that you are well and that that you received my attached email.

I look forward to hearing from you.

Kind regards'

If that doesn't work try telephoning the switchboard to find out whether or not they have a secretary. Send the secretary an email

'Good morning

Sorry to trouble you.

Could you let me know if Pat is in the office? I have sent her/him a couple of emails and cannot trace a reply.

Thanks for your help.'

12.21 *Selling – the necessary skill set*

You do not want to become a stalker or to harass your prospects but you do need to show persistence. Try three times. After that leave it for another day. If you attend the same conferences or events you tend to bump into people again.

Where to network?

12.21 Everywhere and anywhere that mediators, lawyers, accountants, surveyors, insurers, architects, medics, company directors, journalists meet.

So look out for in particular:

- Conferences such as the Chartered Institute of Arbitrators Mediation Symposium which is held each year.
- The annual conferences held by the big trainers such as ADR group and CEDR.
- Workshops, seminars and role-plays that are put on by various organisations for their members such ads those organised by the RICS or Business Mediators Group.
- Support groups (see **Chapter 14**).
- Mediation competitions.

There are more and more mediation competitions being organised. Some are very well-established such as the annual one held in Paris by the International Chamber of Commerce or the ones organised by the International Academy of Dispute Resolution in the USA and other countries.

Many universities now run annual competitions for mediators in the same way that they run moots for would-be barristers.

The organisers often are desperate for both judges and people prepared to act as mediators.

Online networking

12.22 See **Chapter 10** about networking through LinkedIn Twitter and Facebook.

The two tips about following up and keeping in touch apply in Twitterworld as much as in the real world.

But always:
- swap cards;
- follow up;
- keep in touch; and
- always check if they are on Twitter, LinkedIn or Facebook and connect.

Selling for mediators.

12.23 Selling happens when you stop marketing and pitch directly for business. Let us take a practical example.

Are you marketing or selling?

12.24 You have successfully completed some of the marketing tasks described in **Chapter 8**. Your website is up and running. Your blog is established and attracts viewers each month. You digested **Chapter 13** and your new book on mediation has been published and well received. You have been invited to speak about mediation at a conference for in-house counsel.

You prepare your speech (we discuss ways of doing this at paras **13.25–13.36**). It goes down well. The Chairman thanks you and announces that the networking cocktail party will now begin.

Drink in hand you enter the room and several of the audience congratulate you and start talking to you. You respond. You know all about the importance of networking. Everything you have ever heard seen or read about developing a business in professional services emphasises the fundamental importance of networking.

Are you now marketing or selling? Is there actually a difference? (See **Chapter 8**.) Does it matter?

The point of selling is to obtain an order. There is no other reason for doing it. Success is measured solely by the number of orders you obtain. This is true whether you are selling widgets or mediation services. Marketing is about creating the atmosphere or environment in which you can ask for the order.

Be ready to pivot

12.25 In the above you were marketing during the day at the conference when you gave your speech and answered the questions. You join the networking event and you are still marketing. To be sure you have moved from the large group audience to the smaller audience or even to an individual. But you have not asked anybody for an order. While talking to your fellow attendees be poised to pivot from marketing to selling.

At some point during a networking event you are going to have to pivot with at least one person from marketing to selling. If you do that successfully you will feel that the networking party was a good event. If you fail to do it the event is a missed opportunity.

You may not ask for the order there and then but you do ask for a face-to-face encounter, which is where you will be able to ask for the order. Never leave a networking event without at least one provisional appointment for a follow up meeting.

3 stages of selling

12.26 Selling can be seen as a three-stage process:

12.27 *Selling – the necessary skill set*

- Opening
- Exploring
- Closing

All three stages can take place in the same encounter. They may be spread over three separate encounters. In the above scenario arranging the provisional appointment is the first part of opening. Confirming it within the next few days and putting in the diary is the second and final part of opening.

By the time that you meet for coffee/lunch you are halfway there. You have an audience who is ready willing and able to talk to you. In classic sales parlance they are a warm prospect or a qualified lead.

What you now do that you have exchanged pleasantries about the weather the traffic and the coffee? It is simple. You do exactly what you do when you first meet the parties at a mediation in their private room. Remember your initial training. You establish rapport.

Selling on the phone

12.27 With the increase in the use of e-mail for business communication the amount of phone communication has decreased. But you need keep your phone technique sharp, precisely because you have less opportunity to practise it.

When speaking on the phone you are not able to rely upon your body language to the same extent to help you convey your message. Nor will you be able to rely upon observing the other person's body language to interpret the messages that they are receiving (see para **12.23**).

When you have to rely upon your voice alone without any support from body language you have to work harder. The core elements of phone pitching are:

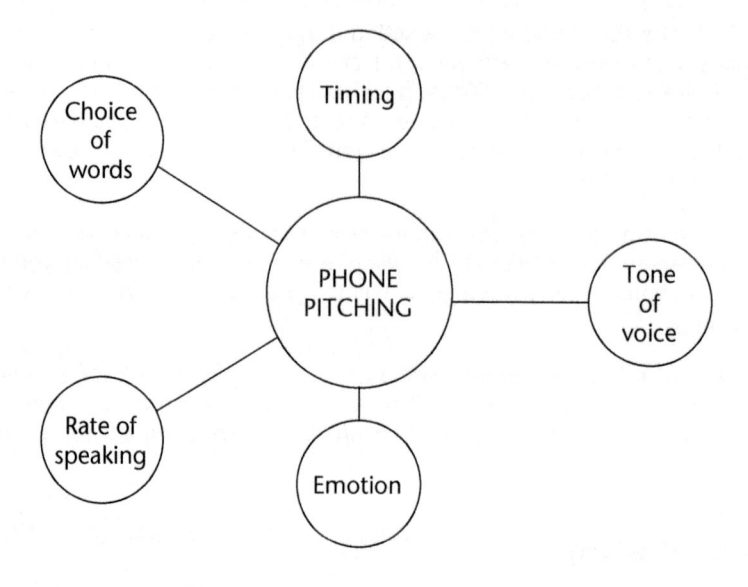

Figure 24

This is sometimes referred to as paralanguage. Professor Albert Mehrabian pioneered research into the relative importance of verbal and non-verbal messages (see *Social Messages* (1971)). His two main conclusions were:

1   There are three elements in any face-to-face communication:
    - words;
    - tone of voice (tonality); and
    - non-verbal behaviour, eg facial expressions.

2   Non-verbal elements are particularly important for communicating feelings and attitudes. They are especially important if there is an inconsistency or discrepancy between what is being said, ie the words spoken and the non-verbal behaviour or the tone of voice. When this happens the listener is more likely to believe the tonality and non-verbal behaviour.

In these circumstances Mehrabian concluded that:

- 55% of the impact is non-verbal or visual;
- 38% of the impact is vocal, such as voice tone and inflection; and
- 7% of the impact is verbal, ie the meaning of the words actually used.

These conclusions have been misinterpreted for many years. Thousands of communication trainers have told their trainees that the 7/38/55 rule applies to all verbal communications. In other words most of the meaning of a message is received by the listener relying upon non-verbal cues rather than verbal ones.

Professor Mehrabian expressly states on his website that: 'Unless a communicator is talking about their feelings or attitudes these equations are not applicable' (www.kadji.com/psy).

Further research has shown that:

- When we are asked to judge the speaker's ability rather than how they were feeling, the verbal element is more important.
- When we are asked to judge whether the speaker was honest or not, the verbal element is the most important.
- The gender of the speaker and the sex of the person being addressed do not appear to influence the relative importance of verbal and non-verbal behaviour.
- Verbal elements tend to dominate in spontaneous conversations and non-verbal in pre-planned or rehearsed communications. So, in presentations as opposed to conversations, the non-verbal element appears to predominate.

So when speaking on the phone you have to choose your words extremely carefully. Make sure that the way in which you are expressing yourself is not incongruent with the words that you are using. If they are then the Mehrabian formula may well apply. This is especially important if you are trying to be persuasive or passionate.

In practice therefore, the rate of speaking becomes more important.

This is not just a question of speaking too fast for people to understand or too slowly to retain people's attention. It is also a question of matching the rate of

12.28 *Selling – the necessary skill set*

speaking to that of the other side. This is because you cannot engage in matching body language. So you match voice speed.

Tone, which includes pitch and inflection, is crucial.

Where the emphasis is placed in a sentence can radically change its meaning, for example:

- He is asking me to leave?
- He is asking *me* to leave!
- *He* is asking *me* to leave!

Persuasion has been defined as a combination of empathy and sincerity. It is easier to convey both empathy and sincerity with words using body language and gesture. On the telephone this is more difficult. One way of doing it is to return to smiling.

Try this:

Put a big cheesy grin on your face. Pick up the telephone and pretend to have an angry conversation.

Difficult?

It cannot be done. As mentioned at para **11.23**, research shows that emotions follow facial expressions. In other words people can make themselves feel happy by smiling.

Observations of skilled telephone negotiators show that they use a lot of facial and hand gestures while speaking on the telephone. They do this even though the listener cannot see them. It still helps them convey the emotional content of the message. Less experienced telephone negotiators may feel self-conscious doing this.

Many experienced mediators say the best mediations are like a conversation. Remember that conversations cannot be conducted in a deadpan monotone.

Body Language

12.28 People communicate whether they want to or not.

Other people's body language

12.29 Body language is seen as a tool for finding out what people really feel and think. It is not possible or sensible to always believe what people say. By using body language we are able to double-check what we are being told.

The difficulties are:

- Anybody who wants to be able to reliably interpret body language has to undergo a great deal of training and practice. If there is any doubt about this take one of the tests available on YouTube. Just interpreting facial expression is much more difficult than might be thought.
- Signals are ambiguous. People may scratch because they have an itch not because they are lying.
- Different people interpret the same signals differently. Confirmation bias, which we are all susceptible to, just makes this worse.

Your own body language

12.30 Many people claim that body language is not a science. But researchers are investigating it and coming up with interesting results. One of the more interesting findings is that mimicry pays.

- Researchers in Holland found that waitresses who repeated word for word the customer's order received 70% bigger tips than waitresses who paraphrased the order.
- It appears that humans have an inbuilt tendency to mimic others. This may have evolved as a survival strategy when we needed to find out who we could trust.
- One way of doing is to match or mirror behaviour.

Mediators are taught the importance of mirroring behaviour. It is another transferable skill when selling.

Try following this three stage process:

1   Observe

Pay attention to what the other person is doing. Are they crossing their legs or arms, leaning backwards and forwards?

2   Pause

Do not immediately copy the behaviour. Pause for 20 seconds. Then imitate the behaviour. So if he leans forward, you lean forward.

3   Relax

When you start imaging you will be very conscious of what you are doing. As you practise, it will become more instinctive. You will probably find that you imitate people all day long without realising. Spend some time looking at other people to see how they interact.

Remember:

- Don't overdo it. You do not want to appear fake and manipulative.
- Imitation is often said to be the sincerest form of flattery.

Researchers at the University of Sussex have found that the following tips are useful in controlling the mood of a meeting

- Keep hands above the table.

12.31 *Selling – the necessary skill set*

- Use palm up batoning to encourage.
- Lean forward to encourage.
- Lean back during drama.

In the end it is the old trio that will see you through: smiling, nodding and eye contact. Practise them in front of the mirror.

Pitching

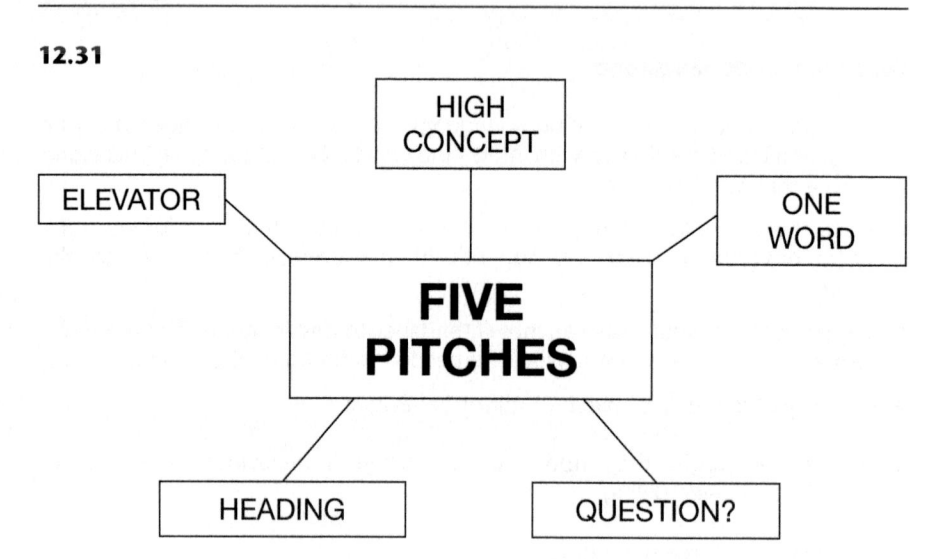

12.31

```
        HIGH
       CONCEPT
ELEVATOR          ONE WORD
       FIVE
      PITCHES
   HEADING    QUESTION?
```

Figure 25

When you make a pitch you are selling. Do not be in any doubt. You are not marketing any more.

At para **7.21** we explained the importance of being clear about your goals and what you are selling and how. Without that clarity you will find hard to pitch successfully.

Try this exercise:

- Write a 250-word description of your business.
- Edit it down to 100 words.
- Edit it down to 50 words.
- Now try it in 10 words.

As discussed at paras **8.08–8.12** mediation is a hard sell. You have to try and emphasise an aspect of what you do that is not going to put off your prospect.

- One solicitor-mediator, fed up with watching people's eyes glaze over when he told them that he was a solicitor and a mediator described himself as a reality therapist. At least people perked up and asked what a reality therapist did.

Selling – the necessary skill set **12.32**

- Another mediator said he replaces nightmares with dreams. People asked what he meant. He explains of course in more prosaic terms that he helps people settle their disputes without the nightmare of litigation or going to trial so that they were free to pursue their dreams.

You need to work on your pitches. How you pitch will depend on your audience. Therefore you need a portfolio of pitches.

5 Pitches

12.32

Dannie Pink summarises the art of pitching in his book on selling.

1 **The elevator pitch**

Everybody tells you to develop one. The idea is to be able to explain your proposal/business/project/yourself to anybody within two minutes at the most. This being the time that two New York journalists worked out was the average time you travel in an elevator between floors.

You have to work on it. Crafting one is not as easy as it sounds. For example, see the blog on the Mediator Network from Roger C Benson a' Mediation Conflict Resolution Consultant 'for a truly excruciating elevator pitch. If you were on the receiving end of it in a lift you would be pressing the alarm to be rescued.

2 **The high concept pitch**

This comes from Hollywood where people do not have time to listen to you in the elevator. They have five seconds in between phone calls.

You need an easy-to-grasp idea. So when the studio boss asks you what your film is about you can say for example 'Snakes on a Plane' or 'A bus with a bomb' (Speed.)

The idea is to be able to write your concept on the back of your business card. That does not mean you use the whole of the card.

So for example the high concept for LinkedIn is 'Facebook for business'. For Twitter it is 'Blogs for ADD sufferers'.

A good high concept pitch is
- Brief: one short sentence is the ideal.
- Uses building blocks that people already know, eg Jaws, space, blog.
- Is not the same as your tagline: eg YouTube's high concept is' Flikr for videos' but their tagline is 'Broadcast Yourself.'

3 **One word pitch**

In the online world of ever-shrinking attention spans and the dash for brevity, Maurice Saatchi, the advertising genius, says that you need one word. This is because only brutally simple ideas get through to people. They travel further and faster.

12.33 *Selling – the necessary skill set*

So for example Barack Obama's presidential campaign strategy was one word: 'Forward'.

What is your one word pitch for mediation? Think about it. Benett G Pitcher, a renowned and highly experienced commercial mediator, in his keynote address to the recent conference organised by the Florence International Mediation Chamber and IMI said his one word was 'Opportunity'.

4 The question pitch

A very successful example of this is the one used by Ronald Reagan in the 1980 presidential campaign when he defeated Jimmy Carter: 'Are you better off now than you were four years ago?'

People are often persuaded more by questions than by statements. Questions make people think more.

5 The heading pitch

This is particularly useful in emails. It is the heading that grabs your attention or not. People read emails because either they look useful or because they are intrigued.

Researchers have found that people who receive lots of emails go for utility. People with fewer emails read them out of curiosity.

Give yourself a chance by being specific.

Instead of: 'Improve your chances of successful outcome at mediation', say '3 tips for successful mediations'.

Overcoming objections

12.33 Prospects will raise objections when being pitched about mediation. See below for a sample of the usual ones. They are the same as the ones clients often bring up when being told by their lawyers that they should consider mediation.

The F Triangle is a helpful device in overcoming them. Fundraisers use it all the time.

```
                    FEEL
                     /\
                    /  \
                   /    \
                  /      \
                 /        \
                /          \
               /            \
              /_____\
           FELT              FOUND
```

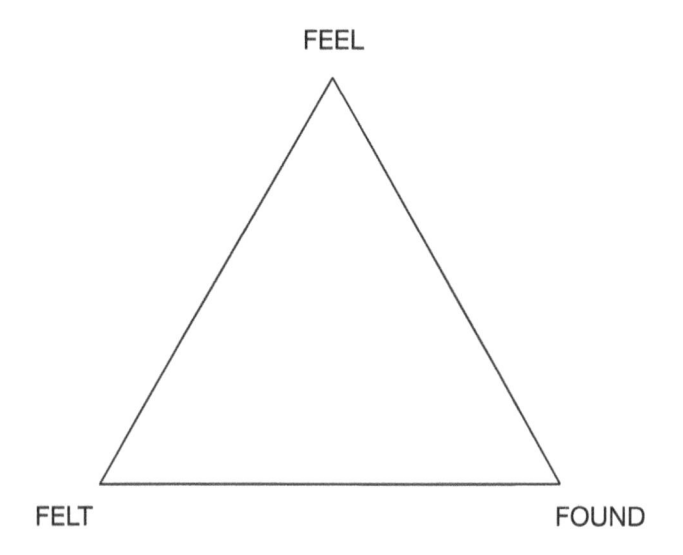

THE F TRIANGLE

Figure 26

Use the three elements to frame a response along these lines:

'I know how you *feel*. Others have told us that they *felt* like that. What we have *found* is that.'

You have to have your pitch ready. Do not try and meet these objections off the cuff. Remember what is was like facing difficult interview questions. You don't want them but you know that they will be coming. Prepare.

Here are some suggestions for dealing with the usual objections.

Timing

OBJECTIONS

12.34

- 'It's too early. We need much more information. They have not even pleaded their case. We need to know exactly what they are saying.'
- 'We need evidential certainty.'
- 'Emotions are still too raw. We need the temperature to cool down.'
- 'It's too late. We have already prepared to go to trial.'
- 'We have incurred all the costs so we might as well go to trial. Everybody knows the details and it made their positions clear. The gap is too wide. We have become too entrenched.'
- 'It will cause delay. We have wasted enough time. We do not want to lose the timetable for the trial date.'

12.35 *Selling – the necessary skill set*

RESPONSES

- 'Mediation is about coming to a fair commercial settlement, which is a reasonable and fair alternative to what might happen at court if the litigation continues.'
- 'In fact it is rare even during or at the end of a trial to have evidential certainty and have all the information you wanted available. People develop their cases as they fight them in court.'
- 'Mediation gives you a good opportunity to assess the opposition directly and hear what it is that they are complaining about, what they want and why. You can do that in an informal and open way, which you will not be able to do through pleadings. You can ask them questions and speak to them in plain everyday English rather than in legalese.'
- 'I understand that emotions are running high in this case. Actually meeting people and letting everyone get things off their chest can be very beneficial. So often at mediations people say "I wish we had had this conversation a year ago".'
- 'Frankly it's never too late to settle. Some cases settle even after the trial has ended and before the judgment is given. There is no reason for there to be any delay. The litigation timetable can continue and you can conduct mediation in parallel. Courts routinely make ADR orders now where that happens rather than there being a stay of the litigation timetable.'
- 'People may think they are too far apart. Some even state in their public positions that they are far apart. But I can tell you that people still settle mediations even where:
    - there is a claim and counterclaim and both sides expect to be net receivers of money; or
    - both sides have put in Part 36 Offers which are poles apart.

    You often find that there is more common ground between the parties than appears in the pleadings and in the correspondence.'

Cost

OBJECTIONS

12.35

- 'It's just an extra layer of cost. Everybody knows what the position is and if they want to settle they can come to us. Or make us an offer.'
- 'We have thought about risk. We have made a part 36 offer. We have protected ourselves on costs. The ball is in their court.'
- 'If the case doesn't settle we would have just wasted time and money.'

RESPONSES

- There are three points on costs:
    - If you settle you will save a lot of costs.
    - If you don't go to mediation you might be penalised on costs even if you win a trial.

- 'If you do go to mediation and it does not settle those costs are not necessarily wasted. Even when mediations have failed the parties and their lawyers often say that it has not been a waste of time because they now understand the other side's case and even more importantly their own better.'
- 'They find it very useful to talk through the situation with an independent third party who in effect is a second pair of eyes and ears.'

Merits

OBJECTIONS

12.36

- 'I have been advised that I have been exceptionally strong case. I have been told we have an 80% chance of winning. They haven't got a case. They are in denial. We just do not understand their case or why they are defending or proceeding.'
- 'I'm entitled to my money. I want my day in court. It's not about the money, it's about the principle. They should not be allowed to get away with this.'
- 'It won't work.'
- 'They won't settle. They are so unreasonable. We have tried before. All they did was tell us that our case was rubbish.'
- 'It's just horse trading. I don't need lawyers or mediators to horse trade. I can do that myself. All that happens is we sit in an airless room for ten hours and then split the difference.'
- 'If we can't do that we just carry on to court. There is no guarantee that this dispute will end.'

RESPONSES

- 'In fact the statistics show that 90% of cases settle at mediation or shortly afterwards. (Check that you have the latest up-to-date figures.)'
- 'Most people who are spending money on lawyers going to court think that they have a strong case. I am often told by both sides that they have been advised by their barrister that they have a 70% or more chance of winning. One of them must be wrong. Maybe both are.'
- 'All cases have a degree of risk. Even if it is only the "mad judge factor".'
- 'And if you are right that they are in denial – and they may be – then ADR can be useful. Some people think that it stands for an Alarming Dose of Reality.'
- 'I agree that sometimes mediation is just horse trading. And if that is what the parties want to do they don't need lawyers or mediators to do it. They can do it themselves. But they haven't so far. Sometimes a third party can encourage them to talk constructively.'
- 'But if the parties want it mediation can be a lot more than horse trading. You know you can have a commercial discussion and come up with ideas and solutions that the court could never give you.'

12.37 *Selling – the necessary skill set*

You as an individual being appointed as a mediator

YOU HAVE NO EXPERIENCE

12.37 'You have not done any mediations before. Why should I be a guinea pig? I can use an experienced mediator.'

RESPONSE

That's true I haven't acted as a lead mediator yet. I'm looking for my chance to start. I have observed several mediations/had assistantships with leading mediators. I feel ready to act as lead mediator now.

I'm keen and I'm hungry. Everybody has to start somewhere and I am asking you to give me a chance to show you what I can do. Are you willing to do that?'

YOU ARE NOT AN EXPERT

'I see that you have done mediations. But you do not have experience in this area. It is technical. I think we want someone who has practised in this area or has done mediations about this sort of subject before.'

RESPONSE

'I agree that I do not have the narrow sector specialism of some of my fellow practitioners. I do have expertise in mediation though and specialise in commercial mediation.'

'In my non-mediation life I have had to learn about new areas quickly. I have had to do the same thing for mediations in other sectors.'

'I've just got two points:
1   Mediation is not expert determination. If you want a technical answer from a technical expert to a technical problem then expert determination may be a better choice for you than mediation.
2   I promise you that if you are willing to appoint me I will read all the material that you send. If there is anything I cannot understand I will ask. You do not pay extra for my preparation. All the preparation is included in my fixed fee.'

YOU ARE TOO EXPENSIVE

'I can get X and Y who are much cheaper.'

RESPONSE

When deciding on your response you have two choices: cut your prices or stick to them.

'I realise that mediation is highly competitive these days. If you are willing to appoint me on this occasion I will match their price.'

OR

'I understand what you say. In mediation as in everything else there's always someone cheaper and someone more expensive.'

'Most people who enquire about my availability do not object to my fees. In fact a lot of them say that I'm very reasonable. Please remember that my fees include:

- Eight hours of mediation.
- All preparation time.
- All travel time and expense (including any overnight accommodation)

There are no hidden extras. I generally find that I am the cheapest person in the room.'

For more on this read **Chapter 16** about how to charge.

I WANT SOMEONE WHO IS GOING TO BANG HEADS TOGETHER.

'Your website says that you are a facilitative mediator. And I have read your blog about importance of acknowledging emotions and letting everybody vent. That all sounds too touchy-feely for me.'

RESPONSE

'I understand what you mean. Before I trained as a mediator and I used to take clients to mediation as a solicitor, I felt the same. Then I found that what commercial mediators really did was not simply tell you the answer based on the law and the facts as a judge would. They were able to explore all and any issues. They do have challenging conversations. They are empathetic but this does not mean that mediators do not engage in robust reality therapy.'

'As a mediator I do act as an agent of reality for all parties there. But I am there not to judge the merits of the dispute but to try and help the parties negotiate a deal. In my experience, and I do not know whether yours is the same, you don't get deals done by arguing. You get them done by discussing proposals.'

'And like it or not our emotions do influence our decision making. Have you read "Thinking, Fast and Slow" by Daniel Kahneman? Brilliant book.'

I WANT SOMEONE WITH GOOD SOFT SKILLS

'My client is very vulnerable. Emotions are running very high in this dispute. The other side are very difficult personalities indeed. We're going to need a velvet gloved diplomat.'

RESPONSE

'I understand your concern about your client. One of the beauties of mediation is that it is not a court room. No one is on trial. No one is cross-examined. I know some lawyers try and do this but I will not allow it.'

12.37 *Selling – the necessary skill set*

'If the clients do not even want to see each other, let alone meet and talk to each other, they do not have to. I know that some mediators insist on a joint opening session for example. I do not.'

'We can decide on the day whether to have an opening session or not.'

'Your client will come under no pressure from me to do anything. All I want them to do is to think about the benefits of settling as opposed to continuing to fight this case. It is for them to decide whether or not it is worth settling. You are there to advise on litigation risk.'

'If at any time anybody's feeling that is all too much we can take a break or even adjourn the mediation.'

'I have dealt with some very vulnerable people including people with learning difficulties, victims of sexual assault, religious or racial discrimination. Some have even been receiving medical treatment for stress and worry. Others have been on the financial brink and facing ruin with all the pressures that that brings.'

'Nearly all those cases still settled on the day'.

I NEED TO SEE REFERENCES

'I see that there are a few on your website. They are anonymous. My clients/my Board expect me to appoint mediators who have been peer-reviewed in listings and directories.'

RESPONSE

'I can assure you that they are all in writing and genuine. If you would like to tell me which ones you think are particularly relevant I will ask the people who provided the reference if I can disclose their identity or ask if you can contact them.

You will also see that I am ranked in XX. Those rankings are based upon written references submitted to the researchers at the directories and personally verified by them.'

YOU HAVE DONE TOO MANY MEDIATIONS FOR THE OTHER SIDE

'I see that you have mediated disputes involving the claimant company twice in the last four years. Their solicitors tell me that you have mediated two this year for them already and about the same number last year. I'm not saying that you're biased of course, but I would prefer someone completely neutral and that none of the parties has ever used before.

RESPONSE

'I understand your position. Thank you for confirming that you do not think I would be biased but I do understand what you say about using someone no one has ever used before.'

I know that there are other solicitors/clients who think the same but mostly people prefer to use someone that they have had experience of before and have confidence in. In fact you find that most mediators get most of their work from referrals and repeat business.

When I was a solicitor I used to want my choice of mediator but in the end I decided that, provided that I knew nothing bad about the mediator proposed by the other side and I had no reason for thinking that he would not get on with my client, I was happy to accept their choice.

The reason was that if they felt comfortable with that mediator it meant that they trusted him and that would mean the process of establishing that level of operational trust which you need for every successful negotiation would be speeded up.

If there is any further information you need please let me know.'

In a nutshell

12.38

- Networks and networking are all.
- Build networks. Practise networking.
- Turn up and join in.
- Fill in your Spider Cards.
- Learn your 5 pitches.
- Rehearse your responses to objections.

Chapter 13

Making a noise

In this chapter you will learn:
- How to make a noise.
- How to blog.
- How to publish an e-book.
- How to write a print book.
- How to podcast.
- How to give a talk.

Profile as brand

13.01 The importance of brand is discussed at para **9.01**. As discussed, individual mediators do not really have 'brands' in the way that corporate mediation providers or other non-mediation services do.

For mediators having a brand means being known to a wide selection of people and having some distinctive characteristics or qualities that they associate with you. For example when mediators and lawyers chat they say things such as:

- 'George is very successful. He did a very good mediation the other day. He is very funny and won the clients over with his jokes.'
- 'Margaret is very clever but she does dwell on the legal points for quite long time before we get down to the commercial realities. But the deal was done and the clients were happy.'
- 'Kevin is good but he thinks that he is still a judge. He cannot resist telling people what he would do if this case came before him as a judge.'
- 'Janet is very good with people. The clients loved her. I thought she was a bit laid-back but we got the deal done.'
- 'Simon is really good but he's so busy I'm not sure he reads the papers as thoroughly as he should. The clients were a bit fed up about the time it took to bring him up to speed.'

13.02 *Making a noise*

How to establish your brand?

13.02 Mediators are told to 'make a noise'. In other words when people talk about mediators you need to be part of the conversation. This is either as a participant or as a subject.

How do you make a noise?

13.03

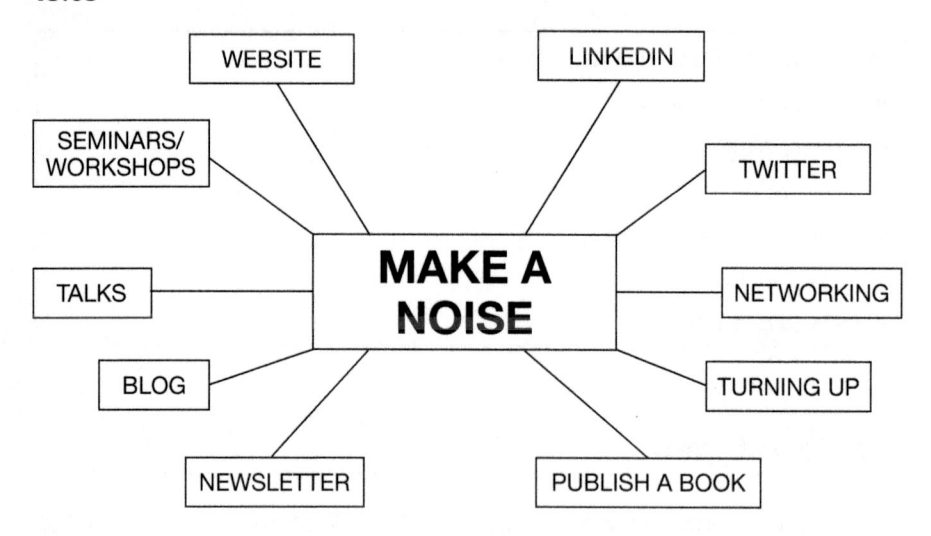

Figure 27

As discussed in **Chapter 1** mediation practice development advisers routinely give this advice. But they do not tell you how you actually do it. It is all very well for social media experts to tell you that you have to become a trusted presence and a go-to person. Write a blog, or, better still, a book, they say. But how do you start?

How to write a blog

13.04
Once you have decided that you are in the business of selling mediation, take the next step and recognise that posting a blog of some sort somewhere is as essential to promoting your business as is answering emails promptly. If you do not do it you will lose business.

Most mediators accept that networking is an essential part of developing their practice. Blogging is another form of networking. This is the essential lesson to grasp. Blogging is about establishing connections. As a format it is:

- about conversing with your readers, not presenting to them.

- more informal and personal than writing articles for trade journals or giving seminars, workshops or lectures.

Why am I doing it?

13.05 Prepare yourself. Be clear why you want to write a blog and who you are writing for.

Ask yourself

- How is this blog going to help you all grow your mediation business? Is it primarily to increase your brand awareness?
- Do you want to sell your mediation services?
- Do you want to connect with other mediators, agents of influence or potential customers?
- Do you want to build a mediation community or group?
- Who are your ideal readers?
- If you were them what would you want to read about? The simple answer is something that is either entertaining or informative.

Seven steps for great blogging.

13.06

1 **Set up a blogging calendar**
   - Write into your diary when your blog will be published.
   - Seven days before that date – you write it.
   - Seven days before *that* date – you start thinking about what you are going to write.
   - Have a running list of blog topics to cover over the next three or four months.
   - Some of these will suggest themselves. For example if you are going to the CMC conference your next blog after that date can be about what happened. What was the news?
   - If you have recently attended a talk or mediation support group, blog about the key topics that were discussed.

2 **Choose your point**
   - Every blog must have a point.
   - You must be able to summarise in one sentence of not more than 140 characters, what it is about.
   - The point is really the takeaway that you want your readers to have when they have finished reading your blog.

3 **Pick your keywords**

   By the time you come to blog you should have worked out what specific keywords you want to include in your online material. See **Chapter 10.**

13.06 *Making a noise*

Do not stuff your blog with keywords. Search engines and readers want more than just a collection of keywords. But make sure that you include some of them:

- in the title
- early on in the blog
- right at the end in the takeaway.

4 Choose your structure

Without structure your blog will just be a meandering essay or a stream of consciousness. Make sure you have headings, subheadings and bullet points.

Here is a suggested template:

CHECKLIST FOR A BLOG

Introduction:

- Say what you are going to discuss. Remember the six key questions the first paragraph sentence should answer: Why, when, who, where and what and how?
- Make your point. Explain it.
- Move on to your next point. Make it. Explain it.
- Keep doing this until you have finished.

Conclusion

- Remind the reader of the key point.
- Repeat the takeaway.

Call to action (CTA).

- A blog without a CTA is a waste of time. You want to promote connections.
- You do this by provoking a reaction.
- Ask for a comment. End with a question. It can be as simple as: 'Do you agree?'

---

5 Choose your length

Opinions among expert bloggers vary. The length will depend on:

- how complicated the topic is.

    A blog about a new Court of Appeal ruling on mediation will merit a longer blog than a comment on someone else's blog that you found interesting and want to share.

- how often you blog.

    If you blog every day or even as some suggest several times a day your blogs will be shorter than if you blog once a month. Daily blogs will be in the 200–300 word range, monthly ones in the 1,000–1,500 word range.

- In practice, given that most people's attention spans are limited, 600–800 words is about right.

6 Include links and mentions

Readers want unique and relevant content.

- The uniqueness comes from you as the blogger.
- Relevant content can be from other sources, either from pages on your website or from links to external sources.

Be generous with your links and acknowledgements.

- Give names of individuals and organisations.
- Don't forget that some people set up Google or social-media alert tracking systems and will be able see that you mentioned them. They will have a look at what you said about them.

7 Respond to comments

Don't forget when you are writing a blog to promote your mediation business to potential customers. It is about your customers. You need to be answering the questions that they are asking. If you do that you will establish connections with your readers.

Always invite your readers to leave comments.

- In this way you obtain free market research about what your customers want.
- You will receive hostile, destructive and even offensive criticism. Always be polite and moderate. Amongst the tsunami of intemperate indignation there might be a germ of a good idea.

The seven deadly sins of the bad blogger

13.07

1 Bad writing

Just because blogs are more informal does not mean that the writing can be casual and sloppy. Mistakes of grammar, punctuation and spelling will put readers off.

2 Laying down the law

Instead of laying down the law invite comments and conversation. Bloggers should put forward an idea with a comment. Blogs are not the finished article with a fully developed thesis. They are more a work in progress and about inviting others to contribute to it.

3 Over promoting

Of course you are trying to sell your services as a mediator. So are all the other mediators in the world. A good way of attracting customers is for them to see you, your website and blog as a resource that they can use and not just as a PR outlet.

13.07 Making a noise

4 Writing as an expert

This means writing for yourself, not for your clients. In the immortal words of public opinion guru Frank Luntz: 'It's not what you say that matters, it's what people hear' (see his book of the same title).

5 Lack of focus

This means badly organised individual blogs. But it also means:

- not having an overall strategy of what your blogs are trying to achieve; or
- not having a recognisable voice or style.

This does not mean that you have to adopt the same approach to every issue or use the same language every time. What it does mean that your individuality – what makes you different from all the other mediators – comes through.

6 Not using technology

There are multiple tools available to bloggers. Apart from the standard text blog there are video interviews, podcasts, infographics RSS feeds etc. How much you can use depends upon your expertise and how much time you can commit to blogging. But the old adage about a picture being worth 1000 words has some validity. Therefore include at least some images even if it is only a photograph of yourself.

7 Binge blogging

- You start to blog. You do a few. You become better at it. It gets easier. You come to like it. You have spare time so you do three or four blogs in a week.
- Then some mediations come your way. You overlook your blog calendar because you have your mediation diary to worry about. You do not blog for 3 months. You have lost your audience.
- Readers like consistency. They will come to expect that on the first Friday every month or every other day you will blog and they will be entertained and informed.

A personal selection of good blogs

www.pgpmediation.com/feed	Phyllis Pollack a US mediator blogs every Friday. A mixture of personal anecdote and hard reportage.
schaumediation.com/	Jan Schau another US mediator blogs every week. More think pieces usually and less hard information.
	Both the above are individual blogs and are well written and informative.
mediate.com	A site which features different blogs every week. A lot of interesting material. The quality and style is very variable. The best is excellent. The less good can be poor.
kluwermediation.com	Similar to the above but with less of a US flavour and more international. Variable style and quality but often very good. Edited by Bill Marsh who is always worth reading.

How to write a book

13.08 Blogging is one thing. Writing a book is an entirely different matter. Ask yourself.

What sort of book is it?

- An e-book: one that you will allow people to download either from your website or through Amazon. Are you going to charge or give it away for free?
- A printed book. Will it be self-published, vanity published or published by a commercial publisher and sold in the traditional way both through bookshops and online?

Why are you writing a book in the first place?

13.09 Do you want to:

- Have some marketing material for potential customers? If you do self-publishing a free e-book may be the answer. But bear in mind that many of these publications called books seem like pamphlets to the reader.
- Establish yourself as a trusted expert. Which do you think is more like to do this: a free 20 page pamphlet or a 250 page book published by a recognised legal or business publisher?
- Get your name out there. If you just want your name to appear when search engines crawl through the oceans of information a self-published e-book may be the answer.

Self-published e-books

13.10 These are conventionally between 60–100 pages long and sold for about £3.99 on Amazon. This is also known as KDP or Kindle Direct Publishing. Amazon is not the only format. You can publish E books via Apple and Barnes & Noble. But Amazon has over 75% of the market.

13.11 Making a noise

Ground rules

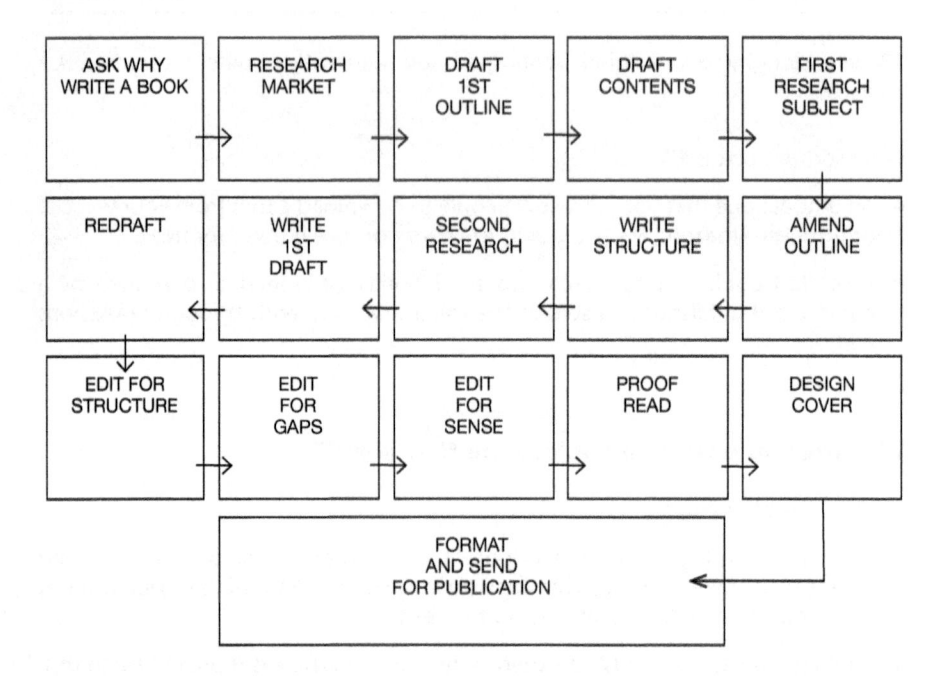

```
ASK WHY        RESEARCH       DRAFT          DRAFT          FIRST
WRITE A BOOK → MARKET      →  1ST         →  CONTENTS    →  RESEARCH
                              OUTLINE                       SUBJECT
                                                              ↓
REDRAFT     ←  WRITE       ←  SECOND      ←  WRITE       ←  AMEND
               1ST            RESEARCH       STRUCTURE       OUTLINE
               DRAFT
  ↓
EDIT FOR    →  EDIT        →  EDIT        →  PROOF       →  DESIGN
STRUCTURE      FOR             FOR            READ           COVER
               GAPS            SENSE
                              ↓
                              FORMAT
                              AND SEND    ←
                              FOR PUBLICATION
```

Figure 28

13.11 Work out how much time you have.

- Writing any sort of book takes time. Even a 25-page e-book is 4,000 words long. Writing that many words in publishable form in less than 15 hours will be difficult. You cannot write hour after hour. The minimum time it will take you is a week.
- A 250 page traditional printed book is more likely to be 100,000-125,000 words. In other words 25-30 e-books. You are looking at six months to complete it.
- Both these time estimates depend upon the amount of research that you have to do.
- Remember that we all underestimate by at least 40% the time it takes to complete a task.

Write an outline

- Start with your idea. Think around it. Getting started can be difficult. Try using a mind map. If you are not sure what these are take a look at Tony Buzan's books and articles about mind maps His book *Mind Maps for Business* is helpful and reader-friendly.
- Write your list of contents. List them as individual chapters showing the topics that you will discuss.
- Having completed the first draft of your outline ask these questions:
  - Who is my audience?
  - What do they want to know?
  - What am I going to tell them?

Having worked this out amend your draft outline.

Establish the structure.

- Structure is everything when writing any sort of book. Once you have worked out the structure stick to it. If you don't you will never finish the book.
- As you write, new thoughts will occur to you. Incorporate them as you go along or make a note in **BOLD CAPS** so that you can incorporate them later. But keep to your original structure.
- Stephen King a successful and prolific writer advises: 'Write now. Fix later.'

Write it

13.12 There comes a time in every author's life when you actually have to start writing. Planning, thinking and researching stops.

Pick a time. You have your outline. Start typing or dictating. Do this for a maximum of 45 minutes. Stop. Make a note of the time and the number of words that you have done. Rest for 5–10 minutes and do another 45 minutes.

Research shows that it is difficult to work at high intensity for more than about 90 minutes or for longer than three sessions of 90 minutes in a day. In other words it is difficult to write at full intensity for more than five hours a day.

Think about yourself and your best work patterns. We all have different circadian rhythm. Some of us are better and more productive first thing in the morning. Others peak later in the day or at night.

Some people really are owls while others are larks. Which are you?

13.13 Whatever is your best period use it to do your writing. Do not fritter away the golden hours on emails and Internet surfing. Do that when you have done your writing.

As you work through the day make a note each time you stop of the time and how many words you have written. Doing this:

- records your rate of progress and shows how many words realistically you can write in an hour.
- builds a sense of momentum, which is encouraging and motivating. Keeping going and sticking at it is the hardest thing about writing.
- stops writer's block from even starting.

Redraft

13.14

- Nobody produces their finished version at the first attempt. Revision is always required.

13.15 *Making a noise*

- Some writers spend all morning working out where to insert a comma and all afternoon working out whether or not to delete it. You are not one of these writers.
- You are not writing great literature. You are writing informational material to establish yourself as an expert on the subject.

Editing

13.15   Edit your first draft. There are three stages;

1   Edit for structure

Look at the overall picture. Read the book to make sure that it flows logically from one section to another. You may change the order of the contents, amalgamate some chapters and subdivide others.

2   Edit for gaps

Go through your notes to yourself. Check quotations. Insert graphics and illustrations.

As you are doing this put yourself in the place of the reader. Ask: Am I going to turn the next page? Am I going to fall asleep?

Think about visuals. Do not have pages of grey text. Break it up with bullet points, charts, diagrams and tables.

3   Edit for sense

Think like the reader. Be a self-critic: does this sentence or paragraph makes sense? Is it too long? Could this section be shorter?

When you started the book you were worried that you might not have enough material. By the time of your first draft you will have too much. Be prepared to cut. Readers prefer short to long books.

Format the text as you go along. Depending on your distribution you will have guidelines to follow.

Insert the table of contents and appendices.

Proofreading

13.16   Check what you have written for accuracy. This means grammatical and spelling as well as factual accuracy. If you are self-publishing you do your own proofreading and fact-checking.

Most writers find it impossible to proofread their own material. Software with built-in grammar and spell checks helps a great deal. But it can produce perfectly spelt and grammatically correct gibberish. You still have to read for sense.

Editing your text can easily take as long as writing it.

Design your front cover

13.17 Keep it simple. Do not use more than two or three colours. There is software to help you.

Prepare your book for publication

13.18 The publisher will have their requirements. If you are self-publishing you will have to convert your text to PDF. As ever there is software to help you do this. Send it to the publisher.

Traditional print media

13.19 Many of the steps described above apply if you are writing a book for print publication either by a vanity publisher or a commercial publisher. In addition you will have to persuade a publisher to accept the book at all. This is much easier with vanity publishers because you pay the costs.

For a commercial publisher you have to pitch your idea by sending a proposal. Here is a template.

Template for a book proposal

Title of the book

Contents of proposal

13.20 Overview: brief statement of what sort of book it is and who the target readers are.

Author
- Description of main qualifications to write the book and relevant background
- Details of any prior publications and public exposure e.g. conferences/podcasts/TV interviews etc
- Reference to website for full profile and information
- Contact details

The market
- Definition of the market
- Estimated size of the market

Why this book at this time?
- Reasons for writing the book this year rather than last year or next year
- What has recently happened or is going to happen to make it topical
- Synopsis of book

13.21 *Making a noise*

Table of contents for the book
- List of chapter headings
- Bullet point list of main topics to be included in each chapter

Competition

Description of rival publications

- Identify by the specific author, nationality and title and publication date of rival works
- Point out differences: eg your book is aimed at the English market the other publications are all written by American authors for the US market.

Sample chapter

- Some publishers want a sample chapter to show the treatment and whether or not you can write in the style they want. Probably not necessary if you are already published either in articles, books or even extended blogs.

Contract

13.21 The publisher will want you to sign a contract. If this is your first book you have limited negotiating power but it is worth bearing in mind the following:

What to ask the Commissioning Editor

13.22

1. Term of licence. Usually the author grants an exclusive licence to the publisher for a period and retains the copyright.
2. How will you promote my book?
3. How will you sell my book? Which territories?. Which formats, eg ebooks?
4. What will the royalties be? This can be tricky. Is it based on the retail price or net receipts. What rate?
5. How many free books will I be given? How much do I have to pay if I want more?
6. Will I be consulted on the cover?
7. Will I be able to liaise directly with the copy editor and make necessary changes at proof stage without charge?
8. Will you pay for a book launch?
9. What happens if this text is not ready by the stipulated date?
10. What is the timetable from delivery of text for copy editor's queries, proofreading and publication?
11. Will you obtain the permissions to use copyrighted material?

How to give a talk or lecture

13.23 All the advice on how to start and develop mediation practice says that you should give talks, seminars and lectures. That is all very well but what about glossophobia?

Glossophobia

13.24 Fear of public speaking is the one of most common phobias. Research has established that statistically many more of us claim that we would prefer death to giving a speech. Jerry Seinfeld joked that at funerals, most people would rather be lying in the coffin than giving the eulogy.

There are several excellent books on making speeches and presentations. For example *The Presentation Coach* by Graham Davies and *The art of speeches and presentations* by Philip Collins.

The lessons from these books are:
- Have a clear central argument
- Tell a story
- Remember it is an artificial exercise. It is a performance. You are trying to give the best version of yourself.

Philip Collins has the following mnemonic: DETAIL. Here is a summary of his advice.

Delivery

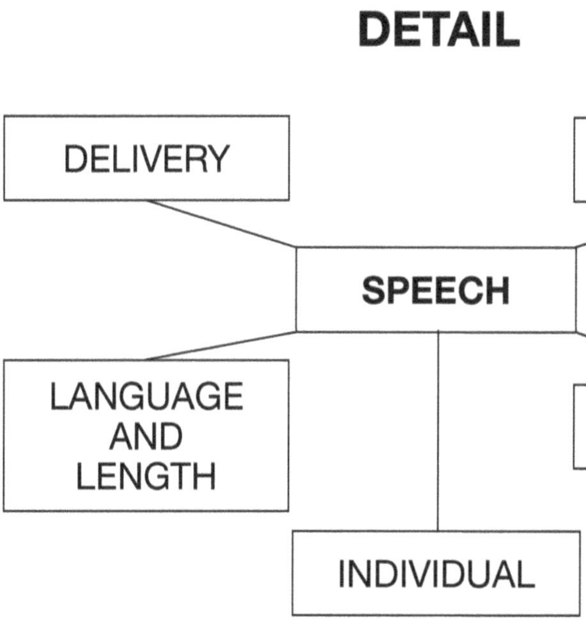

DETAIL

```
     DELIVERY                    EXPECTATION
            \                   /
             \                 /
               SPEECH
             /                 \
            /                   \
   LANGUAGE                      AUDIENCE
   AND
   LENGTH
              INDIVIDUAL
```

Figure 29

13.25 *Making a noise*

13.25 Remember the speech is written to be spoken. You are not writing an essay or an article. You are giving a performance. If you prepare properly and follow these golden rules your material will not let you down.

Stick to the script. Speaking without notes can appear impressive. It is extraordinarily difficult to do. Politicians who appear to do it have spent hours committing the speech to memory.

Don't read out the text. Use cards to prompt you. Always have a full text of the speech with you in case of disaster but do not use it except when catastrophe has struck.

When using your note cards do not speak and read at the same time. Read: pause: look up: engage the audience in eye contact. Only then, speak.

Speeches should not end with a whimper. Do not say 'Thank you for your attention. Does anybody have any questions?'

Always write out your opening paragraph and your closing paragraph. Learn them and stick to them to the letter.

Expectations

13.26 This is just another way of saying what has been repeatedly said in this book about asking who your audience is and what you are doing it for. So work out:
- What your audience's expectations are of you and what your expectations are of them.
- What you expect people to do once they have listened to your speech.
- Is your speech meant to be informative, inspirational or persuasive?
- Will it have traces of all three? Be clear which is to be the dominant element.

Topic

13.27 What is your speech about? If you cannot say what it is about in one sentence you have not got a speech. When you ask yourself what is the topic this does not mean what is the subject. It means what you are going to say about the subject.

Audience

13.28 Who are you trying to address? Who will be there? What is on their mind? What questions do they want answered? What do they already know?

Individual

13.29 This is hard to identify. It means that you are putting forward the best version of yourself.

Language and length

13.30 Keep it simple and clear. Avoid jargon and in-jokes. Choosing the right words and tone becomes much easier once you have worked out the structure of your speech.

Short speeches are better than long ones. You want people to have enough energy and attention left to ask questions once you have finished. Be very clear how long your speech will last. Between five and ten minutes is plenty if you want to stimulate lots of discussion.

Never make it more than 20 minutes. People's attention just wanders.

Finally remember the mantra: Stand up. Speak up. Shut up.

Getting gigs

13.31 Prepare three speeches. They can all be on the same topic. They should be different lengths 5, 10 or 20 minutes.

Ask the organisers if they would like you to give a speech. You can offer a 5-minute filler or a 20-minute main speech. You may of course be invited to speak, just as you may be invited to mediate. All you have to do is wait. But you can end up waiting a long time before anything happens. If you are trying to build a mediation practice you probably cannot afford to wait forever.

If you attend conferences or seminars mingle with other speakers and find out how they were invited. Talk to the organisers and let them know that you are ready, willing and able to give a speech or a presentation. Although you will not be given a star spot there is always the graveyard shift just after lunch to fill.

Seminars and workshops

13.32 These are a particular variety of talk. The three things to consider are:

Do you produce a handout/notes for the audience to take away?

13.33 Handouts which people can collect on the way out are useful. If you tell the audience that there will be one it saves them from writing notes while they are listening to you. You have more chance of catching their eye and interacting.

A handout is also some promotional material which, you never know, might keep you on their radar for a little longer.

Are you going to use PowerPoint?

13.34 Be careful with PowerPoint. Philip Collins advises in his book

> 'I don't ever use slides when I speak and I strongly encourage anyone I write for to ditch them too. They are usually a crutch, but a crutch that helps you to fall over.'

13.35 *Making a noise*

Remember the wise words of Daniel Pink in his book about selling. And after all you are selling when you are giving a seminar or workshop.

> 'PowerPoint is like the weather or reality TV: Everybody complains about it, but nobody does anything about it. No matter where we work, we must endure the blathering of people who anaesthetise us with bullet points and then, in the dark of a conference room, steal our souls and take them into 3-D pie charts.'

Are you interactive?

13.35 Do you want to give a speech or have a conversation with the audience?

It is a matter of style. You can just invite questions as you go along. Or you can actually ask the audience questions. Who thinks that mediation should be evaluative? You can point somebody out and ask 'do you agree with that?'

You might develop a taste for it. Some people just like performing. They love the adrenaline and the applause. Others hate it. They don't do it. Yet they still manage to develop sustainable mediation practices.

But the key question to ask yourself is: is it helping me to promote my business? Speaking to an audience of 20 or even 200 people is one thing. Speaking on the Internet through blogs and LinkedIn and Twitter to hundreds of thousands is another.

There is no doubt that there are mediators who have developed their practice through assiduously giving seminars and talks. They have impressed people with their expertise, usually sector expertise rather than their skill as a mediator, and have received appointments.

Advertising/advertorials

13.36 Some mediators hate to advertise. Others, if they do advertise at all, do it online. They buy a banner advert. Some well-known mediators do it and clearly they think it is worth it otherwise they would not spend their money.

13.37 Others have tried traditional print media. One mediator bought a three-page advertisement in his local paper (outside London). It cost him £120 a month for a prominent position and a photograph. He never knew whether or not it brought him a single enquiry, let alone an appointment. He suspected that it didn't but thinks that he might have received one appointment from a firm of solicitors that he knew because they had learned that he was a mediator by seeing his name in the paper.

Warning: when you ask what the advertising rates are you will be quoted prices from the rate card. Regard the rate card is something to use as a trampoline. The idea is to bounce as far away from it as possible. No advertising executive on a newspaper ever expects to sell any advert off the rate card. They have a wide discretion to do deals and offers in order to secure advertisements.

Making a noise **13.40**

You can start by saying that this is your first time and they will give you a special offer for new advertisers. You can use your negotiating skills which you brushed up when reading **Chapter 1**.

Advertorials are a hybrid between paid ads and blogs or articles. Several mediators have reported that local newspapers and magazines are very keen on content, which is advertorial. All you need to do is contact them, find out what their publishing schedule is, ie when any copy is due, but also more importantly what features or special issues they are planning.

It takes some self-confidence to do this if you've never done it before. But so does being a mediator. Go for it – the worst that can happen is that they say no.

Work out an angle that brings in mediation. Just reading the local newspaper shows that there are lots of disputes and conflicts. That means there is a place for a mediator who can at least explain how mediation can help resolve disputes and conflicts.

Newsletters

13.38 Gurus tell us to send them out. How many people read them? If you are sending them by email, remember para **10.24** – people don't read onscreen, they scan.

A screen-based newsletter is not the same as the traditional four-page hard copy format. Re-read para **13.06** on blogs. Follow those ground rules and you will not go far wrong.

As an alternative consider punchy short update emails such as the one that Charles Powell, a highly successful solicitor mediator sends out each month (see charles.powell@freeths.co.uk).

Podcasts

13.39 More and more people are using podcasts to keep up to date or to learn about new subjects. They are another distribution channel for your brand.

There are two basic types of podcasts: those that you make yourself and those that are made for you by somebody else.

Making your own podcasts

13.40 If you want to make your own podcasts you will need to spend a lot of time learning how to do it. There are very useful websites that will help you, eg wikihow.com/start-your-own-podcast or blogs by Joe Donovan, eg one called 'How to make a successful podcast' in July 2014 (digitaltrends.com/how-to/how-to-make-apodcast/).

13.41 *Making a noise*

An alternative is to approach a company that makes them. They will either make them for you to upload onto your website or onto YouTube or they will ask you to record a podcast for them.

Making podcasts for a publisher

13.41 This is a variation on vanity publishing. You do not usually get paid but you will be given a year's free access to their other podcasts. One company that does this very well is CPDcast (www.cpdcast.com).

Approach them with an idea. If they like it they will book a date in the studio in Fleet Street London. They usually take the form of questions and answers. The interviewer asks you a series of pre-planned questions and you answer them from your speaking notes.

You usually do it for an hour or two at a time. You have to learn to speak clearly but the interviewer and the sound engineer are understanding and helpful.

Making a podcast is literally making a noise and it might raise your profile and get you on somebody's radar.

In a nutshell

13.42

Make a noise.

- You can do it quietly through blogs, books and tweets.
- You can it loudly through conferences, seminars, panels.
- Making a noise is tiring and time consuming. You need the hours and the energy.

Chapter 14

Who can help you?

> In this chapter you will learn about:
> - Mentors.
> - Coaches.
> - Support groups.
> - Co-mediation.
> - References.
> - Referrals.
> - Returns.

Mentors

14.01 Many successful people pay tribute to their mentors.

A mentor is not the same as a role model, coach, inspirational teacher, good friend or confidant. A mentor is someone who can help your career. Someone who can help you achieve what you want to achieve because they have done it before themselves.

In a practical sense, what is mentoring for mediators? Mentoring a mediator who is a self-employed freelance running their own business is not the same as mentoring a junior member of staff in a large organisation and helping them to negotiate their way up the greasy pole.

What can mentors do for you?

14.02
- Provide guidance and possibly advice.
- Be a sounding board.
- Open doors.
- Share their knowledge and experience.

14.03 *Who can help you?*

Be a sounding board

14.03 Mentees often say that this the most useful service a mentor can supply. Many mediators trying to establish their businesses find it very helpful to be able to talk through things with a sympathetic, knowledgeable, critical listener.

Doing this helps you clarify your mind, prioritise your actions and road test your ideas. You will also find it reassuring to know that others have also encountered difficulties along the way and overcome them, or not.

Provide guidance and possibly advice

14.04 Mentors are told that:

- They should not impose their own agenda upon their mentees. They are there to guide rather than teach, to show rather than tell.

- They should listen to what the mentee has to say. Through active listening and intelligent enquiry they will draw out from the mentee what the real issues and problems are and how the mentee thinks they can solve them. If this all sounds to you very much like what mediators do anyway, you are correct. It is. (See para **14.07** on the essential qualities of a good mentor.)

- They may, depending on their temperaments and general view of life, give explicit advice. Generally they will prefer to elicit ideas and information from the mentee and nudge them in the right direction without being prescriptive.

Share knowledge and experience

14.05 Most mediators, by virtue of their temperament and their worldview, are prepared to help people. For mediator-mentors that is often why they became mediators in the first place. Some will happily and freely pass on tricks of the trade that they have developed over the years.

Others will regard them as trade secrets and will not share them. They will point you in the direction of generally available information that might not be known to you. But they will be chary of sharing individual information, which is based upon their own experience and acquired over many years. They will be especially chary if they think that their information gives them a competitive edge.

Open doors

14.06 An experienced mediator who has been practising for several years will simply have a wider range of contacts than the brand-new mediator. Some will not mind sharing their contacts with you. Others will be happy to go further and introduce you to other people with a view to promoting your business. Some will draw the line here. They do not mind giving a bit of general assistance but they are not going to actually help you become a new competitor.

10 things to look for in a mentor

14.07

- **Experience in mediation** – Mentors who have not acted as a mediator and developed their own practices are of limited value. They may now be retired, but at least in the past they have done it. There are lots of trainers, coaches, and personal development specialists who are able to provide motivational support. What you really looking for is a guide through the mediation jungle. Many of these trainers, coaches and personal development specialists have little current or even past mediation experience, which is why they are trainers, coaches and motivational specialists.

- **Confidentiality** – Some people are just better at keeping confidences than others. Some professions require confidentiality to be maintained, for example the legal and medical professions. It is second nature to them. Others merely expect it. Some people are gossips and careless. Some people like to boast. Be alert to these characteristics when talking to potential mentors.

- **Willingness to listen** – Successful experienced mediators should be good at listening. Active listening is a core competency in all mediation training. In fact all mediators do it every time they mediate.

- **Enthusiasm** – Energy and optimism are qualities which mediators are expected to bring to the mediation process. Successful mediators usually do this. Sometimes, unfortunately, mediators, like any other practitioners, become good at what they do and plateau. They start to run on autopilot. They may become blasé. A degree of worldly-wise cynicism from your mentor can be attractive and useful. An unrestricted diet of it will be demotivating.

- **Time** – The adage: 'If you want something done ask a busy person' does not really work with mentors. If their diary is crowded they will be rushed and find it difficult to commit to sessions whether face-to-face, online or over the telephone. Of course successful and busy mediators have to be good at time management. If you do have a mentor who is very busy, steel yourself for some last minute chopping and changing in the diary.

- **Commitment** – You do not want a mentor who is just going through the motions. Measuring commitment is difficult until you have started the process of mentoring. If your mentor habitually cancels appointments, sends emails while with you or rushes off, you know that commitment may not be their strong suit.

- **Curiosity** – Again this is difficult to gauge to start with. To succeed as a mediator you need above average emotional intelligence. If you have that you will pick up whether someone is curious about life from a general conversation with them.

- **Low ego** – Many mediation gurus and coaches emphasise the importance of humility. Being humble is often praised as a good quality in a mediator. Spending time in the company of mediators, especially successful ones, will disclose a surprising lack of humility when they are not mediating. If the mentoring sessions are all about the mentor and not you, find someone with a lower ego level. Listening to war stories as examples of what happens in mediations can be instructive. Listening to 'My Life And Times As The Greatest Mediator In The World' is not.

- **Good contacts** – Successful and experienced mediators are good at developing contacts. The question is whether or not they will be ready, willing and able to

14.08 *Who can help you?*

share them with you. Asking them outright at your first or second meeting will be difficult and is likely to lead to a premature termination of the mentoring relationship. But eventually you will have to ask. They may be reluctant. Do not be surprised if they are.

- **Openness** – Apart from experience and confidentiality this is probably the quality that you most want from a mentor. It is not so much an ability, or skill set as an approach to life. Do they share? Do they want to learn? Do they acknowledge the achievements of others?

The unicorn mentor

14.08 Unfortunately the mentor who has all these ten qualities is like a unicorn. They don't exist. If you are able to tick eight out of the ten boxes you will be doing extremely well. But at least this is a checklist of things to look for when trying to find a mentor.

Mediating, mentoring: aren't they really the same thing?

14.09 At para **11.01** we discussed how mediation skills transfer to marketing and selling skills. Here is another example of the transferability of mediation skills.

The Centre for Lifelong Learning at the University of Warwick lists on its website under the heading 'Mentoring Skills' the range of skills that you will need to employ when participating in a mentor/mentee discussion. There are ten of them.

- Active listening.
- Empathy.
- Paraphrasing.
- Helpful questioning.
- Summarising.
- Focusing.
- Challenging.
- Immediacy.
- Eliciting change talk.
- Balance of power.

Sounds familiar? Of course it does. Mediators are taught the skills in their basic training and practise them every time that they mediate.

Where do you find a mentor?

14.10 In **Chapter 3** we discussed observations. A good place to start looking for a mentor is to ask the mediators who took you along as an observer to their mediations. Hence the need to make a good impression at an observation (see para **3.37**).

Under the family mediator training scheme mediators usually have more opportunities of approaching their supervisor to act as a mentor. Under the family mediation training system, mediators have to appoint a PPC (Professional Practice Consultant) who meets with them at least four times a year. They:

- discuss individual mediations and review files.
- discuss how the mediator's practice is developing.
- under the new regime they will also attend and observe mediations.

The PPC is paid for their time by the mediator.

One very successful family mediator passes on smaller value and simpler mediations to the Mediators who have appointed her as their PPC

The old adage: 'Fish where the fish are' applies to mediators. Mingle with mediators.

You can find them at:

- Conferences
- Workshops
- Masterclasses
- Book launches
- Training sessions
- Lunches
- Breakfast groups
- Mediation competitions

You can find them on:

- Mediation panels
- LinkedIn
- Twitter
- Facebook
- Google
- YouTube
- Websites

You can find them in:

- Bookshops
- Magazines
- Blogs
- Directories

14.11 *Who can help you?*

Or you can find them by:

- Asking other mediators
- Asking people who have been to mediation
- Panels and trainers – some now offer mentoring

Action plan

14.11 Research:

- Contact the mediators who took you on your observations.
- Search LinkedIn for mediators.
- Look in *Chambers* or *Legal 500*.

Prepare:

- Make list of names.
- Investigate their backgrounds on their websites, profiles on mediator panels, LinkedIn, Facebook etc.
- See which ones have written books, articles or blogs.
- Go and listen to them. Read what they write. Mediators who write books, articles and blogs generally want to share their knowledge. They are probably above-average at communication and have some degree of standing and experience. This means that they will tick several of the boxes at para **14.07** above.

Implement:

This is the easiest part. All you have to do is ask. Do not be afraid of asking. Fundraisers will tell you that the main reason people do not make donations is that they are never asked.

What's the worst thing that can happen if you ask? They say no or they ignore you. Disappointing of course. Fatal? Not at all. Re-read para **4.67** on coping with rejection.

Go ahead

14.12

- Make a shortlist of the ones that you like the look of.
- Send them an email saying what you want to talk about and asking when it would be convenient for you to telephone them.
- Diarise when you send the emails. Follow up at appropriate intervals (see paras **12.11–12.13** on following up emails).

Remember, the adage 'Flattery gets you everywhere' also applies to mediators.

Make sure that you open the conversation by telling them how you came to hear of them. For example:

Who can help you? **14.14**

- 'I read your blog about venue selection ... and found it really interesting and helpful.'
- Or 'I saw your listing in Chambers and was impressed by what your client said about ....'
- Or best of all: 'I have bought your new book. I really like it. I think that it is excellent. I will be very grateful for the opportunity to discuss some of the issues that you raised for example... '

As Sunny Bates who makes a living as 'Connector, Entrepreneur, Ignitor of Ideas' says: 'I've never met a person, no matter how well known, who hasn't been flattered by an authentic compliment. Professional love letters work' (see her chapter on '*Networking in a connection economy*' in '*Maximise Your Potential*' by Jocelyn K Glei).

The process

14.13 You have to decide how formal you want the mentorship to be. Some mediation providers are setting up formal mentorship schemes. Formal arrangements will be put in place to regulate:

- Frequency and length of meetings
- Location of meetings
- Length of discussions and follow-up
- Confidentiality
- Method of communication outside meetings

In practice most mentors operate on a much more informal basis with their mentees. Contact, either in person or over the telephone, is more ad hoc. Sometimes people agree after one meeting to meet again in two or three months' time depending on what is required and the time and energy available.

One non-lawyer mediator who is trying to develop his practice meets every other month or so with an experienced commercial lawyer mediator to chat about things and to sample the excellent pies in The Windmill in Mayfair. They take it in turns to pay.

Another non-lawyer mediator contacts an experienced commercial lawyer mediator by email. They exchange views and information. Sometimes they develop the exchange over the telephone and from time to time they catch up with each other by having coffee or lunch.

Both these mediators met their mentors through attending conferences and mediation get-togethers.

In a nutshell

14.14 What you want from a mentor is:
- Active listening and constructive comment

14.15 *Who can help you?*

- Non-judgemental assessments and suggestions
- Introductions to people who can give you work

You will probably receive the first of these straightaway. The second should follow on from your initial meetings.

The third will take more time. In all walks of life when you make a recommendation or introduction you are to an extent staking your own reputation. Any mediator who values his own reputation, which all successful and experienced mediators do because that is what they trade on, will want to have formed a view about your capabilities and values before introducing you. This will not take as long as you fear. Successful mediators after all are good at quickly summing up and assessing people. It's a key skill that they practise every time that they mediate.

Coaching

14.15 Mediators who are parallelists (see **Chapter 4**) often include coaching in their portfolio of services. Coaching is not inherently very different from mentoring. In the context of mediation the key differences are:

- Coaching is more systematic and formal. Mentoring is usually more ad hoc and informal.
- There is more discussion on outcomes and recording next steps in coaching. Mentoring tends to be more open ended.
- Coaching is designed to make the client more accountable for what they say that they are going to do. Mentoring is more about leaving it with the mentee to take the next step and initiate the next contact.
- Most coaching costs money. Most mentoring is free apart from the occasional lunch or drink.

The perpetual motion machine: it exists

14.16 A business has developed of providing coaching to mediators on how to develop their practices as mediators. The coaches charge for sessions whether they are online or in person.

The increasing number of mediators who think that they need coaching because they cannot attract enough work fuels the growth of this industry. This has produced a wonderfully ironic three-stage process

1. Experienced mediators provide coaching to inexperienced mediators who cannot get enough work because there are too many mediators.
2. The same experienced mediators also train new mediators thus producing a fresh supply of inexperienced mediators to the market.
3. Finally they also continue to practise as mediators themselves, thus indirectly restricting the number of mediations available to the people that they have just trained or are in the process of coaching.

It is commercial nirvana: create the problem, sell the cure, make the problem worse, sell more of the cure.

Let it be remembered that many of those providing training and coaching to mediators are doing so to supplement their own income from doing mediations. Would they be doing this if they if there were as busy as they wanted to be mediating? So ask yourself whether this is a good investment of your time money and effort.

Support groups: other mediators

14.17 Mediators as a group tend to be people who get on with other people. They like to talk and ask questions, and are keen to help and learn. At the same time they practise a solitary activity. Most mediators work alone. Some will have mediation observers or assistants present. A few practise co-mediation. But most mediators when they are mediating are doing it by themselves.

Most mediators work on their own in the sense that they are not members of firms or chambers of other mediators. Some are but they are very few and many of the groupings are often in reality marketing organisations. Mediators do not often go into an office and/or chambers every day and discuss things with colleagues.

Even when mediators are able to discuss with fellow practitioners mediation generally or specific issues arising out of mediations there is the constraint of confidentiality. All mediators have to be careful when recounting war stories. Some are inevitably more careful than others.

A successful commercial mediator who has built an excellent practice since he left the Court of Appeal said recently at a gathering of mediators that he would really welcome the opportunity to discuss issues that arise at mediations.

A peculiar feature of the commercial mediation market is that, although other mediators are your competitors, they are also your suppliers. This is because the majority of commercial mediators are lawyers. Not only that; the vast majority of those lawyer mediators are doing mediation part-time. In other words they are still practising as lawyers. This means that they can supply you with work. Hence the need to network with other mediators.

To try and provide this sort of support various groups have been set up.

The Mediators' New Breakfast Club

14.18 This was set up in 2007 by Michael Cover, a barrister mediator. More recently two non-lawyer mediators, David Owen and David Richbell joined Michael in running it.

The aim was to provide a format where mediators (and others) could meet, receive the wisdom of mediators and others involved in mediation by way of an hour's talk by experienced mediators as well as giving fledgling mediators the chance to hear about ways of building their mediation practice.

14.19 *Who can help you?*

Meetings are held in central London usually on the second Wednesday of the month and a nominal charge is made to cover coffee/tea, fruit and pastries. There is no charge to become a member. Attendance counts as CPD for the purpose of the CMC requirements. The invitee list is coordinated by David Owen who will happily add people to it on receiving an email request. His email is dwo@pengaron.co.uk

The club now meets every six to eight weeks in the Punch Tavern in Fleet Street. Meetings start promptly at 8.30am and are over by 9.30am so people can be back at work by 10am. The format is that people arrive before 8 30am, put a £5 note in a mug on the bar, sign their names on the attendance sheet for their CPD points and help themselves to coffee and pastries.

While breakfasting they listen to talks, usually from experienced mediators, on a variety of topics. There is usually one speaker per session. Questions and answers follow. These always have to be cut short.

Many people stay on for a further 30–60 minutes to chat with the speaker or amongst themselves. Business cards are exchanged. Observations are fixed up. Connections are made. It is extremely successful.

David Owen has also organised several other subject groups to cover particular subject areas such as the Property Mediators Breakfast Club and the International Mediation Breakfast Club.

Mediators' Peer Group

14.19 The Mediators' Peer Group (MPG) was set up in 2014 by a small group of mediators who felt that there was not enough support for mediators, particularly 'fledgling' ones. Mediation can be a very lonely existence, particularly where mediators do not take assistants or observers with them.

The group meets every few weeks in central London and provides mediators with the chance to discuss difficult issues which they have faced. Other mediators are able to provide feedback if they have faced the same and similar problems and offer advice on how they tried to overcome them.

In addition discussions take place about how to build a mediation practice. The group is currently organised by Martha Clarke, Linda Davies, Irene Grindell, David Owen and Sheila Thorne. Again a nominal charge is made to cover coffee/tea, fruit and pastries.

David Owen coordinates the invitee list and is happy to add anyone the list are receiving an email request – dwo@pengaron.co.uk. Once you have been to the first event you can go on the mailing list and in the database and be informed automatically of new events and meetings.

Oxford Breakfast Club

14.20 A similar initiative has recently been set up in Oxford by Oxford Mediation who meet on the third Thursday of the month for mediators to meet and talk to each other. See www.oxford-mediation.com.

Clinics

14.21 This sort of mediation clinic is very popular at conferences as well.

- The Association of Northern Mediators, for example, holds mediators' clinics. See their website www.northernmediators.co.uk.

- Andrew Parsons a successful barrister mediator has run an annual clinic for the CIArb for the last seven years in the Winchester area.(ap@portsmouthbar.com).

- The Mediation Peer Group now hold clinic sessions. Attendees sit at tables of 5/6 and discuss problems, situations or issues that have arisen at mediations. People discuss how they would handle them.

Non-mediators also attend these meetings. There are various reasons for doing this:

- To find out what mediation and mediators are like.

- To test the water to see if they would like to become a mediator.

- To talent spot for mediators. A surprising number of barristers and practising solicitors do this. They do not necessarily advertise the fact that they keep their ears and eyes open and make notes.

Where to find them

14.22 Is easy to find out about these events. Go on the CMC website and look for their notices of upcoming events. They post regular 'Mediation Messenger' emails of both CMC and non-CMC events.

Making the most of them

14.23 If you go to any of these types of events the trick is to:

- make sure that you take enough business cards with you;

- engage in active listening and helpful enquiry; and

- go several times.

Many new mediators go once or twice and then give up. You have to commit to going to these types of things for at least one or two years. You will not be able to attend every meeting. But go when you can. Eventually you will get to know people and others will recognise you. Connections will be formed. It takes time and effort.

If you find it difficult to go into rooms full of strangers, make yourself feel at home and engage, you will find it difficult to be a mediator. You must ask yourself whether mediation is for you. As identified in **Chapter 12** mediators find themselves having to get on with a group of suspicious strangers when they turn up at a mediation.

14.24 *Who can help you?*

Co-mediation

14.24 Co-mediation is very popular amongst commentators, trainers and mediators. Outside of community mediation it is not popular amongst mediation customers.

The benefits seem to be obvious. With two mediators the customer can have:

- Gender and ethnic diversity
- Generalist and specialist skills
- Two sets of ears rather than one
- Twice the expertise
- More contact time and less downtime if the mediators see the parties individually and not always as a pair.

But customers do not appear to want it. Some reasons are:

- They are paying twice for the same thing. This is partly true but many mediators now offer two for the price of one. The customer does not pay more – instead each individual mediator is paid less.
- It's double the trouble: an extra set of papers has to be prepared. They may end up having two sets of conversations on the same topics.
- There is a risk of one of the mediators going native if the mediators see parties individually and not always as a pair. One party will see one of the mediators as their mediator in much the same way as you have party-appointed arbitrators.

Even if the customer wants co-mediation there are some practical issues.

Do you mediate only with people that you know well or on an ad hoc basis – as happens in community mediation. Would it be a true co-mediation in the sense of two equals mediating jointly? Or will it be more a case of a senior mediator and an assistant?

Do you mediate as a pair and see the parties together at all times or do you mediate individually? For an interesting discussion of these issues see the article by David Richbell and Jane Gunn in *The Resolver* May 2015.

The best advice is probably:

- Try co-mediation if you have the opportunity whether as a junior/assistant mediator or as equal.
- Find two or three other mediators and get to know them. If they share your general approach to mediation and life you will properly find it easier to co-mediate with them.
- Look for complimentary qualities such as experience, sector expertise or gender and background.
- Have it as part of your offering to the market so that if someone asks you to co-mediate you are ready, willing and able to do so.

Who can help you? **14.29**

References and recommendations

14.25 References and recommendations, together with referrals and returns are all gold dust. Once you start receiving them you have the foundations for a sustainable and viable mediation business.

What are they?

14.26 References are not the same as testimonials or emails and letters of thanks and gratitude. These are private expressions of satisfaction and praise. References are intended to be read by third parties. You can send them on to others or display them on your website.

How to get references

14.27 Some will arrive unsolicited. If you receive one you immediately thank the person who sent it. Ask if you can use it. In particular you want to know whether or not you can quote the sender and/or refer any enquirer to them.

Ask for a reference

14.28 As part of client care you will want to obtain feedback. There are various ways of doing this.

- If you are a member of a panel the mediation provider will have a system for obtaining feedback.
- If you are appointed directly, send your own feedback form or satisfaction questionnaire. If you receive a response follow it up with a request for a reference.
- If any of the parties tell you that they were impressed at the end of the mediation or send an email expressing their thanks and satisfaction, use this as a hook on which to hang a request for a reference or recommendation.

With these sorts of ad hoc case-by-case references or recommendations you are building up a portfolio of them.

You may decide to apply for inclusion on panels or in directories. See how to do this in **Chapter 9**. You will be asked to supply the names of references or recommendations and details of the mediations that you have done. That is when you send a specific request to the parties/ their representatives in your mediations.

LinkedIn

14.29 A popular alternative to sending a written reference or recommendation by email or letter is to post a reference, recommendation or endorsement on your LinkedIn page. Endorsements are nice to have but recommendations really are the glittering prize.

14.30 *Who can help you?*

As a mediator you may also receive requests for references or recommendations. These will usually come from:

- Barristers who have appeared at mediations with you and are applying for promotion to silk or judicial office. Familiarity and experience at mediation is one of the competencies that are expected.
- Barristers and solicitors who are applying for listings in the directories.
- Other mediators.

If you receive a request for a reference or recommendation, reply promptly and positively. But most importantly follow through and do give it. Make yourself available to any interviewers from the directories.

Be as generous and as specific as you can be within the bounds of good conscience and truthfulness.

Think in terms of sound bites and quotable phrases. Think about the sort of reference or recommendation you would like someone to give about you.

Remember that reciprocity is one of Robert Cialdini's Big Six (see **Chapter 11**). And reciprocity underpins references, recommendations, referrals and returns.

Using references and recommendations

14.30 Most mediators include extracts from references or endorsements that they have received on their websites. The big question is whether or not they should be anonymous or not.

Some people have very strong views about this. Stephen Ward for example is adamant that anonymous references or recommendations are worthless. He shares the common suspicion that everybody has about anonymous endorsements and references that are given on the Internet. Anybody can say anything. Nobody can be challenged or policed.

Others, while accepting that this may be true, say that mediation is different. Mediators and parties promise confidentiality towards each other. Mediators should do nothing at all that can identify the parties to a mediation without the parties' express consent. They feel happier with an anonymous description, for example.

- 'I was very impressed in the way that you were able to encourage the parties to bridge the final gap after such a long day of hard negotiation.' *Senior Chancery barrister.*
- 'My clients were delighted with the outcome. They were very suspicious of the whole process but you won their confidence and trust. I'll certainly think of you again in the future.' *Litigation partner in large Midlands firm in a Construction dispute.*

Some mediators make it clear on their websites that they are deliberately adopting a policy of anonymity in order to respect their duty of confidentiality. They provide an assurance that the references are all genuine and, subject to the party's consent, can be inspected if need be.

Supporting applications

14.31 When you apply for membership of a mediation panel, eg the IMI Accredited Mediator Panel or a directory such as *Chambers* or the *Legal 500* you will have to supply references.

You do not just give names of people that you have met while mediating. Write a personal email or letter to a specific person who you would like to supply you a reference. If they agree, they know that their reference will be submitted and that they may be contacted by a researcher to verify or amplify it.

Please understand that not everybody will give a reference. This may be because:

- they do not in fact rate you as highly as you rate yourself or as highly as you think they do;
- they may be miserable and cannot be bothered; or
- more likely they are just too busy and distracted with earning a living themselves.

Even if people say that they will give you a reference, they can be slow in doing it. You have to learn the art of diplomatic harassment.

Referrals

14.32 References and recommendations are good but referrals are even better. This is where somebody actually gives your name to a solicitor or client looking for a mediator.

Please bear in mind the following:

- People cannot give your name unless they know it. That is why it is important to raise your profile and be on as many people's radars as possible (see **Chapter 9**).
- When someone asks if you are available for a mediation, try to find out how they got your name. They may know and be happy to tell you. If they do always send an email to whoever recommended you to thank them.
- Do not be surprised if they do not know. Often junior members of staff who know nothing about the background of the case make enquiries about mediators' availability.

If you feel nervous about asking them at this stage before the job has been confirmed, wait and ask later. You can even do it at the mediation during one of the inevitable lulls or at the end of the day.

Quite often if you have been specifically recommended they will say so in their first email or telephone call.

You in turn may be asked the names of suitable mediators. Do not hold back. Share the names of people that you know. Always make sure that you tell them that you have put their name forward. If you have time, contact them in advance. But usually you have to do it as soon as you are asked.

It is the reciprocity principle again.

14.33 *Who can help you?*

Returns

14.33 Returns are cases which have been accepted by one mediator who at the last moment cannot do it and a replacement has to be found quickly. The term comes from barristers who are booked to appear in court at a hearing or trial. They may even have been paid their brief fee but for some reason they cannot appear and the brief is returned. Hence the phrase.

Returns are common in barristers' chambers. They are much less common amongst mediators. But they do happen. They are more likely to happen if you are a panel member. If the appointed mediator has to withdraw from the mediation the mediation provider will as part of their service find a replacement mediator for the parties. This is when you may be telephoned at very short notice to see if you can step in.

It is important that you make sure that the mediation administrators at your panel do know that you are flexible and ready to take on something at the drop of a hat. It is the A of PEARL: availability. Don't just be available. Make sure that they know you are available.

Occasionally mediators who receive direct bookings may be placed in difficulty. They may already be booked. They may be conflicted out. The case may be too small or the fee too low. All mediators have a list of friendly mediators to whom they can pass on a mediation.

Develop working relationships with some other mediators.

Reputation maintenance

14.34 As you receive endorsements, testimonials and references you need to update your website and your CV/profile to include them. There is no point having a file full of references and testimonials if only you know about them, but nobody else does. Don't boast and brag but do tell people.

Most of your communication comes in via email. Make sure that you systematically print out all your testimonials endorsements and references. Keep them in a separate file. Sometimes you will be asked to send hard copies or scans. You need to protect yourself against computer malfunction.

Remember the R of PEARL: reputation. As the user surveys show, reputation and professional standing are ranked as the first factor that commercial solicitors take into account when choosing a mediator (see **Chapter 6**). References, referrals and returns all build reputations.

Resilience

14.35 Steel yourself. Even when you have pages of glowing recommendations, a stream of referrals and returns there will be many occasions when you are not appointed. Your name has been put forward but they pick someone else.

Re-read para **4.67** about rejection. But what you have to understand is that when you are not selected it is not necessarily because there is anything wrong with you or your profile. It may simply be a display of reactive devaluation. One side automatically rejects the other side's suggestions of mediators. Or each side had their favourite and they ended up choosing a compromise candidate. It happens to everybody no matter how well established and successful you are.

Keep on keeping on.

In a nutshell

14.36

- Join support groups.
- Surf the Internet for mediation get-togethers.
- Turn up and join in.
- Find a mentor.
- Be careful about paying for mediation coaching.
- Ask for and give references.

Chapter 15

Online dispute resolution – ODR

> In this chapter you will learn:
> - What ODR is.
> - How it might change mediation practice.
> - Is it a threat or an opportunity for mediators?

What is Online Dispute Resolution ('ODR')?

15.01 ODR has at least one thing in common with mediation. No one has yet devised a universally accepted definition. There are multiple varieties and variants.

At one level ODR has a simple definition: any method other than face-to-face meeting which uses electronic communication to resolve disputes. By this definition using email or the telephone is ODR. But this is not what all the debate is about.

We can find guidance from two of the great men of ODR, Colin Rule and Ethan Katsh.

Colin Rule set up eBay's electronic dispute resolution system. He said in his 2015 interview on the Mediation Academy website that ODR, as supplied by his new company MODRIA has four elements:

- Problem diagnosis;
- TFN or technology facilitated negotiation;
- Mediation; and
- Evaluation.

Professor Ethan Katsh wrote, with Janet Rifkin, the first book on ODR, '*Online Dispute Resolution: Resolving Disputes in Cyberspace* (2001). His definition is: 'most basically, online dispute resolution is dispute resolution that is supported, facilitated, helped by the use of technology.'

This sounds anodyne but he has gone on to say that ICT is the fourth party in the room.

15.02 *Online dispute resolution – ODR*

Overloaded with acronyms

15.02 Anybody trying to make their way through the thickets of discussion in the blogosphere, twittersphere or just the real world needs to be familiar with the language.

ODR	online dispute resolution
ADR	alternative dispute resolution
ICT	information and communication technologies
TFN	technology facilitated negotiation
AN	automated negotiation
iDR	Internet dispute resolution
eDR	electronic dispute resolution
eADR	electronic ADR
oADR	online ADR
IRL	in real life
C2C	consumer to consumer
B2C	business to consumer
F2F	face to face
MODRIA	modular online dispute resolution implementation assistant
Singularity	the point when computers become more intelligent than human beings. The ETA is 2040.

Types of ODR

Telephone mediation

15.03 This is now well established. The Court Service runs schemes, usually using employed mediators. They offer an hour's free mediation conducted by telephone.

Some private mediation providers also offer telephone mediation. They are usually longer than an hour but rarely exceed three hours. The technology is pretty straightforward, using conference call facilities.

Anecdotally many users said that they were satisfied. They were in the small claims track of the county court. The dispute was resolved at no cost and little effort in the sense that they did not have to go anywhere. They could do it from the telephone at home or on the move.

Not everybody is satisfied with it. At one recent real-life mediation which involved a relatively small monetary claim for discrimination against a disabled person the claimant who was acting for themselves had rejected the suggestion of telephone mediation. They did not want to talk on the telephone. They wanted to meet somebody face-to-face and talk to them man-to-man.

Sometimes the use of the telephone is supplemented by email and Skype.

Users say that they work but not as well as a live face-to-face mediation. If the choice is not to mediate it all or to mediate using Skype then you use Skype.

Virtual rooms

15.04 Several mediation providers offer ODR using screen-based technology. The parties can use this if they have access to a computer, tablet or smartphone so can see and speak to each other.

In essence they are much like a conventional mediations. The differences are:

- The parties interact online.
- Documents are uploaded online.
- Documents are created electronically.

In some ways they are really computerised case management and document production systems.

The technology allows the mediator to speak to all the parties at the same time or privately with just one party at a time.

Algorithmic systems

15.05 These are the systems that Colin Rule and Ethan Katsh are talking about as changing the way in which disputes are settled online. The software captures the information and analyses it and takes a decision online. There is reduced human intervention.

At the moment it is used for example by eBay. Modria, one of the leading suppliers of software, has piloted a scheme with the Dutch Ministry of Justice for online divorce. They are going to trial a scheme in England and Wales with Resolve.

What is the ODR process?

Level One

15.06 ODR at its simplest level can be information management. Parties to the dispute log in online and enter their details about themselves, the nature of the dispute and details of their opponent.

In this way they are simply registering their desire to participate in a dispute resolution using this process. From that stage there can be human intervention in the sense that a mediator/arbitrator is appointed. Communications can be online or through emails. There is nothing new about this. Most communication both before and after traditional facilitative mediations is by email. Very little goes by snail mail these days.

15.07 *Online dispute resolution – ODR*

But the software can go further even in this first stage of what Colin Rule called problem diagnosis. Having collected the basic information the online system, such as Modria, analyses it. Through a series of Q & A's the software can:

- assign the dispute into a particular category of dispute;
- identify options for dealing with it;
- describe the dispute and the different resolution processes;
- give information about the steps involved in how long the process takes; and
- describe how other disputes of this sort have been resolved.

This stage is a triage system. It is not very different from what mediation providers do at the moment when they receive telephone calls and emails from disputants looking for a mediator.

Level Two

15.07 The next level of ODR is more sophisticated. This is what Colin Rule referred to as TFN (Technology Facilitated Negotiation). The technology is the medium for negotiation. There is no human intervention. This is the sense in which Ethan Katsh refers to technology as 'the fourth party in a dispute'. Technology is an independent input into the management of the dispute. So mediation instead of being a traditional three party process becomes a four party process.

This challenges mediation as it is currently practised. ODR enthusiasts predict that as technology advances the role of the fourth party will increase and that of the third party neutral (TPN) will decrease. We are now in the sphere of automated negotiation.

There are various techniques already being used. Examples include:

BLIND BIDDING

15.08 This is usually used where liability is not in dispute and the parties are trying to arrive at a settlement figure.

DOUBLE-BLIND BIDDING

15.09 There are two parties in a dispute. They agree to negotiate. Each side makes secret offers or bids. They are only disclosed if both offers match certain standards. Conventionally each participant submits up to three offers. If the bids of each party come within a predetermined range for example 5% to 30% or for a given amount of money for example £5,000 or £250 a deal is done at the midpoint.

What this system does is encourage the parties to reveal their bottom line offers and demands. By splitting the difference when the amounts are not far apart a deal is achieved.

VISUAL BLIND BIDDING

15.10 The difference between this and Double Blind Bidding is that in Visual Blind Bidding what is kept secret is what the parties are willing to accept.

There can be several parties. They agree to negotiate using the system. They exchange visible proposals. These are usually on the high side or optimistic. But this defines a range of bargaining.

The software generates suggestions that fall within the bargaining range. The parties can continue to exchange proposals if they want to. Or they can make a suggestion to alter the mix. These suggestions are anonymous. The perceived problem of people losing face by accepting a suggestion made by another disputant is avoided.

At the end of the negotiation session if all the parties accept one or more packages (or one or more proposed decision values) there is a resolution. The agreement is determined by the software using an algorithm that rewards the party that moves earliest into the Settlement Zone. This is seen to be less threatening than just splitting a difference.

Insurance companies, which are trying to settle thousands of small claims where there is no real dispute about liability, are enthusiastic supporters of this system.

Level Three

15.11 The third level of sophistication is TFN (Technology Facilitated Negotiation). This is really where the technology becomes the fourth party. Not only does it provide a certain process it can provide the parties with specific advice.

In particular it can carry out sophisticated risk or decision tree analysis. This helps the parties and their advisers to work through the possible permutations.

At this stage there is usually some human intervention. The parties have been through the first two stages. These are conducted entirely online. The second stage of automated negotiation has not worked. They can then if they wish move to the third stage where a mediator is appointed and now participates in their discussions.

The discussions are often carried on through the online medium either through email, Skype so that there can be real time interaction, or by telephone. As an alternative parties can elect to step out of the online process and attend an IRL (In Real LIfe) mediation.

Level Four

15.12 The fourth and final stage of sophistication is where the parties submit their dispute to adjudication by the software. There is no human intervention. The machine tells them what the outcome is.

The software predicts the outcome of the dispute based upon the collection of data on similar disputes that have either been settled in court or through negotiation online and comes up with an expected outcome. The parties can agree to be bound by this. Or they can simply accept it as a non-binding recommendation. This is in practice what evaluative mediators do anyway. The difference is a computer uses software to do it. A human being uses personal experience.

15.13 Online dispute resolution – ODR

What does it mean for mediators?

15.13 The first issue to understand is that when commentators refer to the line between ODR and ADR becoming blurred they do not mean mediation. They mean ADR. As Ethan Katsh said in his 2014 interview with Aled Davies:

> 'I think the field of ADR is coming to recognise that the future is ODR. Maybe that's a bit of an exaggeration, but I think it's inevitable that ODR technology becomes a part of all dispute resolution practice. It has to be. As I said several times, we have these machines that can do things that skilled arbitrators or mediators have to do.'

This sounds considerably less anodyne and in fact almost apocalyptic. But take heart. Professor Karsh is an expert. He is an authority, possibly even *the* authority on ODR. As Robert Cialdini warns: we always have ask ourselves 'How truthful can we expect the expert to be?' In other less provocative words how impartial can we expect any expert to be? (See *Influence Science & Practice*.)

Or as Winston Churchill put it 'Where you stand depends on where you sit.' And Professor Katsh has sat in the ODR chair for the best part of 20 years or more.

ODR in the sense in which Professor Katsh uses the phrase includes adjudication and arbitration. As highlighted in **Chapter 1** the demand for ODR is growing but that does not mean that the demand for mediation is growing commensurately. In fact some think that the growth of ODR will reduce the demand for mediation. That is mediation in the sense of the traditional facilitative model.

The traditional definition which has been referred to namely: 'mediation is a voluntary and confidential process where the parties to the dispute invite a third-party neutral to help them find their own settlement' does not easily accommodate ODR.

So is it a threat or an opportunity?

Advantages of ODR

15.14 Supporters of ODR say that it is:

- *Cheaper*. The fees charged by ODR companies are less than those charged by mediation providers who do face-to-face mediations.
- *More convenient*. People do not have to travel which also saves money. They continue to work from their office or home and log in and out of the online mediation process.
- *More flexible*. People do not have to stay in an office all day just to be at a mediation. The mediation is spread over time. People can participate by email, messaging etc as and when they choose. And there is 24/7 access to the process.
- *Able to provide greater accountability*. One of the problems with conventional mediation is confidentiality. This means that it is difficult to assess how mediators performed and what they did.

- *Able to open up more markets.* Mediators can be situated anywhere in the world and so can the parties. This makes cross-border mediation so much easier. Both the market for the supply of mediators and for the type of mediations is wide open.

- *Able to work with less infrastructure.* This again is a saving on capital costs such as court buildings or mediation suites.

- *Able to provide access to justice for people with claims which are too low in value to justify them incurring conventional legal/mediation costs in pursuing.*

- *Able to remove geographical barriers.* Someone had purchased a pair of trainers in Milan might find it too difficult to sue the manufacture in Slovakia. Not with ODR.

ODR is here

15.15 ODR is described as the next big thing. There are good reasons for this:

- Professor Richard Susskind one of the leading legal futurologists and his committee have produced their Report to the Civil Justice Council on Online Dispute Resolution for Low Value Civil Claims (see htttp://www.judiciary.gov.uk/reviews/on-line-dispute-resolution.

- The Alternative Dispute Resolution for Consumer Disputes (Competent Authorities and Information) Regulations 215/542 are now in force.

- The Alternative Dispute Resolution for Consumer Disputes 2016. This gives effect to the Alternative Dispute Resolution (ADR) Directive.

   What all this means in a nutshell is that traders must provide in their contracts an alternative to consumers for resolving disputes other than litigation through courts. They must also maintain a list of ADR entities who can provide alternative dispute resolution.

- The large retailers are setting up arrangements. Some are outsourcing and some are setting them up in-house. Suppliers of online dispute resolution software such as which Modria and Youstice are busy.

   What this in reality means is that all consumer-trader (C2B) disputes are being shifted towards what is in effect an expanded national ombudsman service. This will largely be paid for by business. In much the same way the Civil Aviation Authority is switching its passenger complaints function to an external ADR system funded by the airlines. So there is a shift towards non-court based resolution. This is ADR.

The question is whether or not it is mediation. In fact it is more likely to be more like adjudication, arbitration or the work of an ombudsman. That is where a decision is taken. An outcome is guaranteed. In **Chapter 8** we investigated why mediation is a hard sell. One of the reasons is that potential users realise that there is no guaranteed outcome.

New approaches are being developed to fill that gap.

15.16 *Online dispute resolution – ODR*

Mediation trainers

15.16 As in mediation, trainers are providing specialised courses in ODR. Most these courses are in fact taught online with some tutors for example being in Hawaii and Chicago and the students may be in London.

They report that most of the people applying for training are non-lawyers. They come from an increasingly diverse background of occupations and ages. More young people are applying for the courses.

Anecdotal evidence suggests that the take-up for actual mediation work as opposed to training is low. Mediation providers are expecting this to all change as the new regulations come into force and have practical application.

The Susskind Future

15.17 The Susskind Report to the Civil Justice Council recommended that a non-criminal dispute court for claims of less than £25,000 should be set up. This would be a new Internet-based court service known as HM Online Court.

This was not a surprise. Perhaps Rolf Dobelli sums up the dilemma best when he says:

> 'If you take your problem to an expert don't expect the overall best solution. Expect an approach that can be solved with the expert's tool kit.'

(See his book *The Art of Thinking Clearly* 2013.)

A three tier process is proposed.

Tier 1 is a classic problem diagnosis. It classifies and categorises the dispute and tells the disputants of their rights and obligations and helps them understand their options and remedies.

Tier 2 is more interesting. This provides online facilitators who will review papers and information provided by the parties and help them through mediation and negotiation. There will be teleconferencing facilities.

The key point is there will be no automated negotiation as described above which provides processes where parties can resolve their dispute without human intervention such as blind bidding.

Tier 3 will provide online judges. These will be full- and part-time members of the judiciary. They will decide cases in whole or in part on the basis of the papers submitted electronically. These will be part of a structured process of online pleading. If necessary this can be supplemented by telephone conference facilities.

What's in it for mediators?

15.18 The report, perhaps optimistically, suggests conducting a pilot with an anticipated full roll-out in 2017.

It is only the first two tiers that are of interest to facilitators who are also mediators.

Paragraph 7.7 of the report is in some ways the most interesting paragraph for the mediation community. It says that it is anticipated 'the facilitator will tend to be more inquisitorial, participative, and advisory than the current mediators' '. In other words far more evaluative than facilitative and far more like conciliation than mediation. See para **2.48**.

Apart from software suppliers, mediation trainers and futurologists how much support is there for this sort of development? Of course the Ministry of Justice is interested in anything that can cut court costs.

The Russian pencil?

15.19 During the Space Race when Russia and the USA were competing for status by launching manned spacecraft they had a problem. Gravity made it difficult for astronauts to write upside down with a pen. So the Americans spent untold dollars on developing new writing equipment to do this. The Russians used a pencil.

The history of government-sponsored IT initiatives has been less than impressive, whether in the legal sector or elsewhere. Why does anybody think that an online HMOC (Her Majesty's Online Court) would be more successfully launched? The acronym ADR stands for many things. It can mean Alarming Dose of Reality.

Some commentators have expressed caution if not doubt about the proposal. For example Professor Christopher Hodges who is Professor of Justice Systems at Oxford has asked how much HMOC would be used. He points out that the numbers of cases in the current small claims system has shrunk from 60,000 in 2001 to 25,000 in 2015. In 2014 500,000 disputes were dealt with by the Ombudsman System (see his article in the *Law Society Gazette* 20 April 2015).

Personal injury claims which are at the moment in a special category of small claim with a limit of £1000 instead of £25,000 are to be part of a new compensation scheme which will largely make clinical negligence litigation extinct.

It is a basic premise of ODR and especially the MODRIA type system that there is a high volume of small value claims. The eBay disputes system is a classic example. There will be other areas of activity where there are many small value claims but how many of these are actually going through the English court system at the moment. Is HMOC an idea whose time has passed before it was born?

Is IT in fact a big expensive solution for a small and reducing problem?

There will be developments. It will be fun to watch them.

Will ODR bring mediators work?

15.20 The supporters of the algorithmic schemes have not produced any evidence to say that their greater use is increasing the amount of work available

15.21 *Online dispute resolution – ODR*

to mediators. In fact they claim that about 90% of disputes are settled without any human intervention at all.

These disputes tend to be low value. But there is a huge volume of them. The market assumes that between 1-3% of all online transactions will produce a dispute.

The providers of telephone and virtual room mediations regard the market as essentially being a stopgap before proceedings are issued in the Small Claims Court. Lawyers are often not involved. Instead enquiries for mediations come from trading standard officers or Citizen Advice Bureaux on behalf of the kinds of people who cannot afford a lawyer.

They think that the consumer regulation will be a game changer. Schemes will be set up by retailers to provide ADR. Mediation will be one of the ADR services provided. The cost will be low.

For scheme mediations, providers are expecting to eventually employ mediators themselves to provide the service in-house rather than use panels.

For the non-scheme mediations, if the volume picks up it might be profitable for mediators. They will not make a lot of money. It only really makes sense for them if they can do several in a day.

Will it make money for mediators?

15.21 The market is trying to find the price point which is going to make sense to customers, themselves and mediators. At the moment there are some anomalies. Nearly all the providers have now introduced a fixed fee time-limited scheme for lower value mediations. This is partly to meet demand created by the increase in court fees but also to provide work for novice mediators (see **Chapter 9**). Most of them are under £10,000 and are to do with complaints about cars.

At the moment with non-scheme online mediations the going rate seems to be that for a dispute with a value of less than £3,000 a mediator would be paid £100 plus VAT. The customer would be charged under £50 plus VAT.

For disputes between £3,000 and £10,000 the customer pays £600 plus VAT and the mediator receives £500. That includes preparation. There is no overtime. It is up to the mediator whether he allows the mediation to continue after three hours but he does not get paid for any more work that he does.

This can produce anomalies. A mediator is paid £500 for a three-hour mediation for a dispute between £3,000 and £10,000. For a live mediation of the same value he will be paid £665 out of the £1000 charged to the customer. So it is more profitable for a mediator to do the 3 hour £500 ODR mediation. It will not be long before the prices are re-aligned.

At least one mediator who attended one of the first ODR specialised training courses has decided that there is more money to be made in selling ODR software then in doing mediations and that is what he is now doing.

Another mediator who attended the same course did one ODR mediation in eight months. He was paid £500 for three hours' work. He does not complain about the rate of pay. If he did two a day every day it that would be the equivalent of £20,000 a month.

But at the moment that is not what is happening. In fact he is worried that having done the training several months ago he is becoming de-skilled in the technology.

Some mediators are pressing ahead with ODR eg. Small Claims Mediation (UK) Ltd offer a telephone mediation service

15.22 Others tried and gave up. For example, Consensus Mediation based in Manchester ran a service called E-mediator for disputes of under £15,000. They now run traditional face-to-face mediations.

Leaving aside the philosophical and moral implications of the security of IT systems and big data algorithms making decisions on people's disputes, what practical effect does all this have for the practitioners of mediation?

In practice if you want to be able to tell people that you conduct online mediation you will have a commercial edge if you can say that you have received specialised training.

You probably also need to join a panel that provides online mediation. In this way you will have access to the software and be covered by their insurance. If you're going to offer online mediation direct you will have two either buy or pay to licence the software.

What do mediators have to do?

Training

15.23 The trainers say that they are providing essential training. The going rate seems to be about £700 plus VAT for a 12-hour course. This is spread over several sessions and is conducted online. There is some live tuition but it is given online in much the same way as a webinar. About half the time is spent on learning how to use the technology. The rest is spent on training mediators how to use new techniques to deal with people online rather than face-to-face in person.

Some mediators who have experience of both online and face-to-face mediation think that the differences are exaggerated. Of course there are the obvious ones such as:

- It takes longer to establish rapport simply because you are not physically present. You cannot shake hands or offer people a cup of tea.
- You cannot use body language in the same way or to the same extent even if you can see the people.
- You are not bouncing in and out of the room energising them in the same way.
- You cannot police who is present. This can give concerns about confidentiality.
- The production of the document recording the settlement still causes problems. Digital signatures are not really used. Ideally the parties should have a printer so

15.24 *Online dispute resolution – ODR*

they can print out the second agreement, sign it and scan it back. The standard provisions in mediation agreements about there being no legally binding agreement until all parties have signed a document incorporating the terms of the settlement may have to be amended.

Some are taking a longer view. The market for online mediation or dispute resolution is not what is happening now, it is what is going to be happening in five or ten years' time. Take the example of divorce. Generations are now growing up who have lived and are living their lives online. They communicate online and they date online. So divorcing online is a natural conclusion.

Five impacts

15.24 How is ODR likely to influence the mediation scene over the next one–three years?

1 To have mediation credibility you will need to be familiar with ODR. You will need to show that you have received specialist training.
2 Mediation using the facilitative model that has been practised and sold for the last 25 years needs updating.
    - The gap between the therapists and the problem solvers, which has been papered over, will become much more obvious.
    - The trend for money claims, which are what most civil and commercial mediations and certainly most consumer disputes are about, is towards a more proactive approach by the mediator.
    - As Susskind's report summarises, the requirement is for mediators to be more inquisitorial and participative.
    - Perhaps after all the evaluative mediators will win the day over the facilitative and transformative colleagues. There is already plenty of evidence of a preference amongst commercial clients for a more evaluative approach.
3 Over the next five years there will be jobs for mediators.
    - Those who are also prepared to be evaluative or be more like ombudsmen will have greater opportunities.
    - Some of these will be in-house as large retailers set up their in-house facilities for providing ADR to meet their obligations under the EU directive. Some and perhaps a greater number will be provided by outside suppliers.
    - There will be more employed mediators.
4 Fees will continue to fall.
    - The difficulty for the business model is going to be the fact that the disputes are low value.
    - That means low ticket, which means low fees and wages.
    - Already we have discussed the downward trend in mediation fees (see paras **2.37–2.29**).
    - This reflects the commoditisation of mediation.

5   Civil and commercial mediators will need to be trained in a wider range of techniques and approaches and be prepared to offer them.

- Technology can provide help in all sorts of ways. You just have to look at the way for example we book hotels, reserve restaurants and run law offices to see that. Telephone mediation has had success. It may expand.
- Skype is routinely used in face-to-face mediations. There are reservations about it. It is only a substitute for having the participant physically present but it can be better than having them absolutely absent from the process.

There are different skills and techniques that a competent mediator has to master. This may not be the Ethan Katsh vision of ODR but it is still ODR. There is no point in being squeamish about the doctrinal purity of mediation if you want to make money in your business as a mediator.

In a nutshell

15.25

- Learn how to conduct ODR
- Treat ODR as a threat and an opportunity.
- ODR will not make mediators lots of money.
- ODR will provide low-paid jobs for in-house and free-lance mediators

Chapter 16

Money

> In this chapter you will learn:
> - How to fix your fees.
> - When you will break even.
> - When to cut your fees.
> - When to charge more.
> - When to give credit.

What should you charge?

16.01 Start with your business plan. If you have read this far in the book without having done your business plan please go back to **Chapter 7** and complete it.

Your business plan will tell you:

- What your expenses will be.
- How long you can cover those expenses without receiving any income.
- What you want to earn in a year.
- How many mediations you can do in a year.
- What your cash flow requirements are.

Cash flow

16.02 Typically your expenses exceed your income in the early days. Do not become despondent if you find that your expenses still exceed your income at the end of 24 months.

Take a look the template business plan and cash flow forecasts at **Figures 17** and **19** in **Chapter 7**. Compare them with the worked example below in **Figure 30**.

16.02 *Money*

3 Year Income & Expenditure Account (forecast)

	Year 1	Year 2	Year 3	Year 4
Receipts				
	£2,500.00	£5,000.00	£12,000.00	
Expenditure				
Training Initial	£3,600.00	nil	nil	
CPD	£240.00	£240.00	£240.00	
Stationery				
Business Cards	£250.00	nil	nil	
Postage	nil	£5.00	£25.00	
Books	£150.00	£25.00	£25.00	
Fees				
CMC	£150.00	£150.00	£150.00	
Panel	£750.00	£750.00	£750.00	
Subs				
Linkedin	£200.00	£200.00	£200.00	
Insurance	£150.00	£150.00	£150.00	
Hotel	£150.00	£150.00	£450.00	
Travel	£250.00	£250.00	£400.00	
Food/ Drink	£750.00	£650.00	£850.00	
Conferences	£500.00	£500.00	£500.00	
Room Hire	£300.00	£300.00	£400.00	
Mobile	£360.00	£360.00	£360.00	
Broadband	£360.00	£360.00	£360.00	
Laptop/ iPad	£1,540.00	nil	nil	
Sundries	£400.00	£10.00	£140.00	
	£10,000.00	£4,000.00	£5,000.00	
Balance a-b	-£7,500.00	-£1,000.00	£7,000.00	
Running Balance	-£7,500.00	-£6,500.00	£500.00	

270

3 Year Income & Expenditure Account (forecast)

	Year 1	Year 2	Year 3	Year 4
Receipts				
Expenditure				
Training Initial				
CPD				
Stationery				
Business Cards				
Postage				
Books				
Fees				
CMC				
Panel				
Subs				
Linkedin				
Insurance				
Hotel				
Travel				
Food/ Drink				
Conferences				
Room Hire				
Mobile				
Broadband				
Laptop/ iPad				
Sundries				
Balance a-b				
Running Balance				

Figure 30

16.03 Money

First year

16.03 The sum shown for total expenditure in the first 12 months totals £10,000 (**Figure 30**).

Assuming that you will only do two paying mediations in this year, you would need to charge £5,000 per mediation to cover this expenditure. For the vast majority of mediators this is fantasy.

Let us assume that, more realistically, you did two mediations each paying £1,250. You are therefore out of pocket by £7,500, ie £10,000–£2,500.

The first 12 months are always likely to be the ones with the heaviest expenditure. This is when you complete your initial training, which will cost anything between £2,000 and £5,000. You could spread the cost, for accountancy purposes, over the first 36 months. But in cash terms that is how much you will be out of pocket.

Second year

16.04 In the second 12 months your annual expenditure will drop. In the example in **Figure 30** it has dropped to £4,000. If you do four mediations at £1,250 each you will now have made a profit in the second 12 months of £1,000, ie £5,000–£4000. Your cumulative loss is now £6,500, ie (£7,500) + £1,000 = (£6,500).

Third year

16.05 Let us assume that in the third year you do eight mediations at £1,500 each. You are more experienced now and charge a higher rate. You will be earning £12,000. If your expenditures increases to £5,000 because you are now busier you are now £7,000 in profit. You are at break-even point with your accumulated loss now transformed in to a small surplus of £500.

Eureka!

In the fourth year on these assumptions you start to make a consistent profit. You have discovered the secret of making money doing mediations.

Of course in practice the assumptions become actual and you can see how, historically, you are doing and how robust your assumptions are. That is why it is essential to record both your budget and actual expenditure and income.

How long can you wait?

16.06 If you are not relying on mediation to pay your bills and you have other sources of income, you can withstand this delay. This is your initial investment in your new business project. By answering the question asked at para **4.63** about how much time money and energy you had to invest in the project you will know whether or not you can afford it.

Money **16.06**

When deciding what to charge, you have to take into account your answers to the following questions:

- When do you have to start making a profit?
- How much profit do you have to make each year?
- What is your expected annual expenditure?
- How many mediations do you expect to do in a year?

When you divide your expenditure by the number of mediations, what is the answer?

That is your average charge per mediation that you need to make in order to make a profit. This is not the same as the fee that you will actually charge. Other factors influence what you charge:

- Do you have a flat fee for a day's work irrespective of the size or complexity of the matter?
- Do you charge the same irrespective of the number of parties involved?
- Does your daily rate include preparation and travel costs and time?
- What is the going rate? Is there an average or market rate that other mediators like you are charging?
- Can you set your own rate or are you part of a panel, appointing body or mediation provider that has its own scale and rates?

Here is some guidance. Remember the latest earnings figures from the CEDR survey (see **Chapter 2**).

- £1,422 was the average fee per commercial mediation charged by less experienced mediators (ie those doing less than ten mediations a year).
- £15,000 is the average annual income for less experienced mediators.
- Most mediators do fewer than ten mediations a year.
- £70,000 is the average annual income for mediators doing 20–30 mediations a year.

To put that in perspective, consider average annual salaries for different professions.

Lawyers

1   In April 2015 a salary benchmarking survey of 400 lawyers carried out by Emolument reported that

Years PQE	Annual salary
0–5 years	£54,000
05–10 years	£76,000
10–15 years	£100,000
15+ years	£181,000

16.07 *Money*

3   The Annual Survey of Hours Earnings compiled by the Office for National Statistics for 2014 shows a different picture.

- The overall average salary of the estimated 21,563,000 people included in the survey was £27,271.
- The average salary for legal professionals was £73,425 and for solicitors £46,576 (based on a sample of 104,000 people).

Non-lawyers

Actuaries /economists/ statisticians	£61,749
Human resource managers/ directors	£56,215
Purchasing managers and directors	£52,083
Sales accounts/ business development managers	£51,576
IT specialist managers	£49,094
IT project / program managers	£48,044
Business, financial/ project manager professionals	£47,095
Management consultants/business analysts	£43,820
Architects	£43,303
Engineering professionals	£41,453
Quantity surveyors	£41,066
Chartered and certificated accountants	£38,692

As a relatively newly-qualified mediator (two years) and former Head of Real Estate Litigation in a large City law firm said: 'You don't go into mediation to make City money. But then you don't have to work City hours.'

It will probably take you about five years before you are doing 20–30 mediations a year.

There are mediators making far more than £70,000 year. The highest earners are making six or seven times that amount. But there are not many of them, as we discussed in **Chapter 2.** This is not to say that you cannot become one of them.

Sell 'em cheap and pile 'em high

16.07 According to Stephen Ward there is plenty of work about for mediators. He told the 2014 Civil Mediation Council Annual Conference in Leeds that 'if you want to be busy be cheap'.

The received wisdom amongst mediation providers is that you cannot charge the same rate for an inexperienced mediator as you can for an experienced mediator. The 2014 CEDR Survey seems to bear this out. There is also plenty of anecdotal evidence of mediators who now command £5,000 a day or more but who, when they started, having recently retired as judges or silks, would go anywhere in the country for £500 a day.

Others point out the dangers of undercutting. You become too cheap and find it difficult to increase your fees as you become more experienced. By offering a low fee you are devaluing yourself and your service. You will become locked into a cycle of low-value low-priced mediations.

Charging low fees does not always work. One non-lawyer mediator, commercially orientated, even offered his barrister contacts to do mediation for no charge at all. He just wanted to obtain experience. The barristers were not interested

Charge more/premium pricing

16.08 If you want to sell yourself at a premium you will not want to lower your charges. You want to be seen as the expert. This expertise can be because of:

- your previous experience in mediation relevant activities, eg as an ambassador or Court of Appeal judge; or
- personal prestige – a former Prime Minister for example who was paid a handsome seven-figure sum for a short but successful mediation.

A recently qualified mediator wants to attract work. She is a former High Court Judge with a high profile in chairing Inquiries. She joined a well-established barristers' chambers, which has an acknowledged specialism in arbitration and are adding mediation to their offering. Although she has no actual mediation experience, her charges are comparatively high to reflect her desire to be seen as an expert offering a premium service. Also the chambers have their own charging structure that they want to maintain.

Be like Stella Artois – reassuringly expensive

16.09 Some people like to hire reassuringly expensive mediators. Some representatives do not want the mediator's fees to be so low as to cast their own charges into an unfavourable light by comparison. This is why some mediators do not publish their rates online. They prefer to negotiate on a case-by-case basis.

How much to ask for

16.10 If you are negotiating a mediation fee ask what the budget is. This is a standard tactic of all salesmen whether selling mediation services, used cars or Eastern carpets. Ask the purchaser what they want to pay before you say what you are prepared to accept.

In practice you will lose more work because your fees are too high than because they are too low.

Much depends on where you are on the Mediation Timeline. If you are starting out and are still trying to complete your first ten mediations, you are in your apprenticeship. You are still in training. There is nothing wrong with charging lower fees for being an apprentice than for being an experienced practitioner. More and more mediation providers recognise this and offer a low cost panel of relatively inexperienced mediators for lower value disputes.

16.11 *Money*

Falling fees

16.11 The fall in fees was identified in **Chapter 1** as one of the current mediation themes (see the CEDR Survey in **Chapter 2**). Generally in the UK over the last five years or so there has been downward pressure on mediation fees. The oversupply of mediators and the effects of the financial crash of 2008 are the two main causes.

In addition to lower headline fees there have been hidden reductions. More mediators are charging a flat fee for the day. They do not charge extra for travel and preparation. Some even charge a flat fee for the whole mediation and do not charge any extra if the mediation overruns the stipulated time.

Most mediators and providers still calculate their charges according to the value of the dispute. Higher value disputes tend to have more parties involved, to require more preparation and generally to be more complex. But this is not always so by any means.

Customer resistance to large bills for preparation is now being encountered. For mediators, preparation consists largely of reading documents. It is not like having to prepare for court. Judging by some of the amounts charged for preparation, some mediators must be very slow readers.

In fact the Commercial Mediation User Group complained that mediators were not preparing enough. They recommended that mediators increased their fees so that they would not be tempted to take on so many mediations and would have the time and the incentive to prepare better. Strangely this suggestion was not generally welcomed by mediators.

Paradoxically one highly successful commercial mediator decided to raise his fees as his clerk thought that he was too busy. What happened? He received more mediations and was even busier.

Is there a going rate?

16.12

A comparison of fees charged by different providers and mediators suggest that there is not.

For example

(Please note that figures quoted are as at July 2015 and are plus VAT.)

ADR Group

Claims under £120,000

£750 per party. Time 8 hours. Total cost £1,500.

£500 per party. Time 4 hours. Total cost £1,000

Additional time £75 per party per hour.

This includes administration, but not room hire which is an additional £350.

> **Clerksroom**
>
> Charge for disputes up to £80,0000 (including their administration fee and free use of rooms).
>
> £500 per party. Time 7 hours. Total cost £1,000
>
> Value £80–250,000
>
> £1250 per party. Time 7 hours. Total cost £2,500
>
> Over £250,000
>
> £1750 per party. Time 7 hours. Total cost £3,500
>
> In all cases additional preparation is chargeable and so is overtime.
>
> **CEDR**
>
> Their low cost option where you do not have a choice of mediator is:
>
> Up to £75,000
>
> £500 per party. Total £1,000
>
> £75,000–£125,000
>
> £1,000 per party Total £2,000
>
> In each case, this is for 3 hours preparation and 7 hours mediation. Additional time is £200 an hour
>
> Otherwise they do not publish their charges.

Cutting fees

16.13 You have set your fee rate. You have given a quote for a mediation. Then you receive the telephone call. 'We would like you to do the mediation but another mediator (sometimes they name him and some surprising names crop up) has quoted a lower fee. Will you do the same?'

Do you cut your fee or not?

There are some mediators who resolutely refuse to reduce their rate once they have given a quote. They tend to be well-established, either as mediators or in a lucrative alternative career. It does not matter to them whether they do this particular mediation or not, or whether they offend the introducer.

Others take a more pragmatic view.

16.14 *Money*

They consider:

- The size of the requested reduction. If it is marginal they will probably agree. They take the view that they are not doing anything else that day and the mediation is a mediation after all. It helps the cash flow and statistics.
- Their relationship with the introducer. Have they done mediations for them before? Do they want to maintain an existing relationship or foster a new one?

Significant reductions are given. Sometimes even by well-established and busy mediators. The market is highly competitive. A long established and well-known barristers' clerk complained recently that a former High Court judge who was now doing commercial mediations was undercutting and as he put 'spoiling the market for everyone'.

There can be dangers in this approach. If you offer a significant reduction to the party proposing you as mediator, the other side can think that you are overly keen to please. They will be asking themselves what sort of influence does the proposing party have over you?

In practice you have to weigh up:

- Are you in the apprenticeship stage? If you are, do the mediation for nothing if necessary. You are still learning your trade. You need to reach ten mediations.
- If you have completed your apprenticeship, what else would you be doing that day. What is the opportunity cost? In reality it is usually small. Do the work. Get the money and the numbers up.
- The value of just doing a mediation. Apart from income and statistics there are two benefits:
  - You practise your skills. Becoming de-skilled or just a little rusty is a real danger for mediators who mediate infrequently or irregularly. To keep up your performance level you need to mediate at least once every other month. Training and simulated mediations help but they are not the real thing. Remember what Confucius said: 'Tell me, I'll forget. Show me I'll remember. Involve me, I'll understand.'
  - You can market yourself. We have already discussed the concept that every mediation is a marketing opportunity, *pace* Aled Davies (see **Preface**). There will usually be two clients, two solicitors and two barristers. That is six qualified leads. And you are being paid to show them what you can do. Mediating is much more effective than giving free breakfast talks to the local business circle.

All-in fee or optional extras?

16.14 The elements that make up the mediation charge are:

- The charge for the mediation day
- Preparation
- Travel time
- Travel expenses
- Hotel expenses

- Room hire
- Admin charges
- Overtime

The charge for the mediation day

16.15 As discussed at para **2.29** the standard day is eight hours. Some providers are now reducing this to seven hours and others are extending it to nine or ten hours. Make sure that you are clear what it is you are providing in the standard mediation day.

This is your basic charge for doing the mediation. You have to consider what else you charge on top.

Preparation

16.16 Most mediators quote a standard mediation fee which includes an element of preparation. Sometimes this is specified, eg three hours. Sometimes their agreement refers to 'reasonable' or 'expected' preparation time.

Any preparation time in excess of the stipulated amount or 'reasonable/expected' amount is chargeable. This is usually at the same hourly rate as for overtime but sometimes it is less.

Some agreements provide that additional preparation will only be undertaken with the express prior approval of all the parties. Others are silent.

Travel time

16.17 Many mediators still charge travel time on top of preparation and mediation contact time. But this is changing and often travel time is often now included.

Travel expenses

16.18 The usual practice is to charge travel expenses on top of preparation and mediation contact time. Again more and more mediators include this within their standard charge.

Some agree to include it within a standard charge within a specified area for example within the M25 or in stated counties.

But many mediators and providers still charge travel expenses even when they do not charge travel time.

16.19 *Money*

Hotel expenses

16.19 Again the usual practice was to charge these in addition to preparation and mediation contact time.

Some mediators take the view that they do not want parties to object to their appointment because they are out of their area. They do not want to be at a price disadvantage compared with local mediators. Therefore they include them within their standard charge.

Room hire

16.20 The usual practice was that the mediation would be held at the premises of one of the legal representatives, either in the solicitors' offices or in counsel's chambers. No charge was made. This changed several years ago and firms and chambers started to charge for the use of their premises during the mediation day. The rate was often lower than purpose-built mediation/arbitration centres or hotels.

Mediators who can offer free or low-cost rooms for the mediation have a competitive advantage (para **7.30**). Some mediators have been known to incorporate the cost of hire into their standard fee. This means that they receive a lower net amount for the mediation but at least they receive something and are appointed in the mediation.

Administration charges

16.21 Most mediation providers make an administration charge. Some show it separately as a fixed amount. Others include it in their charges and deduct it before they pay their mediators their agreed fee.

Individual mediators tend not to make a separate administration charge. They include it in their running costs, which they seek to recover as part of their fees.

Cancellations are an exception. Most mediators provide in their agreements that if there is a cancellation they can charge:

- an administration charge;
- any irrecoverable expenses that they have incurred, eg hotels or travel; and
- any preparation time they have spent.

Overtime

16.22 If the mediation overruns most mediators make an additional charge. Mediators who charge on the basis of a ten-hour day already build in an element of expected overtime.

Some mediators agree a fee for the day. That includes everything no matter how long the mediation lasts. This seems to be a growing trend.

There is no doubt that clients generally prefer a fixed fee. They want to know where they are. This is why more and more firms of accountants and lawyers are having to quote fixed fees. The same applies to mediators.

There are obvious benefits and risks in fixed fees. Mediators just have to decide how much risk they can run. This is really only a consideration once you are out of your apprenticeship.

One benefit of having a fixed daily fee especially for a ten-hour day is that the chances of you having to render supplemental invoices for overtime are reduced. This cuts down on your administration costs.

On the other hand mediations, like work, have a tendency to follow Parkinson's Law and expand to fill the time available. People can simply take ten hours because they have paid for ten hours. If they had paid for eight hours they would have settled within eight hours.

As a mediator, being able to tell people that they are now approaching the overtime zone provides an incentive for them to make up their minds. Being on the clock often encourages parties to speed up.

After sales service

16.23 Your work as a mediator is not concluded when the mediation day is finished. Even if the mediation has settled you may have to:

- Send additional invoices.
- Check that you have been paid.
- Sort out the file and safely dispose of those documents that you are going to destroy.
- Enter details of the mediation in your database/log.
- Email the parties as appropriate.

If the mediation has not produced a settlement you will have more work to do. In addition to the above you must also decide how much you want to be involved in any post-mediation settlement discussions. We discuss this in more detail in **Chapter 19**. You do have to decide whether to charge for any work and if so on what basis.

If the parties want to hold a further day's mediation they will expect to be charged for it. They will expect a lower fee as you have previously mediated the matter and will have less preparation to do.

If you decide to stay involved after the mediation to help the parties conclude a settlement you are taking a risk. Continuing to mediate by email and telephone eats up time. You can never be sure how much time will be needed to help the parties bridge the gap. You can be fairly sure that it will be at least 40% more than you estimate (see para **6.43** about optimism bias). If you do not make it clear at the outset that you will charge for your time you could upset people when you send the bill in later. You could easily forfeit all the goodwill that you have built up.

16.24 *Money*

Many mediation providers stipulate whether or not any after sales service by the mediator is chargeable. Usually it is. You must liaise with your mediation provider as well as the parties or their lawyers if you are going to be involved in any post mediation activity. You do not want to fall out with either the parties, their representatives or your mediation provider (see the Mediation Report Form (Appendix 1) and the template of letters to the parties at para **17.23**).

Remember

16.24 As a rule of thumb for every hour of contact doing the mediation there is an hour of non-contact time, excluding travel but including preparation and pre-and post-mediation administration. You can reduce this by using a mediation provider. But they charge. For example ADR Group charges £150 plus VAT per case. You have to decide whether or not you prefer to do it yourself. You save cash but there is a time cost.

The elephant in the room, which we discussed at para **4.66** is: how do you cost your time? That is the time which you do not spend on mediating, travelling to mediations or preparing for mediations? This is your opportunity cost. You have to quantify it when deciding how much time to spend on pre-mediation contact, eg telephone calls or emails with the parties and their representatives and also after-sales service.

Cash on the nail – do you extend credit?

16.25 Most mediation agreements stipulate that payment for the mediation must be received in advance of the mediation taking place. Some mediation providers take a very hard line on this. If payment has not been received the mediation does not happen.

As an individual mediator, where you are not appointed through a provider, you will have to decide yourself whether or not you insist on cash upfront or whether you are prepared to extend credit.

Obviously being paid upfront is better.

- It removes a degree of uncertainty.
- It concentrates the mind of the parties because they have handed over their money.
- It shows a higher degree of commitment to the process.

Most legal representatives will not object if you insist on payment upfront. In fact it can help them manage their own payment structure with their client. Complications can arise in the following circumstances:

- One party pays in advance and the other does not. What do you do? Do you tell the paying party that the other side has not paid? Do you threaten to cancel the mediation? If you do that you will have to refund what you have received. Will this enhance your reputation with anybody?
- If you are in your apprenticeship you might as well go ahead and take the risk that you will only receive half your fee. At least you carry out a mediation.

And you receive something. This is consistent with regarding your first ten mediations, ie your apprenticeship stage, as paid training.

- If you are out of your apprenticeship the pragmatic view is to go ahead and run the same risk. After all you will derive some benefit from the mediation taking place. You exercise your skills. You have another statistic. You have a marketing opportunity.

- Complications can arise if mediation agreements are not signed before the mediation. They are sent out to the parties in advance. More often than not everybody signs the mediation agreement on the day. A well-drawn mediation agreement will refer to Terms and Conditions of business which are incorporated into the agreement and which operate from the time that the booking is made. You have to be clear that your fees are due and payable before the mediation takes place even if the mediation agreement has not been signed.

- Most mediation agreements stipulate that if the parties have legal representation the legal representative assumes personal liability for the mediator's fees. In the past most mediators were happy to rely upon the fact that the legal representatives who were usually solicitors undertook this liability. They were confident that the solicitors would pay. Sadly this confidence was sometimes misplaced. Relying upon solicitors undertaking to pay is riskier than it used to be.

> **TOP TIP**
>
> - If you decide to wait until the day of the mediation to receive payment because the solicitor says that they will bring a cheque on the day make sure that you ask for the cheque at the beginning of the mediation.
> - The best time to do it is when you see the parties in their private rooms before the mediation formally starts to discuss any matters arising or to have the mediation agreement signed.
> - Hand the mediation agreement round and obtain everyone's signatures.
> - And then ask the solicitor 'Do you have a cheque for me?'

Civilised and professional solicitors do not need to be asked. They hand it over straight away. Others seem to hold back just to test whether you have the nerve to ask them. By asking them you will not offend anybody. And you are showing them that you can grasp nettles and that today is a commercial activity for all concerned. You are not here on a charitable mission. You here to do a job of work.

Overtime

16.26

- If you are not operating on a fixed fee basis you will have to make it clear what your additional charges for overtime are. Spell them out in your mediation agreement. On the day, if you are in danger of overrunning, draw it to the attention of the parties. It is entirely up to them whether they want to continue past the stipulated closing time or not. Usually they do if they think that any sort of progress is being made.

- To make sure that there is not a dispute about how much should be charged for the overtime make sure that the parties sign a document recording the amount

16.27 *Money*

of time spent. A precedent of a Mediation Report Form is at **Appendix1**. Disputes usually arise where the parties agree to carry on, but still finish the day without a settlement. They start looking for someone to blame and that can be the mediator. It also happens if one of the parties suffers from settler's remorse. On reflection they are unhappy with the deal. Once again, they want someone to blame. The usual targets are their own lawyers and the mediator. They rarely blame themselves.

Conditional fee agreements ('CFAs') and funding arrangements

16.27

- Although most CFAs stipulate that the client must pay disbursements, problems can still arise over mediators' fees. Usually it is the claimant who is on a CFA. He may not be expecting to pay anything until the case is concluded either by way of a judgment or settlement.

- The solicitors are not in funds. They are reluctant to use their own money to pay your fees. They often ask you to agree that your invoice will be paid after the mediation has concluded. In other words they are relying upon receiving settlement monies and then paying your fees out of what they receive. Some firms are more trustworthy than others. Take your pick.

Insurers

16.28 They can present a problem. They are involved usually but not always for the defendant. Many insurers operate panels of solicitors to represent them in litigation including mediation. They have financial arrangements. Often there is a billing cycle. You will be told by the solicitors that you will have to fit in with it. In the end you have no choice if you want work but you do have to monitor your outstanding bills (see section on cash flow in **Chapter 17**).

Working for insurers, whether as a lawyer or as a mediator, can be very satisfying but reconcile yourself to the fact that traditionally they have a reputation for being slow payers. Bad debts are rare but so are prompt payments.

Unpaid bills

16.29 Not being paid, or late payment, is much less of a problem for mediators than, for example, for solicitors or barristers. Problems do arise. They usually arise when the solicitor has not been paid by his own client or where the barrister has been instructed on a direct access basis.

Most mediation agreements provide that interest is chargeable on overdue bills. In practice this interest is rarely charged. Sometimes, despite numerous reminders and equally numerous promises the bill remains unpaid. You have a simple question: do you write it off or do you sue?

You have to consider the following:

- How good is the relationship with the firm acting for the client who has not paid? Is there a good reason for non-payment, eg the client goes into insolvent liquidation and your £1,500 is insignificant compared with the solicitors' unpaid bill of £15,000.
- If you issue proceedings you know that you are unlikely to receive any further work from either the client or the solicitor.
- If you decide to write it off you will not offend anybody, provided that your debt chasing tactics have been civilised and courteous. You might receive further work, especially if the introducer feels guilty and liked your style anyway. But do not assume that just because you have been understanding and done them a favour that they will do you a favour in return. As was made clear in the section on negotiation in **Chapter 11** just because you are nice to somebody does not mean that they will be nice to you.

Generally mediators just write off a bad debt. Put it down to the marketing budget.

In a nutshell

16.30

- In the end you can only charge what the market will bear.
- If you have to charge less than you would like, put the cost of the shortfall down to your marketing budget.
- The important thing is to get the mediations in.
- Fees are falling.
- Mediators like other professionals are having to run twice as hard to stand still.
- In practice mediations are more price-sensitive than mediators like to think
- Think hard about providing after sales service without recording the basis in writing.

Chapter 17

Administration

In this chapter you will learn about:
- Key paperwork.
- Terms and conditions.
- Billing.
- Diaries and dates.
- Premises.
- Feedback.
- Complaints handling.
- VAT.
- Tax.
- Insurance.
- Self-employed/employed status.

Administration is boring

17.01 Maladministration is even more boring. As a mediator you have two choices:
- Outsource your administration.
- Do-it-yourself.

Outsourcing:

Panels

17.02 You can outsource some of your administration by becoming a panel member and only accepting appointments from them. Or if you accept mediations directly, route them through a mediation provider who provides administration services to panel members receiving direct appointments. More mediation providers are offering this service (see **Chapter 9**).

If you do this you will be freed from a lot of the logistics of arranging mediations and collecting payment. You will still have to keep some records particularly for your tax and, in due course, VAT returns.

17.03 *Administration*

A virtual office administrator

17.03 They provide a range of services from telephone answering to sending out bills and producing contractual documents.

They all cost money. When you are starting out you probably want to save as much money as possible. Admin is not a big problem to start with but as you become busier it takes up much more time than you think it will.

The rest of this chapter assumes that you are going to do it yourself.

You will need the following essential documents:

- A diary.
- A template mediation agreement (see **Chapter 18**).
- A template terms and conditions (see **Appendix 2**).
- A template mediation report form (aka Time Sheet) (see **Appendix 1**).
- Invoices.
- Business cards.

You also need

- A mobile phone.
- A bank account.

Diary

17.04 This the most important document. That is where you enter the dates of your mediations once they are booked and also dates for potential mediations. It is much easier to have a paper diary in which you can write the dates while on the telephone. This is more reliable than scribbling on scraps of paper and then entering them into your electronic system.

Naturally you will want to sync your paper diary with your electronic calendars on your mobile phone, iPad or laptop.

You will want to be able to know your availability at short notice. So when you are on the move carry a notebook in which you have jotted down the dates that you cannot do in the next three months. People enquiring about mediations are always impressed by prompt responses.

Enter into your diary details of mediation enquiries. You need to chase them up. Quite often people just forget that they ever asked you about availability or even asked you to pencil in a date. You need to be on top of that. Even if they have appointed somebody else simply by asking for an update you remind them of your name.

Mediation agreement

17.05 A commentary on a mediation agreement is contained in **Chapter 18** together with a template. It is only a suggestion. Modify it to suit your particular requirements.

Checklist for a mediation agreement

17.06

1. The agreement is the source of all your authority. Without it you have none. In the agreement the parties agree to:
   - submit their dispute to mediation, which is conducted by you;
   - pay you; and
   - observe confidentiality.
   - Without these key elements you cannot really conduct a mediation. Certainly you cannot conduct a commercial mediation of any complexity.

2. There are organisations, particularly those which carry out pro bono work for community mediations, who do not insist upon the mediation agreement being signed at the beginning of the process. This is most unwise and has led to difficulties when people have decided not to treat the discussions as confidential after all.

3. Always take a copy of the mediation agreement with you to the mediation. Do this even if the parties have signed and returned it in advance. You can never be sure who actually will attend the mediation. Sometimes even the parties' representatives do not know who their clients will bring with them. You need a copy of the agreement so that everybody who attends can sign a schedule which binds them to the confidentiality provisions. This is essential.

4. Take care if you do not insist that the mediation agreement is signed and returned before the mediation. Make it clear in your email accepting the appointment that the terms of the mediation agreement are still binding on the parties from the date of confirming your booking. In particular that the confidentiality provisions apply to all communications with you or through you.

5. Limitation of liability clauses are a contentious matter. Should mediators limit or exclude their liability for their own negligence?

One well-known mediator who is also a busy barrister and mediator advocate does not include an exclusion of liability clause in his own mediation agreement. He also, when representing a party, refuses to appoint a mediator who includes one in his agreement. This might be an affectation because if you have professional indemnity insurance your insurers may well insist, and they often do, that you include an exclusion of liability clause. It may not stand up. But it gives insurers something to argue about.

Terms and conditions

17.07 Some mediators include all their Terms and Conditions (T&Cs) in their mediation agreement. This creates a lengthy and detailed document. Lay clients

17.08 *Administration*

find this off-putting, especially when they are reading it for the first time at the mediation. You will be surprised to find how often, when you ask the parties on the day if they have read the mediation agreement, that they say they had not even seen it.

A better idea is to have your T&Cs as a separate document. Some mediation providers insist that they are also signed and returned before the mediation booking is confirmed. This is not essential. If your T&Cs are displayed on your website, refer to this in the email confirming your appointment. Just say that all bookings are accepted on the basis of your terms and conditions, which can be found on your website and give the link.

Cancellation charges need careful thought. You will find that you are booked for mediations and then unbooked. Dates go in and out of the diary.

A template for T&Cs is in **Appendix 2**

Billing

17.08   You need invoice templates. You can have your own tailor-made template installed on your computer and printed off. This is what most mediators do. Or use one of the ready-made invoice templates that are available as part of your computer software.

Your mediation agreement as well as your T&Cs should provide that payment of your invoices must be made in advance of the mediation (see **Chapter 18**).

When you complete your invoice, remember:
- include a serial number;
- the numbers should be sequential;
- include a date of issue;
- when you become registered for VAT, to include your VAT number; and
- if you incorporate your business as a limited company include the company's registration number

Credit control

17.09   A simple way of keeping track of your bills is to have a lever arch file with a divider. In the front are the bills that are issued. As they are paid you move them from the front part of the file to the back part. That is your paid bills book. You can also see which ones remain unpaid.

In addition you keep a spreadsheet of the mediations that you carry out and the bills that you render. You can do this quite easily in Excel. Or if you prefer do it manually. But do it.

If you do not do this, completing your tax return and in due course your VAT return is much more difficult.

Mediation report form

17.10 Take this form with you to every mediation. It records the time and date of the mediation, when it started and more importantly when it finished. Unless you are operating on a fixed fee basis you will be entitled to charge extra if the mediation overruns its stated time. By having the parties sign the mediation report form at the end of the mediation you obviate any argument when you submit your supplemental invoice.

The mediation report form also records whether or not the mediation has settled and, if it has not, whether you are going to provide any further service. A template mediation report form is contained at **Appendix 1.**

Take at least two copies of the form. If it looks as though the mediation has broken down, or the parties say that they are leaving, you can produce the form and ask them to sign it. You explain that it confirms that the mediation has failed and that no settlement has been agreed.

This often causes the parties to pause and think again. They realise that this really is the end of the process. Do they want that? More often than not they start talking again even after they have signed the form. You can tear it up and fill in the other one when it has settled and they confirm that the mediation has been successful.

Feedback/satisfaction questionnaires

17.11 You want to know what the parties and their representatives thought about your performance. The problem is that once the mediation is over and has settled, the parties and their representatives forget about you. They move on to the next problem. Within a few weeks they will not even be able to remember your name.

Therefore send them a request for feedback as soon as the mediation is completed. Some mediators hand out a feedback form on the day but it is more usual to send it the next day. Mediation providers also send them out. Some contact the parties on the day as soon as they have been told that the mediation has completed to find out what the parties thought about the mediator's performance. Increasingly all this is done online.

Parties and their representatives can be slow in returning feedback forms. Even when they can complete them online they have other things to do. Feedback might be a high priority for you but it is a low one for them.

If you think the mediation went well, keep a note of it. Make sure that you have the full names of the barristers and solicitors involved. These will be the people that you can approach when you need a reference if you apply for membership of a panel or entry into a directory.

Be realistic and resilient. Accept that you cannot please all people all the time. Some mediations just go better than others. Although as a mediator you try and establish

17.12 *Administration*

a rapport with everybody and stay on good terms throughout the day there will be people who do not like you. That is life. Re-read para **4.67** on rejection.

Complaints

17.12 If there is a complaint you must deal with it properly. The golden rule is treat every complaint as a sales opportunity.

Any professional's natural reaction when receiving criticism or a complaint is to defend themselves. Instead do what you encourage the parties at mediations to do. Look at the situation through the other person's eyes.

Thank them for raising the matter. Express regret for the fact that they feel this way. Ask them what they want you to do about it. Within the bounds of reasonableness do it.

Many complaints are prompted when you send the bill for additional time after the mediation has overrun. Parties complain about you taking too long. You were late arriving. You had not properly prepared and so too much time was spent in bringing you up to speed.

Sometimes all that is happening is that the party or their representative is expressing settler's remorse. They feel they have made a bad bargain. They need to blame somebody other than themselves. Or they are now sorry that they did not settle and are regretting the lost opportunity.

Pre-empting complaints

17.13 Certain issues recur in complaints. Be aware of them so that you can try and avoid them.

Common causes for complaints:
- Arriving late.
- Not being properly prepared.
- Being overly aggressive in the pursuit of a settlement.
- Railroading the parties.
- Spending too long with one party and not enough time with another.
- Being too laid-back or, conversely, being too proactive and interventionist.
- Bringing the mediation to a premature end by declaring that settlement was impossible.
- Sitting in your room reading a newspaper instead of being with the parties moving the process along.
- Sitting in your room working on the papers for the next mediation rather than concentrating on the one that you were meant to be doing today.

- Asking challenging questions in a way that suggests you are being critical of the complaining party and exhibiting partiality in favour of the other party.

Settlement fever

17.14 When you start as a mediator you not only want to receive instructions. You also want to achieve settlements. You can easily start to push the parties too fast and too hard towards settlement. With experience you learn to pace yourself better.

Roll with the punches

17.15 When parties and their representatives are being difficult or obstructive you will be tempted to let them know what you think. With time you learn how to challenge this sort of unhelpful behaviour.

At the start it can be difficult. How difficult you find it depends a lot on what you have been doing for your day job so far. But what you must not do is have a row.

Avoid a public bust up. Invite the lawyer to have a private word. Often a frank acknowledgment that you seem to be getting off on the wrong foot can help. Both sides realise that they are perhaps being overzealous, express regret and start again.

If someone overtly criticises you, bite your tongue. Acknowledge what they have said. Express regret that they feel like that. If necessary explain why you have done or said what they have complained of. Be careful not be too self-justificatory. Don't be drawn in to a debate about yourself. Ask them what they want you to do.

Be prepared to ask them outright if they want you to stand down as the mediator and bring the day to an end. Explain that you cannot carry on as mediator if you have lost the confidence of the parties. Usually they say that they do not want this.

If an apology is in order, give it. Do not over-elaborate. Just pick up where you left off and carry on. After all no one told that you that being a mediator was easy.

Reassure them that if they are, for example, complaining that you are asking them too many tough questions, that you are doing exactly the same in the other room.

Suggest that you bring the session to an end for a few minutes so everyone can collect their thoughts and come back to the issue later.

Remember that people can appear to be acting in an obstructive way for all sorts of reasons. They could be:

- Tired.
- Stressed.
- Frustrated.
- Feeling guilty.
- Underprepared.
- Bluffing.

17.16 *Administration*

- Shocked at what they have learned about the strength of their case and their legal costs.
- Suspicious of their client or other legal advisor.

And sometimes that is just the way they are: they are natural bullies who conduct their life in this way.

Premises

17.16 There are:

- The premises where you carry on your business. That would usually be your home, your office if you are still working, a serviced office. You have factored the costs into your business plan.
- The premises where you carry out the mediations. The venues. If you are able to offer premises that is a commercial advantage (see para **7.30**). Usually the parties make the arrangements themselves and hold the mediation in one of the lawyers' offices or chambers.

Compile a list of venues for your area. You can pass this on if the parties are struggling to find somewhere to hold the mediation. This usually only happens if they distrust each other so much that one of them is insisting on a neutral venue.

Checklist of central London venues

17.17 Venues in the London area:

- The Chartered Institute of Arbitrators
- The Law Society
- The Academy of Experts
- The ADR Group
- Littleton Chambers
- Frances Taylor Building
- 128 Fleet Street
- The IDRC

Hotels can also provide facilities. Some have dedicated business centres and suites of meeting rooms (try to avoid using bedrooms). The Hilton and Marriott chains are often available at reasonable rates.

Standard correspondence

17.18 You will need to send emails promptly at different stages in the mediation instruction. Here are some draft templates.

Administration **17.20**

Email/Letter 1

In response to the first enquiry about dates and availability

17.19 Dear X

Thank you for your email of 21 January 2016.

I confirm that I will be delighted to act as mediator in this matter.

The dates that I can currently offer are:

1–10, 15, 17 January

5, 6, 7, 9, 10, 24 February

[*Note you will often be asked for dates to avoid. In fact it is easier if you give them the dates that you can do*]

[*You might need to add*: 'Please note that I have offered some of these dates for other mediations. If there is a difficulty about dates please contact me as the diary changes.']

My standard charges for a full day mediation (which is 8/10 hours) are £2,000. This is normally split between the parties. It includes all preparation, travel time and expense.

Or

My standard charges for a full day mediation (which is 8/10 hours) are £1,000 per party. This includes 3 hours preparation. Additional preparation and travel time and expenses will be charged at £200 an hour.

If the mediation overruns, additional time will be charged at £200 an hour.

Please note that all figures are plus VAT [*or* VAT is not chargeable].

Please also note that all bookings are accepted on the terms of my terms and conditions, which can be found on my website www.xxxxxxx.com

I look forward to hearing from you.

Regards

Email/Letter 2

In response to confirmation that you have been appointed

17.20 Dear X

Thank you for confirming that the mediation is to go ahead on 8 July 2016. I have put the date in the diary.

17.21 *Administration*

Please could you let me have the full name and addresses of the parties and their representatives so that the paperwork can be issued.

I look forward to hearing from you.

Yours

Email/Letter 3

After you have sent out the mediation agreement and the invoices

17.21 This is a letter to both sides.

Dear X and Y

I look forward to meeting you on 8 July 2016.

Please could you let me know if there is any material that you would like me to read before the mediation. If there is could you let me know when you will be sending it.

I am happy to receive material electronically if that is easier at this email address. If you prefer to send it in hard copy form please send it to [*give your address, DX number etc*].

Please could you also let me know when it would be convenient for me to telephone you to have a private and confidential word about the mediation.

I look forward to hearing from you.

Regards

Email/Letter 4

After the mediation

17.22 Write a similar letter to each of the parties' representatives

'Dear X

It was a nice to meet you and your clients on Tuesday.

I'm glad that we were able to achieve a mediated settlement. Thank you for hosting the event [*if they hosted it*].

I enclose a feedback form/questionnaire. I would be very grateful if you could find a moment to complete and return it to me.

Finally, thank you for appointing me on this occasion

Regards

Administration **17.25**

Email/Letter 5

After the mediation if it has not settled

This is a letter written jointly to both sets of representatives.

17.23 'Dear X and Y

It was very good to meet you and your clients yesterday.

I am only sorry that we were not able to reach a settlement. Both parties said that was what they wanted and they worked hard to try and achieve a settlement.

As promised I set out the terms of the offers that were left on the table.

X's client offered:

-
-
-
-

Y's client offered:

-
-
-
-

Each side said their offer was available for acceptance until 12 noon on Friday 15th of July 2016. Acceptance is to be by email from one firm of solicitors to the other.

If I have got anything wrong in recording these offers please let me know by return.

Or where no offers were left on the table.

17.24 I confirm that no offers were left open for acceptance.

I do hope that on reflection the parties will find a way of bridging the gap. If they decide that they can, and if there is anything that I can do to help, please let me know.

Regards

Database

17.25 One of the country's most successful and best established commercial mediators maintains a spreadsheet on which he records the details of every

17.26 *Administration*

mediation that he has conducted. He has now mediated hundreds and his records go back over 15 years.

Although this takes him time, effort and persistence to maintain he has available a huge database of contacts that he has worked with. As discussed in **Chapter 8** on marketing, obtaining work from existing customers is easier than finding new ones.

Having a database like this also helps you deal with enquiries about potential conflicts of interest. You will be asked if you have acted for a particular party in the past or have been appointed by a particular firm. You must give accurate replies.

Do not dissemble.

Bank account

17.26 You can operate your mediation business through your ordinary personal account. But opening a separate bank account for your mediation business is a better option:

- It adds commercial status.
- It enables you to group your mediation income in one place which will make compiling your VAT and tax returns easier.
- It enables you to make payments in relation to your mediation business out of one source which again makes compiling your VAT and tax returns easier.

Remember: always take your bank account details with you. If payment has not been made in advance of the mediation and the parties say that they have forgotten to bring their cheque-book you can ask them to pay electronically. Most solicitors and their clients use online banking these days.

17.27
Health warning: The following paras 17.28–17.41 are for general guidance only and are not advice. The figures given are correct at the time of going to press. You must double check with HMRC or your own advisers. If you need advice, always consult an accountant. That will be money well spent.

VAT: pain, gain or marketing tool?

17.28 There are three figures that you have to bear in mind: **20**, **82** and **150**.

20

The current rate of VAT in the UK is 20%.

This means that if you are VAT registered your charges will be 20% higher than if you are not. If your customers are not VAT registered themselves you can be at a price disadvantage compared with your competitors who are not VAT registered.

82

All registered traders complain about the VAT system. Their duties include keeping VAT records for seven years, submitting VAT returns and receiving visits from the VAT inspector.

It all sounds like bad news. Anyone setting up a new business could be discouraged. But for new mediators the news is good.

You will not have to register for VAT until your annual turnover reaches £82,000. Once it does registration is compulsory.

This is the VAT threshold for the 12 months starting April 2015. It usually goes up each year. Check the latest figures on HMRC VAT Helpline 0843 658 0507 www.hmrctallk.co.uk/vat-helpline/

Calculate your turnover to the end of each month looking back over the last 12 months. If it is likely that your turnover will exceed the threshold limit within the next 30 days you must register for VAT. If you fail to do this you will be liable to a penalty.

Most mediators do not earn anything like the tax threshold amount. If you earn that amount in your first 12 months of practice as a mediator you will be doing extraordinarily well!!

150

Once your annual turnover reaches £150,000 you cease to be eligible for the Flat Rate Scheme. Your VAT administration will become more onerous. But you will be earning enough to employ someone to do it for you.

The Flat Rate Scheme

17.29 This is available for traders who have registered for VAT but whose annual turnover does not exceed £150,000. It is intended to simplify VAT administration for small businesses.

For mediators, who are selling services rather than products, it is advantageous. Especially as you would not normally be buying many items which would be classified as a business expense and therefore reclaimable against VAT.

Under the scheme you charge VAT on your invoices at 20% but pay VAT at a lower rate to HMRC. The rate changes from time to time and varies for different trades and professions.

At the time of going to press the rate for mediators was 14.5%.

In addition in your first year you receive an extra 1%. So the rate for the first 12 months of trading is 13.5%

The difference between 20% and 14.5 % (or 13.5%) you keep as income.

17.30 *Administration*

You still have to fill in a quarterly VAT Return Form. It is much simpler than under the ordinary VAT scheme. You calculate your VAT payable on the amount that you have invoiced that quarter.

Worked example

Mediator pays 13.5% of the gross amount invoiced in the first year and 14.5% in subsequent years.

Amount invoiced £90,000. VAT chargeable @ 20% £18,000. Total gross amount £108,000.

Amount payable to HMRC in first year £14,580.

Amount retained as additional income £ 3,420.

Remember:
- Use the gross amount, ie the invoice amount plus VAT at 20% when calculating your payment.
- Your additional income is taxable.

The advantages of the Flat Rate Scheme are:
- You earn extra income.
- Simplified administration record-keeping.
- An extra 1% retained by you in your first year.

The disadvantages of the Flat Rate Scheme are:
- You cannot claim back any VAT on goods that you buy and expenses that you incur for your business.

Note: You can still reclaim VAT on capital asset purchases over £2,000 provided that they are all on the same receipt. So if for example you are buying IT equipment for your new business, make sure that you buy it all the same time and it totals in excess of £2,000 if you want to reclaim VAT.

Do not join the Flat Rate Scheme if you think that your income is going to exceed £150,000 in your first year. If you do join the scheme and subsequently your income exceeds £230,000 a year you will have to leave the scheme.

VAT as a marketing tool

Higher prices

17.30 As explained above if you are registered for VAT your invoices will be 20% higher than those of your competitors who are not registered for VAT. They have a competitive edge.

This will not be a problem if you are targeting commercial clients. They will almost certainly be registered for VAT. If however you are targeting non-commercial clients many of them will not be registered for VAT.

Kudos

17.31 You need to consider your image or brand. Some mediators think that if they do not charge VAT they will not be taken seriously. If your annual turnover does not exceed £82,000, so the argument runs, you cannot be very busy. After all if your average mediation fee is £2,500 you need to do 33 mediations in a year, or effectively at least three each month. That is much more than most mediators do.

Voluntary registration

17.32 To overcome this problem you have the opportunity of registering for VAT even if your turnover is less than the compulsory registration threshold of £82,000. You can apply for voluntary registration.

HMRC are suspicious of voluntary registration. They do not want traders registering simply to become net receivers of VAT refunds every quarter.

When applying for registration you have to satisfy HMRC that you are running a business or intend to run a business. They are not going to register you if they think you are carrying on a hobby. They will ask for details of your business. They are more impressed if you have a business rather than a home address. But operating from your home is not fatal.

They are impressed if you have already been carrying out some business, ie supplying services, before you apply. This is especially so if you are registering as a sole trader rather than a company. With a company you can always send them a copy of the Certificate of Incorporation as evidence of business intent and activity.

Applying for registration

17.33 You can obtain all the VAT registration forms on the HMRC website.

You will have to register on the Government Gateway portal in order to be able to deal with it online. Online registration is time-consuming and frustrating but in the end it is doable and worthwhile. When you register make sure that you print a copy of your registration notification and of all your passwords.

Remember when you are registered you have to conclude your VAT registration number on all your invoices.

Tax

Sole trader

17.34 This section assumes that you are trading as a sole trader, ie trading by yourself, for yourself, with no partners and not as a limited company. You are

17.34 Administration

personally responsible for any losses that the business makes and all the profits belong to you. You can employ staff. Being a sole trader means that you are responsible for the business, not that you have to work alone.

What this means is that you have to:

- submit your Self-Assessment Tax return; and
- keep records of your invoices rendered and your expenses claimed.

The tax year runs from 6 April to 5 April of the following year. Personal tax is payable each year on 31 January together with payments on account in both January and July of each year.

Under current legislation, once you earn over £100,000 your personal allowance will reduce at the rate of £1 for every £2 of income until this is reduced to 0. In practice your personal allowance disappears once you earn £114,950. Happy are the mediators who find themselves in this position. Please note that the tax allowance is constantly changing and you should consult your accountant for the up-to-date position.

If you trade as a sole trader you must register as a sole trader with HMRC (www.gov.uk/government/organisations/hm-revenue-customs). If you do not you can be liable to a penalty.

Once you are registered you will be sent a Self Assessment Tax Return form by HMRC.

You can choose to submit your return by paper or online. If you do it on paper you have to submit it by 31 October. If you do it online you have to do it by 31 January of the following year.

If you deal with your tax returns online you will need to set up a Government Gateway activation PIN and User ID.

When you register online make sure that you have a UTR number (your unique tax reference.) This is a 10-digit number that must be included on all communications with HMRC.

Do not miss the deadline. Put the dates in your diary. If you miss the 31 January deadline you incur a £100 fine. You may also be charged additional interest on late payment. If you fail to complete your return by 28 February you will also have to pay a 5% surcharge based on the value of the tax you owe.

If you start your business in the tax year 2015/16 this will be your first tax return.

The amount you pay depends on your turnover for the year i.e. the amount that you invoice. Let us assume that you owe £2,000 in tax.

On 31 January 2017 you will pay:

£2,000 – your tax bill for the year.

£1,000 – payment on account of your estimated tax bill for 2016/17 bill.

Therefore the total due is £3,000.

On July 31 2017 you will pay:

A further £1,000 – the other half of your estimated tax bill for 2016/17.

On 31 January 2018:

Your tax bill will be, say £4,000 (let us assume that you have done lots of mediations and your profit has increased).

Less – £2,000 already paid.

To pay – £1,000 tax plus £2,000 being a payment on account, ie half your estimated tax bill for 2017/18.

Limited company

17.35 If you trade through a limited company you pay tax on a different basis.

A limited company is an organisation that you can set up to run your business. It is responsible in its own right for everything it does and its finances are separate from your personal finances. This definition is taken from the www.gov.uk website which contains useful information about choosing a legal structure for your business.

The danger is that when traders operate through a one-man company, frequently they confuse the company and themselves and think of them as just one entity.

This inevitably leads to complications. The company is one legal and taxable entity. You, as its employee and director and shareholder, are another.

The company pays corporation tax. In simple terms this is the amount of the net sales less net expenses.

The company rate for corporation tax is from 1 April 2015 20%.

Worked example

You invoice clients £200,000 excluding VAT. Your expenses are £30,000. You pay tax at XX on the balance of £170,000 profit.

Corporation Tax is due nine months and one day after the company's financial year end.

You have to pay National Insurance Contributions (NIC).

For employers' NIC payments your company will have to pay NI on any salary that you pay yourself over the threshold amount. For details of rates and threshold amounts go the gov.uk website at www.gov.uk - type in national insurance.

17.36 *Administration*

Employees' NIC: you need to pay NI on any salary you pay yourself out the business. This is 12% on anything earned above £149.01 per week until you reach £797 per week. Then you pay 2%.

Remember PAYE income tax, NIC and VAT are all payable quarterly but not always on the same dates. Check with your accountants.

Remember there is no NI payable on dividends: however, there is income tax.

PAYE

17.36 If you are a sole trader your taxes will be sorted out in your tax return at the end of the tax year.

If you trade as a limited company you need to pay your PAYE through the company.

The PAYE will be deducted from the salary that you pay yourself. PAYE is not deducted from any dividends.

You must keep the PAYE that you deduct from your salary in the business bank account until you pay it over to HMRC. You must pay promptly. You cannot use PAYE payments as cash flow for your business.

As a director of your own limited company you need to register for self-assessment in exactly the same way as if you are operating as a sole trader.

Any income taken as salary from your company will be taxed in the same way as if you were an employee of the company.

Dividends

17.37 This is another way of paying yourself from the company. Since you are a shareholder you can pay dividends, which are a portion of the company's earnings.

You can pay dividends at any time provided there are available profits.

The taxation of dividends is more complicated. In broad terms once you have exceeded the combined total of your personal allowances and the basic rate tax band the overall rates are the same as the personal higher tax bracket of 40%.

Take advice from an accountant if you are going to operate through a company.

Sole trader or limited company?

17.38 Before you decide which to do take advice from your accountant. Here is a checklist of the main issues arising when comparing the two methods of carrying on your business.

Sole trader

- Easier and cheaper to start. Choose your business name. Register with HMRC as a sole trader and off you go.
- Less need for an accountant and lower fees if you do need one.
- Your accounts are confidential and private to you, your accountant and HMRC.
- You only need to submit a Self-Assessment Tax Return each year that shows your income, expenditure and profits.
- You pay personal income tax on your profit. This is your income.
- You are personally liable for any business debts.
- There is less opportunity for tax planning, ie reducing your tax bill.

Limited company

- You need to formally set up a limited company, pay the relevant fees and register it with Companies House.
- Greater need for an accountant and higher fees.
- You will need to open a separate business bank account.
- You must file your accounts at Companies House each year. They are open to the public.
- You need to file formal accounts with HMRC and Companies House each year by a deadline. There are penalties for missing deadlines.
- You have to pay corporation tax on the company's profits as well as income tax on any salary you take. If you take dividends you also have to pay income tax on dividends.
- The company, rather than you, is liable for any business debts. Although directors can incur personal liability, for example for underpaid PAYE and NI.
- There is greater scope for tax mitigation.

In a nutshell

17.39

- Trading as a sole trader is simpler and cheaper.
- Trading as a limited company carries more commercial status and provides greater opportunities for minimising your tax bill.
- When starting a business, if you expect to earn less than about £25,000, operating as a sole trader is going to be the best answer. Most mediators, even some of the most successful and long-established ones, trade as sole traders.
- Those mediators who trade as limited companies usually also provide other services such as being a mediation provider or training.

But note

You do have to pay NI as a sole trader. Normally this is Class 2. They are paid every six months on 31 January.

17.40 *Administration*

Your Class 4 National Insurance Contributions are calculated at the same time as your tax return. You pay them with your income tax.

Expenses

17.40 If, as many mediators do, you work from home you want to consider whether you can claim any part of the running costs of your home as a business expense.

The simple answer is that you can, whether you work from home as a limited company or as a sole trader. But before you do consult your accountant.

The HMRC states the rule as:

> 'it is possible to apportion using the cost of a room on a time basis, and to allow the expense of the room during the hours in which it is used exclusively for business purposes, in the same way as it is possible to calculate the business expense of a car which is sometimes used for business and is sometimes used for pleasure.'

You have to seriously consider whether it is worth it.

There are also the simplified expenses rules when flat rates are applied.

You can claim travel expenses against tax. This includes:

- business mileage;
- rail travel; and
- hotel accommodation.

Your business mileage is the travelling for your job. It includes travel to a temporary workplace or meetings. It does not include normal travel between home or anywhere that is a permanent place of work.

You must keep all receipt records of dates, mileage, journey details for your all your business travel, and your car usage. (See www.gov.uk/expenses-if-youre-self-employed/overview.)

The pros and cons of being self-employed

17.41 The advantages include:

- Being your own boss. This suits some people. Others hate it.
- The freedom to choose when and where you work.
- A more direct relationship between the amount of effort you put into your work and the reward you receive.
- Greater flexibility over negotiating your rates of pay.
- Working for more than one person.
- Freelance rates tend to be higher than employee rates.

The disadvantages include:

- You have to do everything. You are responsible for the running of the business.
- You will have fewer resources. You will be the IT department, the cleaning department, the stationery clerk and everything else.
- Credit control means it is difficult to earn big money in the early days. You have to closely watch what is coming and in and what is going out.
- Unless you work from home, you will have to find and pay for premises.
- It can be difficult to rely solely upon freelance/self-employed work as a source of income if you have fixed commitments. You may need to supplement it with a second job.

Being a limited company

17.42 The advantages include:

- Limited liability. As a shareholder you have unlimited liability to contribute to the amount that you agree to put into the company by way of share capital. The liabilities will be the liabilities of the company and in the normal way cannot be transferred to you personally.
- Greater tax planning opportunities. These mainly arise from the fact that as a sole trader all your income earned in a year is taxed in that year. With a limited company you do not have to take out all the money at once and you can build it up in the company until you need it.
- Simplified administration. For small companies the formal requirements have been streamlined. They are not much more onerous than for a sole trader although they are greater and more expensive. You no longer need two people to form a company. The same person can be director, secretary and sole shareholder.

  If you decide that you no longer want to operate as a company you can, after not trading for three months, apply to Companies House to be removed from the register. You complete Form 652a.
- Commercial perception. Some customers prefer to trade with a company. They think that it is somehow more solid and real.
- Ownership. The company is owned by shareholders. Shares can be easily allotted to different people and are easily transferable, subject to the Articles of the company. If you want to bring your spouse or child into the company, as some mediators have done, it is relatively easy to do.

Insurance

17.43 If you accept direct appointments you will need professional indemnity insurance.

Some bodies require it. For example the Civil Mediation Council require it as a qualification. So do other accrediting bodies such as IMI.

17.44 *Administration*

If you want go on a Clerksroom's panel you have to provide evidence of your professional indemnity insurance. Other mediation providers have a block policy that covers their members when they are carrying out mediations arranged through the provider. It is one of the benefits of membership of their panel.

In any case if you intend to comply with the EU Code of Conduct for Mediators you need to have professional indemnity cover. If you do not intend to comply with the EU Code of Conduct of you do have to ask yourself what you are doing mediating at all. See ec.europa.eu/civiljustice/adr/adr_ec_code_conduct_en.pdf.

Professional indemnity cover can easily be arranged through brokers. There are some who regularly advertise for business from mediators for example Oxygen. The cost of professional indemnity cover for mediators is low because the risk is low. It should not cost you more than £200–£250 a year including insurance premium tax.

You need to remember that the professional indemnity insurance is on a claims made basis. This means that the policy that is in force at the date that the claim against you is made responds. It does not matter when the negligent act or omission occurred.

What this means is that you have to keep your professional indemnity cover in place even if you have stopped mediating. This is because the period of limitation for bringing a claim against the mediator is six years. If you decide to retire as a mediator you can buy run-off cover.

If you are a part-time mediator who is also employed, for example by a firm of solicitors or as a barrister, you will already have professional indemnity cover. You need to check whether you are covered by that policy for your work as a mediator. Often you are.

Many mediators regard having a professional indemnity policy as something that they can advertise. It shows a certain status and reliability. You can tell people that you have it. You can even give the policy number and the name of the insurer. What you cannot do is say what the terms are.

What risk do you run?

17.44 Although the CMC and many panels require their members to have professional indemnity insurance the risk of claims being made against mediators is low. This is reflected in the low insurance premiums.

The main areas of potential liability are:

Breach of the mediation agreement

In other words not supplying the level of service that the customers expect under the agreement. For example turning up late and unprepared. Being rude and insisting that the parties settle.

Breach of duty

Not being impartial, deliberately misleading a party, refusing to pass on a proposal or making a mistake when transmitting a proposal to the other side

Breaching confidentiality whether deliberately or inadvertently

For example, leaving confidential papers in one party's room.

Negligence

For example, giving a view on the law which is wrong.

The more evaluative and adjudicated that mediators become the greater the risk of their making a negligent mistake which could lead to actionable loss. They could be just as liable for advising a party to accept a settlement on unfavourable terms as the party's own advisers.

In a nutshell

17.45

- Administration is boring. Maladministration is even worse.
- Keep a spreadsheet of your mediations.
- Keep a file of your bills and chase the unpaid ones.
- If you are doing your own administration do it. If you find yourself not doing it outsource it. It will be cheaper in the long run than having to sort out a mess.
- Buy insurance; do not become paralysed by the risk of being sued.

Chapter 18

Mediation agreement

This chapter covers:

- The standard terms in a Mediation Agreement for civil and commercial mediations.

General

18.01 Your mediation agreement is a crucial document. You derive all your authority from it. If you accept appointments from panels or appointing bodies they will normally issue their own mediation agreement. You do not have to be concerned about producing one for the parties. You need to be familiar with its terms so that you can explain them to the parties at the mediation if they ask.

If you are appointed directly, you will need your own mediation agreement. Look at other mediators' agreements and those used by the well-known mediation providers. You will see what is standard practice. Some agreements will appeal to you more than others. You will quickly discover that some mediation agreements are quite complicated legal-sounding documents. They have been drafted by lawyers for lawyers. Others are written in plain English for non-lawyers.

Which approach you adopt is down to your personal taste and your mediation style.

Send the agreement in advance

18.02 You should always send out your mediation agreement in advance. More often than not the agreement is not signed and sent back in advance of the mediation – it is usually signed on the day. Be prepared to answer questions about the agreement either in advance from lawyers or from the parties on the day. They tend to query the costs recovery clause or the definition of the dispute.

You may be told that a clause in your agreement is not a standard one. Other mediators do things differently. That is why it is important to be familiar with other agreements. They are updated from time to time. Make a note yourself to check them every six or 12 months. Most are freely available on websites.

Some Mediation Agreements are self-contained documents. Others refer to terms and conditions or standard procedures and rules contained in other documents. Of course they have to be read together.

18.03 *Mediation agreement*

Going through the agreement on the day

18.03 A particular problem arises if the parties are not legally represented. You may have to take them through the Mediation Agreement, either on the telephone before the mediation or on the day.

The problem is that on the day of the mediation people are already under pressure. They may be feeling stressed because of the mediation itself. If they have not been to a mediation before they will be receiving a lot of new information. Be patient, because they may not be able to take in the full meaning of the Mediation Agreement quickly.

In the following section there is an analysis of a standard form Mediation Agreement clause by clause. The examples of wording have been taken from mediation agreements that are currently in use.

Standard form Mediation Agreement

18.04 Clause: The parties

THE FOLLOWING PARTIES namely:

1.   (represented by)

2.   (represented by)

(collectively the 'Parties') hereby agree to appoint XXXXXXXXX ('The Mediator'), to administer the mediation of the Dispute on the following terms and conditions:

Comment:

It is essential to make sure that the parties are correctly described. This is particularly important when there are corporate entities or trading names. Exactly the same care has to be taken when drafting commercial agreements. Sometimes as part of a settlement:

- a parent company which is not actually a party to the dispute will join in for example as a guarantor or to promise to procure that something happens
- other group members may agree for example to waive any claims they may have.
- Quite often group companies will have given their authority to the company representative to bind them at the mediation. They may not actually be parties to the mediation agreement. This can be important for the confidentiality provisions. It can therefore be sensible to widen the definition of party by including any related or subsidiary companies etc.

Clause: Mediation rules

1. MEDIATION PROCEDURES

   1.1 The mediation shall be held and conducted according to this Agreement to Mediate ('Agreement').

1.2 The Mediator's standard Terms and Conditions as specified at http://sw com/terms-and-conditions are incorporated into this Agreement. Where there is any conflict between them and this Agreement, the terms of this Agreement shall prevail.

Comment:

One well-known mediation provider expressly provides that the legal representative confirms when he signs his name on the mediation agreement that:

> 'I have advised my client on the meaning and effect of this agreement, and undertake to ensure that my client's fees are paid to XXX in accordance with the terms of this agreement, and acknowledge and agree that my firm is liable for the costs of the mediation in the same way as it is liable for disbursements incurred in the course of litigation and shall be a responsible to and shall indemnify XXX for payment of the fees set out herein in the event of my client's failure to pay pursuant to this agreement.'

Some of the rules contained in procedures can be quite prescriptive. For example: CEDR in the 2014 edition of the Model Mediation Agreement provides in clause 1:

> 'The parties agree to attempt in good faith to settle their dispute at the mediation and to conduct the mediation in accordance with this Agreement and consistent with the CEDR Model Mediation Procedure and the CEDR Code Of Conduct for Mediators current at the date of this Agreement'.

In the Model Procedure the parties agree that they will prepare and exchange a case summary for the mediation specifically and send the mediator one copy of the bundle of documents no less than one week before the date of the mediation. It expressly provides that the good faith of a party may be questioned if they do not submit documents on time.

Another well-known provider stipulates that 'each party will:

- Attempt to agree a bundle of relevant documents ('documents bundle') and supply the mediator with the documents bundle by the date set out in paragraph 3 of the Mediation Details.

- Exchange with each other and supply the mediator with a confidential mediation case summary ('case summary close') by the date set out in paragraph 3 of the mediation details.

The rules of some providers can also be prescriptive about who can attend the mediation. The JAMS rules provide: 'persons other than the parties and their representatives may attend only with the permission of the parties and with the consent of the mediator.'

Clerksroom provides: 'no other person shall attend mediation without the consent of the parties and the mediator'.

By contrast the ADR Group says:

> 'every party should notify ADR Group and other parties involved in mediation of the names of those people intended to be present at the mediation session

18.04 *Mediation agreement*

and indicate their capacity at the mediation is a principal, representative, adviser or otherwise.'

It is for you to decide how prescriptive or permissive you want to be. In the end it does not matter to you as the mediator who attends the mediation, provided that they have the authority to conclude an agreement on behalf of the party they represent and agree to be bound by the confidentiality provisions.

Your life is made easier if the parties send you the material well in advance. You want to be well prepared and you need enough time to complete your preparation. When you're starting off as a mediator you may not be able to be as insistent as more experienced mediators. A safer option is to be user-friendly. Remember that the parties and their lawyers often work under severe time and financial pressures.

Clause: The Dispute

1.3 The Dispute shall mean [all matters in dispute between the Parties arising out of   ].

Comment:

It is important to define the dispute. This serves several purposes:

- It focuses the parties' minds on what they are actually going to discuss and try and settle.
- It helps prevent disputes in the future if either there is no settlement at all, a partial settlement or there is a settlement in this matter but further related matters give rise to litigation.
- In theory there should not be a problem because if there is a settlement the settlement agreement should adequately define what has been settled. In practice most parties want as wide a settlement in its final form as possible. This of course does not always happen.

The reason why the definition of dispute is potentially important is because of the application of the confidentiality provisions (see below). It is not unknown for a party to allege after the mediation that:

- Some sort of admission was made, which was not covered by the without prejudice or confidentiality provisions of the mediation agreement, because what was then being discussed is not what is now being litigated.
- Whatever privilege or confidentiality was attached to the mediation discussions was destroyed by some threat or unconscionable conduct by one of the other parties at the mediation.

Some of these assertions may be genuine but more often they are tactical. They can still cause a lot of time, money and effort to be expended.

In practice there is rarely any dispute about the definition of dispute:

- If proceedings have been started there is usually a simple reference to: 'All matters referred to or arising out of the pleadings in case number XX.'

Mediation agreement **18.04**

- If proceedings have not started, then a little more care has to be taken. Where there has been a pre-action protocol letter and response reference is often made to them.

In mediations where the issues have not been defined so formally either in pleadings or in pre-action protocol exchanges the dispute has sometimes been defined by reference to what has been set out in the position papers/mediation statements or in a list of issues or more particularly detailed or as expanded by the position papers.

If the parties have not agreed a definition of dispute before the mediation make sure that you have ready one or two suggestions along the lines of the above examples. This can help reduce the amount of time spent dithering because people have not thought about it.

Clause: Mediation period

The mediation has been scheduled for an initial period of up to [4/8] hours ('Scheduled Period') starting at ____on _____ at the offices of [   ].

Comment:

It might be thought this would be otiose. However, issues have arisen about when a mediation starts and, more particularly, when it finishes. The significance of this point is not just confined to questions of costs and the mediator's fees. It is also important when considering the scope of confidentiality and formalities for concluding a settlement.

All mediation agreements contain:

- details of when the mediation will begin and how long it will last; and
- provisions for termination of the mediation before the allotted time either by the mediator or any of the parties.

There is usually a provision that the mediation continues after the specified time if the parties want it to continue.

What is not expressly set out is when the mediation will end where there is no settlement reached on the day. Some mediators produce a mediation record form which they ask the parties to sign to confirm the start and finish time of the mediation and that it has not settled. Even in these circumstances questions can arise:

- What happens if the parties agree to leave offers on the table, or to invite the mediator to telephone them the next day to explore settlement? Is the mediation still in session?
- Do the provisions of the mediation agreement about confidentiality and more particularly the formality of concluding a settlement still apply?

There has been litigation on these points. The experienced mediator will make sure the position is clear and agreed by all parties and their advisers and representatives.

Some agreements expressly provide that if the mediator is involved in any subsequent discussions or contact that the provisions of the Mediation Agreement still apply.

18.04 Mediation agreement

The question of when the mediation starts is usually less contentious. It only becomes an issue when one of the parties is late. Someone often asks: when does the time start to run? Be prepared to tell them that the time the mediation started to run from is the specified time in the Mediation Agreement (which at this time has often not yet been signed).

More importantly agreements often specify that its terms apply as soon as the mediator is appointed even if the Mediation Agreement is not signed. This imposes the obligations of confidentiality on all the parties from the start. Experienced mediators will make sure that any pre-mediation conversations that they have with the parties or their representatives are expressly agreed to be confidential.

Clause: Legally binding agreement

Any settlement reached in the Mediation will not be legally binding until it has been reduced to writing and signed by or on behalf of the Parties.'

Comment:

This provision is universal in civil and commercial mediations. It is designed to prevent arguments about whether or not a binding settlement was reached at mediation. All that does is produce satellite litigation, ie litigation about litigation. This defeats the purpose of mediation, which is to bring an end to litigation.

In practice this issue frequently arises. The parties negotiate and make good progress but cannot come to a final detailed settlement. This is often because they run out of time and energy. Sometimes it is because they need further information or to involve someone who is not present at the mediation. Heads of Agreement are proposed. (This is discussed in more detail in **Chapter 19**.)

Everybody needs to be clear and to agree about whether or not this provision continues to apply. The recent case of AB v CD Ltd [2013] EWHC 1376 (TCC) provides a graphic illustration of what happens when it is not spelt out but the mediator stays involved in trying to help the parties conclude a settlement.

Clause: the mediator

The Parties agree that XXXXXXXXXXX will be the Mediator.

Comment:

There is no difficulty in identifying the mediator once appointed. The difficulty is in agreeing who it should be in the first place. This is discussed in more detail in **Chapter 6**. The main point of this clause is to make clear who the contracting parties are.

Self-administered mediations are straightforward. The parties contract each other and the individual mediator. Usually the mediator will want to make clear that he is acting in an individual capacity and any liability that he may have towards the parties is his alone and not that of his firm or any organisation to which he may be connected.

This point really goes to the question of mediator liability, which is discussed in detail in **Chapter 17** and mentioned further below.

Mediation agreement **18.04**

Clause: Limitations of liability

1. 'The Parties recognise that the Mediator is an independent contractor, there is no contract between the Parties and any firm to which the Mediator may be a consultant and no duty of care is owed by any such firm to the Parties.
2. The Parties confirm that they shall not bring any claim against the Mediator for breach of contract, breach of duty or negligence unless the Mediator has acted dishonestly towards them'.

Comment:

This topic is discussed in **Chapter 17**. For the moment it is sufficient to note that different mediators protect and limit their liability in different ways. Not all Mediation Agreements are the same.

Clerksroom for example deals with the liability of the provider as follows:

'Save in the case of gross error or misconduct, the parties agree that they will respect the neutrality of the Mediator and any professional body to which the Mediator may belong, and not bring any claim, demands or proceedings against the Mediator.'

'Further, the parties agree and acknowledge that Clerksroom shall not be liable for any alleged or actual loss or damage arising out of the appointment of the mediator or the conduct of mediation, whether in contract or tort, and agree they will not bring any claim, demands or proceedings against Clerksroom.'

CEDR provides that:

'the parties understand that the Mediator and CEDR do not give legal advice and agree that they will not make any claim against the Mediator or CEDR in connection with this mediation.

ADR Group say that:

'nothing in these rules shall limit or exclude ADR Group's or the mediator's liability for any matter in respect of which it would be unlawful for ADR Group or the mediator to exclude or restrict liability. Subject to that proviso, neither the mediator nor ADR Group shall be liable to the parties for any act or omission in connection with the services provided by them in, or in relation to, the mediation, unless the act or omission is fraudulent or involves wilful misconduct'.

Although some clients will object to the inclusion of a limitation of liability clause most mediation agreements include one.

Clause: Mediation Fees

3.1 The mediation has been scheduled for an initial period of up to [4/8] hours ('Scheduled Period') starting at [ ]on [ ]at the offices of [ ] at a cost of £ per room. All sums referred to in this Agreement are exclusive of Value Added Tax.

18.04 *Mediation agreement*

3.2 The mediation fee ('Mediation Fee') shall consist of:

  (i) the deposit payable for the Scheduled Period in the sum of [£   ] to include also all expected preparation time;

  (ii) the additional sum of £xx.00 plus VAT for each hour (or part thereof) the Mediation exceeds the Scheduled Period up to 12 midnight and at £500 plus VAT for each hour (or part thereof) after then. '

Comment:

Re-read **Chapter 16**, which deals with how you charge.

All mediation agreements contain provisions for the charging of and payment of fees. They are not all the same.

The standard full day mediation has been eight hours for many years. Some mediators now charge on the basis of a nine to ten hour day. This is possibly more realistic as most eight-hour mediations overrun by one or two hours as the parties hone the settlement agreement.

There is a tendency for parties to choose a shorter period. The usual half day is four hours but some parties choose three or five hours. They think that this will be cheaper. Sometimes it is if there is a settlement or the parties close the mediation at the allotted time.

In practice most half-day mediations overrun by an hour or so and sometimes more. This is usually because it takes longer to draft and finalise the settlement agreement than people predict. As a rule of thumb it has been found that, as an example of optimism bias, people underestimate by 40% the amount of time that it will take to complete a task.

Parties rarely walk out at the exact time fixed for the end of the mediation. Discussions usually carry on.

Be clear whether or not you can charge extra if you have not been expressly asked to continue. Some mediation agreements provide that the mediation will continue beyond the stipulated finish time unless the parties say that they do not want to continue. Most mediators ask the parties what they want to do.

Clause: Costs recovery

3.3 This provision shall not disentitle any party to recover the costs of the Mediation in any subsequent assessment of costs whether or not there has been a concluded settlement of the dispute, which is the subject of the Mediation.

An alternative version of this clause which is being more frequently used is:

Each party shall in the first instance bear and pay its own costs and expenses of, incidental to and occasioned by the Mediation but the costs of the parties in respect of, incidental to and occasioned by the Mediation (including the costs of the Mediator and the cost of the mediation venue and the mediation facilities) shall form part of Claim Number XXX (or any future proceedings that may be brought in respect of the Dispute).

Comment:

Nearly all mediation agreements provide that the parties shall split the mediation cost equally. As part of a settlement the paying party may agree to reimburse the mediation cost to the receiving party. Sometimes one of the parties pays all the costs. This usually happens where the potential paying party, for example an insurance company, wants the matter to go to mediation or the other side says it does not have the money. A variation is where one party does not pay the whole of the cost but does pay a higher proportion than 50%.

Most settlements deal with costs by including an amount for them either as part of a global sum or as a contribution. The alternative is for costs to be assessed, if they are not agreed. Where proceedings have started this is a straightforward procedure. If the mediation is taking place before the issue of proceedings this formula can still be used and a later application can be made to the court for costs to be assessed.

If no settlement is reached, this provision preserves the party's position on costs. In other words, if cost orders are made in favour of one of the parties, that party can include the costs of the mediation in the claim for costs that it seeks to recover from the paying party.

Sometimes insurers in particular try to make the costs of the mediation irrecoverable if the case does not settle. In other words costs are not in the case.

Clause: Start and Finish time

3.4 'If the Mediation exceeds the Scheduled Period, the parties acknowledge and agree that any additional time incurred is not included in the deposit amount and that such additional time will be charged for.'

Comment:

Usually the mediator in these circumstances asks the parties to sign a Mediation Report Form recording the start and finish time of the mediation so that there is no argument about how much the additional time should be charged for.

Clause: Overtime

3.5 The Parties are required to inform the Mediator, either before or during the course of the mediation session, if they do not wish to exceed the Scheduled Period.

Comment:

The sensible mediator will remind the authors that the Scheduled Period is about to expire and let them know that he will be charging additional time.

Clause: Legal Aid

3.6 Where a party is CLS Funded, the legal representative acknowledges that authority has been obtained from the Legal Services Commission, and that such authority will cover the full cost of the mediation.

18.04 Mediation agreement

Comment:

With the changes to the legal aid system this is less of a problem in practice than it used to be.

Clause: Expenses

3.7 Incidental expenses (Mediator's travel costs, refreshments etc) and disbursements will be charged at cost.'

Comment:

Given the competitive nature of the mediation market it is more usual to include these in the day rate. Clients usually want to know how much they will have to pay for the mediation and do not like little extras.

If you decide to charge expenses make it clear:

- what your mileage rate will be.
- whether you will be travelling First Class and staying in a 5-star hotel.

From the clients' point of view these expenses can mount up and cause a disproportionate amount of angst.

Clause: Payment of invoices

3.8 The Parties shall pay all invoices within 7 days of receipt by cheque or by electronic transfer to the account shown on the invoice and in any case before the date of the Mediation.

Comment:

Most mediation agreements make the legal representatives liable for the payment of fees and cost of the mediation as well as the clients. Most lawyers require their clients to put them in funds.

Most mediators do not agree that their fees can be paid after the mediation. Occasionally they may do this but it is not as some solicitors argue standard practice.

Clause: Interest

3.9 Interest at the prevailing judgment rate will be charged on overdue amounts.

Comment:

Mediation providers and mediators reserve the right to do this but in practice rarely do so.

Clause: Consulting with legal advisors

4 A party does not require legal representatives to attend the Mediation, but is free to choose whatever representation it wishes.'

Comment:

As mentioned in Chapter 1, one of the developing themes in mediation is the increasing number of mediations that are taking place before proceedings are commenced. More and more parties are also attending mediations without legal representation even if proceedings have been commenced. If proceedings have started and solicitors are on the record it is unusual for there to be no legal representation at all. Experienced users of legal services such as insurers may dispense with legal representation. Sometimes an in-house lawyer attends, or the contract director.

It is increasingly common for there to be only a solicitor or counsel present and not both. If you find out that counsel is going to be at the mediation without a solicitor make sure that he obtains authority from the solicitors to sign the mediation agreement on their behalf as the legal representative of the party.

For smaller disputes and where proceedings have not been started it is common for parties to represent themselves. In family, workplace and community disputes it is the norm for parties to represent themselves and for no legal representatives to be present at all.

Clause: Legal Advice

4.1 Where a party is not legally represented, such party is advised to obtain independent legal advice before, during and after the Mediation and prior to finalising any agreement reached pursuant to the Mediation.

The Parties recognise that the Mediator does not offer legal advice or act as a legal advisor for any of the parties of the Mediation nor will he analyse or protect any party's position or rights.

Comment:

This clause, or something like it, is standard. In practice it may not have much weight at all. Evaluative mediators do give legal opinions where they express their views on the merits of the case. The European Code of Conduct expressly provides that mediators should address any questions of imbalance of power. Most mediators say that they abide by the European Code of Conduct.

In practice this clause is honoured more in the breach than in the observance.

Clause: Private Sessions

5 The Mediator may hold private sessions with one party at a time. These private sessions are designed to improve the Mediator's understanding of the party's position and to facilitate the Mediator in expressing each party's viewpoint to the other side.

Information gained by the Mediator through such a session is confidential unless (a) it is in any event publicly available or (b) the Mediator is authorised by that party to disclose it.

18.04 Mediation agreement

Comment:

Many but by no means all mediation agreements contain a provision that what parties say to a mediator in a private session or caucus will not be disclosed by the mediator to anyone else at the mediation without their consent. It is often assumed that this is the principle upon which the mediation is being conducted.

This clause also makes it clear that the mediator could call for a private section whenever he likes. So can a party. Most civil and commercial mediations are conducted on the caucus basis. In other words most discussions take place in private sessions rather than in joint sessions. There are mediators who prefer to try and conduct as much of the mediation in joint session as possible (see **Chapter 20**).

Clause: Confidentiality

6.1 The Parties recognise that the Mediation is for the purpose of attempting to achieve a negotiated settlement and as such all information provided during the Mediation is without prejudice and will be inadmissible in any litigation or arbitration of the dispute.

Evidence, which is otherwise admissible, shall not be rendered inadmissible as a result of its use in the Mediation.

The Parties will not issue a witness summons or otherwise require the Mediator or any other person attending the Mediation under the auspices of the Mediator to testify or produce records, notes or any other information or material whatsoever in any future or continuing proceedings.

All documents, statements, information and other material produced prior to or during the course of the Mediation, save to the extent that these documents have been disclosed already and are in the domain of the litigation, whether in writing or orally, shall be held in confidence by the parties and shall be used solely for the purposes of the Mediation.

Comment:

Mediation is promoted as a confidential process. So is arbitration. The question of how confidential mediation really is in practice is not as straightforward as the wording of these provisions would suggest. This is discussed in more detail in Mediation Advocacy (Bloomsbury Professional, 2015), Ch 12. The key points to note are:

- You as the mediator cannot be called as a witness.
- Documents produced for the purpose of the mediation are not disclosable unless they would be disclosable in any event.
- Any document that would be disclosable under the normal rules of disclosure is not protected from disclosure by the fact that it was referred to or used at the mediation.

The safe working assumption is that what occurs at mediation is covered by the ordinary rules on 'without prejudice' communications. There is no special privilege called 'mediation privilege' as a matter of law, but there might be an extra duty of confidentiality as a matter of the contract between the parties contained in the mediation agreement.

Clause: Pre-mediation confidentiality

6.2 Any communication by or through the Mediator before the commencement of the Mediation or after its termination shall, unless expressly agreed in writing by the Parties, be subject to the same confidentiality provisions as set out elsewhere in this Agreement.

Comment:

This point has already been discussed in relation to confidentiality above.

Clause: Termination of the Mediation

7 Either of the Parties or the Mediator shall be entitled, in their absolute discretion, to terminate the mediation at any time without giving a reason.

Comment:

This provision is not as straightforward as it appears. This is because the courts have had regard to whether or not a party's conduct at the mediation was reasonable or not. But refusing to negotiate at all, or walking out after a short time for no apparent reason, may fall into the category of unreasonable conduct. It may also amount to a breach of the warranty of good faith, which is contained in most mediation agreements. See below.

This is more a problem for the parties than for you as the mediator. But you might feel it necessary to draw the parties' attention to it if the prospect of a premature and unilateral termination of the mediation arises.

Mediators who want to end the mediation before the allotted time must in practice have a good reason for doing it otherwise they may be in breach of contract. Complaints have been made against mediators who have done this and fees have been reimbursed. Some clauses are rather fuller for example:

'Mediations shall terminate when:

- A written settlement agreement is executed by the parties, or
- A written notice of withdrawal is given by any party, or the time set for the mediation has expired without agreement for continuation or resumption, or the mediator decides and notifies the parties that continuing the mediation is unlikely to result in a settlement, or as undesirable or inappropriate to any other reason.'

(Independent Mediators)

In most mediations one of the parties and sometimes both tell the mediator at some point that they might as well terminate the mediation and leave. This is almost always an expression of extreme frustration. Usually the mediator does not agree with them and asks them to stay. Usually they do and usually a settlement is reached. This is discussed at **Chapter 20**.

18.04 *Mediation agreement*

Clause: Warranty

8 The legal representatives warrant that:

- they have carried out all necessary checks as recommended by the Law Society and/or the Bar Council to verify their clients' identity; and

- advised their clients of the obligations of disclosure on the part of legal advisors and/or mediators under the Proceeds of Crime Act 2002 (POCA).'

Comment:

This is a warranty given by the legal representatives. The rules about mediators making disclosure under POCA have been much relaxed. But most commercial mediators will have encountered some complex arrangements, which were not easy to fathom. A private word with the lawyers usually ensues.

Clause: Authority

9 The parties warrant that they or their representatives have full authority to negotiate and enter into a legally binding settlement agreement disposing of the dispute at the Mediation.

Comment:

The question of authority in mediations is one that arises very frequently in practice. The whole purpose of the mediation is to achieve finality by negotiating a legally binding settlement on the day. This means that there has to be someone present who can do this.

Clause: Signature of this Agreement

10 This agreement is to be signed by the instructed legal representative of each party attending the Mediation (if represented) on behalf of that party.

The legal representative is liable for the fees of the Mediation in the same way as they are liable for disbursements incurred in the course of litigation.

Comment:

This makes the solicitor liable for the mediator's fees. Always collect money on account.

Signed	Signed ....
....	Representative
Name	Name ....
Signed	Signed ....
	Representative
Name	Name ....

Accepted to act as Mediator;

```
Date ......................................................
Signed ...............................................
('the Mediator')

Observer

Signed ...............................................

Other Attendees

............................................................


............................................................

............................................................
```

Who sign only for the purposes of confirming their agreement to be bound by the provisions of Clause 6.

In a nutshell

18.05

- Always send the Mediation Agreement out in advance.
- Always have it signed before the mediation starts.
- Review other mediators' agreements. Update yours so that it is in line with market practice.

Chapter 19

Settlement agreement

> This chapter covers:
> - How to record the settlement.
> - Heads of terms.
> - *Tomlin* orders.
> - Settlement agreements.

The danger zone

19.01 After a long day the parties have shaken hands. The deal is done. Except that it is not. Nearly every mediation agreement stipulates that the parties are not legally bound until they have signed a document recording settlement.

But the clients think that the job is done. They are either:

- Relaxing and congratulating themselves on getting a deal. The danger is that they now switch off and lose interest. They become impatient and want to go home and celebrate. They exert pressure on their representatives to draft a settlement agreement quickly.

Or

- They are carrying out a post-mortem on whether or not they should really have agreed and are asking themselves whether the deal can be improved even now. They are not switched off. They are switching themselves back on to full negotiation mode. They will be putting pressure on their representatives to improve the deal during the drafting.

Mediators know that it always takes longer for the parties to draft the settlement document than they think. This is because:

- There is the well-established optimism bias that leads people to habitually underestimate by about 40% how long it will take them to complete any task.
- There is the tendency for drafting to take longer as people concentrate on the detail.
- There is a temptation for lawyers, even if there is no pressure from their clients to do so, to try and improve the deal for their clients in the drafting. All professionals want to try and do a good job for their clients but late-night perfectionism and generalised anxiety creeps in.

19.01 *Settlement agreement*

- People are tired.

The mediator has four tasks at this time:

- Keeping the momentum going.
- Monitoring the drafting of the settlement agreement. This is much easier of course if counsel is present. They usually take on the job.
- Keeping the clients engaged and on-side. If the advocates are out of the room drafting the settlement agreement the clients can feel alone and slightly abandoned. Experienced mediators are alert to this danger and go to chat to them.
- Avoiding post-mortems. Do not get drawn into discussions about the settlement unless the lawyers ask for your comments. Never discuss it with the clients in their lawyers' absence.

Who should do the drafting?

- If barristers are present on either side they should do it.

  They are more experienced in drafting settlement agreements and consent orders and they like doing it. If only one barrister is present ask him to do it.

- If no barristers are present then the team with the largest legal representation should do it.

  If there are two representatives the more senior can draft the agreement while the more junior keeps chatting to the clients to make sure they stay engaged and on-side.

- If the mediation is being held in the offices of one side's solicitors or barristers they usually undertake the drafting because they have access to the technology.
- If one side has brought a draft agreement that gives them a head start and they should finish off the first draft.
- If one party is represented and the other is unrepresented, the representative should do the drafting.
- If the parties are not represented you will end up doing it. That is why you need to be familiar with the contents of *Tomlin* orders and settlement agreements. A *Tomlin* order is a particular type of consent order which has several advantages for both claimants and defendants (see para **19.17**).

Drafting by committee is never a good idea. This is true in any circumstances and is particularly true at mediation. It is much better if one person prepares a draft for consideration by everyone. Amendments can be discussed and agreed.

The Practical Law Dispute Resolution section advises that 'it may be helpful to convene a joint meeting, to allow the parties to sit at the table and finalise the agreement' (see uk.practicallaw.com).

In practice this is not a good idea, for the reasons given above. All that happens is that the negotiations reopen and continue. Once an agreement has been agreed in principle it is essential to have it recorded in writing as soon as possible. When the parties can see exactly what they are agreeing, then amendments can be made and details clarified.

Usually mediators do not involve themselves in drafting until there is a disagreement over a particular provision or wording.

Draftsmen should remember at all times that their clients have come to a settlement. The clients want finality and they do not want to stay all night.

Heads of agreement: a solution or a problem?

19.02 The preference at nearly every mediation is for the parties who have settled to sign a completed agreement. They want to walk away knowing that everything has been done and finality has been achieved. This is however, not always possible.

People run out of time

19.03 Decision-makers have to leave to catch trains. The case handler at the insurers needs to be telephoned for final consent and he has left for the day.

People run out of energy

19.04 This is far more common than running out of time. People just get too tired. This can affect barristers and solicitors who are being asked to produce and approve detailed documentation. It is especially significant if, as part of the settlement, parties agree to do something different, for example exchange shares in a company or transfer land. The legal documents required to give effect to these transactions are probably not available at the mediation.

The unexpected occurs

19.05 The litigators who are present may not feel sufficiently familiar with the area of law to be able to give advice. Of course well-prepared advocates will have foreseen this and every other possibility. But even the best prepared advocates can be caught out by the imaginative twists and turns that negotiation can take.

In extreme cases the parties, having been in a dispute, and with a broken relationship, effect a reconciliation and decide to enter into, eg a fresh licence agreement or a new supply contract. In their new-found commercial enthusiasm they want the paperwork signed now before everybody changes their minds. The contracts lawyers have all gone home. What to do?

People run out of authority

19.06 It is unrealistic to expect that the representatives of corporate bodies, insurers or funders have been given unlimited authority to settle. Even if they have been given a limited authority it may still be subject to ratification by a higher level of seniority. In these circumstances the best that can be achieved is a contingent or conditional agreement.

19.07   *Settlement agreement*

Legally binding or not?

19.07   At this stage someone suggests that Heads of Agreement be signed. The essential question is whether they are intended to be legally binding or not.

If they are intended to be legally binding:

- they must be clearer and fuller than if they are not;
- the advocates have to make sure that they are capable of having legal effect; and
- all the usual formalities and ingredients for a legally binding contract have to be observed and included: ie offer, acceptance, consideration, certainty, and intention to be bound.

If they are not intended to be legally binding what is their purpose?

- They serve as a record of the stage that negotiations had reached.
- They are an indication of a degree of psychological commitment but there is no legal obligation to complete an agreement on these terms.

Non-binding heads of agreement give the parties the opportunity for second thoughts and renegotiation. Nobody can complain if this happens.

Improving the deal in the drafting

19.08   This always happens. It is only a matter of degree. Sometimes the draftsmen are striving after perfection and precision. Often they are trying to renegotiate. Where parties are not represented the temptation to renegotiate part of the deal is almost irresistible.

At all times bear the following in mind:

- Most clients think that the deal is done and want to go home.
- Some clients will want their representative effectively to renegotiate parts of the deal during the drafting. They must be warned of the dangers of doing this. In the end advocates must follow their clients' instructions. But if this happens expect a long night.
- It is the clients who are paying for your time as well as their representatives' time.
- In most mediations the process of convergence during the negotiation towards settlement improves relations which were fractured at the start of the day. Generally people feel better about each other. Warn the draftsmen of the dangers of poisoning relations by prolonged disputes over drafting. Their clients may want to do business again with each other in the future or at least be able to nod at each other in the street.
- As time passes people become tired. They go around and around in circles about the same issue. There is a danger that the draftsmen start a mini war and demonise each other. There is a risk of contagion. They start to quarrel and have negative feelings towards each other. This is particularly true if the lawyers think

that they have not had sufficient opportunity to display their lawyerly expertise during the commercially influenced day. Their clients may start to be infected. This is where you as mediator step in.

Your role

19.09

- Calm, patient persistence is what is required. You will also be tired and increasingly frustrated at the backtracking, nitpicking and second-guessing that is going on. Whatever you do, contain your irritation and smile understandingly.
- Remind the parties how much progress they have made. Encourage the parties to stand back and take the macro rather than the micro view.
- Ask whoever is raising an objection or issue to be as specific as possible about their concerns. Get them to crystallise the concerns in front of their clients. Often it is just a general unease that somehow they may be overlooking something.
- Always ask whoever raises the problem how they would like it solved.
- In the end you may well have to ask: is this a deal breaker? Before you do, try and encourage the parties to say whether or not the points that they are raising are really about things they would *like* to achieve or about things that *must* be achieved. There is always the distinction to be drawn throughout any negotiation between what is desirable and what is essential. As the day draws on and blood sugar levels fall people can lose sight of this distinction.

If a final settlement cannot be reached you may end up with heads of terms. You need to be aware of some of the dangers.

Heads of terms: avoiding pitfalls

Include all relevant terms

19.10 Apart from the usual ones about parties, dates, consideration etc it is essential to include a provision making it expressly clear how any proceedings are going to be disposed of. This emerged from the case of *Brown v Rice & Anor* [2007] EWHC 625 (Ch).

This was a case between a Trustee in Bankruptcy and the bankrupt's wife over a property. The case did not settle at mediation but both parties left offers open until the next day. There was a dispute about whether or not an offer had been accepted and therefore a deeply binding settlement concluded. The judge found that no legally binding offer could have been made because the terms of the offers left on the table did not specify how the action would be disposed of.

Everyone signs

19.11 Given the circumstances in which Heads of Agreement and offers are produced, ie late at night when everybody is exhausted, it is a good idea to

19.12 *Settlement agreement*

make sure that all those involved in the decision-making sign the document. This includes the clients and legal representatives including counsel. This makes it harder for anybody to say afterwards that they did not understand what was being said. Sensible draftsmen also include an acknowledgement from the client that they have been advised on the terms and meaning of the agreement and an acknowledgement from the advisers that they have in fact given this advice.

Sleep easy clause

19.12 It is a sensible precaution to include a clause that obliges everybody to act in good faith to amend any obvious mistakes or omissions in the document. This is separate from the clause that imposes an obligation on the parties to perfect the document, eg by entering into a deed of security in a form to be agreed and in the absence of agreement to be settled by conveyancing Counsel.

Take a selection of these boilerplate clauses to the mediation so that they are available as and when needed.

Whole agreement clause

19.13 In the mediation agreement the parties agree to meet to mediate in good faith. It can be dangerous to assume that everybody is doing that. People sometimes tell lies. The way to deal with this is either to provide that all material terms are contained in the agreement and that no reliance has been placed on any representations or information not contained in the agreement. In other words a whole agreement clause.

In practice this can be difficult to achieve at the end of a hard day's negotiation. The better approach is to identify the key information relied upon and for it be warranted as correct.

Contingent agreements

19.14 Occasionally a final settlement agreement can be drawn up, whether as part of a consent order or as a standalone document, that is still dependent on another event. For example:

- Further approval from the Board of Directors which has to sign off.
- A further step has to be taken, for example the surveyor may have to draw up a detailed plan before the contractor can re-site the garden fence.

In these circumstances include a warranty by the party taking the further step that they will do it within a specified time and that if it is a case of seeking approval that they will recommend that approval be given.

Where a further step has to be taken jointly, for example instructing a surveyor, both parties should warrant that they will cooperate in good faith to do this by a fixed date. If one of the parties does not cooperate they are deemed to have consented to the choice or instruction of the other party.

Conditional agreements

19.15 These are distinguished from contingent agreements, although of course they are to an extent contingent because they are not final, completed agreements. Here the provisions are triggered by something happening. As soon as it does everything else flows. For example a pension provider agrees to start making payments as soon as the claimant's financial adviser tells them of the identity of the new provider.

The parties will want to be as certain as they can that the condition is something that can be met in the future. But there must be a backup provision if the condition cannot be met. This usually happens because of an unexpected change in circumstances. For example a government change to the rules for pension transfers, which no one had foreseen.

Pre-action mediations

19.16 If proceedings have not been started the settlement document will have to be a settlement agreement which will not be incorporated into a consent order of the court. This means that the default provisions will have to be drafted differently because the parties will not have the benefit of the enforcement methods under for example, a *Tomlin Order*.

Post-action mediations

19.17 The settlement is nearly always incorporated into a consent order. The usual form of consent order is a *Tomlin* Order. This has the advantage for the parties of not being a judgment. This can be particularly valuable to the paying party who does not want a judgment registered against him, which he would have to disclose to a potential lender if he has to raise finance to fund the settlement.

For the receiving party the two advantages of a *Tomlin* Order are conventionally:

- It is not necessary to commence a fresh action in order to enforce the settlement. The usual wording provides that: 'All proceedings be stayed except the purpose of carrying to give effect the terms of the schedule.'
- The terms can be confidential. In a *Tomlin* Order the order is on the face of the document and refers to the terms contained in a schedule. Until October 2014 the schedule was attached to the order. Although it could be expressed to be confidential it was kept on the court file. In fact because it was open to public inspection confidential schedules were often disclosed.

The solution to this problem was to refer in the schedule to a document signed and dated by the parties. That was not filed at court. The usual wording it is:

In the order: 'on the terms of settlement contained in a document signed by the parties and dated XXX retained by Messrs YYY '

On the document: 'this is the document containing the terms of settlement referred to in a consent order signed on XXX' signed by YY and ZZ dated XX.

19.17 Settlement agreement

Remember the Chancery Direction with effect from 2 January 2015. See ww.judiciary.gov.uk/judges-and- masters-orders-final 02012015.

APPENDIX 1

IN THE HIGH COURT OF JUSTICE Claim No: 123456

CHANCERY DIVISION

Mr/Mrs Justice [name] or Master [name]

[day, month, year]

between:

ABCDEFG

Claimants

and

(1) HIJKLMNOP

(2) QRSTUV

Defendants

ORDER

UPON the application of [party] by notice dated 2

AND UPON HEARING [names of the advocates and/or those given permission to address the court] for the Claimant and the first Defendant and the second Defendant in person

IT IS ORDERED that:

1. ....

2. ....

2

To be adapted as appropriate. Where, for example, an application has been made by a Part 8 claim form, the recital should read:

'UPON the application of [party] by Part 8 Claim Form dated .....'

An order made following the trial of a Part 7 claim should recite:

'UPON THE TRIAL of this claim'.

3. This order shall be served by the Claimant on the Defendants

Service of the order

The court has provided a sealed copy of this order to the serving party:

ABC Solicitors LLP at [address] [reference]

Interest

19.18 The receiving party should be aware that interest does not automatically accrue on any late payments due under a *Tomlin* Order. This is because it is not a judgment. If there is default in paying and a judgment is entered, interest will automatically accrue. It is therefore important to provide that interest will be payable on any late payments in any event.

Sealing the order

19.19 There is a fee to pay to court on the sealing of the order (at the time of going to press it is £50). There is no point in arguing about who is going to arrange for the order to be sealed. Usually the claimant is the receiving party and is anxious that the order be sealed as soon as possible. It is slightly demeaning to suggest that the other side can pay the fee.

Checklist for settlement agreement

Who is to be a party to the agreement?

Who is the client settling with?

19.20 Are there other parties who you would like to bind into the settlement? For example, a defendant should endeavour to ensure all claimants and potential claimants are tied in.

As with defining the parties to the Mediation Agreement particular care should be taken with identifying group companies.

Otherwise the benefits of reaching a settlement may be lost when a similar claim comes in from a related, but not explicitly identified, party.

Third parties

19.21 What about any relevant third parties, for example, joint tortfeasors. Are they to be released from future claims, or are rights to bring claims against others being preserved?

What about sideways litigation, where the parties to the settlement become involved in further litigation where one of them takes action against a third party who joins in the other.

Consider including non-sue clauses or at least an indemnity from the litigating party for all costs, expenses and damages etc.

What is the scope of claims being settled?

19.22 What claims does the settlement agreement cover? For example how do you deal with existing, but unknown, claims and with future claims.

19.23 Settlement agreement

Formalities

19.23 What formal requirements are necessary to ensure a binding settlement? For example, does the agreement need to be in writing or in a deed (for example, where no consideration is passing).

Consider execution formalities and whether the execution clause will be effective to bind the parties.

Disposal of court proceedings

19.24 Deal with notification to the court and the formalities required to dispose of any court proceedings. Is the action being stayed, dismissed, discontinued or discontinued on agreed terms (so that enforcement can take place within the existing court proceedings)?

Warranties

19.25 One or both of the parties may have relied upon information provided by the other or an assumed set of facts or circumstances when deciding whether or not to make this settlement agreement. If this was fundamental to their decision, consider including a warranty that the information relied upon was accurate and complete.

A very common example is when the paying party pleads poverty. The receiving party relies on this information when assessing the recoverability risk. The paying party is often asked to warrant that its statement of assets and liabilities is true.

Is settlement conditional or unconditional?

19.26 For example, settlement may be conditional on payment so that the agreement only becomes binding and effective on the payment of the settlement sum.

Default provisions

19.27 Will the innocent party be able to enter judgment for the full amount relief claimed in the proceedings if there is breach of the settlement terms?

Payment arrangements

19.28 What about the method and timing of payments. For example, it may take time for the paying party to raise the settlement funds and/or have the payment approved, but the timing of the payment may be highly significant to the client. How will payment by instalments be structured?

Interest on late payments

19.29 Are express provisions for interest on late payments needed?

Tax implications of the settlement

19.30 Check whether the settlement payment attracts VAT or has any further tax implications.

Legal costs

19.31 Make express provision for the parties' legal costs under the settlement, remembering to deal with any existing costs orders in the proceedings.

Confidentiality

19.32 Is an express confidentiality provision required in the settlement agreement? Should there be a carve out?

In some cases, an agreed form of joint public statement, to be issued on conclusion of the settlement, can be beneficial.

Governing law and jurisdiction

19.33 As with any contract, issues of jurisdiction and governing law of the contract and the forum for any claims should be carefully considered.

Capacity and authority to settle

19.34 Ensure that the person(s) who will be signing the settlement agreement has authority to bind the company and to enter into the agreement, and include relevant provisions in the settlement agreement dealing with this.

Resolving disputes

19.35 The whole point about having written agreements is to remove the chances of further argument and dispute. Sometimes, even with the best drafted agreement, there can be genuine disagreement about what it means. Some mediators volunteer to adjudicate on any such disputes. If that is what the parties want, then:

- it must be included in the settlement agreement to have binding effect; and
- the mediator's charges should be defined along with the power, if any, he has to make a decision as to who should pay his charges.

Joint and several liability

19.36 If the parties have joint liability they are each liable for the full amount. If they have several liability they are only liable for their respective share.

19.37 *Settlement agreement*

Joint and several liability is a hybrid: the defendants are jointly liable to the claimant but as between themselves their liabilities are several. Therefore, if the claimant pursues only one defendant and recovers the whole amount due, that defendant can pursue the other defendants for their contribution.

Several defendants

19.37 The question of joint and several liability is more likely to be of interest to the defendants than the claimants in practice. Those advising defendants should bear in mind the Civil Liability (Contribution) Act 1978.

Section 1 provides that a person who is liable for damages suffered by another may recover a contribution from any other person who is liable in respect of the same damage.

The term 'liable in respect of the same damage' is given its natural and ordinary meaning, not the extended meaning previously given by the courts until the case of *Royal Brompton Hospital NHS Trust v Hammond (No 3)* [2002]UKHL 14.

Section 1(4) provides that a person who has made, or agreed to make, a payment in a bone fide settlement of any claim against them in respect of any damage is entitled to recover a contribution from a person who is liable for the same damage provided that the former 'would have been liable assuming that the factual base of the claim against him could be established'.

It is essential to remember that this section only applies to a claim for damage and not one for debt. A joint or joint and several debtor who has settled the claim by paying the whole amount can recover a contribution from the other debtors by way of restitution.

Advisers must be careful when making a settlement in a multi-party action, if the paying party intends to recover some or all the settlement amount from other parties. In those circumstances, a settlement may subsequently be held to have been unreasonable if the action for a contribution is defended. The case of *John F Hunt Demolition Ltd v ASME Engineering* [2007] EWHC 1501 (TCC) illustrates this.

Advisers also need to remember that if a party settles a claim it will not cap liability for a contribution to the damages under the 1978 Act. This is why care has been taken in connection to what has been described as sideways litigation. The case of *Carillion JM Ltd v Phi Group Ltd* [2011] EWHC 1379 (TCC) is an illustration of the problem.

Claimants beware

19.38 Claimants' advisers must be careful not to inadvertently lose or waive their right to a recovery from other potential defendants.

Section 3 of the Civil Liability (Contribution) Act 1978 provides that:

> 'Judgment recovered against any person liable in respect of any debt or damage shall not be applied to an action, alter the continuance of an

action, against any other person who is (apart from any such bar) jointly liable with him in respect of the same debt or damage.'

It is thought that judgment includes a consent order.

Section 3 will not apply if a settlement is reached but there is no subsequent judgment. If this happens release of one jointly liable tortfeasor or contractor will release all the others unless in the settlement agreement there is an express or possibly an implied reservation of the claimant's rights to pursue them.

In a nutshell

19.39

- If the parties want finality on the day they have to sign on the day.
- Heads of Agreement cause more problems than they solve.
- As mediator try and avoid being involved in the drafting. But recognise that you will be to some extent at most mediations.
- Always be prepared to help if the parties run into difficulties over the drafting.

Chapter 20

Help I've got a mediation

> In this chapter you will learn:
> - What to do before your first mediation.
> - How to defrost your technique.
> - What to do when you arrive at the mediation venue.
> - What to say in your opening statement.
> - How to conduct the joint opening session (with scripts).
> - How to manage the process during the day.
> - How to conclude the mediation.
>
> This chapter is a checklist for the first time mediator and for the more experienced mediator wanting a refresher.

Refreshing yourself – feeling a bit rusty

20.01 Many mediators find that if they are not mediating regularly they can lose their self-confidence. As mentioned at para **4.11** you can quickly become deskilled. If you have done mediations before, but not for some time, you may feel a little out of touch and rusty. This chapter is designed to help you get back up to speed.

You will have heard or read much of it before. Treat the chapter as revision notes. They highlight key facts and points that can easily drop to the back of your mind instead of being at the front.

First mediation: help

20.02 Even experienced litigators when facing their first mediation ask questions which appear minor to experienced mediators. For example a senior litigation partner in a large City firm was preparing for his first mediation. The dispute was a low value one with two unrepresented parties. He simply wanted to know who prepared the settlement agreement and how it was done.

You will find the answer to this question and other similarly troubling matters in this chapter.

20.03 *Help I've got a mediation*

Read through the following questions to decide which ones you need to check up on (see para **20.09**).

1 Do I speak to the parties first?
2 What do I talk about in my first conversation?
3 What is the purpose of these conversations?
4 Do I need to read the mediation papers?
5 What do I need to take with me?
6 What do I wear?
7 Where am I going?
8 What time do I arrive at the venue?
9 What do I do when I get to the venue?
10 When do I introduce myself?
11 What do I do first?
12 When do I go and see the parties?
13 What do I do when I have my preliminary chat with the parties?
14 What if someone does not want a Joint Opening Session?
15 What do I do and say in the Joint Opening Session?
16 What do I say in my opening statement?
17 What do I do when I've finished my opening statement?
18 What do I do while the parties are giving their opening statements?
19 What do I do in the first round of caucuses?
20 When do I ask for their first offer?
21 Who do I ask to go first?
22 What do we do about lunch?
23 What do I do if we reach a deadlock?
24 We have settled: who writes the settlement agreement?
25 The parties have signed: how do I say goodbye?

The mediation lifejacket

20.03 As explained in **Chapter 3** if you trained in the UK you will have been taught the facilitative model of mediation. Your trainers gave you a definition of mediation that was something like:

> 'Mediation is a confidential and voluntary process where the parties to a dispute invite a third-party neutral to help them find their own solution to their problem.'

They would have told you:

- That the dispute belongs to the parties and the process belongs to you as the mediator.
- Not to be evaluative.
- That there are three stages in the mediation process: education/exploration, exchange and formulation.
- That your job is to move the parties through the process from positions through interests to needs (PIN).
- Of the importance of active listening and open questioning.
- That success at mediation does not mean that that the mediation results in a settlement.

Your four lifebelts

The safe model

20.04 First, there is nothing wrong with this safe model.

In practice many mediators depart from it. More and more customers want mediators to be more evaluative and interventionist than the safe model allows. This does not matter. If you stick to the safe model you will not do harm to the parties and you will keep yourself out of trouble.

When you become more experienced as a mediator you can develop your own style and model. Customers will either buy it or they won't.

The three stages:

(1) Education/exploration.

You ask the parties what is important to them and why. Some trainers describe this as educating the parties about their dispute. Take care. If you are too pedagogic, expect some resistance as the parties feel that they are being patronised. Adopting a more exploratory role is safer.

Your three core questions are:

- What is important to you?
- Why is it important to you?
- How would you like to achieve this?

You may of course do this over more than one exploratory session.

(2) Exchange

You help the parties to exchange information, comments and questions. Much of this will be information that the parties say that they need to know before they can form a view on what would constitute a fair settlement. This may be straightforward factual information to update their understanding. For example what is the current value of the property in dispute? Does the other side have a plan showing the boundary? Has the expert report been received?

20.05 *Help I've got a mediation*

Other questions can be more contentious and in fact be interrogations rather than information requests such as: do they understand how weak their case is?

Having conducted this exchange of comments, information and views – subject always to the constraints of confidentiality – you encourage the parties to formulate proposals.

(3) Formulation

This is where the parties, having explained their positions and scored their points off each other, explore whether or not they can devise proposals that would be acceptable to themselves and the other side.

Your trainers warned you of the dangers of premature proposals. Under the safe model there must be a full exploration of the issues before the parties can discuss proposals. This is why in mediations starting at 10am the first offers are often not received until 4pm.

In practice parties and their lawyers often want to have figures on the table much sooner than this and are increasingly impatient about being led through detailed discussions of the issues.

Using the six questions

20.05 Remember ask open question not closed ones. They are:

Who, What, When, Why, Where and How.

> **TOP TIP**
> - Go easy on asking 'Why'. Repeated 'why' questions can seem hostile.
> - Instead of asking repeatedly: '**why** is this issue important to you?' vary it with '**how** will this issue influence your decision?' Or **how** is this issue important to you?'

Re-read para **11.20** for a more detailed discussion.

Smiling

20.06 As the legendary American mediator, Leila Love says: 'You are never completely dressed without a smile.'

Re-read para **11.23** about smiles.

Remember, smiling:
- puts you in a positive frame of mind;
- sends a positive message to people who see your smile; and
- relaxes and reassures you and all around you.

Every time you walk back into a private session, knock on the door, go in and smile. When you conclude a private session ask them what information you can disclose to the side. They tell you. Nod, thank them and smile.

Three maxims

20.07 Here are three suggestions for sayings that you can use at every mediation:

Help I've got a mediation **20.08**

- 'Not every negotiation is a mediation. But every mediation is a negotiation.'
- 'Settlements do not get made by arguing but by discussing proposals.'
- 'People do not do deals for your reasons. They do them for their own reasons. You need to understand each other's reasons.'

They may be clichés but no one can dispute them. Keeping these in mind will help you hold on to your structure for the process on the day if the waters turn choppy.

First stage

20.08 Check the steps in this flowchart.

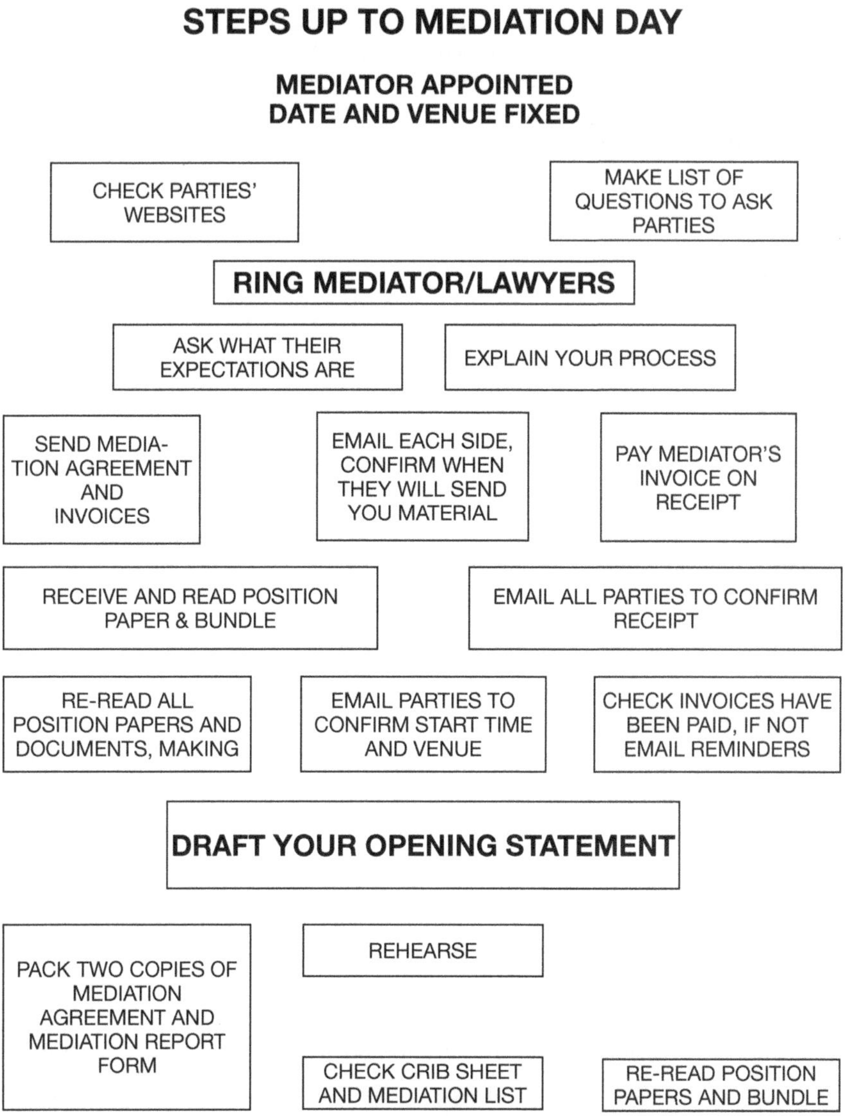

STEPS UP TO MEDIATION DAY

**MEDIATOR APPOINTED
DATE AND VENUE FIXED**

- CHECK PARTIES' WEBSITES
- MAKE LIST OF QUESTIONS TO ASK PARTIES

RING MEDIATOR/LAWYERS

- ASK WHAT THEIR EXPECTATIONS ARE
- EXPLAIN YOUR PROCESS
- SEND MEDIATION AGREEMENT AND INVOICES
- EMAIL EACH SIDE, CONFIRM WHEN THEY WILL SEND YOU MATERIAL
- PAY MEDIATOR'S INVOICE ON RECEIPT
- RECEIVE AND READ POSITION PAPER & BUNDLE
- EMAIL ALL PARTIES TO CONFIRM RECEIPT
- RE-READ ALL POSITION PAPERS AND DOCUMENTS, MAKING
- EMAIL PARTIES TO CONFIRM START TIME AND VENUE
- CHECK INVOICES HAVE BEEN PAID, IF NOT EMAIL REMINDERS

DRAFT YOUR OPENING STATEMENT

- PACK TWO COPIES OF MEDIATION AGREEMENT AND MEDIATION REPORT FORM
- REHEARSE
- CHECK CRIB SHEET AND MEDIATION LIST
- RE-READ POSITION PAPERS AND BUNDLE

Figure 31a

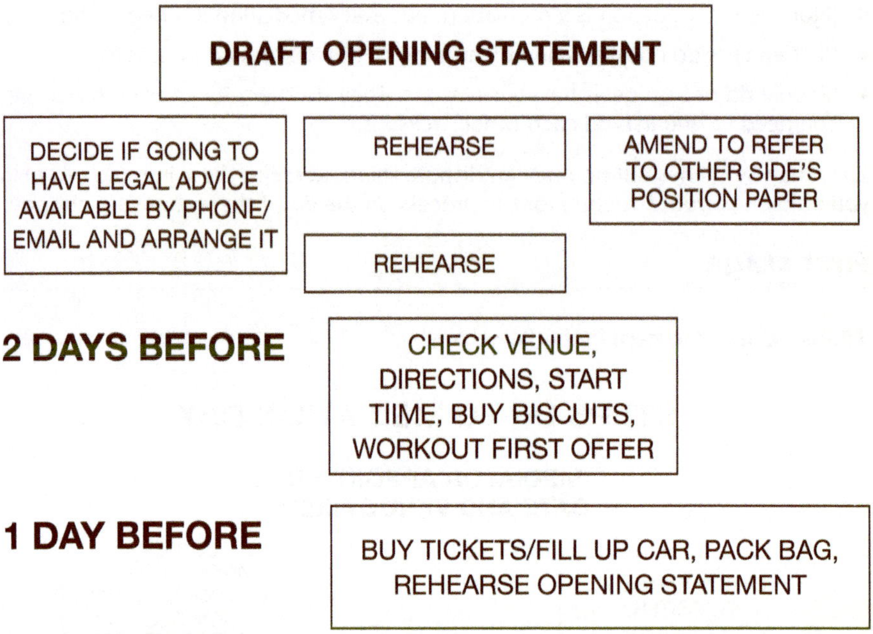

20.09 *Help I've got a mediation*

```
                    ┌─────────────────────────┐
                    │ DRAFT OPENING STATEMENT │
                    └─────────────────────────┘
```

| DECIDE IF GOING TO HAVE LEGAL ADVICE AVAILABLE BY PHONE/EMAIL AND ARRANGE IT | REHEARSE | AMEND TO REFER TO OTHER SIDE'S POSITION PAPER |

REHEARSE

2 DAYS BEFORE CHECK VENUE, DIRECTIONS, START TIIME, BUY BISCUITS, WORKOUT FIRST OFFER

1 DAY BEFORE BUY TICKETS/FILL UP CAR, PACK BAG, REHEARSE OPENING STATEMENT

Figure 31b

Mediation crib sheet

20.09

> Here is a list of things that you must remember to do on the day.
> - Have the mediation agreement signed by everybody. Make sure all attendees sign the confidentiality section.
> - Fill in the definition of 'Dispute' in the mediation agreement.
> - Ask, right at the beginning, whether anybody has time limits.
> - During each private session remind everybody that what they say is completely confidential.
> - Ask at the end of each session: 'What can I tell the other side about what we have discussed in this session?'
> - Ask: 'Can I tell them that?' if you hear something that you think is particularly significant.
> - Write down in your notebook the terms and time of every offer made.
> - Always ask when discussing proposals/suggestions/offers: 'Is that an offer you want me to put to them? Always write it down. Always read it out to them before you leave the room.
> - In your mind walk yourself through the stages of the mediation day. BOX
> - A copy of the CRIB SHEET is at **Appendix 3** for you to photocopy and take with you.

Fast track through the mediation stages

20.10 This guides you through the stages of a civil and a commercial mediation and assumes:

- a full day's mediation lasting eight hours;
- a dispute between two parties;
- a neutral venue with a start time of 10am;
- a mediator using the facilitative model with caucuses and simultaneous not sequential exchange of offers; and
- a working lunch.

Stage	Activity	Time
1	Parties arrive	9.00–9.30
2	Mediator introduces himself and has private chats with each of the parties in their rooms	9.30–10.00
3	Mediation begins with Joint opening session	10.00–10.30
4	Joint opening session ends: Private sessions (caucuses) begin	10.30–12.30
5	First Exchange of Offers	12.30–13.00
6	Lunch: parties continue working and consider each other's First Offers	13.00–13.30
7	Second exchange of offers	13.30–14.45
8	Private sessions continue	14.45–15.30
9	The Wall	15.30–15–45
10	Review sessions either joint or private	15.45–16.15
11	Further private sessions including face-to-face meetings of lawyers or clients with each other	16.15–16.45
12	The end game: Final Offers. Offers accepted.	16.45–17.00
13	Drafting settlement agreement	17.00–17.45
14	Signatures and copy documents	17.45–18.00
15	Farewells	18.00

Variations

20.11 This timetable is illustrative and not prescriptive in any way. Mediation is a flexible process. The time splits are only indicative. But they are based on several hundred mediations.

FAQs for your first mediation

20.12

Q1 Do I speak to the parties first?

20.13 *Help I've got a mediation*

Yes.

Send an email to each of the parties:

- introducing yourself;
- asking them if there is any material that they want you to read beforehand; and
- asking when it would be a convenient time for you to call them to have a private and confidential discussion.

See templates at paras **17.19–17.21**.

Do not wait

- for them to contact you;
- until you have received material from them; or
- until the mediation agreement has been signed.

It does not matter which party you telephone first. But

- Tell them that everything that is said in the conversation is confidential between you. Confidentiality applies even if they have not yet signed and returned the mediation agreement.
- Speak to all parties. Have the same sort of conversation with all sides.
- Do not disclose to one side what you have discussed with the other unless you have been expressly asked to do so.
- You may be asked by one representative to specifically find out something from the other side. For example, they may ask you to:
  - Tell the other side that they are expecting to see up-to-date information on a particular matter, for example a valuation of property or costs schedules.
  - Obtain confirmation that there will be a representative present on the other side who will have authority to settle on the day.

When you have spoken to both sides send a joint email to both of them:

- thanking them for their time;
- confirming the venue and start time;
- saying that you are looking forward to meeting them and their clients; and
- giving your mobile number in case problems arise.

20.13

Q2 What do I talk about in my first conversation?

If the parties have legal representation you will be talking with their solicitors.

When you do emphasise that the conversation is on a confidential basis. Tell them that you want to:

- Introduce yourself and explain who you are.

- Explain how you normally go about mediation, what your approach is and what process you normally follow. Ask them if that meets their expectations or whether there is another approach that they would prefer.
- Ask who is coming from their side and about their experience of mediation.
- Tell them what time you will be arriving at the venue, ie at least 30 minutes before the start time so that you can deal with the paperwork and any issues that their clients want to raise. Ask them when they will be arriving.
- Ask them if there any points or issues that they would like you to be aware of at this stage.

20.14

Q3 What is the purpose of these conversations?

For you, to establish rapport with each side and to learn something about the solicitors. Usually they will explain what their client is like and any difficulties or issues that they have with them. Some, even at this stage, will ask for your help in persuading their client to come round.

They often also tell you that:

- They have reservations about the other side's intentions to negotiate in good faith about settlement.
- They are concerned that the other side will not have authority to settle. They frequently ask whether you as the mediator know who is definitely going to attend from the other side.
- They have doubts about whether or not it would be a good idea to have a Joint Opening Session. This may be because they think that their own client is vulnerable in some way and they do not want them to be exposed to unnecessary pressure from the other side. Or, they think that the other side will be so antagonistic or legalistic that the session will just degenerate into a slanging match.

This all helps to start building rapport.

For the parties, these early discussions allow them the opportunity of:

- Finding out what you are like.
- Asking your advice and guidance.
- Explaining any concerns that they have about the process or their clients
- Setting the agenda and hopefully, from their point of view, winning you over to their side.
- Marking your card by identifying issues or problems that they think you will have to deal with.

20.15

Q4 Do I need to read the mediation papers?

Yes you certainly do.

20.16 *Help I've got a mediation*

Some mediators say that:
- There is no need to work through mediation bundles. They are never referred to at the mediation. Skimming them is enough.
- You should never read the papers at all. Instead allow the parties to tell their story in their own words at the mediation.

You are a novice mediator, so do not try and fly by the seat of your pants at this stage. Wait until you have done 200+ mediations before you are tempted to wing it.

Read the material. Usually the bundle of documents is sent in hard copy, although digital copies are increasingly popular. Work through the bundle making notes as you go and flag important pages.

The bundle usually arrives before the mediation statements. When you receive them read them thoroughly and work through the bundle again.

In your mediation notebook list the key questions that occur to you. This helps you to focus your attention. Sometimes during discussions at the mediation you can say that the same question had already occurred to you and refer to your list. This impresses the parties.

Quite often there will be simple queries such as
- What happened at the last Case Management Conference?
- Has the threatened application to strike out been made?
- What are the costs to date and what is the estimate of costs going forward?

Others will be more substantive and searching. By the time you arrive at the mediation you should be able to highlight the issues.

20.16

Q5 What do I need to take with me?

Pack your mediation kit. Make sure that you take with you:
- The mediation agreement (see **Chapter 18**).
- The mediation report form (see **Appendix 1**).
- Your opening statement for use in the joint opening session (see para **20.27**).
- Address and telephone number of the venue
- Your iPad/laptop and chargers.
- Your mobile phone.
- Mediation notebook.
- Highlighters and pens.
- Calculator.
- Memory stick.
- Post-it notes.
- Tissues.

- Biscuits: for when the hospitality at the venue runs out.
- Your mediation crib sheet (see para **20.09**).

A template of this list is at **Appendix 4** so that you can copy it and take it with you.

20.17

Q6 What do I wear?

The subject of dress is discussed in more detail in **Chapters 11** and **12**.

> **TOP TIP**
> - Dress up not down.
> - Dress modestly.
> - Men. Wear a tie. It is easier to take a tie off than to put one on. As the day progresses men can loosen their ties as everyone loosens up. Jackets can be taken off as a sign of serious intent to really be involved.
> - Women. As one very successful female family mediator says: dress like a professional person.

20.18

Q7 Where am I going?

Make sure:

- That you know where the venue is. It is not always obvious.
- That you know how to get to the venue from the train station or, if you are driving, where you can park. Ask the person hosting the venue. Sometimes the most convenient railway station is not the most obvious one.

> **TOP TIP**
> Resist offers to be collected by the parties or one of the lawyers. If the other side see you arriving in a car with their opposition they will be suspicious.

20.19

Q8 What time do I arrive at the venue?

- Never be late. Always arrive by the time that you say that you will. Make sure that this is at least 30 minutes before the stated start time of the mediation.
- If the mediation is at a neutral venue, arrive before the parties. If it is being hosted by one of the parties, arrive before the visiting party.
- Travel the night before and stay in a hotel if necessary in order to be there on time.
- Catch the train before the obvious choice. Build in spare time. Do not assume that taxis will always be available at the station. Check and pre-book if necessary.

20.20

Q9 What do I do when I get to the venue?

20.21 *Help I've got a mediation*

MEDIATION DAY

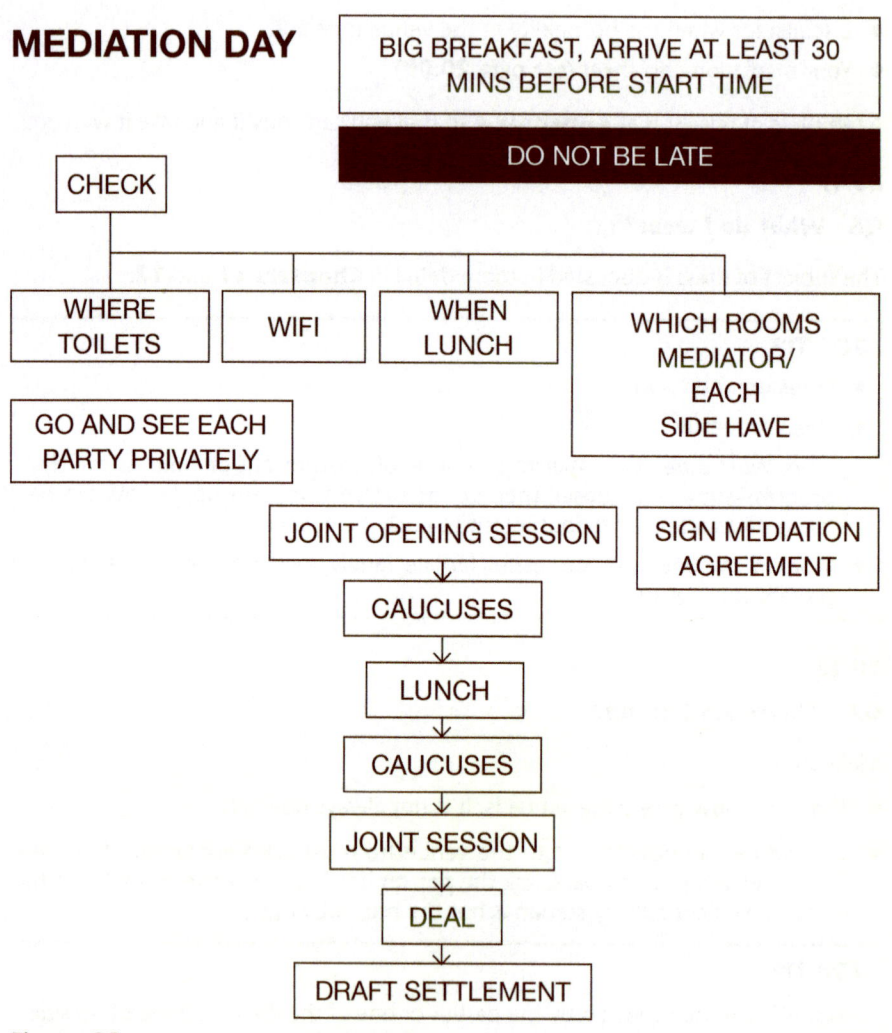

```
BIG BREAKFAST, ARRIVE AT LEAST 30
MINS BEFORE START TIME

DO NOT BE LATE

CHECK
 ├── WHERE TOILETS
 ├── WIFI
 ├── WHEN LUNCH
 └── WHICH ROOMS MEDIATOR/EACH SIDE HAVE

GO AND SEE EACH PARTY PRIVATELY

JOINT OPENING SESSION        SIGN MEDIATION AGREEMENT
        ↓
     CAUCUSES
        ↓
      LUNCH
        ↓
     CAUCUSES
        ↓
   JOINT SESSION
        ↓
       DEAL
        ↓
  DRAFT SETTLEMENT
```

Figure 32

- Introduce yourself to the receptionist and find out who else has already arrived.
- If the mediation is at a neutral venue the receptionist will normally show you to your room. If it is being hosted by one of the parties someone will come and collect you and take you to your room.
- Ask where the toilets are.

20.21

Q10 When do I introduce myself?

- If you find yourself in the waiting area with some of the parties and/or their representatives be careful about introducing yourself.
- If everybody is present you can introduce yourself to both sides without one party thinking that you are favouring the other.

Help I've got a mediation **20.23**

- If only one party has arrived try not to introduce yourself in case the other party suddenly turns up and find you talking to their opponents. They will be worried that you are being nobbled or are showing favouritism.

- Sometimes you will already know some of the attendees. Smile and nod. If need be simply tell them that you will come and introduce yourself when everybody is ready.

- If one of the parties is present and waiting for their solicitor and they recognise you go and say hello. Tell them that you will come and talk to them when their lawyers have arrived. You will be surprised how often people visit your website and know what you look like.

- Do not travel up in the lift with just one of the parties. You will all find it stilted and embarrassing at best. At worst when you arrive you discover that the other party is sitting in the reception area. They see you step out of the lift with their opponents and assume the worst.

- Don't forget that the parties demonise each other at mediation. Be careful that you do not become demonised by association.

20.22

Q11 What do I do first?

- Find out which rooms the parties are in and make a note of the numbers. Some modern office blocks are difficult to navigate and all the corridors look the same.

- Check that the room for the Joint Opening Session has enough chairs for the number of people present. Parties often turn up with unexpected numbers on the day.

- Decide where you want to sit. Many mediators especially barristers and judges like to sit at the head of the table, with the parties on either side opposite each other.

- Others prefer to sit in the middle of the table with the parties around them so that the opposing teams are not staring at each other.

- Often the layout of the room dictates how you have to arrange the seating.

Check:

- That there is water on the table for those who will be doing the speaking.

- That you know how the blinds work as in modern all glass buildings direct sunlight can be a problem.

- That you know how the air conditioning controls work.

- That the rooms are soundproof.

- Where the toilets are – and that the parties know.

20.23

Q12 When do I go and see the parties?

20.24 *Help I've got a mediation*

- As soon as you have sorted yourself out ask if anybody has arrived. Find out where their room is. Knock on the door and introduce yourself.
- If the whole team is present you can then go through your preliminary chat routine (see **Q13**).
- If some of the team has not arrived introduce yourself to those who are there. Say that you will go back to your room – tell them the number. Ask them to let you know when everybody is ready and you will come and attend to the paperwork etc.
- There is no particular order in which you go and see the parties. It is a question of who is ready first.

20.24

Q13 What do I do when I have my preliminary chat with the parties?

Remember the CRIB SHEET. You need to cover the following points:

- Have the mediation agreement signed.
- Fill in the definition of the Dispute.
- Make sure that everybody knows your name and that you know everybody else's name. If you mis-hear a name, ask them to repeat it. Nothing is worse for rapport building than calling someone by the wrong name.
- Explain briefly the purpose of the mediation, ie to make peace not war.
- Ask if they want a Joint Opening Session.
- Ask if there are any issues or questions they want to raise with you at this stage.
- Take this opportunity to start establishing rapport. Be prepared to make small talk. In fact in these early few minutes when people are forming first impressions there is no small talk. It is all big talk because it is all important. Pay attention to what they are saying. Show respect by not rushing them.

20.25

Q14 What if someone does not want a Joint Opening Session?

The safe mediation model assumes that there will be a Joint Opening Session (also known as a plenary session). This is where all the parties and their lawyers sit in the same room with the mediator.

Ask why they do not want one. If appropriate explain the benefits of a Joint Opening Session for you and for them.

A Joint Opening Session allows you to:

- Introduce yourself to everybody and to make sure that everyone knows who everyone is and why they are at the mediation.

- Explain the purpose of mediation and the ground rules for the day, eg that mediation is voluntary, confidential and without prejudice.
- Set the mood for settlement discussions.

A Joint Opening Session gives give each party the opportunity:

- To say what they want to the other for the purpose of the mediation.
- To make sure that they have been heard and acknowledged and to impress the other side as a genuine human being and a strong witness.

There are sometimes good reasons for not wanting a Joint Session:

- There has been a history of intimidation or extreme confrontation and one of the clients is feeling stressed by it. Sometimes clients are under medical care as a result of the other side's conduct.
- Relations are so bad between the parties that they will not be able to restrain themselves from engaging in public and angry arguments.
- The subject matter of the dispute is sensitive and people still feel embarrassed, eg in a sexual harassment case.
- The parties do not want one. They want to get down to it. They tell you that there is no need for a Joint Opening Session because there have already been extensive settlement negotiations, which have failed. Both parties are confident that they know all the relevant facts and also each other's positions very well. They just want to start the negotiation.
- If a party, and particularly a professional, says that they do not want to have a Joint Opening Session it is worthwhile exploring why they are reluctant. Sometimes it is because:
  - They have not prepared properly and do not want to be found out.
  - More often, and this is particularly true with barristers, they want to challenge your authority and assert control over the process.

Do not insist on a Joint Opening Session.

Some very successful and experienced mediators insist on having one. They are even prepared to have a row with the parties before the mediation gets underway. They may feel able to throw their weight around in this way. You are not in that position.

The better view is that if a party does not want a Joint Opening Session they are entitled not to have one. They are paying after all. For most parties, if not for their advisers, mediation is quite stressful enough. Why add another layer of stress by insisting on a Joint Opening Session?

20.26

Q15 What do I do and say in the Joint Opening Session?

Remember that the purpose of a Joint Opening Session is to:
- Allow you as the mediator to introduce yourself to everybody and to make sure that everyone knows who everybody is and why they are at the mediation.

20.27 *Help I've got a mediation*

- Explain the purpose of mediation and the ground rules for the day, eg that mediation is voluntary, confidential and without prejudice.
- Set the mood for settlement discussions.
- Give each party the opportunity to say what they want to the other for the purpose of the mediation.

Before you bring the parties together in the room where you going to hold the Joint Opening Session take a moment to arrange yourself.

- Choose your seat and make sure that you have your papers in front of you on the table.
- Have a note pad to hand to jot down any point which you think is important from any of the parties or their representatives.
- Make sure that you have a glass of water to hand. You are nervous. Your mouth will be dry. Talking and tension makes it drier. Take a sip in mid speech if you need to. Just say 'Excuse me' and have a drink. This also gives you a moment to think.
- Check through your opening statement.

Then you launch into your opening, which you have prepared.

20.27

Q16 What do I say in my opening statement?

Here are two examples of a mediator's opening statements.

Example 1

This is an example of mediator's opening statement for a civil and commercial mediation, where the mediator has had preliminary discussions with the parties in their rooms

'Good morning everyone.

1   Before we start please can we make sure all the mobiles are switched off. Thank you .

2   My name is XX and I'm the mediator. This is ZZ and she is an observer. I would like to thank you for agreeing that ZZ can attend to observe today. I should stress that she is observing me not you.

3   I realise that some of you know each other. But for the record could we just go round the table and say who you are and why you are here.

4   I would like say a few things. I have already discussed some of these with some of you but I like everyone to hear them at the same time.

5   The only purpose of being here today is to try and reach a settlement. There is no other purpose. This is not a rehearsal for trial. We are here to make peace today not war. That requires a slightly different skillset and mindset.

6   In my experience, and I've done over [300/25] of these mediations now, you need three things to mediate:

7 The first is the authority to settle. [*Turn to the client and their representatives and address the question directly to each of them.*] Do you have the authority to settle? Do you have to ring anybody before making a decision? Funders/insurers/family members?

8 The second is the will to settle. You have been in business – you know what that means. You give a point and take a point. Think flexibly. Sometimes you have to think the unthinkable. Just repeating your best points over and over again doesn't usually work.

9 Thirdly you need the confidence to know that if you are prepared to make a concession today to get a deal done it will not be thrown back in your face. As I have explained, everything today is without prejudice. It is also confidential. I do want to emphasise that. What you tell us, when I and ZZ are with you in a private session, stays with us unless and until you tell me that I can disclose it to the other side. But generally what happens here today remains confidential between the people who are here today.

10 As I said we are to make peace today not to fight. If you want to fight you can go to court. In my experience most mediations fall into three stages:

11 The advocacy stage [*and I say this with all due respect to the advocates that are here today – if barristers are present*] when you tell me all the points that you will tell the judge if the case doesn't settle.

12 The problem-solving stage, where you look to see if you have the building blocks to build a platform for settlement. If you want to settle can you do it?

13 Having deciding that, then you have you move to the third stage – negotiating the final figures and words.

14 Frankly the sooner that you can move from advocacy mode into problem-solving mode the more chance you give yourselves of securing a settlement today.

15 I'm not here as a judge. I'm not going to tell you that you are right and they are wrong. My job is to try and find out what are the obstacles to settlement. You tell me that you want to settle. What is stopping you? Let's get the obstacles out in the open.

16 You do not have to convince me of anything other than you are here in good faith to try and settle. I ask you to do two things:

17 The first is to price the risk of doing better elsewhere. Your lawyers can advise you about litigation risk and discount.

18 The second is more for the clients and is a commercial and personal question. What is the benefit of settlement to you? Today you can have certainty if you want it. If you want finality you can also have that, but you will have to sign the settlement agreement today as I have explained

19 I ask you to think about these two factors and do the calculations because they will benchmark any proposals that are put on the table today. In my experience – and I do not know whether yours is the same – settlements are made, not by arguing with each other, but by discussing proposals.

20 I like the parties if at all possible to have exchanged proposals before the sandwiches arrive.

21 In a moment I'm going to ask the parties if they want to say anything, always bearing in mind that we are here to make peace not war. Position papers have been exchanged and we can all read and write.

20.27 *Help I've got a mediation*

22 All I ask is that the listeners bite their tongues, no matter how defamatory, inflammatory or just plain wrong you think the speaker is. Everybody gets a chance to have their say today.

23 Finally I would ask you a favour. This is a voluntary process. Anybody can leave at any time. All I ask is that you give me ten minutes' notice before you walk out.

24 To finish, some words of encouragement. I am told that worldwide 70% of mediations produce a settlement on the day. So the statistics are in your favour.

25 Who would like to go first? It's usually the claimants.'

Example 2

This is an example of mediator's opening statement for a civil mediation where the mediator has not had preliminary chats with each of the parties.

'1 Good morning, allow me to introduce myself, my name is XXXX please call me XX. What is your name and how would you like to be addressed?

2 I like to have the clients sitting next to me is that all right?

3 I have the mediation agreement here. [*Hand round to all to sign.*] I assume that you have all read it and had it explained to you. If you have not, please ask me any questions.

[4 *Wait until everyone has signed it and then you sign and date it.*]

5 First, a few housekeeping points.

6 Each party has their own room which is yours for today. Is everything all right for you? We also have the use of this room until [am/pm].

7 Toilets; the gents are [............] and the ladies are [...........].

8 We have coffee, tea and water. Lunch is been arranged for [........]. [*Or* The sandwiches are due to arrive at   .]

9 The telephone number here is [   ] in case of any emergency.

10 If there's a fire alarm the fire escape is at [.........] [*and give location*].

11 Please turn off all mobile phones or at least put them on silent. I do realise that some of you will need to stay in touch with the office.

12 Are you all comfortable? Is the air conditioning OK?

13 Does anybody have any time limits? Any childcare constraints or to catch planes/trains?

14 Let me explain who I am and my role today. Some of you already know me. I am [the litigation head at solicitors ..../head of   chambers for 30 years/sat as a High Court judge].

15 I'm not here today as a judge or advocate. I'm here to facilitate you finding your own settlement to your dispute. This is your day. I will do what you wish.

Or

16 I am here to manage the process. You find your way through the problem to eventual settlement, with my help, but I'm in charge of the process.

Help I've got a mediation **20.27**

17 And crucially I ask you not interrupt me during my statement. After I have made my statement I will ask each of the parties to make their opening statement.

18 I will take notes while you are speaking and I may interrupt you just to make sure that my understanding is correct. Apart from that I'm asking that nobody says anything to anybody when the other side is speaking.

19 If there's anything that you would like to say during the other side's opening statement please could you make a note. We can deal with it at the end.

20 As I said before, we are not conducting a trial today. No one is on trial. I'm not a judge today.

21 I do want to give you my solemn undertaking that I am independent. I have no connection with any of the parties here. If anybody thinks that there is any reason why I cannot act as an independent and neutral third party today please say so now.

22 I would like to explain the mediation processes. Mediation has been practised for thousands of years. It is not a new thing. In fact it is something that everybody does every day. We all mediate with children, neighbours, colleagues, bosses. It is a process of trying to achieve a settlement.

23 What is different about today is that I am here as a neutral third party to help you. As I have already said, I'm not here as a judge to say who is right and who is wrong. You all have lawyers who have given their advice. You do not need another lawyer's opinion.

24 However, I will be asking some reality-testing questions. These may seem challenging to you but they are designed to help me understand your position and to explain the other side's position to me. During the course of the day I will shuttle back and forwards between you. I will be acting as a messenger much of the time and I ask you not to shoot the messenger.

25 Mediation is proving very successful. About 75% of cases that come to mediation result in a settlement. And I'm here to help you achieve your settlement to your dispute.

26 I just want to explain your rights and entitlements.

Confidentiality

27 Everything happens here today is confidential. By that I mean when I am in a private session with you I will not disclose anything you tell me until you tell me that I can.

28 Also what happens here in any joint session, including this one, must stay confidential. You can't discuss it with anybody else, except of course your legal advisers. Is that clear? Does that give anyone a problem? No going on the Internet and talking about it in the wine bar? Good.

29 It is also without prejudice. This is not quite the same thing as confidentiality. What is means is that if are prepared to make a concession here today to try and get a deal done, and it doesn't work, the concession cannot be referred to later. You cannot call me as a witness. People have tried in the past and have failed.

30 The process is also voluntary.

31 This means that you can leave at any time. You can terminate the mediation without giving a reason. So can I. I don't do it very often. All I would ask is

20.27 *Help I've got a mediation*

that if you do decide you want to leave please could you give me ten minutes' notice before you leave.

32 I do realise that sometimes people get frustrated at mediations and think that no progress has been made, or can be made. They therefore want to terminate the process. In my experience that is often premature. Surprising things can happen late in the day. And please remember that nobody gets a settlement on the day by walking out.

33 If we start to approach the scheduled time which is [6pm] for the end of the mediation and we have not settled I will ask if you wish to continue. I do charge by the hour after the scheduled time for finishing.

Neutrality and impartiality

34 As I have already said to you, I am independent. I have no personal involvement in the facts of this case nor any interest in the outcome. It may be that you think that I am spending too much time in the other room and not enough with you. Please do not get worried by that. I'm only doing it because I think that it is necessary to try and identify the common ground and the issues that we have to deal with today in order to achieve a settlement.

35 I will not be giving you any advice today. You have lawyers present. If you need any further advice, for example from your barristers, your accountants or your tax advisers then you can obtain it. You can either adjourn today or you can contact them by email or telephone. If you do that you must make sure that they are aware that the confidentiality provisions in the mediation agreement are also binding on them.

36 This session we are having now is the joint opening session. I shall shortly ask the parties if there is anything you want to say.

37 Please bear in mind that you have exchanged documentation and that we are here to try and achieve a settlement. But you may put your case as you wish.

38 All I ask is that you respect the other side and behave in a courteous and polite manner. I know the emotions are high and sometimes tempers get lost. But can we please agree that there will be no displays of bad temper, swearing or abuse?

39 One thing that you have today is the chance to review your case. This is one of the most valuable things a mediation can bring to you. The way a case or dispute looks on day one is not the same as it looks on day 101. And it is never the same as it looks on the first day of trial.

40 You have the opportunity today to achieve your own settlement. You can work out solutions to problems that no judge could give you, even if you were to win at trial. What will happen, if you do not settle today using your own abilities, is that a settlement will be imposed upon you by a judge. One of you will definitely not like it and it may be that both of you won't like it much.

41 As I said I'm not here as a judge but I have read the papers and I am an experienced lawyer and it does seem to me that the issues that we are going to have to address today are:

42 [*Itemise them.*]

43 We do need to sort this out.

44 I now ask the claimants what they would like to say.'

20.28

Q17 What do I do when I've finished my opening statement?

You say: 'Would anybody like to say anything?' Usually the claimants go first and then you indicate the claimant.

When they have finished you say 'Thank you' and ask if anybody else on their side wants to say anything.

Then turn to the other party and ask them what they want to say.

20.29

Q18 What do I do while the parties are giving their opening statements?

There are three different schools of thought:

1. You look at the speaker and engage in active listening.

   You do not take notes but communicate through your attention that you are taking it in and paying regard to what is being said.

   Using your peripheral vision, you check what impact is being made on the other side. Keep in mind everyone will be trying to read you as well.

2. You do the above but you also make notes as you go along of the key points as they occur to you. The danger of this is that people will try and read into your note-taking what you think is significant.

3. You take a full note as the speaker is speaking. The advantage of this:

   - He can see that you are paying attention.
   - You will not forget what he said and can refer to it later during the mediation.
   - People cannot read you in the same way as when you are looking around the table or at the speaker.
   - There is less chance of you giving anything away by your facial expression or body language.

20.30

Q19 What do I do in the first round of caucuses?

Remind yourself of the three-stage process of mediation. In the first caucus you are building rapport and, most of all, trying to find out what is important for the parties. What elements, from their point of view, have to be included in a settlement?

- Try to keep the caucus to about 30/40 minutes and then go and see the other party.
- Sometimes this is not possible because the lay client wants to tell you their story. They want to vent. If they do this you probably have to let them carry on but do not overrun.

20.31 *Help I've got a mediation*

- Never let the first caucus be more than an hour long otherwise the other room will feel neglected.

20.31

Q20 When do I ask them for their first offer?

There are as many ways of eliciting offers as there are mediators.

There are three main approaches.

1 Avoid premature offers

   Some mediators are worried about the dangers of premature offers. They want a full exchange of information and a debate of the issues before anybody makes any sort of offer. Their fears are:

   - Premature offers will not take sufficient account of what the other side has explained about their own interests, position and needs.
   - Parties will not have a chance to vent their emotions. Therefore they will be more restricted and guarded in their offer.
   - The mantra is that unexpressed emotions sabotage settlements. In other words people have to get things off their chests before they can clear their minds and think about settlement.
   - Unless there has been this full exploration there is a danger that the offers will be superficial and not address what the parties really need in order to achieve resolution.

2 Let the parties decide

   Other mediators think that you let the parties decide when they are ready. Bearing in mind that:

   - Paying parties are always slower to want to make an offer than the receiving party.
   - This is why insurers traditionally do not want to make an offer until 3.30 in the afternoon.

3 The sooner the better

   Other mediators think that the dangers of premature proposals and offers are exaggerated:

   - There are even greater dangers with delayed proposals and offers.
   - They believe that settlements are not achieved by discussion and exploration, which is often a euphemism for arguing, but by discussing and consideration of proposals. They therefore encourage an early exchange of proposals.
   - Occasionally mediators (including one of the busiest mediators in the UK) ask parties what their proposal for settlement is in the first caucus. This is rare but as the mediator you will want to find out how well the parties have prepared for this mediation by thinking about settlement. You will be disappointed how little the parties consider the terms and structure of settlements as opposed to the terms and structure of arguments.

20.32

Q21 Who do I ask to go first?

Should offers be made sequentially or simultaneously?

Traditionally one party makes an offer and the other makes a counter-offer. You as the mediator go back and forth playing 'settlement tennis'.

Many people are reluctant to go first. They ignore the theory of 'anchoring'. Research shows that the person who names their figure first has more influence on the outcome. All subsequent figures are judged in relation to the first figure.

Most people tell you that they want to hear from the other side first. They use phrases like 'We do not want to bid against ourselves' or 'We do not want to enter into a Dutch auction'.

20.33

Q22 What do we do about lunch?

Establish early on when you arrive whether or not sandwiches have been ordered and, if so, when they will be available. If not ask the parties what arrangements they want to make.

There are three schools of thought:

1. Have lunch brought in for the parties to eat in their own rooms and keep on working. This maintains the momentum.
2. Have lunch brought in and all the parties eat together.
   - The theory is that this will encourage parties to interact and help lower the barriers to settlement.
   - Momentum is maintained but in a different way. Many deals are concluded over a meal in normal commercial life.
   - But it is a sad fact of mediation life that the parties do not usually want to be together in the same room, let alone break bread together.
3. The parties make their own arrangements and go out for something to eat.
   - This can disrupt momentum.
   - Suggest that they go out at different times.
   - You can still be working with one party while the other is having lunch.
   - When they return you pick up with them while the others go out for lunch.
   - The advantage of going out is that it gives people a break. For many clients mediation is stressful, claustrophobic and pressured. Fresh air and a walk can help them absorb the new information that they have received, clear their minds and re-energise them for the afternoon session.

20.34

Q23 What do I do if we reach a deadlock?

Tell everyone that 'running into the wall' happens in all mediations. If people can stick with it and have faith in the process, progress can still be made.

20.35 *Help I've got a mediation*

Remind them that nobody achieves a settlement by walking out and since they have paid for eight hours of your time they might as well use it.

Suggest:

- A review session.
- Lawyer-to-lawyer meetings
- Principal-to-principal meetings.
- A private session with the representatives to see if they can tell you what is holding things up in their room.
- Sealed bids.

20.35

Q24 We have settled: who writes the settlement agreement?

- As the mediator, you do not write the settlement agreement. Let the parties' lawyers/representatives do it.
- Only become involved if they become stuck over the wording and you have a mini-mediation over the drafting.
- The only exception is where the parties do not have any legal representation either physically present or on the end of a telephone or email. In this case you have no choice.
- This is when you pull out your templates for *Tomlin* Orders and settlement agreements (see **Chapter 18**).

20.36

Q25 The parties have signed how do I say goodbye?

Try to avoid a signing ceremony. This just gives people another chance to try and have the last word, which can undo a whole day's carefully crafted negotiation and drafting.

Once the draft is agreed take it to one room for signature and then to the other.

Ask how many copies the parties want and have them made either by the venue organiser or by the host.

Make sure they sign your Mediation Report Form confirming that the mediation has settled. Check that you have written in the start and finish times so that you will be able to charge any overtime (see para **20.16**).

Ask the parties whether they want to say goodbye to each other. Sometimes they are very keen to do this. Other times they absolutely do not want to even see each other, let alone shake each other's hands and say goodbye.

More usually, they are waiting for a cue from you. Always politely try to encourage them to shake hands. Don't insist on it, Just remind them that most people feel better if they do. It is the classier option. And after all in many walks of life what goes round comes round.

Avoid stage managing moments of theatre and gathering everyone into the same room for a speech of congratulations. It can all go wrong.

In practice most of the time the parties just want to go home. Usually they will say good-bye to each other and shake hands.

Say good night to everyone. Congratulate them.

Go home. Write up your mediation log. Congratulate yourself. If this is your first settled mediation, you will remember this day for the rest of your mediation career.

Remember

20.37

- Prepare and then prepare again and then again. Rehearsal is essential for a confident opening statement.
- Sports psychologists train players and competitors to visualise how they will perform. Do the same for the mediation. It works and it helps.
- Practise what you are going to say. Do it in front to of a mirror so that you can see your body language, particularly your hands and eyes.
- Time yourself and mark the time splits on your notes.
- Keep smiling at all times and in all circumstances.

In a nutshell

20.38

- Keep dipping into this chapter.
- Rehearse.
- Remember: if it does not settle it's down to them. If it does settle it's down to you.
- Go for it. You will enjoy it.

Chapter 21

Conclusion – bringing it all together

Kissing frogs and strangling babies

21.01 You have got this far so you are ready to accelerate along the Mediation Timeline whatever your entry point is (**Figure 4** at para **1.16**).

You need to put it into action.

You need two things:

- Action Grids.
- The PEARL qualities.

Action Grids

21.02 These help you to actually do what you know that you have to do to promote yourself: turn up, tweet, network, blog, phone calls. The big problem is time. You have other things to do. Unless you timetable actions they will be crowded out. You have to ring fence slots.

Remember **Chapter 13**: to establish an internet presence you have to blog, tweet and update regularly. In other words set a routine.

PLAN, DO, REVIEW:

Make some Grids: for a week, a month, a quarter and a year.

	\multicolumn{7}{c	}{Weekly Grid}
	Tweet	LinkedIn	Email	Blog	P/call	Turn up	Spider cards
Mon							
Tues							
Wed							
Thurs							
Fri							
Sat							
Sun							

21.03 *Conclusion – bringing it all together*

Monthly grid							
	Tweet	LinkedIn	Email	Blog	P/call	Turn up	Spider cards
Week 1							
Week 2							
Week 3							
Week 4							

Quarterly grid							
	Tweet	LinkedIn	Email	Blog	P/call	Turn up	Spider cards
January							
February							
March							
April							
May							
June							
July							
August							
September							
October							
November							
December							

Figure 33

Fill it in – when you are going to do something and check how you are doing.

- every other day on the daily grid;
- once a week on the weekly grid; and
- once a month on the quarterly grid.

The Pearl Qualities

21.03 Doing mediations is hard and draining. Trying to attract mediations is harder and even more draining. For both you need to have the PEARL Qualities.

Conclusion – bringing it all together **21.03**

```
                    ENTHUSIASM/
                    ENERGY
PERSEVERANCE/                          ATTITUDE/
PATIENCE                               APTITUDE

                    PEARL
                    QUALITIES

LUCK/                                  RECIPROCITY/
LOVE                                   RESILIENCE
```

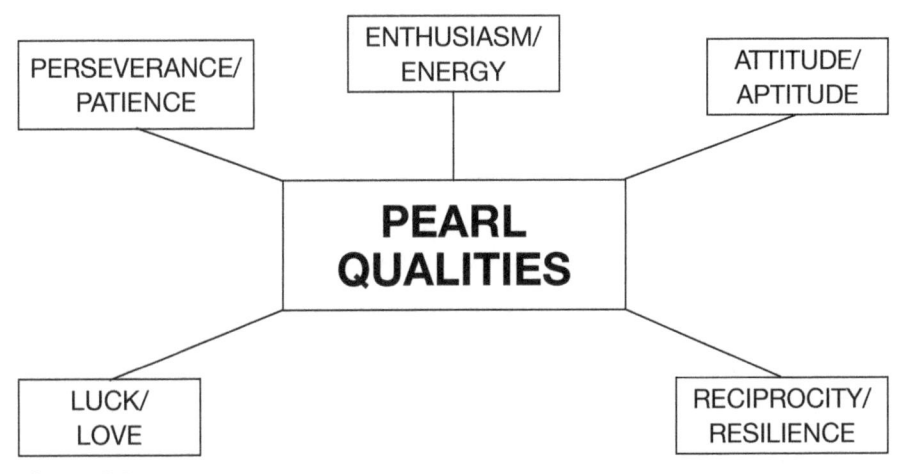

Figure 34

You need:

Patience/Perseverance

Be prepared to give your mediation project three years (see para **4.56**).

Being a mediator and building a practice takes time. Lots of it. Aled Davies' Top Tip to spend the first 100 minutes of every single day on a mediation marketing activity is impossible for most people. But spend some time and effort on a mediation promotion activity every day. Well, six days a week. You can allow yourself one day off. Try and do this even if you only tweet or email someone saying that you want to catch up with them.

But even as a part time activity promoting yourself as a mediator will take at least ten hours a month/two hours a week on average. That is not counting any time actually spent doing mediations.

On average try to spend the equivalent of 20 minutes a day as a minimum on blogging, tweeting, making phone calls, going to meetings or attending conferences and workshops etc.

Plan what you are going to do. Stick at it. The only way to do this is to keep a log/diary/record of what you intend to do and what you in fact do. If you do not use Action Grids make sure that you have a mediation diary or year planner. Enter the blogs you are going to draft and post, the workshops and breakfast meetings that you are going to attend, the phone calls that you are going to make, the contacts that you are going to get in touch with and make sure you do them.

Enthusiasm/Energy

To keep promoting yourself and to hustle for work in the face of continual frustration and disappointment and rejection is extraordinarily difficult. That is why you have to honestly complete the self-audits at **Figure 9** and **Figure 17** (**Chapters 4** and **7**). Do you have the necessary commitment and resources available to invest in this project? You need to be sure in your own mind.

21.03 Conclusion – bringing it all together

As a mediator you tell then parties to see the bigger picture, to think outside the box. Do the same thing yourself. Use your imagination.

For example: one newly accredited mediator was also a young solicitor who had set up his own practice. Most of his clients came from his ethnic community. He tried to promote mediation amongst them. They were suspicious of this new concept. The take-up was small. So he offered it for free. He told his contacts to bring their disputes and he would mediate for nothing. All he asked of them was to tell their friends and bring them along to mediate when they had a dispute.

It is not only novice mediators who show imagination. One of the UK's best known commercial mediators, John Sturrock, put on a show about mediation at the Edinburgh Festival in 2015. Another stellar commercial mediator, Bill Wood, made a video for his website where he explains the mediation process to his dog. Viewers love it. There is no truth in the rumour that the dog has been asked to do more mediations than his owner has.

Attitude/Aptitude

You cannot realistically build a civil and commercial mediation practice if you stick rigidly to the safe model of mediation that you were taught on your initial training course (see **Chapter 5**). Be flexible. You may even have to strangle babies.

Flexibility comes with self-confidence – knowing when to do something different and sensing how far to go. Self-confidence comes with experience.

But having a business like attitude will help you. Upholding the doctrinal purity and the One True Way of mediation will make the job of growing your business as a civil and commercial mediator longer and harder.

Reciprocity/Resilience

To save wear and tear on your psyche and nervous system adjust your expectations. Be realistic. Hence the importance of not only completing the self-audits at **Figures 9** and **17** but also the business plan at **Figure 19**.

Be frank with people. Perfuming your profile a little is expected (see **Chapter 9**) but do not pretend that you are more experienced than you are. You need to build rapport and win trust. Deceiving people will not help you do this.

Instead if you are in front of someone with lots of work in their gift, eg a litigation partner or claims manager tell them frankly that you have not done many, or indeed any, mediations. Say that you asking for their help to get started. You just want a chance to show them what you can do.

You will be surprised at how positively people will respond.

Remember:
- The motto in the **Preface** 'Dare to share'. Give out knowledge and information in your posts. Offer suggestions to others for observations, panels, workshops etc. Pass on names and contacts.

- Cialdini's Big Six (**Chapter 11**) – Reciprocity is crucially important in building a business.
- **Chapter 4** at para **4.67** on rejection. After all failure is only success deferred.

Luck/Love

Venture capitalists who are continually on the lookout for projects to invest in talk about having to kiss lots of frogs before finding a prince. The same is true of mediators. You have to have hundreds of conversations face-to-face, by email, Twitter, Linkedin or phone with lawyers, panels, editors, finance directors, HR professionals, barristers, accountants etc in order to be appointed to mediations.

Often luck is no more than the intelligent appreciation of opportunities. You have to put yourself in the Opportunity Flow. Remember the importance of turning up.

You may not like doing it but go where the mediations and the mediators are. You may have to kiss lots of frogs but eventually ... .

Some amber lights

Re-invent yourself

21.04 It is all well and good for established commentators and trainers to tell you to re-invent yourself. But when you just been accredited and have not actually done a mediation you are not even a mediator yet. There is nothing to re-invent.

Re-inventing yourself as a Conflict Resolution Professional is much easier when you have some mediation experience.

Extra training courses

Some newly accredited mediators disappointed and impatient at the lack of mediations go on more training courses. They take conversion courses to become workplace or family mediators. Or they train to become coaches.

All this takes time and costs money. Be careful that you do not become distracted and fall into the trap of believing that mediating role-plays in training rooms is being a mediator.

Remember also to be aware of the danger of diluting your offering by offering too many services (see **Chapter 4** on parallelists).

Over-investing

At the inaugural meeting of the Peer Mediation Group (see **Chapter 14**) during the discussion on the difficulty of getting mediations a speaker from the floor said: 'I am passionate about mediation. I live and breathe mediation and I am frustrated that I cannot mediate.' Another speaker said 'I am devoted to mediation. My

21.05 *Conclusion – bringing it all together*

whole family is. My dad is a mediator. My mum is a mediator. And I'm a mediator. We talk about it morning, noon and night.' She too was frustrated by the lack of mediations.

Mediators with this level of personal investment in mediation are risking not only frustration but disillusionment. Pace yourself. Building a mediation practice is not a sprint, it is a steeplechase over three years.

Takeaways

21.05 Keep in mind these Takeaways as you move along the Mediation Timeline (**Figure 4** at para **1.16**) and become a snowballer.

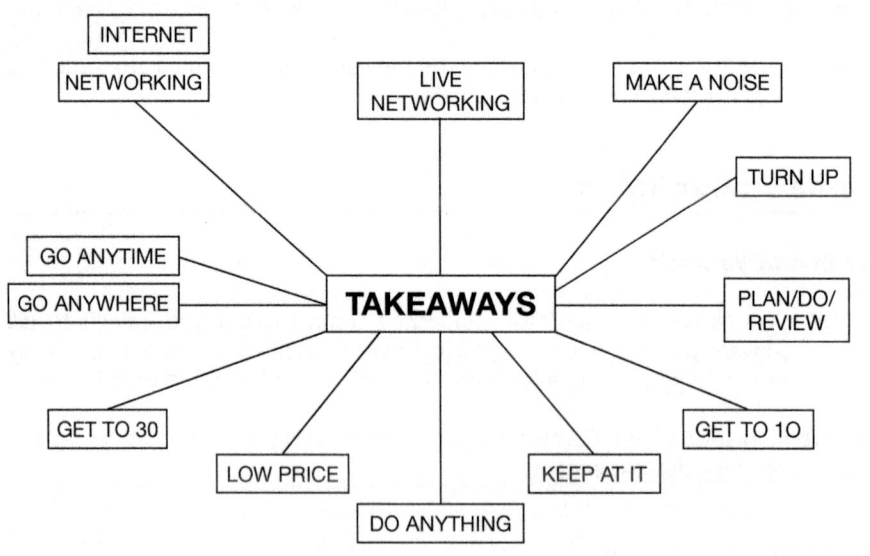

Figure 35

The buzz

21.06 When you do a mediation and you see the relief and the gratitude on people's faces because a settlement has been reached – a settlement which they had not been able to achieve themselves or through their lawyers – you will know that it has been worthwhile. Mediating is not always pleasant but you will find it stimulating, rewarding and good fun. And you can make some money.

| GO FOR IT | PLAN, DO, REVIEW | GIVE IT 3 YEARS |

Appendix 1

Mediation record form

Please sign and return this Form to the Mediator once the Mediation has concluded.

CASE NAME: ....

Date of Mediation ....

Time Mediation Commenced ....

Timed Mediation Concluded ....

Did the Mediation Settle? Yes/No

If the Mediation did not settle, will a further mediation session be required?   Yes/No

Does the Mediator anticipate charging for any post mediation support?   Yes/No

Signing this document confirms agreement to the above details:

Claimant

Signed ....

Printed ....

Claimant's Representative

Signed ....

Printed ....

Defendant

Signed ....

Printed ....

Defendant's Representative

Signed ....

Printed ....

Mediator

Signed ....

Printed ....

Appendix 2

Mediation crib sheet

- Have the Mediation Agreement signed by everybody. Make sure all attendees sign the confidentiality section.
- Fill in the definition of 'Dispute' in the Mediation Agreement.
- Ask, right at the beginning, whether anybody has time limits.
- During each private session remind everybody that what they say is completely confidential.
- Ask at the end of each session: 'What can I tell the other side about what we have discussed in this session?'
- Ask: 'Can I tell them that?' if you hear something that you think is particularly significant.
- Write down in your notebook the terms and time of every offer made.
- Always ask when discussing proposals/suggestions/offers: 'Is that an offer you want me to put to them?' Always write it down. Always read it out to them before you leave the room.
- Have your Mediation Report Form signed.
- In your mind walk yourself through the stages of the mediation day.

Appendix 3

Mediation Terms and Conditions

These terms and conditions must be read in conjunction with the Mediation Agreement sent to the parties and are incorporated into the Agreement. If there is any conflict between these terms and conditions and the Mediation Agreement the latter shall prevail.

Liability for the mediation fees

1. Unless the parties agree otherwise, they will pay in equal shares the mediation fee and any other expenses.
2. Responsibility for the fee and expenses rests with the solicitors where instructed, or with the individual party if unrepresented.
3. The amount in dispute will be calculated as the value of the claim and any counterclaim. The fee will be set accordingly. If during a mediation, it becomes apparent that the amount in dispute is higher than the amount notified, I reserve the right to invoice the parties for any additional mediation fees payable.

Cancellation policy

The following charges are payable. If the mediation is:

1. Postponed but re-booked within four weeks only irrecoverable expenses such as venue cancellation fees or travel costs already incurred will be charged.
2. Cancelled more than seven days before it is due to take place, there will be no cancellation fee, except for any irrecoverable expenses (eg venue cancellation fees) and any preparation time already spent by me.
3. Cancelled less than seven days, before it is due to take place, any irrecoverable expenses (eg venue cancellation fees) and 100% of the Deposit.
4. Preparation time is charged at the hourly rate for additional time shown in the mediation agreement.

Invoicing

1. In most mediation instructions, two invoices will be issued.
   - Deposit invoice - for the costs of the scheduled period or fixed fee and any venue costs.
   - Balance invoice - for any additional mediation time or venue fees if not previously invoiced.

Appendix 3

2   The Deposit invoice is payable no later than seven working days in advance of the mediation or in full upon receipt if issued within seven days prior to mediation, as a precondition to the mediation taking place.

3   Where a Deposit invoice is not settled in full prior to the mediation I may allow the mediation to proceed subject to the instructing solicitor undertaking in writing to settle the full amount of the invoice, if still unpaid by the client, within two days of the date of the mediation.

4   All other invoices (including the Balance invoice) are payable in full within seven days of the date of issue, unless agreement is reached to the contrary.

5   All fees are exclusive of VAT.

Appendix 4

Mediation kit

- The Mediation Agreement (**Chapter 18**).
- The mediation report form (**Appendix 1**).
- Opening statement for use in the joint opening session (para **20.27**).
- Address and telephone number of the venue
- iPad/laptop and charger.
- Mobile phone and charger.
- Mediation notebook.
- Highlighters and pens.
- Calculator.
- Memory stick.
- Post-it notes.
- Tissues.
- Biscuits: for when the hospitality at the venue runs out.
- Mediation Crib Sheet (**Appendix 3**)

Index

[*all references are to paragraph number*]

A

Accreditation
assessment, 3.34–3.35
continuing professional
   development, 3.11, 3.39
insurance, 3.12
mediation providers and trainers
   accreditation, 3.14
   approaches, 3.23–3.30
   cost, 3.15
   experience, 3.21
   generally, 3.03–3.04
   materials, 3.19
   minimum assessment criteria, 3.08
   minimum requirements, 3.06
   monitoring, 3.09–3.10
   names of individuals, 3.20
   observations, 3.09–3.10
   practical experience, 3.22
   pre-training reading and work, 3.18
   regulation, 3.05
   supervision, 3.09–3.10
   timing, 3.16
   venue, 3.17
observations
   generally, 3.36–3.38
   introduction, 3.09–3.10
requirements, 3.06
training, 3.01–3.02

Administration
bank accounts, 17.26
billing, 17.08–17.09
business cards, 17.03
business plan, and, 7.37
complaints
   generally, 17.12–17.15
   pre-empting, 17.13
database, 17.25
diary, 17.04

Administration – *contd*
emails, 17.18–17.24
expenses, 17.40
feedback questionnaire, 17.11
insurance, 17.43–17.44
introduction, 17.01
invoices, 17.08–17.09
mediation agreement
   checklist, 17.06
   introduction, 17.05
mediation report form
   generally, 17.10
   template, Appendix 1
outsourcing requirements, 17.02–17.02
panel member, as, 17.02
premises
   central London venues, 17.17
   generally, 17.16
professional indemnity insurance, 17.43–17.44
satisfaction questionnaire, 17.11
self-employment, 17.41
standard correspondence, 17.18–17.24
tax
   choice of business medium, 17.38
   dividends, 17.37
   expenses, 17.40
   limited companies, 17.35
   PAYE, 17.36
   sole traders, 17.34
   summary, 17.39
terms and conditions
   generally, 17.07
   template, Appendix 2
VAT
   Flat Rate Scheme, 17.29
   generally, 17.28

Index

Administration – *contd*
  VAT – *contd*
    marketing tool, as, 17.30–17.33
    rate, 17.28
    registration, 17.32–17.33
    thresholds, 17.28
  virtual office, 17.03
Advertorials
  branding, and, 13.36–13.37
Ageism
  barriers to entry, 2.03–2.06
Appointers
  insurers, 6.08
  introduction, 6.04
  lawyers to the parties, 6.06
  panel, 6.07
  parties, 6.05
Approved suppliers
  choosing a mediator, and, 6.23
Arbitration
  generally, 5.36
Arb/Med
  generally, 5.32
Authoritative interventions
  generally, 5.29

B

Back-up plan
  generally, 7.38
Bank accounts
  generally, 17.26
Barriers to entry
  ageism, 2.03–2.06
  geography, 2.18
  introduction, 2.02
  lack of demand, 2.17
  legalism, 2.08–2.11
  monopolies, 2.16
  oversupply, 2.14
  price, 2.15
  professional bodies and fees, 2.13
  sexism, 2.07
  summary, 2.19–2.20
  training cost, 2.12
Barristers
  choosing a mediator, and, 6.21
Blogs
  introduction, 13.04
  problem areas, 13.07
  purpose, 13.05
  structure, 13.06

Body language
  selling, and, 12.28–12.30
Books
  e-books
    cover design, 13.17
    editing, 13.15
    ground rules, 13.11
    introduction, 13.10
    preparation for publication, 13.18
    proofreading, 13.16
    redrafting, 13.14
    structure, 13.11
    timing, 13.12–13.13
  introduction, 13.08
  print media
    contents of proposal, 13.20
    contracts, 13.21–13.22
    introduction, 13.19
    proposal template, 13.20
    title, 13.20
  purpose, 13.09
Brands
  advertorials, 13.36–13.37
  blogs
    introduction, 13.04
    problem areas, 13.07
    purpose, 13.05
    structure, 13.06
  books
    e-books, 13.10–13.18
    introduction, 13.08
    print media, 13.19–13.21
    purpose, 13.09
  e-books
    cover design, 13.17
    editing, 13.15
    ground rules, 13.11
    introduction, 13.10
    preparation for publication, 13.18
    proofreading, 13.16
    redrafting, 13.14
    structure, 13.11
    timing, 13.12–13.13
  establishing, 13.02–13.03
  introduction, 8.06
  marketing, and, 8.06
  newsletters, 13.38
  podcasts
    introduction, 13.39
    publisher, for a, 13.41
    self-production, 13.40
  print books
    contents of proposal, 13.20

Brands – *contd*
  print books – *contd*
    contracts, 13.21–13.22
    introduction, 13.19
    proposal template, 13.20
    title, 13.20
  self-published e-books, 13.10–13.18
  seminars and workshops
    handouts and notes, 13.33
    interactivity, 13.35
    introduction, 13.32
    PowerPoint presentations, 13.34
  talks and lectures
    audience, 13.28
    delivery, 13.25
    duration, 13.30
    expectations, 13.26
    glossophobia, 13.24
    introduction, 13.23
    invitations, 13.31
    language, 13.30
    personal presentation, 13.29
    topics, 13.27
  writing books, 13.08–13.21
Business cards
  generally, 17.03
Business plan
  advantages, 7.04–7.10
  back-up arrangements, 7.38
  costs
    accounting, 7.36
    IT, 7.35
    legal, 7.36
    start-up, 7.30–7.31
  form and content
    acronyms, 7.20
    goals, 7.21–7.22
    introduction, 7.19
  importance, 7.12–7.18
  introduction, 7.01
  narrative plan, 7.27
  remuneration expectations, 7.32
  resource needs
    accounting, 7.36
    administration, 7.37
    available time, 7.34
    IT, 7.35
    legal, 7.36
  segmenting the market, and, 7.28–7.29
  size and length, 7.11
  start-up costs, 7.30–7.31
  template, 7.23–7.26

Business plan – *contd*
  use, 7.02–7.03
  workload, 7.33

C

Change mediation
  generally, 5.38
Choosing a mediator
  approved suppliers, 6.23
  barristers, 6.21
  CMC registers, 6.18
  directories, 6.16
  FMC registers, 6.18
  Internet searches, 6.17
  individuals, 6.22
  introduction, 6.10
  'little black book', 6.23
  marketing groups, 6.20
  previous experience, 6.13
  principal factors, 6.11–6.23
  recommendations, 6.14
  registers, 6.18–6.19
  solicitors, 6.21
  'talent spotting', 6.15
Civil Mediation Council
  accreditation, and, 3.03
Clients
  appointers
    insurers, 6.08
    introduction, 6.04
    lawyers to the parties, 6.06
    panel, 6.07
    parties, 6.05
  choosing a mediator
    approved suppliers, 6.23
    barristers, 6.21
    CMC registers, 6.18
    directories, 6.16
    FMC registers, 6.18
    Internet searches, 6.17
    individuals, 6.22
    introduction, 6.10
    'little black book', 6.23
    marketing groups, 6.20
    previous experience, 6.13
    principal factors, 6.11–6.23
    recommendations, 6.14
    registers, 6.18–6.19
    solicitors, 6.21
    'talent spotting', 6.15
  identification of
    appointers, 6.04–6.08

Index

Clients – *contd*
  identification of – *contd*
    introduction, 6.01
    parties, 6.02–6.03
    needs of, 6.09
Clinics
  generally, 14.21
  location, 14.22
  use, 14.23
Closed questions
  selling, and, 11.22
CMC registers
  choosing a mediator, and, 6.18
Coaching
  and see **Mentoring**
  generally, 14.15–14.16
  introduction, 5.38
Co-mediation
  generally, 14.24
Complaints
  generally, 17.12–17.15
  pre-empting, 17.13
Confidentiality
  settlement agreements, and, 19.32
Continuing professional development (CPD)
  generally, 3.11, 3.39
Costs
  settlement agreements, and, 19.31
Costs of business
  accounting, 7.36
  IT, 7.35
  legal, 7.36
  start-up, 7.30–7.31
CV
  achievements, 9.11–9.18
  content, 9.05–9.19
  courses, 9.11
  education, 9.15
  feedback, 9.17
  form, 9.05
  introduction, 9.02
  languages, 9.16
  length, 9.05
  non-mediation experience, 9.09
  personal interests, 9.18
  publications, 9.12
  rankings, 9.10
  rules, 9.03–9.04
  speaking, 9.14
  structure, 9.03
  testimonials, 9.17
  training, 9.13

D

Database
  generally, 17.25
Deal mediations
  generally, 5.38
Database
  generally, 17.25
Diary
  generally, 17.04
'Directive' mediation
  choosing between styles, and, 5.23–5.26
  generally, 5.21
Directories
  choosing a mediator, and, 6.16
  profile, and, 9.30–9.31
Dividends
  tax, and, 17.37

E

Earnings
  and see **Remuneration**
  advance payment, 16.25
  business plan, and, 7.32
  cash flow, 16.02–16.06
  charging levels, 16.07–16.11
  elements, 16.14–16.24
  funding, 16.27–16.28
  overtime, 16.26
  unpaid bills, 16.29
e-books
  cover design, 13.17
  editing, 13.15
  ground rules, 13.11
  introduction, 13.10
  preparation for publication, 13.18
  proofreading, 13.16
  redrafting, 13.14
  structure, 13.11
  timing, 13.12–13.13
'Elicitative' mediation
  choosing between styles, and, 5.23–5.26
  generally, 5.21
Emails
  generally, 17.18–17.24
Evaluative mediation
  choosing between styles, and, 5.23–5.26
  current role, 5.21
  introduction, 5.09

Evaluative mediation – *contd*
  meaning of 'evaluative', 5.12
  practice, in, 5.10–5.11
Expenses
  tax, and, 17.40
Feedback questionnaire
  generally, 17.11

F

Facebook
  generally, 10.41
  introduction, 10.03
Facilitative interventions
  generally, 5.30
Facilitative mediation
  background, 5.02–5.03
  choosing between styles, and, 5.23–5.26
  exchange stage, 5.07
  exploration stage, 5.06
  formulation stage, 5.08
  introduction, 5.04
  key elements, 5.04
  practice, in, 5.05
  stages, 5.06–5.08
Feedback
  generally, 14.27
  use, 14.29–14.30
Flat Rate Scheme
  VAT, and, 17.29
FMC registers
  choosing a mediator, and, 6.18

G

Geography
  barriers to entry, 2.18
Governing law
  settlement agreements, and, 19.33

H

Handouts and notes
  seminars and workshops, and, 13.33
Heron model/analysis
  authoritative, 5.29
  facilitative, 5.30
  generally, 5.28
  introduction, 5.27

I

Indicative mediation
  generally, 5.20

Insurance
  mediation training providers, and, 3.12
  mediators, and, 17.43–17.44
Insurers
  appointers of mediators, as, 6.08
Interest
  settlement agreements, and
    generally, 19.18
    late payments, on, 19.29
Internet searches
  choosing a mediator, and, 6.17
Interventions
  authoritative, 5.29
  facilitative, 5.30
  Heron model/analysis, 5.28
  introduction, 5.27
Invoices
  generally, 17.08–17.09

L

Lack of demand
  barriers to entry, 2.17
Lawyers to the parties
  appointers of mediators, as, 6.06
Lectures and talks
  audience, 13.28
  delivery, 13.25
  duration, 13.30
  expectations, 13.26
  glossophobia, 13.24
  introduction, 13.23
  invitations, 13.31
  language, 13.30
  personal presentation, 13.29
  topics, 13.27
Legalism
  barriers to entry, 2.08–2.11
Limited companies
  advantages and disadvantages, 17.42
  choice of business medium, 17.38
  tax, 17.35
LinkedIn
  generally, 10.05
  introduction, 10.02–10.03
  references and recommendations, and, 14.28
  setting up, 10.05

M

Marketing
  barriers, 8.07–8.13

Index

Marketing – *contd*
brands
advertorials, 13.36–13.37
blogs, 13.04–13.07
e-books, 13.10–13.18
establishing, 13.02–13.03
introduction, 8.06
newsletters, 13.38
podcasts, 13.39–13.41
print media, 13.19–13.21
seminars and workshops, 13.32–13.35
talks and lectures, 13.23–13.31
writing books, 13.08–13.21
checklist of tools, 8.14
CV
achievements, 9.11–9.18
content, 9.05–9.19
courses, 9.11
education, 9.15
feedback, 9.17
form, 9.05
introduction, 9.02
languages, 9.16
length, 9.05
non-mediation experience, 9.09
personal interests, 9.18
publications, 9.12
rankings, 9.10
rules, 9.03–9.04
speaking, 9.14
structure, 9.03
testimonials, 9.17
training, 9.13
differences from selling, 8.04
general, 8.01–8.16
groups
choosing a mediator, 6.20
reputation, 9.29
introduction, 8.01
marketing groups, 9.29
panels of mediators
access, 9.22
administrators, 9.25
advantages, 9.28
business model, 9.27
functions, 9.23
introduction, 9.21
problem areas, 8.08–8.11
profile of mediator
brand, as, 13.01–13.42
CV, as, 9.02–9.19
general, 9.01–9.33

Marketing – *contd*
profile of mediator – *contd*
reputation, 9.20
reputation
directories, 9.30–9.31
introduction, 9.20
marketing groups, 9.29
panels of mediators, 9.21–9.28
selling
active listening, 11.15–11.18
authority, 11.10–11.12
closed questions, 11.22
clothing, 11.12
commitment, 11.03
conditioning and association, 11.09
consistency, 11.03
flattery of people, 11.07–11.08
introduction, 11.01
liking a person, 11.05–11.09
methods of influence, 11.02–11.13
open questions, 11.20–11.21
opening up, 11.24
rapport building, 11.14
reciprocation, 11.02
scarcity, 11.13
similarities between people, 11.06
skill set, 12.01–12.38
smiling, 11.23
social proof, 11.04
talking, 11.19–11.22
titles, 11.11
use of transferable skills, 11.14–11.24
social media
basic requirements, 10.02
Facebook, 10.41
introduction, 10.01–10.04
LinkedIn, 10.05
Twitter, 10.06–10.09
website, 10.10–10.40
VUCA, 8.02
Marketing groups
choosing a mediator, and, 6.20
reputation, and, 9.29
MEDALOA
generally, 5.34
Med/Arb
generally, 5.33
Mediation
barriers to entry
ageism, 2.03–2.06

Mediation – *contd*
barriers to entry – *contd*
geography, 2.18
introduction, 2.02
lack of demand, 2.17
legalism, 2.08–2.11
monopolies, 2.16
oversupply, 2.14
price, 2.15
professional bodies and fees, 2.13
sexism, 2.07
summary, 2.19–2.20
training cost, 2.12
career, as a
advantages and disadvantages, 4.02–4.14
ambitions, 4.44–4.49
careerists, 4.28–4.39
coping with rejection, 4.55–4.56
cost, 4.51–4.53
early starters, 4.29–4.32
introduction, 4.01
'moonlighting', 4.15–4.27
parallelists, 4.40–4.43
route map, 4.50
switchers, 4.33–4.39
'cottage industry', as, 2.42–2.43
future trends, 2.46–2.55
introduction, 2.01
procedure checklist, 20.01–20.38
profession, as, 2.40–2.41
types and styles available, 5.02–5.39
Mediation after last offer arbitration (MEDALOA)
generally, 5.34
Mediation agreements
checklist, 17.06
generally, 18.01
introduction, 17.05
lack of representation, 18.03
sending in advance, 18.02
standard form, 18.04
Mediation report forms
generally, 17.10
template, Appendix 1
Mediation providers and trainers
accreditation, 3.14
approaches, 3.23–3.30
cost, 3.15
experience, 3.21
generally, 3.03–3.04
materials, 3.19
minimum assessment criteria, 3.08

Mediation providers and trainers – *contd*
minimum requirements, 3.06
monitoring, 3.09–3.10
names of individuals, 3.20
observations
generally, 3.36–3.38
introduction, 3.09–3.10
practical experience, 3.22
pre-training reading and work, 3.18
regulation, 3.05
supervision, 3.09–3.10
timing, 3.16
venue, 3.17
Mediators
accreditation
and see **Accreditation**
generally, 3.01–3.40
ambitions, 4.44–4.49
careerists, 4.28–4.39
conflict advisers, and, 2.44
coping with rejection, 4.55–4.56
demographic data, 2.31–2.32
direct access, 2.45
early starters, 4.29–4.32
expansion of numbers, 2.23
generally, 2.21
'moonlighting', 4.15–4.27
non-lawyers, 2.24–2.25
numbers, 2.30
parallelists, 4.40–4.43
regulation, 2.33–2.39
remuneration, 2.26–2.29
role, 1.01–1.07
switchers, 4.33–4.39
women, 2.22
Mediator's recommendations
generally, 5.35
Mediators' New Breakfast Club
generally, 14.18
Mediators' Peer Group
generally, 14.19
Mentoring
and see **Coaching**
advice, 14.04
experience, 14.05
guidance, 14.04
identifying, 14.10–14.13
introduction, 14.01
knowledge, 14.05
opening doors, 14.06
process, 14.13–14.14

Mentoring – *contd*
  provision of guidance and advice, 14.04
  qualities and skills, 14.07–14.09
  role, 14.02–14.06
  sharing knowledge and experience, 14.05
  sounding board, as, 14.03
Monopolies
  barriers to entry, 2.16

N

Narrative mediation
  deconstruction stage, 5.17
  engagement stage, 5.16
  generally, 5.14
  reconstruction stage, 5.18
  relevance for commercial situations, 5.19
  stages, 5.15–5.18
Networking
  displacement activity, as, 12.03
  follow up, 12.14–12.21
  introduction, 12.01–12.05
  making appointments, 12.14–12.20
  online, 12.22
  opportunity flow, 12.08
  place, 12.21
  plan, 12.06–12.13
  remembering names, 12.13
  spider cards, 12.07
  tips, 12.09–12.20
  venues, 12.21
Newsletters
  branding, and, 13.38

O

Observations
  generally, 3.36–3.38
  introduction, 3.09–3.10
Ombudsman
  generally, 5.37
Online dispute resolution (ODR)
  advantages, 15.14
  algorithmic systems, 15.05
  blind bidding, 15.08
  double-blind bidding, 15.09
  eBay EDR system, 15.01
  effect on mediators, 15.13–15.21
  future trends, 2.55
  generally, 15.01

Online dispute resolution (ODR)
  – *contd*
  impact, 15.24
  information management, 15.06
  introduction, 1.06
  meaning, 15.01
  mediation trainers, 15.16
  'next big thing', as, 15.15
  opportunity for mediators, as, 15.14
  process
    information management, 15.06
    software adjudication, 15.12
    TFN, 15.07–15.11
  Skype, 15.03
  software adjudication, 15.12
  Susskind Report, 15.17
  technology-facilitated negotiation
    blind bidding, 15.08
    double-blind bidding, 15.09
    introduction, 15.07
    visual blind bidding, 15.10
  telephone mediation, 15.03
  terminology, 15.02
  threat to mediators, as, 15.14
  training, 15.23
  types, 15.03–15.05
  virtual rooms, 15.04
  visual blind bidding, 15.10
Open questions
  selling, and, 11.20–11.21
Outsourcing
  administration, and, 17.02–17.02
Oversupply
  barriers to entry, 2.14
Oxford Breakfast Club
  generally, 14.20

P

Panels
  access, 9.22
  administrators, 9.25
  advantages, 9.28
  appointers of mediators, as, 6.07
  business model, 9.27
  functions, 9.23
  introduction, 9.21
Parties
  appointers of mediators, as, 6.05
PAYE
  generally, 17.36
PEARL
  generally, 1.17

PEARL – *contd*
  reputation, 14.33
  returns, 14.32
Pitching
  cost, 12.35
  generally, 12.31
  individual characteristics, 12.37
  merits, 12.36
  overcoming objections, 12.33–12.37
  timing, 12.34
  types, 12.32
Podcasts
  introduction, 13.39
  publisher, for a, 13.41
  self-production, 13.40
PowerPoint presentations
  seminars and workshops, and, 13.34
Premises
  central London venues, 17.17
  generally, 17.16
Previous experience
  choosing a mediator, and, 6.13
Price
  barriers to entry, 2.15
Print books
  contents of proposal, 13.20
  contracts, 13.21–13.22
  introduction, 13.19
  proposal template, 13.20
  title, 13.20
Professional bodies and fees
  barriers to entry, 2.13
Professional indemnity insurance
  generally, 17.43–17.44
Profile of mediator
  brand, as
    advertorials, 13.36–13.37
    blogs, 13.04–13.07
    e-books, 13.10–13.18
    establishing, 13.02–13.03
    introduction, 8.06
    newsletters, 13.38
    podcasts, 13.39–13.41
    print media, 13.19–13.21
    seminars and workshops, 13.32–13.35
    talks and lectures, 13.23–13.31
    writing books, 13.08–13.21
  CV, as
    achievements, 9.11–9.18
    content, 9.05–9.19
    courses, 9.11

Profile of mediator – *contd*
  CV, as – *contd*
    education, 9.15
    feedback, 9.17
    form, 9.05
    introduction, 9.02
    languages, 9.16
    length, 9.05
    non-mediation experience, 9.09
    personal interests, 9.18
    publications, 9.12
    rankings, 9.10
    rules, 9.03–9.04
    speaking, 9.14
    structure, 9.03
    testimonials, 9.17
    training, 9.13
  general, 9.01–9.33
  panels of mediators
    access, 9.22
    administrators, 9.25
    advantages, 9.28
    business model, 9.27
    functions, 9.23
    introduction, 9.21
  referrals, and, 14.31
  reputation
    directories, 9.30–9.31
    introduction, 9.20
    marketing groups, 9.29
    panels of mediators, 9.21–9.28

R

Recommendations
  choosing a mediator, and, 6.14
  generally, 5.35
References and recommendations
  feedback, from, 14.27
  introduction, 14.25
  LinkedIn, 14.28
  meaning, 14.26
  obtaining, 14.27–14.28
  use, 14.29–14.30
Referrals
  generally, 14.31
Registers
  choosing a mediator, and, 6.18–6.19
Rejection
  generally, 4.55–4.56
  mentoring, 14.11
  resilience, 14.34
  returns, 14.32

Index

Remuneration
administration charges, 16.21
advance payment, 16.25
asking rate, 16.10
business plan, and, 7.32
cash flow, 16.02–16.06
charging levels, 16.07–16.11
conditional fee agreements, and, 16.27
credit periods, 16.25
cutting fees, 16.13
day fee, 16.15
elements, 16.14–16.22
expenses, 16.18–16.20
funding, and
  conditional fee agreements, 16.27
  insurers, 16.28
  unpaid bills, 16.29
generally, 2.26–2.29
hotel expenses, 16.19
initial year charges, 16.02–16.06
insurance, and, 16.28
introduction, 16.01
low fees, 16.07
non-contact time, 16.24
overtime, 16.22, 16.26
post-mediation administration, 16.23
premium pricing, 16.08–16.09
preparation, 16.16
rates, 16.12
room hire, 16.20
travel expenses, 16.18
travel time, 16.17
unpaid bills, 16.29

Reputation
directories, 9.30–9.31
introduction, 9.20
maintenance of, 14.33
marketing groups, 9.29
panels of mediators
  access, 9.22
  administrators, 9.25
  advantages, 9.28
  business model, 9.27
  functions, 9.23
  introduction, 9.21

Resilience
generally, 14.34

Returns
generally, 14.32

S

Satisfaction questionnaire
generally, 17.11

Search Engine Optimisation
websites, and, 10.40

Segmenting the market
business plan, and, 7.28–7.29
focus, 6.50–6.51
generally, 6.48
mediators, for, 6.49

Self-employment
generally, 17.41

Selling
active listening, 11.15–11.18
appointments, 12.14–12.20
authority, 11.10–11.12
body language, 12.28–12.30
closed questions, 11.22
clothing, 11.12
commitment, 11.03
conditioning and association, 11.09
consistency, 11.03
differences from marketing, 8.04
flattery of people, 11.07–11.08
follow up, 12.14–12.21
generally, 5.01
introduction, 11.01
liking a person, 11.05–11.09
methods of selling, 12.23–12.27
methods of influence, 11.02–11.13
networking
  displacement activity, as, 12.03
  follow up, 12.14–12.21
  introduction, 12.01–12.05
  making appointments, 12.14–12.20
  online, 12.22
  opportunity flow, 12.08
  place, 12.21
  plan, 12.06–12.13
  remembering names, 12.13
  spider cards, 12.07
  tips, 12.09–12.20
  venues, 12.21
open questions, 11.20–11.21
opening up, 11.24
phone, by, 12.27
pitching
  cost, 12.35
  generally, 12.31
  individual characteristics, 12.37
  merits, 12.36

Selling – *contd*
  pitching – *contd*
    overcoming objections, 12.33–12.37
    timing, 12.34
    types, 12.32
  'pivot', 12.25
  rapport building, 11.14
  reciprocation, 11.02
  scarcity, 11.13
  similarities between people, 11.06
  skill set
    body language, 12.28–12.30
    follow up, 12.14–12.21
    networking, 12.01–12.22
    methods of selling, 12.23–12.27
    pitching, 12.31–12.37
  smiling, 11.23
  social proof, 11.04
  stages, 12.26
  styles of mediation available, 5.02–5.39
  talking, 11.19–11.22
  telephone, by, 12.27
  titles, 11.11
  use of transferable skills, 11.14–11.24
Seminars and workshops
  handouts and notes, 13.33
  interactivity, 13.35
  introduction, 13.32
  PowerPoint presentations, 13.34
Settlement agreements
  authority, 19.34
  capacity to settle, 19.34
  checklist, 19.20–19.2
  conditional agreements, 19.15
  confidentiality, 19.32
  contingent agreements, 19.14
  costs, 19.31
  default provisions, 19.27
  disposal of court proceedings, 19.24
  formalities, 19.23
  governing law, 19.33
  interest
    generally, 19.18
    late payments, on, 19.29
  introduction, 19.01
  joint and several liability, 19.36
  jurisdiction, 19.33
  late payment interest, 19.29
  legal costs, 19.31
  mediator's role, 19.09

Settlement agreements – *contd*
  parties, 19.20
  payment arrangements, 19.28
  pitfalls, 19.10–19.13
  post-action mediations, 19.17
  pre-action mediations, 19.16
  problem areas, 19.02–19.08
  resolving disputes, 19.35
  scope of claims, 19.22
  sealing order, 19.19
  several defendants, 19.37
  signature, 19.11
  tax implications, 19.30
  third parties, 19.21
  Tomlin orders, 19.17
  unconditional, 17.26
  waiver of right to recovery, and, 19.38
  warranties, 19.25
  whole agreement clause, 19.13
Sexism
  barriers to entry, 2.07
Social media
  basic requirements, 10.02
  Facebook
    generally, 10.41
    introduction, 10.03
  introduction, 10.01–10.04
  LinkedIn
    generally, 10.05
    introduction, 10.02–10.03
    setting up, 10.05
  Twitter
    generally, 10.06–10.09
    introduction, 10.02–10.03
    setting up, 10.06
    things to avoid, 10.09
    use, 10.08
    tweets, 10.07
  website
    content, 10.24–10.28
    creation, 10.13
    design issues, 10.14
    generally, 10.10–10.12
    Google Analytics, 10.37–10.38
    hosting, 10.15
    introduction, 10.02–10.03
    maintenance, 10.16–10.23
    purpose, 10.14
    refreshing, 10.26–10.27
    Search Engine Optimisation, 10.40
    statistics, 10.37–10.39
    updating, 10.28–10.36

Index

Social media – *contd*
  website – *contd*
    writing rules, 10.25
    YouTube, 10.03
Sole traders
  advantages and disadvantages, 17.41
  choice of business medium, 17.38
  tax, 17.34
Solicitors
  choosing a mediator, and, 6.21
Support groups
  generally, 14.17
  Mediators' New Breakfast Club, 14.18
  Mediators' Peer Group, 14.19
  Oxford Breakfast Club, 14.20

T

Talks and lectures
  audience, 13.28
  delivery, 13.25
  duration, 13.30
  expectations, 13.26
  glossophobia, 13.24
  introduction, 13.23
  invitations, 13.31
  language, 13.30
  personal presentation, 13.29
  topics, 13.27
Tax
  choice of business medium, 17.38
  dividends, 17.37
  expenses, 17.40
  limited companies, 17.35
  PAYE, 17.36
  settlement agreements, and, 19.30
  sole traders, 17.34
  summary, 17.39
Terms and conditions
  generally, 17.07
  template, Appendix 2
Tomlin orders
  settlement, and, 19.17
Training cost
  barriers to entry, 2.12
Transformative mediation
  generally, 5.13
  relevance for commercial situations, 5.19
Twitter
  generally, 10.06–10.09

Twitter – *contd*
  introduction, 10.02–10.03
  setting up, 10.06
  things to avoid, 10.09
  use, 10.08
  tweets, 10.07

V

VAT
  Flat Rate Scheme, 17.29
  generally, 17.28
  marketing tool, as, 17.30–17.33
  rate, 17.28
  registration, 17.32–17.33
  thresholds, 17.28
Virtual office
  administration, and, 17.03
VUCA
  marketing, and, 8.02

W

Warranties
  settlement agreements, and, 19.25
Websites
  content, 10.24–10.28
  creation, 10.13
  design issues, 10.14
  generally, 10.10–10.12
  Google Analytics, 10.37–10.38
  hosting, 10.15
  introduction, 10.02–10.03
  maintenance, 10.16–10.23
  purpose, 10.14
  refreshing, 10.26–10.27
  Search Engine Optimisation, 10.40
  statistics, 10.37–10.39
  updating, 10.28–10.36
  writing rules, 10.25
Whole agreement clause
  settlement agreements, and, 19.13
Workplace mediations
  generally, 5.38
Workshops and seminars
  handouts and notes, 13.33
  interactivity, 13.35
  introduction, 13.32
  PowerPoint presentations, 13.34

Y

YouTube
  generally, 10.03